W9-AFB-820

THE NEW BOOK OF KNOWLEDGE ANNUAL

HIGHLIGHTING EVENTS OF 1972

THE NEW BOOK OF KNOWLEDGE ANNUAL

THE YOUNG PEOPLE'S BOOK OF THE YEAR

ISBN 0-7172-0604-1
The Library of Congress Catalog Card Number: 40-3092

PRINTED IN THE UNITED STATES OF AMERICA

CONTENTS

CONTRIBUTORS

BARBER, Alden G.
Chief Scout Executive, Boy Scouts of America
BOY SCOUTS OF AMERICA

BENNETT, Jay
Senior Editor, *The New Book of Knowledge* and *Lands and Peoples* encyclopedias; author of young adult novels, including *The Killing Tree* and *Wear a Long Black Coat* THE MOST DISHONEST THING

BOHLE, Bruce
Usage Editor, American Heritage Dictionaries
NEW WORDS IN DICTIONARY INDEX

BRAYNARD, Frank O.
Program Director, South Street Seaport Museum; author of books and articles on ships and shipping
SOUTH STREET SEAPORT

BRUNDAGE, Avery
President (1952–72), International Olympic Committee THE 1972 OLYMPIC GAMES

CRONKITE, Walter
CBS News Correspondent
EVENTS AROUND THE WORLD

DAUER, Rosamond
Poet OWLS
MATTHEW HAD A MONSTER

FLANDERS, Stephen C.
News Correspondent, WCBS Radio
THE 1972 PRESIDENTIAL ELECTION
YOUTH IN POLITICS

FLETCHER, James C.
Administrator, National Aeronautics and Space Administration (NASA) TO JUPITER—AND BEYOND

GARDNER, Harvey
Managing Editor, Gold Medal Books; contributing reviewer for *The New York Times Book Review, The Saturday Review* ALL ABOUT BIKES

GOKHALE, Balkrishna G.
Professor of history and Director, Asian Studies Program, Wake Forest University; author, *Ancient India, The Making of the Indian Nation, Asoka Maurya* BANGLADESH

GOLDBERG, Hy
Co-ordinator of sports information, NBC Sports; frequent winner of New Jersey Sports Writer of the Year award SPORTS

GUREVICH, Vladimir
Novosti Press Agency (U.S.S.R.)
SOVIET BALLET SCHOOLS

HARP, Sybil C.
Editor, *Creative Crafts* magazine
FUN WITH HANDICRAFTS

HERST, Herman, Jr.
Author, *Fun and Profit in Stamp Collecting, Nassau Street* STAMP COLLECTING

HINDS, Harold R.
Manager, Maplevale Organic Farm; Associate Editor, *Northwind;* co-author (with Wilfred Hathaway), *Wild Flowers of Cape Cod*
YOUTH IN ECOLOGY

HONIG, Joel
Musician; music reviewer; contributor to *Opera News* YOUNG PEOPLE'S CONCERTS

HUSSAIN, Farooq
Tutor-lecturer, Graduate School, Architectural Association School of Architecture (London); author, *Living Underwater* MAN UNDERWATER

JACOBSON, Daniel
Director, Social Science Teaching Institute; Professor of geography and education, Michigan State University; author, *Great Indian Tribes, The First Americans*
CULTURE OF THE NORTH AMERICAN INDIANS

KATHMANN, Richard
Artist; co-director of the environmental art project, Chicago River Spectacle Company
ART AND MACHINES

KNOX, Richard G.
Director of Public Relations Department, Girl Scouts of the United States of America
GIRL SCOUTS OF THE U.S.A.

KURTZ, Henry I.
Associate Editor, *Lands and Peoples;* author, *John and Sebastian Cabot* THE QUEEN'S GUARDS

MARGO, Elisabeth
Author, *Taming the Forty-niner*
A RAILROAD UNDERGROUND

MILNE, Robert Scott
Free-lance writer; member, Society of American Travel Writers WHITEWATER BOATING

MISHLER, Clifford
Editor, *Coins Magazine* and *Numismatic News*
COIN COLLECTING

MITCHELL, John G.
Editor in Chief, Sierra Club Publications
THE CAMPING BOOM

MURPHY, Lydia
Social worker, Gloucester City (England) Social Services Department ARCHEOLOGICAL DIGS

PUTMAN, Richard E.
General Electric Company TELEVISION

REUWEE, A. Daniel
Director of Information, Future Farmers of America
FUTURE FARMERS OF AMERICA

ROSENTHAL, Sylvia
Author, *Live High on Low Fat*
COOKING CHINESE STYLE

SCHNEIDER, Leo
Science Editor, *The New Book of Knowledge;* Author, *You and Your Cells, Lifeline: The Story of Your Circulatory System*
A STONE AGE PEOPLE

SHAPP, Charles
Assistant Superintendent of Schools, New York City
A CHAMPIONSHIP CHESS MATCH

SHAW, Arnold
Author, *The Rock Revolution, The World of Soul, The Street That Never Slept*
THE MUSIC SCENE

STAPLETON, E. J.
Director of Public Information, Boys' Clubs of America BOYS' CLUBS

STASIO, Marilyn
Theater critic, *Cue* magazine; author, *Broadway's Beautiful Losers* STREET THEATER

STRACY, Alan
Grolier International
Consultant, THE ART OF BEAUTIFUL HANDWRITING

TEDESCHI, Richard
Instructor in French language and literature, University of Massachusetts (Amherst)
IT'S FUN TO HAVE A PET

VAUGHAN, E. Dean
Director, 4-H and Youth Development Division, Federal Extension Service, U.S. Department of Agriculture 4-H CLUBS

VERTER, Leslie
Public Relations Coordinator, Camp Fire Girls, Inc.
CAMP FIRE GIRLS

VITIELLO, Gregory
Senior Writer, Children's Television Workshop (NET) THROUGH MY EYES

EVENTS AROUND

THE WORLD

In many respects 1972 was a year in which it became especially clear that we live in a very small world, where all men and all nations are indeed neighbors and one nation's conflicts become the genuine concern of all. This fact was made vividly and terribly clear when Arab guerrillas, seeking to bargain for the release of Arab prisoners held in Israel, entered the Olympic Village in Munich, West Germany, where the summer Olympic Games were in progress, and killed 2 Israeli team members while taking 9 others hostage. In the tension-filled occurrences that followed, 14 persons (including the 9 Israeli hostages) lost their lives. This terrifying incident, growing as it did out of the long conflict between Israel and the Arab world and played out on the stage of a great international gathering, proved dramatically and tragically the ever-closer connections among people.

President Richard M. Nixon, in carrying out his promised visits to the People's Republic of China and the Soviet Union, gave dramatic and happier evidence of the new kind of world in which we live. It was startling to recall in 1972 how impossible the President's genuinely friendly visits would have been, politically and practically, just a few years ago.

People all over the world continued to be concerned about the bitter internal conflict raging in Northern Ireland, with all of its overtones of religious and social strife. In the course of the year, Britain suspended home rule in Northern Ireland in a new attempt to seek governmental solutions to the deeply rooted problems that have led to the conflict.

The United States, too, dealt with long-term and serious international conflict as negotiations to end the war in Vietnam came close—but not, at year's end, close enough—to a settlement. The hopes of the world were lifted by the advance in the diplomatic negotiations despite the continuation of the conflict.

In a victory of major proportions, President Nixon won re-election in 1972, defeating Democratic candidate George McGovern. The dimensions of his landslide victory gave the President a strong mandate for his domestic and foreign policies.

A world that had only recently entered the space age saw the last planned lunar mission carried out with great success by Apollo 17 and its crew. With an eye to the future of mankind, the astronauts unveiled a "world peace plaque" and dedicated a rock on the moon to the youth of the world before leaving the moon.

WALTER CRONKITE

President Nixon reviews an honor guard during ceremony at Peking Airport.

A VISIT TO CHINA

It was a night to remember. The Great Hall of the People in Peking was decorated with a large American flag in honor of the occasion. The banquet tables were covered with flowers and the first dishes of a lavish eight-course meal. President Richard Nixon walked from table to table, raising his glass of *mao tai,* a Chinese liqueur, in a salute to his Chinese Communist hosts. In the background, the People's Liberation Army Band began to play a familiar tune—"America the Beautiful."

The gesture was one of the many friendly acts that marked President Nixon's historic 8-day visit to the People's Republic of China in February of 1972. A new era of history opened up during that eventful week. The most powerful capitalist nation in the world and the most populous Communist nation moved a step closer to peaceful co-existence.

The road that brought them together had been a long and hard one to travel. Twenty years earlier, the United States and China had been locked in armed conflict in Korea. Since then, a "cold war" had existed between the two countries. Even while President Nixon was in China, the rival powers were supporting opposite sides in the Indochina war. Only a year before his visit, the Chinese had denounced the President as "the most ferocious and cruel chieftain of imperialism."

But because of recent political developments, both countries had decided to lessen the tension that has existed between them since the Communists came to power in China in 1949. Experienced China watchers felt that the timing of the trip was important. During the United States military buildup in Vietnam in the mid-1960's, China felt itself threatened by the presence of tens of thousands of American troops in Southeast Asia. President Nixon's withdrawal of United States ground combat forces eliminated that threat.

At the same time, China's relations with its rival Communist superpower, the Soviet Union, had worsened. Chinese and Russian troops face each other on opposite sides of the 6,000-mile Sino-Soviet frontier. In 1969, Chinese and Russian troops fought several small battles in a disputed border region. China and the Soviet Union are also competing for the leadership of the Communist world. The Chinese now see the Russians rather than the Americans as their principal enemy. By improving relations with the United States, the Chinese can turn their full attention to their conflict with the Russians.

From the American point of view, the Nixon trip held out several promises. It was hoped that improved United States–Chinese relations would lead to an early settlement of the long and costly Vietnam War. There was also the long-range prospect for both nations of cultural exchanges and increased trade.

Mrs. Nixon meets glassware-factory workers.

The Nixons pay a visit to China's most famous historic landmark, the Great Wall.

Months of careful planning preceded President Nixon's trip. Virtually every detail had been arranged before the presidential jet took off from Washington on the 11,500-mile journey to Peking. At 11:30 A.M. Peking time, on February 21, 1972, the President's plane taxied to a halt at Peking airport. Moments later President and Mrs. Nixon stepped from the giant jet plane and were greeted by Chinese Premier Chou En-lai.

A WARM WELCOME

The opening ceremonies were brief and simple. There were no speeches and no cheering crowds. The President reviewed an honor guard, and then his motorcade sped into the city. Some American newsmen thought that the official greeting at the airport was more polite than friendly. But experienced China watchers felt otherwise. They pointed out that the 500-man honor guard of the People's Liberation Army was the largest in memory. The fact that every senior leader of the Chinese Government, except Chairman Mao Tse-tung, was present at the airport was considered another special gesture of respect.

If there was any doubt about the friendliness of the Chinese reception, it was quickly laid to rest by Chairman Mao himself. Shortly after his arrival at the State Guest House in Peking, the President received an invitation to visit Chairman Mao at his private residence in Peking's Imperial City. Normally, the Chinese leader sees visiting dignitaries at the end of their stay in China. In breaking this tradition, Chairman Mao was telling the world that President Nixon's visit was a very special event. Newspapers everywhere carried front-page photos of a smiling Chairman Mao shaking hands with the President and chatting cordially with him over tea.

The visit to Chairman Mao was the beginning of a week-long social whirl. At a 3-hour state banquet the following evening, President Nixon and Premier Chou En-lai exchanged toasts of friendship. Premier Chou termed the President's visit "a positive move and an event unprecedented in the history of relations between China and the United States."

While admitting there were serious differences between the two nations, Chou stated that these should not prevent the establishment of "normal state relations" based on respect for each other's territory and sovereignty. He concluded by toasting "the friendships between the Chinese and American peoples."

President Nixon replied by declaring: "There is no reason for us to be enemies. Neither of us seeks the territory of the other. Neither of us seeks domination over the other." The President quoted Chairman Mao's statement: "So many deeds cry out to be done, and always urgently. . . . Seize the day." Then he added, "This is the day for our two peoples to rise to the heights of greatness which can build a new and a better world."

In the days that followed, President and Mrs. Nixon visited the Great Wall of China and the legendary Ming Tombs, where many Ming dynasty emperors are buried. They also attended a special performance of a Chinese ballet called *The Red Detachment of Women.* The President was enthusiastic about the performance and praised it for its "excellent dancing and music and really superb acting." On another evening, the Nixons were treated to a brilliant display of gymnastics and of table tennis. (Table tennis is the Chinese national sport.)

While the President and Premier Chou held policy talks, Mrs. Nixon visited an agricultural commune, a glassware factory, and the Peking Zoo. She later announced that the Chinese were sending two giant pandas in return for two musk-oxen being sent to China by the Americans.

POLITICAL STUMBLING BLOCKS

But the friendship and harmony that were displayed at public appearances and social functions did not mean that major political differences had been settled. The Chinese press referred to the talks held by Premier Chou and President Nixon as "serious and frank"—a phrase often used in Communist countries to indicate sharp disagreements.

Near the end of the President's visit, a 1,500-word joint communiqué was issued. The carefully worded statement noted that there were serious differences of opinion on many subjects. Among the areas of disagreement were the future of Taiwan, which is the island home of the Nationalist Republic of

President Nixon is warmly greeted by Communist Party Chairman Mao Tse-tung.

China, and the terms of a Vietnam settlement. But, on the positive side, the communiqué expressed the desire of both parties to encourage "the progressive development of trade" as well as "people-to-people contact and exchanges." The communiqué also called for the creation of "normal state relations." (The United States and China currently have no formal diplomatic ties.)

World reaction to the visit was mixed, though mainly favorable. Most European countries, especially those allied with the United States, applauded President Nixon's statesmanship. Praising the visit, one German newspaper commented: "The structure of international affairs is being reshaped." A Rumanian Communist publication called Nixon's visit "an important positive act."

Some nations, particularly in Asia, were less enthusiastic. India's Prime Minister Indira Gandhi cautiously remarked: "If the meetings between the American and Chinese leaders are meant to forge friendship, it is welcome to us." But she added that India "will not be bound by any such decision which seeks to dictate terms to Asian countries." On Taiwan, there was a growing fear that the United States was abandoning its longtime ally Nationalist China. Taiwan's National Assembly adopted a resolution stating that the Nixon visit "deeply and greatly hurts the interests of the Republic of China."

Most Americans were hopeful that the President's trip would lead to better relations between China and the United States, and that it would improve chances of world peace.

The charming Ling-Ling nibbles playfully at bamboo leaves.

ANIMAL AMBASSADORS

They steal your very heart away with their gentleness, their playfulness, and just the way they look—like small bears wearing clown-suits. Their names are Ling-Ling and Hsing-Hsing, and they have come all the way from distant China. For Ling-Ling and Hsing-Hsing are the giant pandas that were given to the United States by the people of the vast People's Republic of China. They were given as an expression of goodwill and warm friendship, following President Nixon's diplomatic trip to China.

They both now live in quite spacious quarters set aside for them in the National Zoological Park in Washington, D.C. Without a doubt they are the most pampered and protected pets in the entire United States. They were also the most sought after. When the news was announced that China was going to give the pandas, many zoos throughout the country eagerly bid for them. However, it was finally decided by President Nixon that Hsing-Hsing and Ling-Ling belonged in the nation's zoo in Washington.

For hours on end, thousands of men, women, and children, especially children, line up to see this rare and delightful pair. Then they go home and talk to other people, especially children, about Ling-Ling and Hsing-Hsing and how wonderful they were to see.

Ling-Ling, the girl panda, puts on a brilliant show all her own. Hsing-Hsing is a shy boy panda who keeps to himself and quietly chews his bamboo shoots.

Ling-Ling seems to know full well why so many people have come to see her. For she performs with great charm and an almost innocent cunning. She is always aware of the laughter and happy cries of the children. She gambols about the grass with her favorite toy, a metal beer keg. Ling-Ling pushes the keg along, tumbles it about, and then suddenly decides to lie down on it. And as she lies there, her eyes go casually, oh so casually, to where the people are. Sometimes she will take a tin plate and hold it to her face and play hide-and-seek with it. Then, seeming to tire of all her play, she will go over to a log and ease herself down onto it, looking like a black-and-white cuddly teddy bear.

Hsing-Hsing sits in his corner or else climbs up the bole of a slim bamboo tree and just stays there and thinks. Thinks about where he

Hsing-Hsing, the male panda, holds a stick deftly in his heavy paw.

has come from and where he is now. For pandas come from the damp bamboo forests of the Tibetan Plateau in southwest China. The Chinese word for a panda is *beishung*, meaning "the white bear." Hsing-Hsing, who weighed 74 pounds when he arrived in the United States, will be about 6 feet long and weigh some 300 pounds when he grows up.

The people of the United States, in return for the pandas, sent to the Chinese two burly but solemnly delightful musk-oxen, named Milton and Matilda.

Milton and Matilda are as rare to the Chinese people as the pandas are to the people of the United States. No Chinese zoo had a musk-ox until Milton and Matilda arrived. Musk-oxen live in the Arctic climate areas of the North American continent. They are about 5 feet long and can reach a weight of 600 pounds. Whenever they are threatened by wolves, the musk-oxen form a circle about their young calves, and then lower their massive heads, sharp horns ready to gore the enemy.

It is fairly certain that the Chinese people will get to love Milton and Matilda just as in the United States the people have taken Hsing-Hsing and Ling-Ling to their hearts.

Milton, the male musk-ox, sports a new harness for his journey to China.

COOKING, CHINESE STYLE

From the earliest times, heads of state have honored their important visitors with a sumptuous banquet or feast. This tradition was observed when President Nixon visited China. On the night of their arrival in Peking, the President and the First Lady were guests of honor at a 3-hour-long banquet given by Premier Chou En-lai. The banquet was held in the huge, red-carpeted Great Hall of the People. Later that week, the President was host at dinner for about 700 Chinese and American guests. Both banquets included a steady procession of courses, for it is the custom that Chinese banquets offer more food than can be eaten.

President Nixon's visit to China aroused fresh interest in Chinese cookery, long considered one of the world's finest cuisines. From Tel Aviv to Hong Kong, and throughout North and South America, millions of people are familiar with dishes such as won-ton soup, a clear broth in which float meat-filled dumplings; crisp barbecued spareribs; and mouth-watering mixtures of morsels of meat and crunchy vegetables bathed in a thick, shiny sauce.

By now it is common knowledge that chow mein means fried noodles, and that chop suey is unknown in China. However, chop suey can be considered Chinese, since it was invented by a Chinese-American cook who wanted to use up leftover vegetables. And who has not heard that shrimp with "lobster sauce" contains no lobster? The sauce was meant to be served with lobster. It is also no secret that thousand-year-old eggs, a favorite appetizer in China, are really no more than 100 days old. To prepare them, uncooked eggs are wrapped in a kind of clay containing lime, rolled in rice chaff, and permitted to age.

But it would be inaccurate to lump together all of China's kitchen triumphs under the one heading of Chinese cooking. China is a vast land that produces all kinds of foods. Each region has its specialties, and whenever a cook from a particular region left to go to another country, he carried his kitchen secrets with him.

In America, the best-known type of Chinese cooking is Cantonese. The first Chinese restaurant was opened about 100 years ago in San Francisco by a Chinese from Canton, and Cantonese style came to stand for Chinese cooking. It remained unchallenged as the most popular form of Chinese food until about 10 years ago, when the fiery hot specialties of Szechwan, located in southern China, found their way to other shores. Shanghai, China's largest city, and Fukien have contributed their specialties. And from Hunan, in the center of the southeast temperate zone of China, comes another type of food—spicy and often peppery, but not as hot as Szechwan cooking.

Restaurants offering specialties from all the regions of China are known as mandarin. Mandarin style is so-named because this type of menu was the favorite of the mandarins, the class of high-ranking officials under the Chinese Empire.

Although ingredients and seasonings may vary from one region of China to another, the basic methods of food preparation do not. Most cooks in China do not have streamlined kitchens with gas or electric ranges that supply heat at the touch of a button. Wood, charcoal, twigs, leaves, or anything that can be gathered, dried, and burned is used as cooking fuel. To use as little fuel as possible, the Chinese cut meat and vegetables into small pieces so they will cook faster. There are few ovens in China, so foods are generally fried or steamed. Most pastries are bought from cake shops, but many kinds of steamed cakes are made at home.

Butter is rarely used in cooking, for China has always had a scarcity of dairy products. Peanut, soybean, and sesame oils are among the most commonly used cooking fats.

Chinese food is well known for its special seasonings and flavorings—sauces, herbs, spices, and garnishes. While these seasonings vary from region to region, the one ingredient almost always used in Chinese cooking is soy sauce, a dark, salty liquid made from soybeans.

For a feast or banquet the Chinese do not serve dessert at the end of the meal, but fit it in somewhere after the middle. Throughout President Nixon's dinner for his Chinese hosts, a steady stream of pastries was served. But in ordinary family meals there is often no dessert.

It is a Western custom to pour tea throughout dinner. Many Chinese banquets do not include tea at all, and if it is served, it comes at the end of the meal. Traditionally, soup ends the Chinese meal; they feel that soup refreshes the mouth and helps to wash down the food.

All Chinese cooking, whether for a feast or for everyday meals, has one basic object, and that is to please the palate. For the Chinese believe that good food is an important part of good living.

President Nixon (*center*) and Chinese Premier Chou En-lai (*left*) exchange toasts at a magnificent traditional banquet given in Hangchow.

A CHINESE FOLKTALE

There was once a bricklayer. He was handsome, hardworking—and poor. One bright and sunny day he was busy repairing the wall of the house of a very rich man, when he saw, in the flashing light of the sun, the beautiful daughter of the rich man. Right then and there he decided that he must have this girl for his very own.

"I want you for my wife," he said to the gently smiling girl.

"You must ask my father," she said, while all the time her eyes looked lovingly into his.

"I want your daughter for my wife," he said to the father.

"You do?" asked the father and he began to laugh.

"I will be a good husband to her and a good son-in-law to you."

The father laughed some more and then shook his head.

"You will be nothing of the kind. Not until you bring me three treasures."

"What are they?"

"A strand of red hair 3 yards long, a golden rooster that has one foot, and a pearl that glows like the sun even in the middle of the night."

"I will get them."

The rich man laughed until his sides almost burst, for he knew that nowhere in the wide world were such treasures to be found.

But the young man was in love and determined to find the treasures. He spent many days on strange roads, seeking the unusual treasures, but he could not find even one of them. One evening as he sat wearily and hopelessly under an old tree, the thought came to him that he should ask the Great Buddha for help. Instantly, he arose and started the long journey to the Sacred Temple of the Great Buddha.

The very next night he stopped to rest at a house where an old woman lived with her only son. When she learned that the bricklayer was on his way to the Sacred Temple, she asked a favor of him.

"My son cannot speak. Please ask the Buddha what can be done to make him speak."

"I will ask him," said the bricklayer, and he set forth on his journey. The very next evening he stopped at a lonely farm. The farmer was very kind to the weary traveler and then asked a favor of him.

"Why is there not a grain of rice left in my storehouse? I filled it at the last harvest."

"I will ask the Buddha," the bricklayer promised, and went on his way.

He came to a broad river. There was no bridge he could walk across and no ferryboat on which he could sail across. Suddenly a huge snake arose from the waters of the river and smiled graciously at him.

"I will take you across if you will ask the Buddha a question."

"What is it?"

"I have been in this river 500 years. Why have I not become a spirit?"

"Have you been a good snake?"

"Exceptionally good."

"Then I will ask the Buddha."

When the young man finally came to the Sacred Temple of the Great Buddha, he was so tired that he lay down and went to sleep. As he slept, he dreamed that the Buddha came to him and said, "I will answer your questions. The old woman's son cannot speak because there is a red strand 3 yards long in his hair. A golden rooster with only one foot eats all the farmer's rice. A pearl that glows in the night lies in the head of the snake and prevents him from becoming a spirit."

In the morning when the bricklayer awoke, he was sure that his questions had truly been answered. He knelt and thanked the Buddha and then went on his way.

When he came to the broad river, the snake was anxiously waiting for him. He took the traveler across the river.

"Now I shall make you a spirit by plucking out the pearl from your head," said the bricklayer.

The instant the pearl was removed, the snake became a spirit and flew up into the blue sky. The bricklayer glanced at the pearl that was now in his hand and it was glowing.

When he came to the lonely farm, he said to the anxious farmer, "There is a golden rooster hiding in your storehouse. He eats all the rice."

The farmer found the golden rooster with the single foot and gave him to the traveler. And as he did so, the storehouse began to fill with rice.

"Let me cut the red strand that is 3 yards long from your son's hair," said the bricklayer to the old woman when he reached her house.

Colorfully dressed attendants carried the bride in an enclosed litter in a stately Chinese wedding procession of centuries gone by.

"Is that what the Buddha said to do?"

"Yes."

"Then do it."

And the instant the long strand of red hair was cut from the boy's head, he began to speak.

"Good-by and good luck to you," said his happy mother.

And indeed the bricklayer did have very good luck. For when he came to the rich father and showed him the three treasures, there was nothing the man could do but say, "Now you can have my daughter for your bride."

And there was nothing for the blushing young daughter to do but say, "And now I shall be your bride."

And there was nothing for the happy young bricklayer to do but say, "I shall be a devoted husband to you. And a good son-in-law to you, dear father."

And indeed he was.

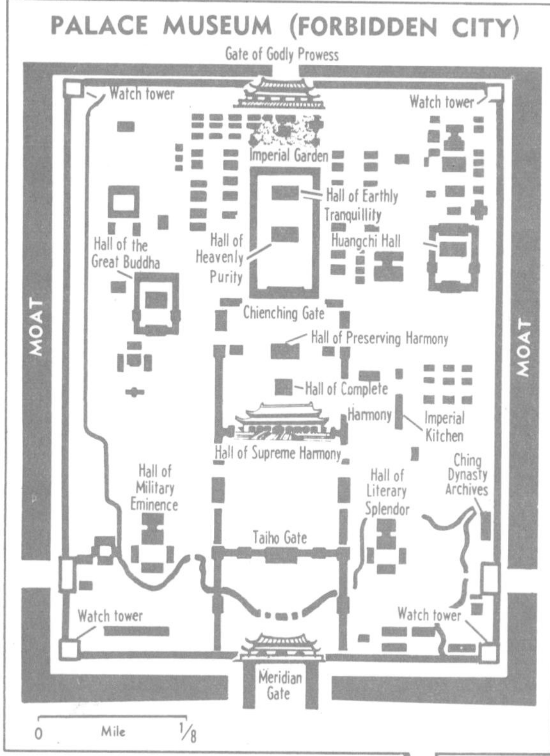

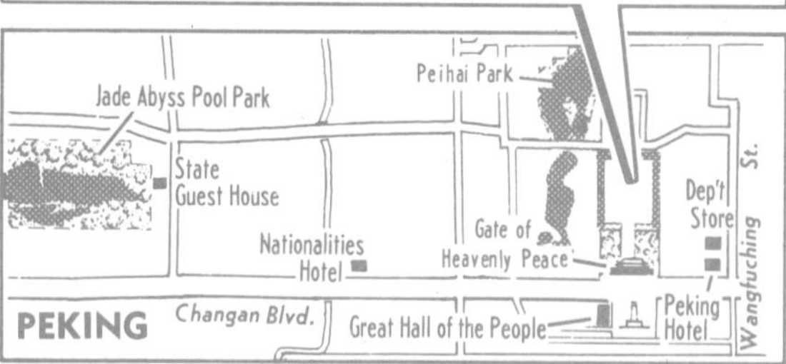

A plan of the Forbidden City.

THE FORBIDDEN CITY

The Forbidden City of Peking is like a precious pearl inside a jewel box inside a larger jewel box. The larger jewel box is an old, walled part of Peking called the Inner City. The smaller jewel box inside it is an area known as the Imperial City, where members of the emperor's court lived. And the pearl itself is the Forbidden City, 250 acres of palace and gardens, where China's Ming and Ching (or Manchu) emperors lived from 1421 until 1912.

In 1912 the last of the emperors was overthrown, and China became a republic. Today there are government offices in the Imperial City, and the old palaces and halls of the Forbidden City are now a part of the Palace Museum.

The Forbidden City was closed to the general public during China's Cultural Revolution, which began in 1966. But in 1971 a new phase in Chinese diplomacy began, and the City was reopened.

Water still flows in the broad moat surrounding the Forbidden City, and a wine red protecting wall stands more than 35 feet high. Upon each corner of the wall stands a yellow-roofed watchtower. (This wall was repainted in preparation for President Nixon's visit.)

Four entrance gates, one on each side of the wall, lead into the city. The largest is the Meridian Gate. As the visitor passes through the Meridian Gate he faces a large, paved courtyard in the middle of which a canal, the Golden Stream, flows under five marble bridges.

The visitor must then go through the Taiho Gate and cross still another courtyard before he arrives at the three great ceremonial halls, the heart of the Forbidden City.

All three halls stand on a white marble terrace. Their walls and columns are red, and their roofs are of yellow tile. The first of the great halls is the Hall of Supreme Harmony. It was here that the emperor had his throne, and it was here that the most formal ceremonies, such as those in honor of the New Year or the emperor's birthday, were held. In the dimness of the vast hall the richly carved throne, its dark wood gleaming, rests on a platform 6 feet high. Tall statues of cranes, the symbol of long life, stand at either side of the throne. Dark lacquerwork, gilt columns, red columns, and blue cloisonné pillars and urns are all part of the interior.

To the north of the Hall of Supreme Harmony is a smaller, square hall, known as the Hall of Complete Harmony. The emperor rested here before he appeared at the ceremonies held in the larger hall.

North of the Hall of Complete Harmony is the Hall of Preserving Harmony, which was once the scene of imperial banquets.

To the east and west of these three halls are

Five marble bridges adorn the courtyard that leads to the Taiho Gate.

other courtyards and buildings, laid out in a perfectly balanced design. The Hall of Military Eminence once housed the imperial printing presses, and the Hall of Literary Splendor formerly held the imperial collection of books.

A gate known as Chienching (Gate of Heavenly Purity) leads from the last of the great halls to rear palaces in an inner courtyard. At one time the emperor's bedroom was in the first of these, the Hall of Heavenly Purity. Later the palace became a reception room for foreign ambassadors.

Ming empresses lived in another of the rear palaces, the Hall of Earthly Tranquillity. Later Ching emperors and empresses spent their wedding nights here. The bridal chamber was painted and furnished in red for happiness. Another section of this palace was used for performing sacrifices to the gods of the imperial kitchen. It is said that as many as 1,300 pigs a year were offered to the kitchen gods.

From the rear palaces still another gate—the Gate of Earthly Tranquillity—leads into the Imperial Garden. There are fountains in the garden and a small man-made mountain complete with a cave.

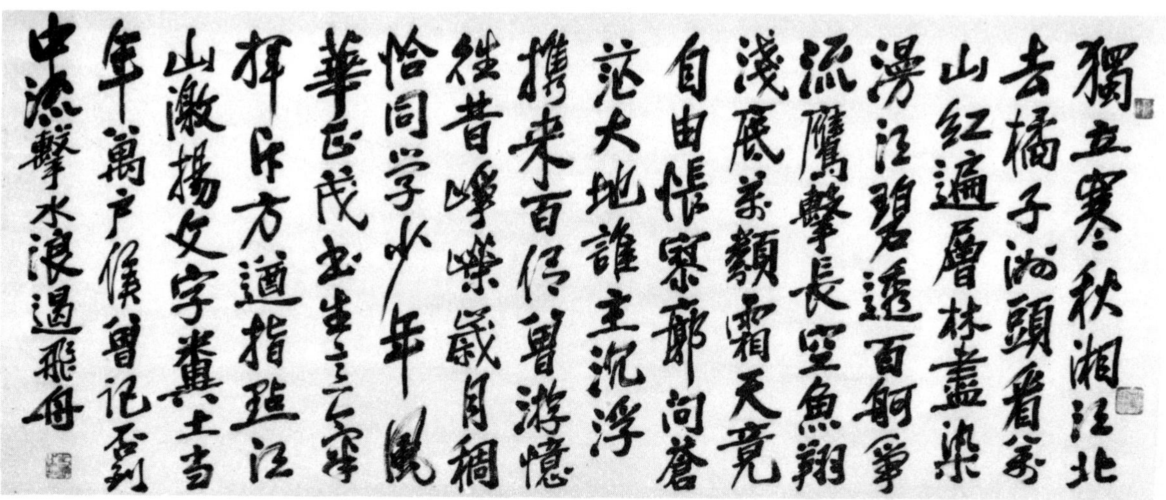

A poem about his school days by Mao Tse-tung. The calligrapher is Fang Chao-ling.

THE ART OF BEAUTIFUL HANDWRITING

If you were going to school in China, you wouldn't have to learn an alphabet. But you would have to do something much harder. You would have to learn to read and write the symbols for hundreds of words.

Chinese words are not made up of individual letters, but are represented by symbols. These are known as characters. Each one is made up of different strokes written with a brush inside an imaginary square. To form sentences the characters are written in a column from the top of the page downward, and from the right-hand side of the page to the left.

At least that is the traditional way of writing. But many changes are taking place. In some of the printed material now appearing, for example, the sentences are arranged across the page as they are in English. Usually these are written and read from right to left. Students taking notes and people writing informal letters may write not only across the page, but from left to right, as well. Most people under the age of 35 write in this way. But an older person may prefer to write the traditional way.

The art of beautiful handwriting is called calligraphy. From ancient times, the Chinese have considered fine handwriting a great art, and a person who is able to write beautifully is very much respected.

The Chinese have so much regard for this art form that they hang examples of fine calligraphy in their homes. Often these examples are a line or two of poetry. The characters are valued not only for the meaning they express, but for their beauty. A well-written character has both balance and a feeling of movement. The Chinese admiration for calligraphy is a little like a Westerner's admiration for abstract art.

The beginnings of Chinese writing go back several thousand years—to about the 28th century B.C. (Egyptian picture writing developed at about the same time.) The earliest characters were simple pictures of things. One style of Chinese writing was well established by the 18th century B.C. This is the style named shell-and-bone because examples of it have been found engraved on tortoise shells and animal bones. Through the centuries a number of other writing styles developed.

In Chinese there are about 40,000 characters. Each character stands for a one-syllable word. To read and write, a person must know 3,000 or 4,000 characters.

The thousands of Chinese characters fall into several categories. Some characters look roughly like the objects they represent.

Another group of characters consists of symbols that suggest the meaning of the word.

Tan, or "dawn," is represented by the symbol for the sun drawn above a line, which is the horizon.

Some characters are made up of two or more symbols that add up to a new meaning when they are put together. "Woman" and "child" combined form "good."

The largest number of characters fall into a group called phonetic compounds. In this group, one part of the character gives the meaning, and one part gives the pronunciation. *Ya,* or "crow," is made up of two elements. One gives the pronunciation, "ya," and one part is the symbol for "bird." (To the Chinese the crow's call is ya-ya instead of caw-caw.)

Just as a tennis player practices until he masters certain basic strokes, a calligrapher practices until he masters seven basic brushstrokes. All Chinese characters are made up of some combination of these strokes. The basic brushstrokes are: a horizontal line, a dot, a vertical line, a sharp curve, a stroke sweeping down from right to left, one sweeping down from left to right, and another stroke sweeping down, but not quite so sharply, from left to right.

The necessary writing equipment consists of a brush, a brush stand, ink, and an inkstone. These are known as the Four Treasures of the Room of Literature. The writing brush has a reed or bamboo handle and a writing tip of animal hair, often rabbit's or sheep's hair. When it is used, the brush is held upright without any tilt.

The ink—always black—is not liquid, but solid. It is made of lampblack mixed with a kind of gum, which is heated and allowed to harden. The mixture is shaped into small sticks.

The inkstone is a flat stone with a small hollow in the center. When a person is ready to write, he grinds some ink with a little water in the hollow of the inkstone; using his left hand, he slowly moves the tip of the ink stick around and around on the inkstone. It is part of the calligrapher's art to judge exactly how much ink to grind. He should have just enough for the project he plans.

And when he starts to write—usually on a long scroll—he must be absolutely sure of what he is doing. There is no such thing as going back over a character to correct a mistake. Each stroke must be written quickly, without pausing, and perfectly—the first time.

Everyday writing in Chinese is a very different matter from the fine art of calligraphy. If a student sits down to do his homework, for example, he doesn't use a brush, or grind ink, or write on a long scroll. Neither does a mother when she writes a note to the teacher. They are much more likely to use a ball-point pen or a pencil and write on ordinary notepaper. If you're planning to write a poem, though, a ball-point pen will never do. For that, you will still need a brush and ink.

Chinese characters of one type look somewhat like the objects they represent. On the left is the sun, and on the right the moon.

Some characters consist of symbols that suggest a word's meaning. *Tan,* or "dawn," is made up of the symbol for the sun above the horizon.

Two or more characters can be combined, and the result is a new meaning. The characters for "woman" and "child" combined form "good."

One part of a character may give meaning, and one part sound. The two parts of *ya,* or "crow," give the meaning "bird," and the sound "ya."

President Nixon signing U.S.–Soviet space pact.

A VISIT TO THE SOVIET UNION

Following his successful visit to the People's Republic of China in February, 1972, President Richard Nixon began another important journey 3 months later. This time his goal was Moscow and a full-scale summit meeting with the leaders of the Soviet Union. Unlike the China visit, where the President was cast in the role of high-level tourist, his mission to Moscow was more of a political business trip. In China there had been a holiday air, with carefully staged public displays of friendship and a constant round of parties, banquets, and sightseeing trips. The Russian excursion was quite different. Here the emphasis was on practical accomplishments. The Soviet and American leaders engaged in lengthy policy talks and signed a series of treaties covering such areas as mutual arms limitation, technical exchanges, and joint space exploration.

Almost from the moment the presidential jet touched down at Moscow's Vnukovo Airport, on May 22, the mood was set for a week of serious discussions and sessions of hard bargaining. After a short welcoming ceremony at the airport, the President and Mrs. Nixon were whisked off by motorcade to spacious quarters in Terem Palace, inside the walls of the Kremlin. The thousands of Russians who lined Lenin Prospect hoping to see the American President got only a brief glimpse as the big Russian limousine sped by.

The Nixons hardly had time to unpack their bags before the President was invited to hold an unscheduled meeting with Communist Party chief Leonid Brezhnev. The two leaders conferred for nearly 2 hours, mapping out a schedule for the policy discussions that were to be held in the following days.

But although the Russian and American leaders were businesslike in their approach, the social side was not forgotten. At a cocktail party in magnificent St. George's Hall in the Great Kremlin Palace, the President and his Soviet hosts exchanged pleasantries while sipping vodka and eating caviar.

Later that evening a state dinner was given in President Nixon's honor. The menu of this sumptuous meal included venison, beef, and pheasant, and champagne and a variety of other wines. There were the usual formal toasts. In his remarks, Soviet President Nikolai Podgorny expressed a desire for a "radical turn toward relaxation of tensions." Calling President Nixon's visit "a momentous event," he declared that the Soviet Union wanted "not merely good but friendly relations between the U.S.S.R. and the U.S." President Nixon replied by saying: "We meet to begin a new age in the relationship between our two great and powerful nations."

In a cordial vein, one of the Soviet leaders told his American guest: "Mr. President, just before your plane landed there was a warm shower; then the sun came out. The peasants

The Nixons attend the Bolshoi Theater for a performance of *Swan Lake*.

call this a 'mushroom rain' because it makes the mushrooms grow. It is a good omen for crops, and we hope that today's rain is a good omen for our meetings as well."

It seemed that it had been a good omen, for during the next few days a large number of treaties and other pacts were agreed upon. Actually, the groundwork had been done months earlier during preliminary negotiations. These had included advance meetings between Soviet officials and Henry Kissinger, the presidential adviser on national security affairs. But there were still many details to be resolved by President Nixon and his Soviet counterparts during their intensive talks.

IMPORTANT AGREEMENTS

Among the many agreements, the arms limitation pacts were clearly the most important. Two arms agreements were signed by President Nixon and General Secretary Brezhnev. The first limited the number of anti–ballistic missile (ABM) systems each country could have. Both the Soviet Union and the United States were permitted to have two systems: one to protect their capital cities, and a second to defend a part of each nation's offensive missile force.

A second arms pact, called an interim agreement, put specific restraints on the offensive missile forces the two nations could maintain. Under the terms of the 5-year agreement, the two countries were limited to those offensive missiles already in existence or under construction. Both parties pledged not to construct new intercontinental ballistic missile (ICBM) launchers after July 1, 1972. Each side was permitted to keep a fixed number of offensive missiles and missile-launching submarines.

President Nixon hailed the arms pacts as "an enormously important agreement," and added, "It is only an indication of what can happen in the future as we work together toward peace in the world." Soviet Premier Aleksei Kosygin expressed a similar view when he called the treaty "a great victory for the Soviet and American peoples in the matter of easing international tension . . . ."

Although the signing of the arms limitation pacts was the high point of the President's visit, several other important agreements were worked out by the two sides.

Medical Research

By the terms of this agreement the Soviet Union and the United States will exchange medical equipment, newly developed drugs, and information. Teams of American specialists will visit the Soviet Union, and Russian medical experts will come to the United States. There may be joint research efforts in the fields of cancer and heart disease. A 10-man joint commission will be established to co-ordinate these exchange programs.

Protection of the Environment

The two countries will exchange specialists and information dealing with various environmental problems, such as air, water, and noise pollution. This is the first treaty dealing with the environment signed by the United States.

Science and Technology

American business firms and Soviet agencies will be able to develop joint technical projects for mutual profit. The pact provides for the exchange of technical data and scientific material. Global communications is considered a likely area for joint American-Soviet activity. A joint commission will meet twice a year.

Space Exploration

The two nations agreed to "develop co-operation in the fields of space meteorology, study of the natural environment, exploration of near earth space, the moon and the planets, and space biology and medicine." The principal feature of the pact was the announcement of a joint space mission to be carried out in 1975. At that time, a U.S. Apollo spacecraft will rendezvous and link up with a Soviet Soyuz spacecraft. Such joint ventures could lead to combined expeditions to other planets and an end to the space race.

Incidents on the High Seas

In recent years, there have been a number of incidents in which U.S. and Soviet warships nearly collided while deliberately maneuvering close to each other. To avoid such dangerous confrontations, the pact forbade ships and planes of the two nations from engaging in mock attack and other activities that might cause an incident.

Mutual Trade

This was the one major area where the two sides failed to reach a definite agreement. What did come out of the meetings was the formation of a joint trade commission to iron out differences and supervise the future expansion of U.S.–Soviet commerce. A major stumbling block is the question of Soviet repayment of World War II lend-lease debts. The Russians have offered $300,000,000 in payment, while the United States is asking for about $1,000,000,000.

▶ AMBASSADORS OF GOOD WILL

In between treaty signings, President Nixon did manage to squeeze in a few social and ceremonial activities. On the morning of May 24, he laid a wreath at the Tomb of the Unknown Soldier in Moscow. Soviet television cameras recorded the event. The following evening he and Mrs. Nixon attended a performance of *Swan Lake* by the famed Bolshoi Ballet.

On May 28, President Nixon addressed the Russian people over Soviet television. It was the first time an American president had ever spoken directly to the Russian people in this manner. In his speech, President Nixon pointed out that the Soviet Union and the United States had never fought a war against each other. "As great powers," he noted, "we will sometimes be competitors, but we need never be enemies."

He went on to say: "If we continue in the spirit of serious purpose that has marked our discussions this week, these agreements can start us on a new road of co-operation for the

Mrs. Nixon listens attentively as a Russian schoolgirl recites a poem.

benefit of our people, for the benefit of all people."

The President concluded his remarks by recalling his visit to Leningrad—which had been besieged by the Nazis in World War II. There, he had read the diary of a young girl named Tanya Savicheva, who had lost her entire family during the siege. President Nixon repeated what he had expressed in an earlier speech, that the high-level meetings taking place would help to achieve "that kind of world in which the little Tanyas and their brothers and sisters will be able to grow up in a world of peace and friendship."

While the President attended to affairs of state, Mrs. Nixon was given the role of goodwill ambassador. She visited Moscow's massive GUM department store, where she made several purchases, and was taken on a tour of several Russian schools. As a former schoolteacher, the First Lady enjoyed the opportunity to sit in on Russian classes. At one school, she presented a gift of some American basketballs to the school team. Mrs. Nixon also attended a performance of the Moscow State Circus and shook hands with a performing bear.

Wherever she went, the First Lady received praise for her charm and gracious manner. Mrs. Andrei Gromyko, wife of the Soviet Foreign Minister, remarked: "I have known the wives of several American presidents, but Mrs. Nixon is the nicest."

All in all, the summit meeting was considered a great success. While many problems remained unresolved, the superpowers had taken steps to ease tension and improve the political climate in a world troubled by war and social unrest. On the immediate practical side, the stage was set for increased cultural, scientific, and economic exchanges between the two countries.

During his stay, President Nixon expressed his hope that there would be more such productive summit meetings in the future. "We look forward to the time when we shall be able to welcome you in our country," he told the Soviet leaders. "This is the first meeting. There will be others."

Teen-age ballet students rehearse in the Churlionis School of Arts, Vilna.

SOVIET BALLET SCHOOLS

Every spring, thousands of girls and boys, from Vilna to Vladivostok, try out for admission to one of the famous ballet schools of the Soviet Union. There are 19 of these schools. They are located in major cities, including the capitals of all 15 republics of the U.S.S.R.

Parents usually go along for moral support the day of the tryouts. The youngest applicants are only 10 and the oldest, 13. The entrance examinations are long and hard, and competition is as fierce as a wind from the Baltic. At the ballet school in Moscow, for example, there are as many as 2,000 applicants for 20 vacant places.

The eagerness of the young people—boys, as well as girls—to be accepted into a ballet school indicates the enormous popularity of the art in the Soviet Union. The Russian people have a highly trained taste and great love for the ballet.

Ballet began in Italy, but some of the greatest dancers and choreographers of all time have been Russians. The legendary dancers Anna Pavlova and Vaslav Nijinsky were both born in Russia in the late 1800's, and such popular ballets as *Swan Lake* and *The Sleeping Beauty, Scheherazade* and *Petrouchka* were created in Russia by choreographers Marius Petipa and Michel Fokine.

Today in the Soviet Union 4,500 boys and girls are enrolled in ballet schools. Thousands more young people study ballet, but in ballet studios or in groups run on a voluntary basis. The best known of such groups are those at

A class on the stage of the Bolshoi Theater.

Rehearsal time in a ballet studio in Moscow.

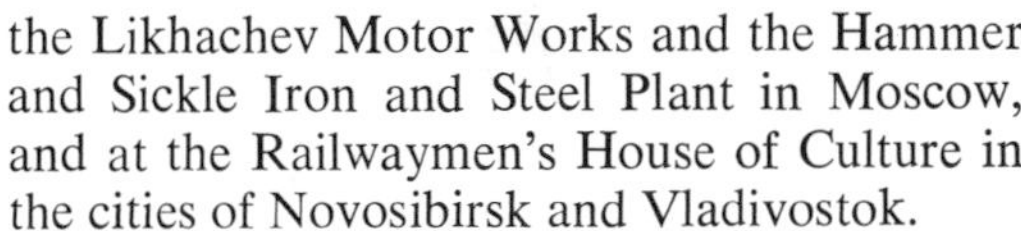

the Likhachev Motor Works and the Hammer and Sickle Iron and Steel Plant in Moscow, and at the Railwaymen's House of Culture in the cities of Novosibirsk and Vladivostok.

The 19 ballet schools, however, are the major centers of choreographic education in the U.S.S.R. The largest of the schools is the Moscow Academic Choreographic School at the Bolshoi Theater, with a student body of about 600. (The Bolshoi is the world-famous Soviet ballet theater.) The second largest ballet school is the Leningrad Academic State Choreographic School, with 400 students. These are also the oldest ballet schools in the country. Both of these schools were founded in the 18th century.

THE ENTRANCE EXAMINATIONS

Not everyone who would like to enroll in a ballet school gets as far as the entrance examinations in the spring. Many hopeful candidates are screened out earlier.

In the course of the year, experienced teachers hold preliminary reviews of young talents. To some, the teachers are forced to give a disappointing verdict. To the lucky ones who pass the preliminary review, the teachers give advice on the best way to prepare for the coming exams.

The actual entrance examinations are divided into three rounds. In the first round, examiners check the physical appearance (face and figure) of the applicants and their professional aptitude: leap, flexibility, and step. In the second round, a medical commission examines each applicant's skeleton and muscles, the inner ear (which controls balance), and the eyesight.

The boys and girls who pass these two rounds move on to the third and hardest round. They face a commission that determines their artistic abilities. The candidates are asked to do several simple ballet steps, to sing something, and to improvise a dance to music.

THE COURSE OF INSTRUCTION

In the Soviet Union, girls and boys start elementary school when they are 7. To enroll in a ballet school, a student must be 10 years old and must have completed the first 3 years of elementary school. The length of instruction in ballet school is another 8 years.

Those whose abilities are spotted somewhat later may enter a ballet school at the age of 12 or 13, after they have finished 5 years of regular school. For this group, the term at the ballet school is 6 years. Instruction is free for both groups.

Classes in all schools in the Soviet Union begin on September 1. The schedule in the Moscow Academic Choreographic School is a good example of the way a ballet student's time is organized.

Classes start promptly at nine. The morning hours are devoted to specialized subjects: folk, historical, and everyday dances and classical ballet; training in breathing (for junior classes); the art of makeup; and music. The afternoon classes are devoted to general subjects: mathematics, history, biology, a foreign language, and similar courses. The workload is heavy, but after each class hour there is a 10- to 15-minute break.

At the school in Moscow, students take all their classes—dance, as well as general, subjects—in the same building. But the general subjects are taught in specially equipped study rooms. The school also has a place for sports. They are very popular here. There are some restrictions, though, on sports for ballet students. Activities like football and horseback riding, which may lead to serious injuries, are not encouraged.

A hot dinner is served in the afternoon, and classes end at five. Some students live at home. Those who come from other cities board at the school.

DANCE LESSONS

The hours devoted to dance lessons are, of course, a high point of the day. In the school in Moscow there are 20 large halls in which these lessons are given. Boys and girls are instructed separately.

All students, no matter how old they are or how long they have been in ballet school, take 2 hours of instruction in classical ballet every day.

The instructors proceed slowly and carefully so that their young students do not injure themselves by doing too much too soon. Standing on the tips of the toes is allowed only after a student has been in the school 6 to 8 months. Lessons on the tips of the toes are not given every day. They are given no oftener than every other day.

Junior pupils learn simple dance elements, which they perform at a very slow tempo. As their instruction progresses, these elements become more complicated, and the tempo quickens.

For their classical ballet lessons junior girls wear *pomanelki*. These are sleeveless tops and shorts. Older girls generally wear short beige or white dresses with wide shoulder straps. Boys wear costumes consisting of sleeveless tops and tights.

An important element in ballet training is practice, and this includes more than daily sessions at the bar. Practice also means learning to appear in public. Pupils in the Moscow Choreographic School often have the opportunity to appear before an audience. Ballet students take part in almost every presentation of the Bolshoi Theater. Pupils of the Moscow ballet school also give performances and concerts of their own in the theater building, and they make concert tours of the U.S.S.R. and other countries.

WHAT DOES THE FUTURE HOLD?

It requires dedication, discipline, and lots of hard work to study ballet seriously. Not everyone who enrolls in a ballet school is able to cope with all of these demands, and somewhere along the line a number of students drop out. As a rule, only two thirds of those who enroll in a ballet school will actually graduate from it.

But for those who do complete their professional training the future is bright with opportunities. Many graduates join ballet companies, including the company of the Bolshoi

Each ballet school pupil receives individual criticism and comment.

The youngest girls of the Moscow Academic Choreographic School.

There's time to relax and to chat for a few minutes between classes. Here students of the Churlionis School of Arts take their break.

Theater. Some of today's great Soviet stars—Ekaterina Maksimova, Vladimir Vasilyev, Nina Sorokina, Natalya Bessmertnova, Yury Vladimirov, Yelena Ryabinkina, and others—are graduates of the Moscow Academic Choreographic School.

Not all ballet school graduates become performers, however. Some become ballet masters; some become orchestra leaders; and others, teachers. Many young people who left their home cities to study go back to their homes after graduation. There they join local theaters, studios, and ballet schools. Still others become specialists in the theory and history of ballet.

Each year the graduates move out into the world of ballet. And each year in the spring a fresh crop of boys and girls, their faces shining with hope, appear to take the examinations for ballet school.

Vladimir Gurevich
Novosti Press Agency

Fencing helps ballet students develop speed and lightness of movement.

Mrs. Richard M. Nixon greets students at the Moscow Academic Choreographic School. They gave her ballet shoes and a tutu during her May, 1972, visit.

A RUSSIAN FOLKTALE

The Stubborn Shepherd

Many, many years ago there was a powerful and fierce czar, who ruled his country with an iron hand. Everybody feared him. Everybody trembled in his presence. The Czar was so feared that whenever he sneezed everyone in the kingdom—everyone—had to say "To your good health." There was not a person in the entire length and breadth of the land who did not say it—except for one fellow, a young shepherd. He would not say "To your good health" when the Czar sneezed.

This state of affairs went on for quite a while. But one day the Czar found out about the young shepherd. He ordered him brought to the palace at once.

The Czar sat on his throne and gazed fiercely down at the shepherd. Then, in a low and calm tone, he ordered, "Say at once, 'To my good health!' "

"To my good health!"

"To mine. To mine, you fool!"

"To mine, to mine, Your Majesty."

"But to mine. To my own," shouted the Czar, and he rose from his throne, a tall and awe-inspiring figure.

"Of course," said the shepherd calmly. "To my own."

The Czar came close to the young shepherd and roared, "Say 'To your health, Your Majesty.' Or you will die!"

The shepherd shook his head. "Not until I marry your daughter."

Now the Czar's daughter was as pretty as a snow flower, and she smiled shyly at the young shepherd. But the Czar did not smile at all. He had the shepherd thrown into a deep pit with a very hungry bear. And then everybody went away and left the shepherd to his fate.

But there was something about the stubborn shepherd that touched the heart of the hungry bear. For the bear just sat back and stared at the shepherd all the night through, and did not harm him in any way. In the morning, the Czar came and found his most stubborn subject, the bold young shepherd, still alive.

"Well?" said the Czar.

"Not until I marry your daughter."

So this time the shepherd was thrown into a den of wild boars. Everyone was sure the shepherd was in for trouble. But he wasn't. For the moment those savage and hungry beasts saw him, they all gathered around him and stared. That is how the Czar found the shepherd in the morning—surrounded by a circle of adoring and fascinated wild boars.

"Well?" stormed the Czar, who was growing more desperate and furious by the moment.

"Your daughter."

"Never!"

The Czar had once been given a present of two lions. They were his favorite pets, and they were savage and bloodthirsty. He had the young shepherd thrown to the lions.

The fierce lions did not attack the shepherd. Instead, they spent the whole night licking his face with joy and delight.

Now the Czar decided on a new way of dealing with his stubborn and unruly subject.

"Come with me," he said to the young shepherd.

They rode along in the royal coach until they came to a forest that had tree upon tree of sparkling silver.

"This is all yours," the Czar assured him, "if you say 'To your good health, Your Majesty.' "

The wedding of the Czar's daughter and the shepherd can only be imagined. But even a simple Russian wedding of long ago looked royal as the bride and groom, wearing crowns, stood before the priest in his splendid vestments.

The shepherd looked at the sparkling silver forest. He would have given almost anything to own it.

Yet he said, "No."

The Czar and the young shepherd rode on and on until they came to a huge castle of pure gold. When the sun shone upon it, it was truly dazzling.

"Say it and you shall have both the silver forest and the golden castle."

The shepherd hesitated. "No," he finally said.

The Czar and the shepherd rode on and on until they came to a lake. On the lake floated thousands of small boxes, and in the boxes were jewels of every description. The shepherd looked at the jewels in astonishment.

The Czar smiled, for now he was sure that he had won.

"Say it and you shall have it all: the silver forest, the golden castle, and all of these precious jewels."

Slowly the shepherd shook his head. "I love your daughter and I will marry her."

Slowly, slowly the Czar came to a great decision.

"All right, you may marry her. But you will say, 'To your good health, Your Majesty'?"

"Yes."

The wedding of the Czar's daughter and the young shepherd was the grandest wedding ever seen in Russia. Such rejoicing and such feasting and so many songs! Everybody was happy. The Czar was so happy that he began to sneeze. And everybody said what they had to say—"To your very good health, Your Majesty!" And then there was a great silence and all the faces, from the Czar on down, were turned to the stubborn young shepherd.

First, he gave his pretty bride a kiss. Then he turned to the Czar and said in a loud voice, "To your very good health, Your Majesty!"

And everybody cheered and cheered. For all I know, they are still cheering.

RUSSIAN ARTS AND CRAFTS

On the night of January 12, 1972, a fascinating art show opened at the Corcoran Gallery of Art in Washington, D.C. It was very unusual and unique. The show, entitled Soviet Union: Arts and Crafts in Ancient Times and Today, was the most costly art exhibition ever sent to the United States by the Soviet Union. There were more than 2,000 examples of Russian art, dating from the 5th century B.C. to as recently as 1972.

The exhibition traveled to five other American cities during the year, ending its tour at the Metropolitan Museum of Art in New York City. The exhibition was part of an exchange program carried on every two years between the United States and the Soviet Union. This cultural exchange was first started in 1959 and has done much to help the Soviet people and the American people know each other better. In return for the Soviet contribution in 1972, the United States sent a show called Research and Development, U.S.A. to the Soviet Union.

The Soviet exhibition was impressive and interesting. It attracted many visitors in all six cities. Americans have always been interested in folk arts and crafts, both their own and those of other nations. Americans themselves have a strong and rich tradition of arts and crafts that goes back to earliest colonial days. And it was evident that the show was planned to meet this interest. "Our aim is to show the American people the crafts and folk arts of all the Soviet Republics," said Anatoly Dyuzhev, First Secretary of the Soviet Embassy in Washington. "Folk arts and crafts create new life and help to educate our people. . . . They symbolize the friendship between all nations of our country."

But most of all the show impressed all who saw it with the evidence of a continuing tradition in Russian culture. Works of art that dated far back into Russian history seemed to relate to works that were created only a year or two ago. Forms may have changed from century to century, but they always seem to keep what is most beautiful and most practical for everyday life.

Among the highlights of the show was a pre-Christian Scythian gold plaque that dates back to the 5th century B.C. Of great beauty, the plaque shows a vigorous eagle carrying off a hare. As was to be expected, there were a number of magnificent icons, richly colored religious scenes and images painted on wood. The painting of icons was Russia's most

A gaily painted clay toy from the Kirov region.

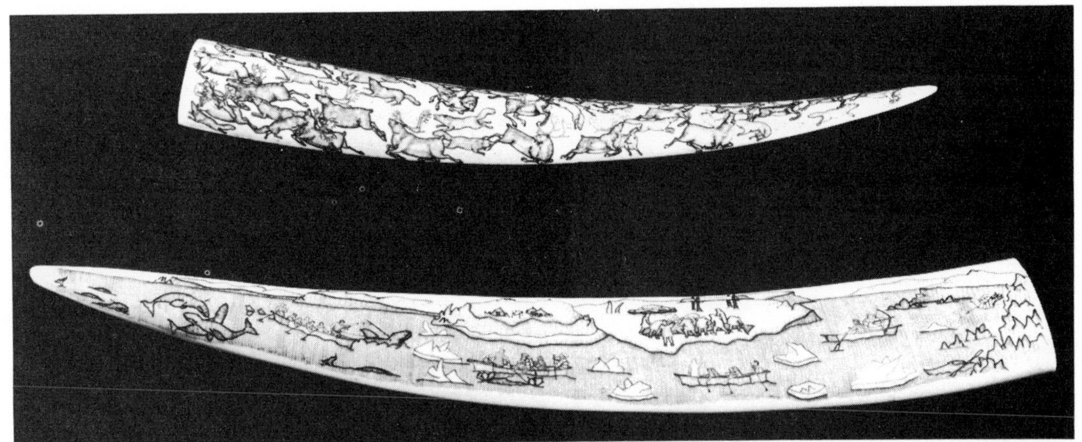

Engraved walrus tusks: hunting scenes (*top*), hunting the whale (*bottom*).

famous art form for centuries. A particularly striking icon in the exhibition was a 14th-century representation of the Prophet Elijah. It shows the biblical figure in the fiery chariot on his dramatic flight to heaven.

There were many other treasures in the exhibition. There was a gold chalice set with emeralds that was made for the mother of Czar Peter the Great. There was also a saddle that was made for Ivan the Terrible. The seat and flaps are encrusted with gold embroidery and gleaming gems. Looking at it, one can easily imagine the fierce Russian Czar seated on a white charger, ready to lead his soldiers into battle.

The show had many things to delight children. There was a beautiful collection of clay whistle-toys that were created by an old woman who lives in a northern Russian village. This old grandmother digs her own clay and then molds and bakes the toys on an iron griddle. Some of the motifs and designs she paints on the toys have been traced back nearly 4,000 years.

There were a number of doll-like figures of peasants in the exhibition that were done with delicate taste and humor. Some of the other objects that seemed to attract the most viewers were the rugs from Kazakhstan, the ceramics from Dagestan, the Latvian tapestries, and the lace from Vologda.

All in all, the show seemed to achieve its aim of getting the American people to understand the Russian people better through their arts and crafts.

A thick felt appliqué rug.

A silver filigree vase from Armenia.

The Russian bears are a star attraction: they are so well trained that they can perform almost as skillfully as human acrobats.

THE RUSSIAN CIRCUS

The children come and sit wide-eyed, mouths open. They are lost in a world of magic, a world of brilliant color and excitement. It is the world of the circus.

The circus in the Soviet Union is the same as any other circus the world over. And yet it is not the same. For it has a very intimate quality; there is only one ring, and so every act draws the full attention of the audience.

Nearly all the Russian circuses have an abundance of animal acts. The most famous is the Russian bear. In the old days these circus bears were taught to wrestle and to show how fierce and strong they were. But now a change has come about. Papa Bear rides a motorcycle and then gracefully jumps off and hops onto a bicycle and pedals to his heart's content. Mama Bear drives a car. And then, most thrilling of all, the whole bear family get together and play a game of ice hockey.

The Russians have added new forms to their circuses. They now have a Circus on

Ice and a Water Circus. It is here, at the Circus on Ice, that the bears put on skates, grasp hockey sticks, and play ice hockey. All of the other acts at this circus are performed on ice. At the Water Circus all of the acts are performed in a large pool. One of the most exciting moments comes when three huge tigers play water polo with their beautiful trainer.

Of course, a circus is not a circus without its clowns. The Soviet circuses have many outstanding funnymen. Perhaps the best known of all is Popov, who is called the "Sunny Clown." He has a golden crop of hair and a radiantly smiling face, and his simpleheartedness seems to charm everyone.

Karandash—whose name means "pencil"—is a naïve, sweetly sentimental, and blundering little man. He has been likened to Charlie Chaplin. And Yuri Nikulin, another clown, is at times comic and then sad and doleful, like the American clown Emmett Kelly.

There are acrobats, trapeze artists, and pole balancers. The Soviet circus is different and it is the same as other circuses. It is the joyous gathering place of the young.

The Kiselev acrobats (*above*) perform a difficult balancing act; and clowns (*center*) sing and play musical instruments to amuse the audience.

CHILDREN'S THEATER

Exciting and imaginative, theater for children in the Soviet Union is a highly developed art form that is as professional and popular as theater for adults. The Russians, firmly believing that plays for young people should be more than just entertainment, have learned to use the stage to tell children about the world around them.

About 1920, theaters giving performances exclusively for young people began to appear in all the major cities of the Soviet Union. In the 1930's, theaters were started on collective and state farms in rural areas. Today there are mime, puppet, and dramatic companies performing in almost every city, town, and village of Russia.

Young people's theater in the Soviet Union is divided into three groups. There are separate performances for small children, for adolescents, and for older teen-agers. For 5- and 6-year-olds, for example, there are 110 professional puppet companies, as well as companies of live performers who act out fairy tales and legends. For older audiences, plays about school, factory, and collective farm life are popular. In addition, classics and transla-

The merry jester capers and prances in *The Tale of the Fisherman and the Golden Fish.*

***The Tale of the Dead Princess and the Seven Braves:* The sun smiles on the new day . . .**

OF THE SOVIET UNION

tions of foreign plays are in the repertory of most companies.

Young Russians are provided with unusually beautiful spectacles. The best choreographers direct the dancing, the finest composers write the music, and the most talented artists design the costumes and sets. The productions are among the most colorful and artistic in the world. Scripts are written especially for the children's theater by some of the Soviet Union's leading authors. Many of the roles are portrayed by the best actors and actresses of the Russian stage.

All children's theaters in the Soviet Union are completely supported by the government. In planning a new production, the preferences of audiences are always kept in mind, and their help is often sought in the selection of scripts. Teachers and students are frequently asked for their opinions, and some theater companies have young people's student councils to approve a script.

One of the largest professional children's theater companies in the Soviet Union, and one of the best known in the world, is the Central Children's Theater of Moscow. This group, founded in 1921, has a staff of about 350 people, its own building, and a permanent company of about 80 actors.

Two of the most popular of the company's productions are *The Tale of the Fisherman and the Golden Fish* and *The Tale of the Dead Princess and the Seven Braves.*

Every Russian child loves the story of the fisherman that begins with the words "There lived an old man and his wife by the very blue sea." The Children's Theater has transformed this familiar tale into an enchanting stage production that combines music, dance, and drama. The story, well known to American children as *The Fisherman and His Wife,* ends on a strong moral note, with the merry jester warning the audience against the evils of greed and envy.

The Tale of the Dead Princess and the Seven Braves is a version of the Grimm Brothers' *Snow White and the Seven Dwarfs.* Pushkin's tale is about a wicked queen who poisons her stepdaughter and has her body placed in a glass coffin. The handsome Prince Yelisei, who loves the princess, finds the coffin, shatters it, and restores the princess to life. The Russian version stresses the power of love, the virtue of loyalty, and the triumph of good over evil.

. . . and the fearless Seven Braves boldly march out.

President Richard Nixon and Vice-President Spiro Agnew rejoice in their victory.

THE 1972 PRESIDENTIAL ELECTION

Presidential primaries are elimination contests. The candidates who survive the primaries enter the "semifinals" at the national conventions. The conventions pick the finalists who will represent the two major parties, and it is these two candidates who run against each other in the presidential election. In 1972 the Democratic presidential nominee was Senator George McGovern of South Dakota. The Republican nominee was President Richard Nixon, running for a second 4-year term.

President Nixon faced only token opposition in his bid for the GOP nomination. Presidents in office who run for re-election are traditionally given the nomination at their party's national convention. Sometimes, as in the case of President Lyndon Johnson in 1968, the chief executive decides he does not want to stay in office. His party must then turn to other potential candidates.

THE PRIMARIES

In January, 1972, there were six major Democratic candidates for the presidential nomination. They were Senator Hubert Humphrey of Minnesota, Senator Edmund

Muskie of Maine, Senator George McGovern of South Dakota, Senator Henry Jackson of Washington, Mayor John Lindsay of New York City, and Governor George Wallace of Alabama. The names of former Senator Eugene McCarthy of Minnesota and Representative Wilbur Mills of Arkansas were entered in a few key primaries.

By June, all but three had dropped out, or had been eliminated in contests that began in March in New Hampshire and ended in June in California and New York. In July, Senator McGovern went into the Democratic national convention at Miami Beach, Florida, with the greatest number of delegates. Still in the race were Humphrey, Muskie, and Wallace. But Governor Wallace had been shot and disabled during an attempt on his life at Laurel, Maryland, in May. He was physically unable to run for president even if nominated.

The American presidential primaries have been called "savage contests"—and "savage" is not too strong a word. Candidates travel hundreds, even thousands, of miles a day, eating on the run, speaking at one rally after another, planning strategy, getting by with almost no sleep. In addition to enduring this physical punishment, candidates must raise millions of dollars to pay for TV and radio time; newspaper ads; staff salaries; the chartering of planes, buses, and cars; the renting of halls and auditoriums; and outlays for postage and telephones.

The men and women in these primary contests must also face a constant barrage of criticism of their ideas, and attacks on their personalities, by their opponents. Hanging over them is the constant fear of losing so badly in any given primary that they can no longer stay in the race.

The prize is great. For the man who occupies the White House has the power, influence, and opportunity to affect the lives of all Americans—and to change the times in which we live. The primaries have been called a clumsy, wasteful method of picking the men who will run for president. There is some truth to these charges. But the individual state primary system—when compared with a proposed national primary—still gives unknown candidates, who may have little money, a chance to take the first step up the presidential ladder.

In 1972, President Nixon entered some of the Republican primaries. His only real opposition came from Republican Congressman

Senator Hubert Humphrey greets well-wishers after a campaign news conference in Los Angeles.

Senator Edmund Muskie campaigns in Milwaukee before the Wisconsin presidential primary.

A shower of balloons falls over the convention floor as President Nixon is renominated.

Paul McCloskey of California, an ardent antiwar candidate. McCloskey ran against Mr. Nixon in the March 7 New Hampshire primary. Mr. Nixon got 69 percent of the vote, McCloskey only 20 percent. Three days later, on March 10, McCloskey formally withdrew from the race.

The last primary was held in New York on June 20. That ended the preliminaries. Next came the national conventions of the two major parties, the second major step in an American presidential campaign.

THE WATERGATE AFFAIR

Before the conventions took place, an incident occurred at an office-apartment building called the Watergate, in Washington, D.C. On June 17, 1972, at 2:00 A.M., five men were caught after they broke into the sixth-floor headquarters of the Democratic National Committee. One of the five men was James W. McCord, Jr., security chief for the Committee for the Re-election of the President—the agency set up to raise money to re-elect President Nixon. The five men had in their possession a large sum of money and electronic bugging equipment. When surprised by building guards, the men were in the act of removing telephone bugs used for eavesdropping on and recording conversations going in and out of the Democratic Headquarters. Some Democrats charged that high Republican officials, including President Nixon, had known of the raid beforehand.

Democratic delegates react wildly to Senator McGovern's nomination.

However, the White House denied any connection with the Watergate raid. And although it was a new and potentially dangerous type of political spying in this country, "the Watergate issue" did not arouse the public. Most straw polls indicated that voters considered Watergate the sort of political shenanigans that both parties engage in during an election campaign. The Republicans just happened to be caught in the act.

THE CONVENTIONS

Both major parties held their 1972 national conventions at Miami Beach, Florida. The Democrats met from July 10 through July 14, the Republicans from August 21 through August 23.

At the Democratic convention, 1,509 delegate votes were needed to win the nomination. Senator George McGovern entered the convention with nearly enough votes to clinch the presidential nomination. His closest rivals were Senator Hubert Humphrey, Governor George Wallace, and Senator Edmund Muskie.

Attempts were made to form a "stop McGovern" coalition by those who opposed McGovern's candidacy. But when McGovern's forces—using brilliant tactics on the floor of the convention—won control of California's 271 delegates, the battle was over.

The Democratic convention was historic in that the delegates represented a much broader segment of the general population than ever before. Twenty-three percent of the Democratic delegates were under 30 years of age; 15 percent of the delegates were black; and 36 percent were women.

The convention nominated George McGovern for president, and Missouri Senator Thomas Eagleton as his running mate. Some observers thought it was a strong, well-balanced ticket. But a few days after the convention, it was revealed that Senator Eagleton had undergone electric shock treatments twice for mental depression in the 1960's.

There was no implication that Eagleton had not been cured. Nevertheless, it was learned that the vice-presidential candidate had withheld his past medical history at the time McGovern aides had asked him if there was anything in his record that could hurt him or the ticket. At first, McGovern said he was "1,000 percent" behind Eagleton. But within 10 days Eagleton was dropped from the ticket by mutual agreement. Shortly afterward, the Democratic National Committee named Sargent Shriver to take Eagleton's place. But the "Eagleton affair" created doubts about McGovern's competence as a leader, and undoubtedly hurt his candidacy.

The Republican convention in August contained no surprises. President Nixon had already indicated that his Vice-President, Spiro Agnew, would remain on the ticket. The Republicans ran their well-planned convention with almost split-second timing in a deliberate effort to contrast their method with the more chaotic Democratic convention.

CAMPAIGNING FOR PRESIDENT

Traditionally, a presidential campaign begins after Labor Day. But with his prestige badly hurt by the Eagleton affair, Senator McGovern began to campaign even before the Republican convention had adjourned. History showed that his efforts were wasted.

The McGovern-Shriver ticket showed a dip

Thomas Eagleton withdraws his candidacy.

Sargent Shriver joins the Democratic ticket.

in the straw polls during August. McGovern supporters claimed they would close the gap with the GOP after the first week in September. They discounted the loss of the most powerful labor figure in the nation, AFL-CIO President George Meany. Meany, who had backed Senator Humphrey, decided to "sit out" the election, withholding his endorsement from both McGovern and Nixon. Although rank-and-file union members vote as they please, the Meany endorsement would have meant millions of dollars in campaign funds—something McGovern badly needed.

By the first week in September, McGovern was trailing the President by 30 points in the major polls. Mr. Nixon did no formal campaigning, but his role as president gave him access to the public anytime he wanted it. McGovern continued his grinding round of trips back and forth across the country, but trouble continued to dog his steps.

Newspapers and radio and television news shows carried reports of insubordination on the part of key McGovern aides. One embarrassing incident involved Pierre Salinger. While on a trip to Paris, Salinger conferred with the North Vietnamese peace negotiators on behalf, he said, of Senator McGovern. Asked about the Salinger visit, the Senator denied that he had authorized any such approach to the North Vietnamese. Three hours after his denial, Senator McGovern issued a press release praising Salinger's efforts to promote peace by meeting with the North Vietnamese in Paris.

Doubts about Senator McGovern began to grow in the public mind and were reflected in the straw polls. Much of the doubt seemed to be based on a lack of public confidence in McGovern's ability to lead and control his staff, his party, and ultimately the country. There were also many who thought he was too "radical" in his approach to social and economic problems.

Vice President Spiro Agnew greets admirers while campaigning in Columbus, Ohio.

Senator George McGovern on the campaign trail.

The issue of the war in Vietnam also began to fade as peace talks continued. Except for Air Force and Navy pilots, few American military personnel were being killed or wounded. No longer were men being drafted for combat service, and public concern over the war was at its lowest point since President Nixon had first taken office. The muting of the war issue hurt McGovern, who had first won public attention as a leading foe of American involvement in Vietnam.

On October 26, 1972, Dr. Henry Kissinger, the President's top adviser on national security, confirmed a Hanoi radio report that virtually complete agreement had been reached on a Vietnam cease-fire. Kissinger said that a few details remained to be ironed out but that peace could be expected within a few weeks at the latest.

Hanoi later set an October 31, 1972, deadline for signing a cease-fire, but the deadline came and went without an agreement. Senator McGovern promptly accused President Nixon of having "pretended" to be near a negotiated settlement. The Democratic nominee charged that President Nixon's actions were part of a re-election strategy based on "cruel political deception." He also claimed that the President had refused to accept, without revision, an agreement his own aides had negotiated with the North Vietnamese.

The President denied McGovern's charges and insisted that a basic truce agreement had been reached to cover all of Indochina. Nixon emphasized that no truce would be signed before Election Day. As the President pointed out in a speech at Providence, Rhode Island: "We are going to end this war in a way that will lay the foundations of peace in the years to come."

President Nixon makes a rare campaign appearance, on Liberty Island in New York.

A NIXON LANDSLIDE

Apparently the American people decided that President Nixon was sincere in his efforts to end the war. On November 7, they re-elected him president by an overwhelming margin. President Nixon won 49 states and rolled up a total of 521 electoral votes. McGovern won only one state—Massachusetts—and the District of Columbia, with a total of 17 electoral votes. Nixon received 47,042,923 popular votes, McGovern 29,071,356. President Nixon's victory was one of the greatest political landslides in American history.

The 1972 presidential election was a very important election. Reforms within the Democratic Party led to far greater participation of women and minority groups in the making of party policy. The Republicans also began to recruit more young people and women into the GOP.

Unlike such popular presidents as Dwight Eisenhower and John Kennedy, President Nixon is respected for his competence rather than for his personal style. But as the President himself once noted, he would rather be respected than liked.

Most American voters apparently felt that President Nixon had shown himself to be a skillful leader, particularly in foreign affairs, during his first 4-year term. They had more confidence in him as the better qualified of the two candidates to lead the nation for the next 4 years. Senator McGovern, on the other hand, was liked and admired for his personal qualities of sincerity and honesty. But he projected an image of indecisiveness and inadequate leadership ability. The American people chose the candidate who they felt was more competent to bear the heavy burden of the presidency.

The new electorate, 18- to 20-year-olds, register to vote.

YOUTH IN POLITICS

For the first time in American history the youth vote—voters between the ages of 18 and 24—was of major importance in a presidential election. When the Twenty-sixth Amendment was ratified in 1971, it made millions of young people, 18 through 20 years of age, eligible to vote in all elections. In 1972, some 11,000,000 18-to-20 year olds would be able to cast their first ballots.

The big question in the minds of Republican and Democratic leaders was, Which major party would these young people choose when they registered? One survey indicated that about half of the new voters considered themselves to be Democrats, and under 20 percent favored the Republican Party. An official of one of the parties said, "If you ask a new voter what he is, he's as likely to say 'Capricorn' or 'Leo' as anything else!"

Some political experts had predicted that many of these new young voters wouldn't bother to register to vote in the 1972 presidential election. When registration ended in the fall, only 6,400,000 of the 18-to-20 year olds, about half of those eligible, had registered. Even so, the voter registration drive, conducted by nonpartisan groups as well as by supporters of the two major parties, had had impressive numerical results.

One and one half million new voters were enrolled in Texas, 500,000 in Pennsylvania, and 1,400,000 in New York. Ohio registered 1,000,000 new voters between the ages of 18 and 24. In Illinois more than 400,000 young voters were enrolled.

College students received the most publicity among the new voters, and they were most often the ones who were interviewed on television news shows. But of the entire 18-to-24 age group, the vast majority do not attend school. Sixty-three percent of the young men and 47 percent of the young women are out working.

The young people most likely to vote are college graduates, white-collar workers, and people with high incomes. The young people least likely to vote are blacks, people with only a grade or high school education, blue-collar workers, and people with low incomes.

It was in the 1968 presidential campaign that young people in large numbers made their first impact on American presidential politics. Tens of thousands of college students worked for Senator Eugene McCarthy of Minnesota, beginning with the New Hampshire primary in March, 1968, and up until the Democratic convention in Chicago in August. Many thousands of other young people worked equally hard for Senator Robert F. Kennedy of New York, until his assassination in Los Angeles in June, 1968. Opposition to American involvement in the war in Vietnam was the biggest motive of much of the youth activity in the 1968 campaign.

Young people were involved once again in the 1972 primaries, but the atmosphere was very different from that of the previous campaign. The American troop strength in South Vietnam had dropped from 560,000 men in 1968 to well below 100,000 men. It was expected that only 40,000 American servicemen would remain in Vietnam by the time of the election.

The argument was no longer centered on American battlefield deaths but on the question of how to get out of South Vietnam as rapidly as possible. President Richard M. Nixon held out against any agreement to end the war until the release of all American prisoners of war held by the North Vietnamese was assured.

The Democratic opposition—led by senators George McGovern, Edmund Muskie, and Hubert Humphrey—accused the Nixon administration of needlessly dragging on the war because it still hoped to win a military victory in Vietnam. They pointed to the fact that 20,000 Americans had died in the war since President Nixon had taken office, and that his administration had failed to find a way out of the conflict.

Many college youths flocked to the Democratic standard in the winter and spring of 1972. Most supported the candidacy of Senator George McGovern of South Dakota. These young people were given key posts on the McGovern primary campaign staffs. Many people under 25 attended the Democratic national convention at Miami Beach, Florida, where Senator McGovern was nominated for the presidency. The Youth Caucus at the Democratic convention played a role in writing the Democratic Party platform. They also planned the strategy when the McGovern supporters battled on the floor of the convention to win the 271 California delegates vital to McGovern's nomination.

However, a number of the young people who took part in the Democratic convention

A first-time voter is being shown how to operate a voting machine.

later stated that they were disturbed by the way the California delegates were secured. Some of the young idealists called it a return to the "Old Politics" of wheeling and dealing. While it did not seem important at the time, this may have caused a shift in youthful support for Senator McGovern.

Initially, Senator McGovern tried to involve young people in his campaign by stressing idealistic issues—such as his proposal to withdraw all U.S. military forces from Vietnam immediately if elected president. McGovern made full use of youthful talent and appeared to have a greater rapport with young people than his Republican opponent. College students in particular were impressed by McGovern's honesty and decency.

McGovern may be a decent man, but he was also a politician who wanted to win an election. As the campaign progressed, he was forced to make compromises. For his youthful

Young people help their favorite candidate by distributing literature and preparing posters.

supporters, the first serious disappointment came when McGovern abruptly dropped his running mate, Senator Thomas Eagleton of Missouri. McGovern's decision came after it was disclosed that Eagleton had undergone shock treatments for mental depression several years earlier. Some young McGovernites were offended by the way McGovern hesitated about the decision. First he stated that he backed Eagleton "1,000 percent," but then, after keeping him dangling for several days, he replaced Eagleton with R. Sargent Shriver.

Faced by waning support after the "Eagleton affair," McGovern turned in desperation to the old-line party regulars. They were the same people who had been swept aside by the youthful forces of McGovern's "New Politics" at the Democratic national convention. Now McGovern went out to woo these men. He visited former President Lyndon Johnson and paid several calls on Mayor Richard Daley of Chicago. It was later learned that he had also sought the support of Governor George Wallace of Alabama.

As the party regulars began to move into the McGovern fold, many of his younger followers lost their enthusiasm. Their disenchantment with McGovern was a serious blow to his campaign.

The Republican Party also made a big push to attract young voters to its ranks. Youthful GOP volunteers canvassed their neighborhoods, urging support of President Nixon. They also helped in voter registration campaigns, and were active in the fund-raising efforts of the state committees to re-elect the president. President Nixon, aware of the importance of the youth vote, made several pleas for young voter support. During the Republican convention in Miami, the President made a special appearance at a GOP rock-concert rally, where the well-known entertainer Sammy Davis, Jr., was performing. A large contingent of "Young Voters for the President" were present at the convention.

Commenting on the new voters, a political analyst named Richard Scammon noted that "young people by and large are considerably more liberal and Democratic than the country at large." On the other hand, political pollster George Gallop predicted that voters who were college students would split roughly 50–50

Envelope stuffing is a very important job in an election campaign.

between President Nixon and Senator McGovern. With the exception of college students, President Nixon did just as well or better than Senator McGovern among young voters. Another point that came out of the 1968 and 1972 elections is that young people are less likely to vote than their elders unless they are deeply stirred by some issue or candidate. Sixty-two percent of all the eligible voters exercised their right in 1968. But among 21- to 24-year-olds, the figure was only 51 percent.

The lack of voting interest is greatest among young working people. Unlike college students, youthful workers often do not have the leisure time to become actively involved in politics. Generally, they tend to follow the same voting patterns as their parents. If the household has been Democrat, they vote for the Democratic candidates. In the 1972 campaign, the polls indicated that most young blue-collar workers tended to favor President Nixon. However, many young workers expressed the view that people in their position could do little to create political or social change.

Bayard Rustin, a black leader in the labor movement, put it this way: "The system works for those who use it." But he added that there are many people, including members of minority groups and the poor, "who have not been allowed to use it and they have no knowledge of how to go about using it." Nevertheless, the voter registration drives of 1972 saw a lessening of indifference among young voters. The 6,400,000 new voters who registered showed that they cared enough about the American political system to take part in it.

Today young people are having an increasing impact on local and state elections. Some are running for office themselves. One town in Iowa has a 19-year-old mayor. Students have been elected to the city councils of several college towns. In general, young people share most of the ideals and goals of the general population. But there is one major difference: They are usually more eager for change and more open to new ideas than older people. During the next ten years, about 4,000,000 people will come of voting age each year. There is no doubt that this ever-expanding bloc of young voters will play a significant role and have a strong voice in American politics.

STEPHEN C. FLANDERS
News Correspondent,
WCBS Radio

BANGLADESH

Born out of the ashes of what was once East Pakistan, Bangladesh is the newest of the nations of the world. With an estimated 75,000,000 people, it ranks eighth in population among the world's nations. It lies in the northeastern corner of the Indian subcontinent, at the head of the Bay of Bengal, and is bordered by India on the west, the north, and the northeast and by Burma on the southeast.

THE PEOPLE

The people of Bangladesh are a mixture of Indo-Aryan, Mongoloid, and Dravidian elements. The two major divisions among the people are the Bengalis of the plains and the hill tribes who live in the Chittagong Hills in the east. Most of the people are Muslims. Hindus form the largest minority group, about 10 percent, and there are smaller numbers of Buddhists, Christians, and animists.

The Bengalis. The average Bengali is short and dark, with sharp features and a slender build. He has a vibrant personality. He is dreamy, emotional, changeable, and alert. He is poetical in his choice of words and articulate in his speech. He delights in argument, in the subtlety of ideas, and in ceaseless conversation. By nature he is tolerant, but he can be aroused to frenzied action when seized by indignation or passionate loyalty to an ideal. He is gentle and easygoing but is capable of hard and sustained work when called upon to do so.

Village life. The basic unit of life in Bangladesh is the village. It is usually located along the course of a river or canal with rice fields nearby. Communication between villages is chiefly by boat. There are thousands of these, of all sizes and shapes, and they travel up and down the rivers carrying people and goods. One of the most enchanting sights is a riverboat tossed on the gentle ripples of the water and framed in the rising or setting sun.

The people are poor; the average per capita income is estimated to be only between $70 and $75 a year. But they are by no means gloomy, and a smile comes readily to their lips. The everyday diet consists of rice and fish with some vegetables. The typical house is a slight structure, generally built of reeds, bamboo, and mats and plastered with clay or mud.

The usual dress for men is the lungi, a length of colored cotton cloth worn wrapped around the waist and stretching to the ankles. At work the men wear it tucked up to the knees. Women wear the sari, a long, often very colorful garment, which is draped around the body from the shoulders to the ankles. With their slim figures, graceful walk, and dark wistful eyes, the Bengali women are attractive in their own way. Traditionally, Muslim women cover their faces, especially when strangers are around.

FACTS AND FIGURES

PEOPLE'S REPUBLIC OF BANGLADESH is the official name of the country. Bangladesh means Bengal Nation.

CAPITAL: Dacca.

LOCATION: South Asia. **Latitude**—26° 38′ N to 20° 46′ N. **Longitude**—92° 41′ E to 88° 02′ E. **Area**—55,126 sq. mi.

PHYSICAL FEATURES: Highest point—Keokradong (4,034 ft.). **Lowest point**—sea level. **Chief rivers**—Ganges, Brahmaputra.

POPULATION: 75,000,000 (estimate).

LANGUAGE: Bengali, English.

RELIGION: Islam (predominant).

GOVERNMENT: Republic. Independent since 1971. **Head of state**—president. **Head of government**—prime minister. **International co-operation**—Commonwealth of Nations.

NATIONAL ANTHEM: "My Golden Bengal."

ECONOMY: Agricultural products—rice, jute, tea, mangoes, pineapples, coconuts, bananas, oilseeds. **Industries and products**—jute manufacturing, handicrafts, various light industries. **Chief exports**—jute and jute manufactures, fish, tea, tobacco, timber. **Chief imports**—metals, petroleum, coal, machinery, textiles. **Monetary unit**—taka.

THE LAND

Bangladesh has an area of 55,126 square miles. It is a land of low plains crisscrossed by rivers, of which the most important are the Ganges and the Brahmaputra and their

A Bengali selling red peppers in a marketplace.

tributaries. It is a tropical land where there is no real winter, for the average mean temperatures range from over 60 degrees to over 90 degrees Fahrenheit. It is also a land of torrential monsoon rains—which fall from June to September—and violent winds called cyclones. These often bring heavy flooding and death and devastation to wide areas. (The cyclone of 1970 is reported to have killed 500,000 people.) In its gentler aspects, it is a pleasant, rather lazy land of many small villages. There are fewer than a dozen major urban centers. Of these, the most important are Dacca, the capital, with a population of about 1,250,000 (counting suburbs and surrounding towns), and Chittagong, which is the chief port.

THE ECONOMY

Bangladesh is an agricultural country. The main food crop is rice. Jute and tea are the major commercial crops. Bangladesh is the world's leading exporter of jute, a fiber used to make sacks, burlap, and twine. Jute forms the basis of the country's foreign earnings. Mangoes, pineapples, coconuts, and bananas are also grown. Linseed and mustard seed provide much of the oil used for cooking. What industry there is consists mainly of jute mills and processing and consumer industries.

Bangladesh is not rich in minerals, and the lack of large-scale deposits of coal, petroleum, or natural gas makes firewood the major source of fuel. The country's hydroelectric

A farmer watering his rice fields. Rice is the staple food in Bangladesh.

Left: Riverboats are a common form of transportation. *Above:* A typical small Bangladesh village.

potential is considerable but much of it still awaits development.

The size of the average farm is small and the farming methods used are old-fashioned. Bangladesh is one of the most densely populated areas in the world and the population is rising at a rate of 2.5 percent a year. At this rate, unless agriculture is modernized and effective means of population control are adopted, the country will not be able to feed its people adequately.

The many rivers and canals are both a blessing and a problem. They provide the chief means of transportation of people and goods. But to be used efficiently they require effective methods of flood-control and mechanization. The great hydroelectric potential of the country can be utilized for industrial growth only if the rivers are harnessed. This would enable Bangladesh to provide power for industrialization. But such projects require vast amounts of money, which the new nation, poor as it is, cannot easily supply.

HISTORY

The history of Bangladesh can be told briefly. Originally it was part of the larger Bengal region of eastern India and its historical roots are deep in the ancient past. Successive groups of invaders ruled over the land—Turks, Moguls, and lastly the British. In 1947, when India gained its independence from Great Britain, East Bengal became part of the new nation of Pakistan. The creation

Bicycles and pedicabs crowd the busy city of Dacca, the capital of Bangladesh.

of Pakistan was a result of the demands of the Muslim League for an independent and separate nation for those parts of the former British Indian Empire where the Muslims were a majority.

The new nation of Pakistan was born with a built-in flaw. It was composed of two parts, East Pakistan and West Pakistan, separated by some 1,000 miles of Indian territory. Other problems served to undermine the new state. The two parts of Pakistan were completely different in the makeup of their peoples and in their cultures. In addition, all aspects of Pakistani national life came to be dominated by groups from West Pakistan. East Pakistan turned out to be a fertile field for commercial investments, but the Bengalis charged that most of the profits were drained off to West Pakistan. The West Pakistan leadership was accused of neglecting the interests of the Eastern region and treating it as a colony. The East Pakistanis also complained that they were not receiving their fair share of political power, which they claimed on the basis of having over 55 percent of the total population of the nation.

Other issues led to frustration and discontent among the Bengalis of Pakistan. The government at first refused to accept Bengali as one of the national languages. Popularly elected local governments in the East were dismissed on charges of wanting to secede from Pakistan. Bengali leaders were imprisoned as traitors. There were frequent riots, and a long period of military rule (from 1958 to 1971) created dangerous tensions in the East.

The climax came in the elections of 1971. The Awami League, led by Sheikh Mujibur Rahman, won most of the seats in the East Pakistan provincial legislature and a majority of the seats in the national legislature. This would have given Sheikh Mujib a decisive role in Pakistani politics. It was a situation unacceptable to General Yahya Khan, the leader of the national government, and Zulfikar Ali Bhutto, who had emerged as the leader of the Pakistan People's Party, the majority party in West Pakistan. Particularly objectionable to them was the Awami League's Six Point Program, which included self-government for the Eastern region. West Pakistani leaders believed this would lead to the dismemberment of Pakistan.

The Birth of Bangladesh. Negotiations for the establishment of civilian rule and the drafting of a new constitution proved fruitless, setting off widespread riots in the East. The West Pakistan army retaliated with brutal suppression during which, it is charged, millions of people lost their lives and hundreds of villages were destroyed. Some 10,000,000 Bengalis, mostly Hindus, are believed to have fled to India as refugees, placing an intolerable burden on the Indian economy. As a result India became involved in what was essentially a civil war between East and West Pakistan.

The Bengalis, helped in part by India, had organized their own guerrilla forces, called the Muktibahini. The guerrillas cut communications and ambushed West Pakistani troops in widespread areas of East Pakistan. Incidents mounted until, in December 1971, India and Pakistan went to war in both the Eastern and Western regions. The war was swift. In less than 2 weeks the Indian Army, with the aid of the Bengali guerrillas, had compelled the Pakistani forces to surrender. The Bangladesh provisional government, which had been formed earlier in India, arrived in Dacca and took over control of the new nation.

Sheikh Mujibur Rahman, who had been arrested and imprisoned in West Pakistan, was released by Zulfikar Ali Bhutto, who became president of Pakistan, following the downfall of General Yahya Khan. On January 10, 1972, Sheikh Mujib arrived in Dacca and became prime minister of Bangladesh. After some 10 months of bloodshed and destruction, the new nation of Bangladesh ("Bengal Nation") had come into existence.

As the new flag fluttered over Dacca, the people began to bury their dead and rebuild their shattered lives. The refugees began to trickle back. The new nation was recognized by most of the nations of the world. The first agony of nationhood was over, but although there is great promise for Bangladesh, great problems remain.

Balkrishna G. Gokhale
Director, Asian Studies Program
Wake Forest University

WORLD OF SCIENCE

The waters off Hawaii . . . a lovely corner of man's new frontier—the sea.

MAN UNDERWATER

In 1870 an exciting adventure story by a popular French writer was published, and started an interested public thinking about a mysterious world under the sea. The adventure story—we would now call it science fiction—was *20,000 Leagues Under the Sea.* The author was a remarkable man named Jules Verne.

Verne's description of the exploits of Captain Nemo and his crew aboard their fabulous submarine, the *Nautilus,* actually inspired many inventors, who attempted to build some of the make-believe apparatus Verne had described in his book. The book also made the general public think, for the first time, that man might be able to live underwater.

The crew of Captain Nemo's submarine ate only food from the sea. It was prepared from exotic seaweeds and unusual fish, as well as from such conventional delicacies as squid and octopus. The *Nautilus* herself was an inspiring submarine. Her oxygen supply was generated on board by a complex electrical treatment of seawater. All the crew were provided with devices like the modern aqualung, which enabled them to walk about on the ocean floor. Since the appearance of Verne's novel, many inventors, explorers, and scientists have actually made Verne's fantasy come true. They have gone on to study many basic questions that man has long had about the nature of the world's oceans and the uses man might make of them.

▶ MODERN NEMOS WITH PROBLEMS

In September, 1962, the first experiments in living under the sea took place. One experiment was in the Caribbean and was directed by the American inventor Edwin Link. The other was directed by Jacques Cousteau, a Frenchman, and was carried out in the Mediterranean. Both experiments were a result of studies, made by U.S. Navy scientist George Bond, on the effects of deep dives on humans.

The most striking thing about Bond's work was that it seemed to show a way to overcome some of the basic problems of deep dives. In order to return to the surface from depth, a diver must decompress all the gas that his body tissues have absorbed in the increased pressure of his undersea environment. The deeper the dive, the greater the pressure—and the longer the time required by the body to decompress to surface atmospheric pressure. If a diver does not decompress properly, the results are dramatic—and unpleasant. His blood stream fills with little gas bubbles that have been released too quickly. These bubbles can clot around the joints and cause severe attacks of pain and stiffness. Divers have nicknamed this condition "the bends."

Man has entered the world beneath the sea.

The easiest way to understand the effects of the bends (properly called decompression sickness) is to imagine the diver's body as a bottle filled with a carbonated soft drink; the contents of the bottle would represent his bloodstream. If the cap of the bottle is removed slowly (without shaking the bottle), bubbles will rise gently through the liquid until it has gone flat. This would represent a gradual, trouble-free decompression. However, if the bottle is shaken before it is opened (similar to a diver's coming up from a great depth too quickly), most of the drink turns to froth, and is lost when the cap is removed. This would represent a very serious decompression accident which could take the life of the diver or cause permanent injury.

Bond decided that there must be a limit to which the tissues of the human body will absorb the gas that the divers breathe under pressure at any given depth. After this point, the decompression time would remain the same regardless of how long a diver remained down. This idea was proved true when experiments were made with dogs, with goats (which are used because their lungs are about the same size as human lungs), and, finally, with humans.

Once techniques were developed for diving and returning to the surface without risking the bends or other complications, further experiments—in prolonged, deep dives—were

Jacques Cousteau's diving saucers have explored the sea at ever-greater depths. Above: A saucer is readied for lowering. Below: The descent begins.

An artist's drawing shows the U.S. Navy's amazing underwater experimental station Sealab III. Aquanauts like those depicted here performed tasks both inside and outside their underwater habitat and research laboratory.

begun. Many of the problems scientists knew about at the beginning of the experiments have been solved. Other, unexpected problems have caused real trouble.

Of the problems scientists knew about at the beginning, that of adjusting to a new and alien underwater world has not been as great as some scientists feared. Men and women have proved to be equally good oceanauts. Oceanauts do not have to be supermen. They do have to be calm, even-tempered people who think things out coolly in difficult situations and emergencies that often occur in dives. Strength of character seems to be much more valuable than sheer physical strength in the underwater world.

BREATHING UNDERWATER

One of the real difficulties in deep dives involved the air divers breathe. Most of the air humans breathe on land—and underwater—is inert nitrogen. However, under pressure at depths of about 150 feet, nitrogen becomes a narcotic and causes hallucinations and a dangerous feeling of contentment and well-being. In fact, a diver in this condition might feel he no longer needed his aqualung. The feeling that divers experience in these circumstances is called "rapture of the deep." The medical name for the condition is nitrogen narcosis. Nitrogen narcosis can be avoided if the diver has in his air supply a gas that is lighter than nitrogen. Helium and hydrogen both fit this description. Until recently, helium has been used with oxygen by divers in preference to hydrogen, which can explode when mixed with oxygen.

Although helium is widely used in underwater experiments, it has its drawbacks, too. It is not as effective at very great depths as it might be. Research teams are now experimenting with hydrogen at greater depths. A diver very far down needs only a 2 percent oxygen mixture, and that, when mixed with

An aquanaut from Tektite II, an undersea habitat, enters a personnel transfer capsule which will take him to a decompression chamber on the surface.

hydrogen, is not explosive. At great depths, however, oxygen itself is a problem. Too little oxygen underwater is poisonous to a diver's system. Too much oxygen can cause fainting. Fainting underwater is very dangerous. When someone faints on land, the force of gravity helps to restore the normal circulation of the blood. This helps the person who has fainted to recover. Underwater, the body of the diver is almost weightless—like that of an astronaut in space. Therefore circulation is not helped by gravity, and the person who faints underwater cannot recover as quickly as the person who faints on the surface because circulation is not restored as quickly.

Why is there a smaller percentage of oxygen in the total volume of gas breathed underwater than in that breathed on the surface? Because, regardless of depth, the body only requires the equivalent of one atmosphere (air at the surface) of oxygen in its breathing mixture. If this volume was in a balloon and was taken underwater to a depth of 30 feet, the balloon would be half the size it had been on the surface, because of the increased pressure. In the same way, by the time a diver reaches depth, he is breathing gas under increased pressure, and the amount of oxygen he needs for adequate respiration makes up a progressively smaller part of his total breathing mixture.

OTHER HAZARDS

In an undersea "house" or laboratory, the atmosphere is very important. It is delicately balanced and can be seriously changed by an ordinary, everyday problem like burning the toast at breakfast. Even toast burned on land gives off potentially lethal carbon monoxide—but so little that it does not matter. However, in an underwater house, even a tiny amount of carbon monoxide in the atmosphere could be dangerous.

The kind of food that oceanauts eat is very carefully planned. The planning is based partly on how much energy they need for the work they must do. Smelly cheeses and other fermented foods pollute an underwater atmosphere and have to be avoided. Helium, if it is used in the underwater house, conducts heat much faster than air does. Therefore room temperatures underwater must be somewhat higher than normal.

Often an undersea habitat or house gets very damp. This can be uncomfortable for the oceanauts and can cause skin conditions. Every single item used in an underwater house must be examined carefully to see if it might

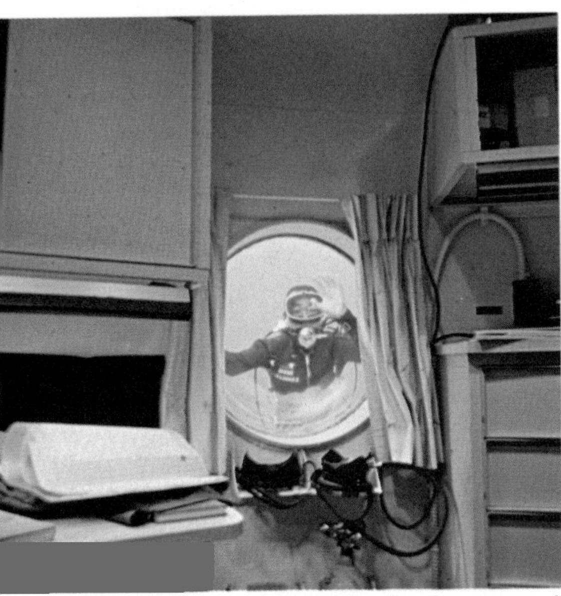

On the outside looking in: An aquanaut surveys his undersea home, Tektite II.

Two Tektite aquanauts at work and at play in their laboratory–control center.

cause trouble under pressure or when exposed to the synthetic atmosphere of the habitat. For example, photographs give off a very strong smell of the chemicals with which they were developed when they are taken undersea. Some printing inks have strong odors in underwater atmospheres. Some books, magazines, and newspapers are therefore unsuitable for use underwater. Television tubes, which are gas-filled like light bulbs, do not work in undersea habitats unless they are specially protected from the helium in the atmosphere. Wristwatches that are to be worn in undersea habitats must also be protected against the expansion of helium under pressure. Scientists have devised special valves for watches to be worn at great depths. The valves release excess helium before it can expand enough to destroy the watch.

There are even problems with the aqualung which is so widely used in underwater exploration and experimentation. It cannot regulate the proportions of gases in the breathing mixture. But in deep dives, for all of the reasons we have discussed, the diver must have this balance regulated very carefully. If the balance is not maintained, the diver may suffer from oxygen poisoning. There is now a device that seems to have solved some of the problems of regulation. It is called the electrolung and employs electronic sensors.

Electronic sensors that can monitor oxygen content were originally developed for the NASA Mercury spaceflight program. They have become a vital part of the electrolung, which is essentially a closed-circuit aqualung system. Electrolung was built by two marine biologists who wanted to increase the depth and duration of their dives.

As the diver's body uses oxygen, the sensors make sure that the proper amount of oxygen is injected into his breathing mixture. A "scrubber," or filtering system, absorbs carbon dioxide. In using the electrolung, the diver wears meters on his wrist that indicate the quantities of gases in the breathing mix. An alarm rings if his oxygen goes out of the control range. There are backup sensors and an override switch on the oxygen tank so that in an emergency the diver can replace the automatic breathing system with a manual one. There is also 10 percent of oxygen in the second of the electrolung's two tanks. This additional quantity of oxygen serves as a backup supply of breathing gas until the diver gets up to a depth of 10 meters (about 30 feet). At that depth he can safely switch to pure oxygen or surface.

Man can now hunt for his food underwater, just as Jules Verne predicted.

MAN–FISH

Scientists have even considered giving man artificial gills so that he can breathe underwater as fish do. However, the operation necessary for giving a man gills has not yet been performed—and may never be. For one thing, there seems to be no way the gills could be taken away when they were no longer needed. Scientists have also been unwilling to risk the ethical and psychological problems that might arise with the creation of a man-fish. However, the scientific possibility of making man a liquid breather does exist.

The ways both land animals and underwater creatures respire are really quite similar. Both men and fish exchange carbon dioxide for oxygen by means of semipermeable membranes in air or water. In man, these membranes are in his lungs. In fish, they are in the gills. The real differences lie in the density of air as contrasted with that of water and in the speed at which the exchange can take place. Because of these differences, it now seems that a man-fish would have to work much too hard to obtain from water the oxygen he would need.

Man's survival on earth has depended, in part, on his ability to adapt to new environments. As a result, man's biological structure—in spite of its complexity—is versatile. Man can tolerate extreme changes in his environment. There must be some amount of psychological and physiological adaption if man wants to live and work under the sea. In the Age of Exploration, men like Marco Polo and Christopher Columbus went to places and cultures that were completely alien to the European world they knew. They had to make adjustments to the new worlds they discovered —and they made them successfully. In some cases, their wanderings and their discoveries were spread out over many years. By contrast, sky divers in free fall are exposed to complicated—if not terrifying—environmental stresses. However, these stresses usually last for less than 60 seconds.

The real danger in the body's adapting to underwater conditions is that the process sometimes means the acceptance of conditions that are not really desirable or even necesary. Men involved in underwater experiments sometimes put up with everything and anything short of disaster in order to see their project through. However, it is on the basis of these experiments that the development of the world's seas and oceans will be planned. Therefore it is important that real human values and the special and unique quality of life be taken into consideration as underwater living moves out of the laboratory and into everyday reality.

Since the early experiments in underwater living were begun 10 years ago, man has already learned many valuable lessons. The vast potential of mineral, biological, and physical resources in the oceans of the world is very real. But man is beginning to learn that these resources have been somewhat misunderstood—or even overrated in some cases. Because of his haste to tap the resources of the oceans, man runs the danger of exploitation and pollution. The oceans are vital to life on earth and form an extremely sensitive life system. If man should throw the system off by exploitation and pollution, he could cause irreversible changes in ocean ecology. The lives of millions of sea creatures could be affected and so could man's own life.

If man is to live with—and in—his oceans, he needs to know even more about them. The understanding and research of scientists and marine technologists are not sufficient. Every aspect of human imagination, education, sensibility, and ingenuity is needed to make life under and around the sea good for all mankind.

FAROOQ HUSSAIN
Author, *Underwater Living*

A woman aquanaut in the Tektite program takes photographs underwater. She is breathing with the aid of an electrolung. The mesh bag she has is for carrying samples of undersea life back to Tektite II.

SCIENCE EXPERIMENTS

Johnny has a dog whose name is Hannibal. One day Hannibal managed to slip his leash, and nearly lost his life as a result. Hannibal ran from behind a parked truck into the path of an oncoming car. It was the dog's good luck that the driver of the car was alert. He quickly braked and just barely stopped short of the frightened Hannibal's nose.

Stopping a car is a complicated process. Several steps have taken place by the time the driver actually presses the brake pedal. These steps involve the driver's brain, nerves, and muscles. All of them work together with split-second timing.

Hannibal's sudden appearance in front of the car alerted the driver to a dangerous situation. A nerve impulse, or message, traveled through nerves connecting his eyes with his brain. (It is the brain that recognizes danger, and acts.) A second nerve impulse flashed, this time from the brain to the muscles of the leg. It told the muscles to press the brake pedal. (The muscles do as they are ordered.)

The time it takes to react to a situation is called **reaction time**. It varies from one person to another. It also varies in the same person. For example, reaction time is faster when you are rested than when you are tired.

Reaction time can be measured with great accuracy by special machines. You can make a "machine" that will roughly measure your reaction time.

TESTING YOUR REACTION TIME

1. Ask somebody to hold the ruler at the 12-inch mark. You hold your thumb and forefinger, spread apart, at the 1-inch mark. 2. Then your friend lets go of the ruler without warning you. Catch the ruler by bringing your thumb and forefinger together. At what mark did you catch the ruler? 3. Try it several times and take an average of the results. If you caught the ruler at the 5½-inch mark (which is about average), your reaction time is approximately .150 second. If you caught it at the 3-inch mark, your reaction time is about .100 second and is faster than average. If you caught the ruler at the 10⅞-inch mark, your reaction time is .225 second and is slower than average.

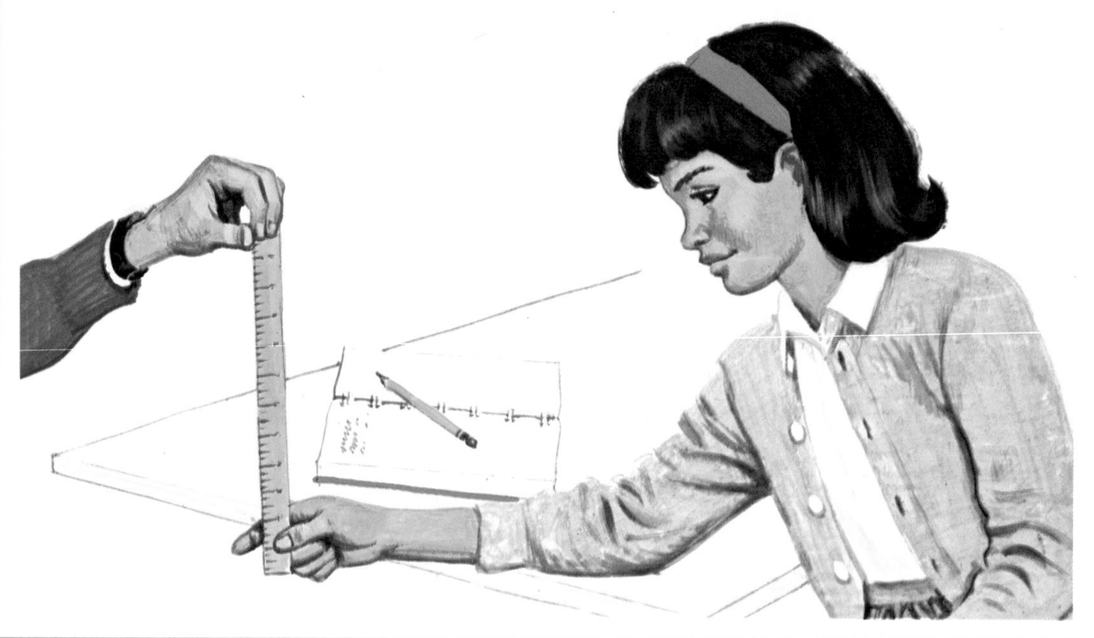

CONDUCTING RADIO WAVES

You will need a small, battery-operated transistor radio. You will also need some objects made of different materials, such as glass, paper, wood, and aluminum foil, to enclose the radio. (Ice-cream bags are made of paper with a coating of aluminum. "Tin" cans are made of steel coated with tin, or are all of aluminum.)

Turn on the radio and tune in a station. Then enclose your radio in one of the objects. Suppose you can still hear the program. This means that the radio waves can pass through the object into the radio. If you can't hear the radio, it means that the waves are not passing through the object.

Keep a record of your results.

Have you ever wondered how a radio broadcast reaches you? The radio station may be hundreds of miles away, yet somehow voices and music reach you clearly. Do they come through the wire that plugs into the wall socket? That can't be, for battery-operated transistor radios don't have such a wire.

This is what happens in the broadcasting station: A microphone detects the sounds of voices or music and changes them into electrical currents. The currents are strengthened (amplified) and are fed into the antenna of a sender, or transmitter. The currents flash out of the antenna in all directions, traveling at a speed of 186,000 miles per second. These are radio waves.

The process is reversed when the radio waves reach your set. The radio changes the waves back into electrical currents, which are fed into the speaker of your set. The speaker changes the currents into sound waves.

Of course, you can't hear anything if the waves don't reach your radio. Have you noticed that a radio may go silent in a tunnel or under a bridge? Here is an experiment that will enable you to learn which kinds of materials block radio waves, and which kinds allow the waves to pass through.

Archeologists working at this site in England have exposed the guard chamber of an ancient hill fort. The bridge of earth (center) is called a balk.

ARCHEOLOGICAL DIGS

Archeologists try to discover how people lived in former times by studying the traces of their belongings and their buildings that have survived. Sometimes very old castles and palaces have remained standing. However, when buildings of interest to archeologists have been destroyed, or have been leveled in order to make way for new structures on top of them, they can only be studied by the archeologists' having a look beneath the soil. Archeologists also look for objects that were buried by our ancestors on purpose. These were either valuable objects buried for safe-keeping, or personal belongings buried with a dead person in a burial mound or ancient graveyard.

An archeological excavation is the method of planned and careful digging to uncover ancient structures and to find objects surviving from early times. These excavations are popularly called "digs."

Excavation helps us to learn what ancient settlements were like to live in. It also enables archeologists to make a time scale for a site used over many years. Each group that has used a specific site at some time in history leaves a layer of refuse and building rubble, which is buried by a layer made by later inhabitants. As archeologists work down through the ground, removing each layer in turn, they often discover objects that come from earlier and earlier times.

Digs are not just treasure hunts. They have to be organized and planned in advance because as much evidence as possible about a site must be collected from it while the dig is going on. Archeologists are careful about keeping track of what they find, and of what the site looks like at each stage of digging. Recording is very important because a dig is a form of destruction. A site can never be put back together in quite the same shape it was in to start with.

Digs are like scientific experiments because they start out to prove a hunch an archeologist may have about a site. Unlike experiments in chemistry or physics, they can never be precisely repeated, although sections of sites can be left unexplored for later archeologists. But like all scientists, archeologists make careful reports of what they find.

Archeologists have found a prehistoric Indian village at the Koster Site in Illinois. Above: A worker checks the carefully marked layers of a cut. Below: Archeologists and students work in the main excavation at Koster.

▸ FINDING A SITE

It is not difficult for an archeologist to find the type of site he wants to dig. It may actually be on the map of the region in which it is located. If it is in England, it might be labeled "Roman Camp," or if it is in the United States, it might be labeled "Indian Village." Sometimes people in an area know that mysterious bumps and hollows in their fields are old settlements, because of objects they have found that were pushed to the surface by burrowing animals or by plows. Some sites can be located by examining aerial photographs of the region. From the air, sites may appear as round or square shapes in fields, formed by the grass growing unevenly on disturbed soil. These shapes are often invisible to someone standing on the ground. Sometimes sites appear by accident when workers dig a trench for a pipeline or excavate for the foundation of a building.

Archeologists can get further information about the layout of a site by using instruments that test the differences in the surface caused by buried structures or filled-in pits. One of these instruments is called a **resistivity meter**. The meter is used to test differences, or variations, in the ground's ability to conduct electricity. Another instrument used by archeologists mapping a site is the **proton magnetometer**. This instrument is used to test the changes in the magnetism of the earth caused by what lies underneath the surface. There are also machines like mine detectors that locate buried metal objects.

▸ THE DIG BEGINS

The director of a dig usually begins by surveying and leveling the site. An assistant then draws charts of the site's shape and layout. These charts are used as guides when the time comes to draw plans of the cuttings, or dug areas. To make this easier, the site is laid out in a grid pattern, with numbered stakes in the ground at, say, 25-foot intervals. These stakes are then guides for locating special areas. Finds can be identified by using a reference system like the one on a street map.

These students (*above*) do some vital and educational dirty work at Koster—digging. Every detail of the location and appearance of an ancient skull (*below*) is recorded carefully.

There are many ways to open cuttings on a site. At first, the digging may be in trial squares or trenches. These small areas can show bits of large features, and show that the dig is on the right track. Then the trial holes can be made into larger trenches. On small sites, such as a burial mound, or barrow, or at sites where the layers of soil are very deep and complicated, archeologists open large box-shaped cuttings. These boxes may be joined by knocking out the gangways of soil, or balks, which separate them. The balks are important because they show each layer of soil and refuse in cross section. Diggers keep them straight and neat, and use them as guides when stripping layers.

Trenches running in parallel strips across a field may show sections of buildings, and give a rough idea of what a large settlement was like. However, this method is useful only where the topsoil is very shallow, and where there are many people on hand to help. Another way of opening a large area is to start with many box-shaped cuttings, and to extend them in any direction.

DIGGING IN

Most digging is done by hand. In some cases, bulldozers may be used at some point in the dig, but hand digging is the rule, and people on a dig use a variety of tools. They use picks, spades, and shovels (with care) to remove large amounts of soil and rock. They have to watch what they are doing, and sometimes sift the unwanted soil, which can then be thrown into a wheelbarrow and carted away. When they get to a layer with a large number of finds, or where caution is called for, diggers get down on their hands and knees and use hand picks and small coal shovels, and carry the dirt to the wheelbarrow in buckets. The trowel is one of the most important tools of all for an archeologist. He uses a sturdy builder's trowel, rather than the familiar gardening trowel, which is fragile. The digger puts great strain on his trowel as he steadily peels his way through rough soil, a layer at a time. Along with a trowel, diggers often use a brush, to dust off layers and to get the soil out of rocky crevices. Some diggers use a tablespoon to scoop soil out of deep, narrow holes. For delicate finds, such as thin pottery and skeletons, there are a number of smaller tools, such as penknives, doctors' tongue depressors, and small paintbrushes used to clean finds before photographing.

Diggers come from all walks of life. They may be high school or college students, or people on vacation from office or factory jobs. They have to be strong and healthy to work such long and hard hours, and they have to be able to work as members of a team.

Diggers work in groups under foremen or supervisors, who assist the director. To avoid getting in one another's way, diggers often dig in "lanes," or yard-wide paths. They often move backward as they work so that they will not disrupt cleaned surfaces. When a digger finds an object, he places it in a tray or bag. Each find is labeled to show in which level of the dig it was found. All finds from each layer are kept separate from finds from other layers.

Archeologists know a lot about pottery, which most peoples have made for daily use. They have a rough idea of the order in which different types of pottery were used by given peoples. If an archeologist found, for instance, a bead and a bit of pottery in the same layer, he could place the bead in a time scale because he would probably know the age of the bit of pottery. Pottery can be used for guessing roughly the dates of buildings found in the same layer. There is also a time scale for flint arrowheads and for some metal objects.

In most sites, the objects that have lasted over the years represent only a small number of the articles used by the inhabitants. Many finds are very much decayed. However, some soils can actually preserve objects. Acid peat bogs, with their marshy conditions, preserve wood and vegetable matter such as rush matting or cloth. Some peat bogs even preserve leather and skin. So it is a mistake to think that because wooden plates and cups are not found in a clay or sandy soil, these objects did not exist, and the inhabitants used only pottery.

OTHER DISCOVERIES

Archeologists are not just interested in collecting and labeling objects. They also take samples of soil from the cuttings for study by experts using laboratory methods. Where there are traces of animal or vegetable matter, samples can be sent for radiocarbon analysis. This is a way of dating a thing by testing the proportion in it of an isotope, carbon 14.

While digging, examining finds, and sampling are all going on, the director and his assistants are busy recording their discoveries by making drawings and by taking photographs.

As the dig comes to its close, the time comes for the diggers to clean up the area of the dig. On many digs, the soil is dumped back into the cuttings, and turf placed over the top. This is done to keep the lower levels from weathering by wind and rain, and to allow a field to go back to its former use. When digs take place in a town or city, they have to be filled in for safety's sake.

No excavation ends with the final filling in of the cuttings. The director is left with huge amounts of information to think over and to organize. This information is often included in an article for publication in a magazine or book.

And what, you may ask, happens to the finds? By rights, they usually belong to the owner of the land, who may, and often does, present them to a museum for others to go and see for themselves.

LYDIA MURPHY
Gloucester City (England)
Social Services Department

Apprentice archeologists transform a building into a museum to display their Koster finds.

THE CINDERELLA SLIPPERS

> Her godmother just touched her with the wand, and at the same instant her clothes were turned into cloth of gold and silver, all beset with jewels. This done, she gave her a pair of glass slippers, the prettiest in the whole world. Being thus decked out, Cinderella climbed into her coach. . . .
>
> From the folktale *Cinderella*

The story of Cinderella and her glass slippers is well known to millions of children. Of course, glass slippers exist only in fairy tales. Well, not quite. Recently four German youths made a unique find—an actual pair of glass slippers.

The dainty slippers, dating back to the 3rd century, were uncovered by amateur archeologists at a construction site in Cologne, West Germany. The Cinderella in this case was probably the wife of a glassblower. Her Prince Charming had placed the slippers in her coffin before burial.

It was the custom in those days to bury shoes with the dead so that their souls could wander in comfort. People believed that if this was done, the spirits of the dead would not come back to haunt the living.

Cologne in the 3rd century was a frontier outpost of the Roman Empire, and a center of the glassblowing trade. The city's glassblowers were noted for their beautiful work. The 9-inch slippers, one slightly smaller than the other, had apparently been made from two bottles.

A pair of glass slippers recently found in Cologne, Germany, by amateur archeologists.

In order to convert them into slippers, the glassblower pinched the bottles in the middle and flattened them in part. He then added sandal straps and strips of blue and white glass for a decorative effect. A crude pair of glass slippers was thus fashioned.

The slippers were discovered as a result of construction work in a section of the city near the Rhine River. Power shovels and bulldozers were being used to dig out the foundation of a new building.

One of the machines turned up an old coffin, which the four youths spotted as they were walking through the site. The stone-encased coffin had special niches cut into it for the slippers.

This was the first time glass shoes had been found in an ancient grave. In the past, stone and wooden shoes had been unearthed. As far as the experts know, this is the only pair of glass shoes that has survived from ancient times.

Unfortunately, the four amateur archeologists who made the discovery found themselves in trouble. City law requires that all archeological finds must be reported to the police within 24 hours. The Cologne Museum has first rights to buy such relics. The price paid is then divided between the finder and the person who owns the land where the object was discovered.

Instead of reporting the find, the youths tried to make off with their prize. But an informer turned them in, and the slippers were recovered. Maybe Cinderella's fairy godmother was watching over them!

A HAN DISCOVERY

The 1972 discovery of a 2,100-year-old tomb near the city of Changsha, China, has opened the door to an important era of the past. The tomb contained the well-preserved body of a Chinese noblewoman, who lived under the Han dynasty (which ruled China from 202 B.C. to A.D. 220).

It was during the Han dynasty that China became a united country. Small rival states were brought under the control of a central government. A national legal code and a single written language were adopted. China became a great empire during this period. It was a generally peaceful and prosperous time, in which the arts flourished.

The newly excavated tomb has provided archeologists with a rich knowledge of the culture of the Han dynasty. The ornate coffin that was found in the tomb actually consisted of six coffins, one inside another. Around the inner coffin, in which the woman's body had been placed, was a beautifully decorated silk covering, 7 feet long and 3 feet wide. On it were paintings depicting Chinese legends and scenes of everyday life of that time. Experts consider the cover to be the most valuable piece of Chinese silk ever found.

The body of the woman, who is believed to have been about 50 years old when she died, was wrapped in 20 silk garments of different patterns and styles. The body was so well preserved that the woman's facial features were still recognizable. A reddish fluid had been put into the coffin. It is believed to be a chemical used to preserve bodies.

Near the coffin was a banquet table loaded with a variety of foods, all of which were still identifiable. Included were melons, eggs, rice cakes, and peaches. Among the more than 1,000 items in the tomb were wooden figurines, pieces of pottery, and bamboo utensils.

In its account of the discovery, the Communist Party newspaper *Jenmin Jih Pao* stated: "These are the most important and extremely rare relics recently found. They are of great value in studying the history, culture, handicrafts, agriculture, medicine, and preservatives of that age."

In recent years a number of other Han dynasty tombs have been found. A group of Chinese soldiers discovered a network of tombs on Lingshan mountain in 1968. The chambers of these tombs were tremendous in size. The smallest of them was large enough to hold the remains of several chariots and a number of horses.

Each of the tombs on Lingshan mountain had a grand hall, several smaller side chambers, and a burial chamber. The tombs were sealed "by pouring molten iron between two parallel brick walls to make walls of iron."

An ornate coffin recently found in an ancient tomb near Changsha, China.

TWO ANCIENT STATUES

In the 5th century B.C., a Persian army invaded Greece, which was then enjoying its golden age. As the Persian troops advanced toward the city of Athens, many Greeks hid their valuables and fled to the hills. Twenty-five miles southeast of Athens, in the midst of lush vineyards, stood the town of Myrrhinous. In one of the surrounding fields a Greek family buried two beautifully carved and painted statues to keep them from falling into the hands of the Persians.

In 1972, Greek archeologists discovered the hiding place. Although some 2,500 years had passed, the statues were only slightly worn and damaged. They had been placed in a shallow pit facing each other. The statues are of a young man and a young woman, who were probably brother and sister. Experts hailed them as masterpieces of ancient art.

Archeologists unearth ancient Greek statues.

In describing them, the director of antiquities in Athens stated: "These are funeral statues that stood over tombs. They probably belonged to the same family, who buried them to protect them from the invading Persians around 490 B.C."

By a stroke of luck, the base of one of the statues had been found earlier and had been stored in the Athens Epigraphic Museum. On it was inscribed the artist's name. He had signed the statue as follows: "Aristion the Parian made me." (A Parian is someone from the Greek island of Paros.) The sculptor has received generous praise from art experts. "He is undoubtedly a great master," one of them remarked.

Both statues are made of fine white marble. They are typical of the formal style of the Archaic period of Greek sculpture. The young man is presented standing stiffly, with his arms at his sides and one leg slightly forward. Both feet and the right hand are missing. During that era it was customary to paint statues so that they would appear more lifelike. The hair of this statue still shows traces of its original red coloring.

The young woman is shown wearing a long, pleated gown with short sleeves. The dress is decorated with colored rosettes. Along the hemline there is a leaf-like design in red, black, and yellow. On her head the woman wears a band of lotuses and daisies. Her long hair is yellowish in color and falls in curls over her shoulders. She is adorned with bracelets, a necklace, and other jewelry.

The statue of the woman is considered the best-preserved sculpture of that period ever found. Except for some damage to the nose, the statue is in an almost perfect state. According to the experts, repair work will not be difficult.

Meanwhile, archeologists are continuing to excavate the area around Merenda, as the ancient town of Myrrhinous is now called. As one of them remarked, "We hope to be able to find the graves on which the two statues stood 2,500 years ago."

DIGGING UP AN ACRE OF TROUBLE

It started out as just another dig for relics of the past. An archeology professor and a group of students found some bones in an ancient Indian graveyard and took them back to their Pennsylvania college for further study. It was a perfectly innocent archeological field trip. Who could possibly care about the removal of a few ancient bones?

As it turned out, the six tribes of the Iroquois Indian Confederacy cared very much. They let out a war whoop that was heard from New York to Pennsylvania. There were letters of protest, angry words from tribal leaders, and a general uproar that continued until the bones were returned to the Iroquois Indian reservation. Before the dust cleared and the conflict was resolved, the white man once again had found himself in the midst of an Indian war. Fortunately, this one was only a war of words.

The trouble began in the summer of 1972, when Professor Peter Miller and 18 students were working in an Indian burial ground on the hillside of a farm in upstate New York. Professor Miller, who teaches archeology at Kutztown State College in Pennsylvania, had previously dug up a 600-year-old Iroquois longhouse (an Indian communal dwelling made of bark) in that part of the state. This time he and his students uncovered the bones. They are believed to be from 10 skeletons of Indian men and women buried about A.D. 800. A total of 43 skeletons are thought to lie in the burial ground, which is located a few miles south of the St. Lawrence River, in the town of Depauville.

While Professor Miller and his group were digging up the graves, the Iroquois Indian Confederacy was holding a conference. The tribal leaders were outraged when they learned what was going on. According to Indian religious beliefs, the spirits of the dead cannot rest in peace if their remains are disturbed.

The chiefs took immediate legal action. A court order was obtained prohibiting the archeologists from digging in the burial ground. But when the Indians arrived at the graves to serve the court order, they found that the professor and his students had already departed with the bones. The Indians were infuriated.

Chief Lloyd Elm of the Onondaga tribe summed up the feelings of his fellow Indians when he declared: "I've been living on the Onondaga reservation for 37 years, and I've seen a lot of things. I've seen the government take land away, a little at a time. But this is the most deplorable act I've seen committed against the Iroquois Confederation."

A Mohawk chief had this to say: "A final resting ground of our ancestors has been destroyed by the immoral and sacrilegious actions of a group of unknowing and apparently unconcerned white scientists."

Following the discovery that the bones had been removed, the Iroquois sent telegrams of protest to the governors of New York and Pennsylvania. In addition, a three-man Indian delegation traveled to Kutztown State College to recover the bones. The delegation met with Professor Miller, who was embarrassed about the entire matter. "He was quite apologetic," one of the Indians reported later. The professor agreed that it was "the proper thing" to return the bones and handed them over to the members of the delegation.

On August 4, the bones were taken back to the Onondaga Indian reservation, where they were reburied 2 days later. A short ceremony was held at the reservation cemetery by the chiefs of the Iroquois Confederacy.

No further legal action was taken against Professor Miller. But the Indians are hoping to get a law passed that would prevent anyone from digging up their sacred burial grounds and removing the relics of their ancestors.

In the meantime, the Indians may try to buy the parcel of land that includes the Depauville burial ground. A steelworker named James Enderton currently owns the 160-acre farm where the burial ground is located. Enderton, who bought the farm from an Indian in 1965, was thinking of building a swimming pool on the site of the graveyard. But he has said that he would be willing to sell the land to the Indians if they wanted it and were willing to pay a fair price.

TO JUPITER—AND BEYOND

How many times have you searched the night sky, wondering about the millions of stars that dot the heavens? Several of those bright lights look like drifting stars, traveling about the darkness. But they aren't wandering stars. These lights that slowly change their position among the star patterns of the sky are called planets. The planets in our solar system—Mercury, Venus, Earth, Mars, Jupiter, Saturn, Uranus, Neptune, and Pluto—are all captives of our star, the sun. They travel around the sun in orbits, or fixed paths.

Blast off: On March 2, 1972, Pioneer 10 began its long journey to Jupiter—and beyond.

Since the beginning of time, man has had a great curiosity about the celestial bodies. Early man thought that the stars and planets were gods who controlled the lives of human beings. Hunters and shepherds used the stars as guides, and learned to foretell the seasons by what they saw in the sky.

Thousands of years ago, astronomy, the science of the universe, was used in determining the length of the year, telling time accurately, and drawing up the first calendars. Astrologers, who were also astronomers, studied the movements of the sun, moon, and planets, and began compiling information about the heavenly bodies. They were able to work out the positions of the sun and moon each month. The rising and setting of the sun were used to mark out the length of a day.

Through the centuries, the studies of such renowned astronomers as Copernicus, Brahe, Kepler, and Galileo helped us to learn a great deal about our distant neighbors the planets. The earliest astronomers used only their eyes to search and chart the heavens. Later, telescopes, cameras, spectrographs, and other tools were used, and exciting discoveries were made about our universe.

Modern technology has enabled man to further broaden his knowledge of our vast solar system. In 1969 the whole world watched with astonishment as an American astronaut took his first step on the moon. With this historic deed a resounding success, the National Aeronautics and Space Administration (NASA) turned its attention to other ambitious space missions. The next major projects were to be the exploration of the outer planets by unmanned spacecraft.

THE PLANET JUPITER

Jupiter is the largest planet in our solar system. Seen from Earth, it is the second brightest planet and fourth brightest celestial body in the sky. (Venus is brighter.)

For centuries the bizarre and spectacular planet of Jupiter has interested scientists. Its

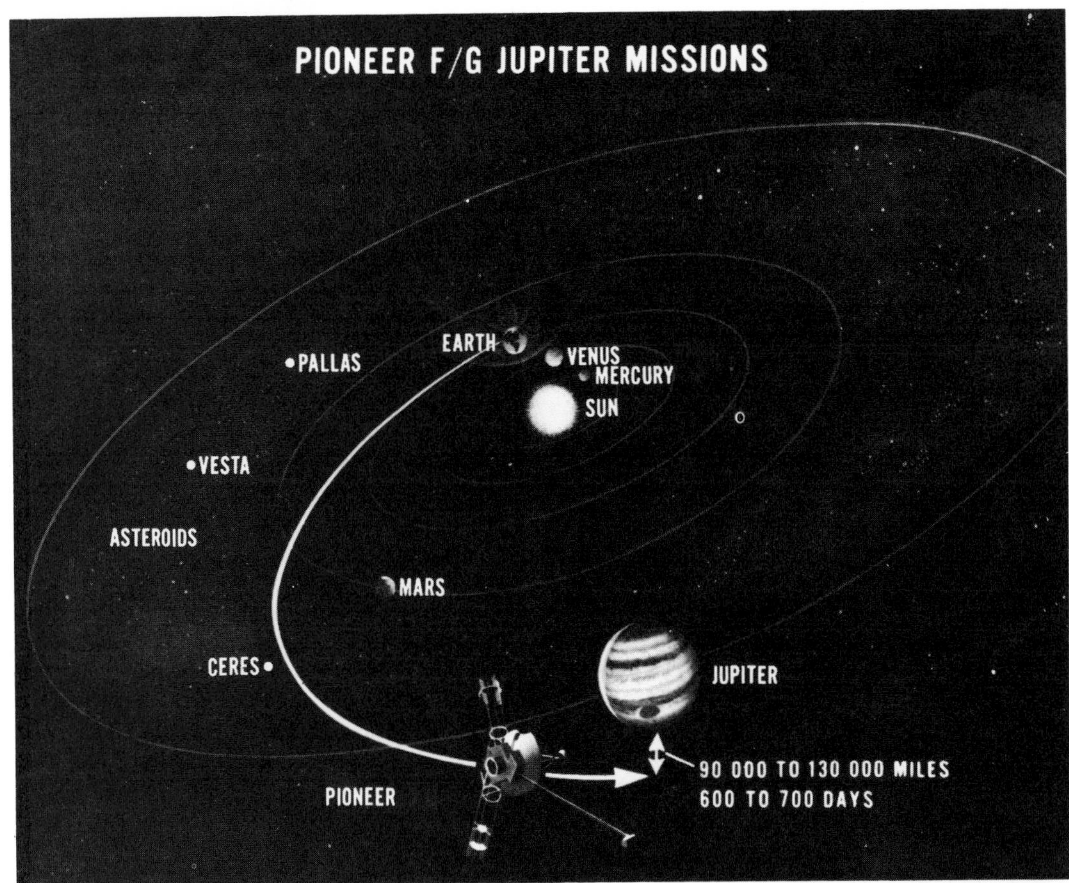

Pioneer 10 had to take care to avoid hitting the asteroids as it passed through the Asteroid Belt, one of the most hazardous parts of the journey.

mass is 318 times the mass of Earth, and its volume is 1,000 times Earth's. Jupiter has 12 natural satellites, or moons. It takes almost 12 years for Jupiter to complete one orbit around the sun.

Jupiter appears to have its own source of energy: the planet gives out more energy than it absorbs from the sun. Scientists wonder what the source of this energy is. Also, floating in space like a yellow-orange and blue-gray striped ball, the planet may actually contain the elements necessary for producing life.

THE FLIGHT OF PIONEER 10

On March 2, 1972, Pioneer 10 was launched by an Atlas-Centaur rocket from Cape Kennedy, Florida. Destination: the remote outer planets and beyond. The primary objective of the journey, however, is to explore the mysterious planet of Jupiter.

The journey to Jupiter, an incredible distance of 620,000,000 miles, will take about 22 months to complete. This is the longest interplanetary voyage of the space age. The craft is expected to arrive near the planet early in December, 1973.

The Jupiter-bound Pioneer 10 spacecraft is providing NASA with a series of firsts in space exploration. Never before has a spacecraft been required to travel so fast and so far, and to work so long. The unmanned Pioneer 10 is the first craft to be placed in a flight that will eventually take it from our solar system into interstellar space. The 570-pound vehicle is also the first craft to have flown beyond Mars and to have entered the hazardous Asteroid Belt—that vast space between the orbits of Mars and Jupiter. This was one of

A model of Pioneer 10 is set on a shake table to see if it can withstand launch vibrations.

the most critical periods of the long journey. The Asteroid Belt is not just empty space. The enormous gap contains thousands of tiny asteroids (planets), all of which the spacecraft carefully had to avoid hitting.

If everything goes according to plan, Pioneer will be the first craft to take closeup photographs of Jupiter. The actual flyby will last approximately 1 week. During the first 2 days, the planet will be viewed in full sunlight. As the craft draws nearer to its target, more and more of Jupiter's surface will be in darkness. When Pioneer 10 is at the nearest point (about 90,000 miles from Jupiter), almost 60 percent of the planet will be dark.

The spacecraft will pass out of Earth's view for a time as it swings behind Jupiter. During this period, all communications between the craft and Earth will stop. If all systems are still working properly when the craft emerges from behind the planet, the remaining scheduled scientific experiment will begin.

Because the distance between Jupiter and Earth is so great, it will take 45 minutes for radio commands to reach the craft, and 45 minutes for data to reach Earth. If the experiments are successful, scientists will learn about Jupiter's magnetic fields, its radiation belts, the measurements of its atmosphere, and the planet's heat balance. It is also hoped that Pioneer will be able to shed some light on the famous Great Red Spot of Jupiter. The 30,000-mile-long and 7,000-mile-wide mysterious spot moves from year to year, and its brightness changes. Scientists do not know the cause of the color and movement. Some of them think the spot may be the result of storms in Jupiter's atmosphere. Since 1665, the Great Red Spot has disappeared completely several times. It seems to brighten and darken at 30-year intervals.

When Pioneer 10 has completed its surveillance of the planet, the spacecraft will make use of Jupiter's gravity to continue on its way toward the orbit of Uranus, some 2,000,000,000 (billion) miles from Earth. During this part of the long journey, the spacecraft is programed to send back to Earth valuable data about the sun's atmosphere, and about any interstellar phenomena it might encounter.

THE ENDLESS JOURNEY

Scientists are looking ahead with long-range plans for the journey of Pioneer. The small radio on board the craft may continue transmitting until Pioneer crosses the orbit of Uranus. Beyond this point, communications with the craft will cease. The distance is just too great.

In 1980, the Pioneer spacecraft, having left our solar system, will continue its journey through the outer reaches of the Milky Way galaxy and on endlessly through space.

And this leads to one of the most exciting but uncertain missions of Pioneer 10. In one of the first scientific attempts by man to communicate with intelligent beings elsewhere, the spacecraft is carrying a special pictorial aluminum plaque. It is designed to show scientists of some distant civilization when the spacecraft was launched, from where, and by what

An artist's conception of how the Pioneer 10 spacecraft will appear as it orbits Jupiter, which at its nearest point will be 90,000 miles away.

kind of beings. The plaque is engraved with the figures of man and woman, and diagrams indicating the position of Earth and facts about our solar system. However, as hoped for as this objective might be, scientists agree that chances of finding other planetary civilizations are very remote.

THE MISSION SO FAR

By the end of 1972, Pioneer 10 had traveled nearly half of its journey, encountering virtually no problems. All of its systems were in good working order, and the fuel reserves for course changes were about twice what is needed. Ten of the eleven experiments were running well and continuously. The eleventh test will be used to record heat emissions while the craft is flying by Jupiter.

The flight of Pioneer has thus far provided NASA officials with more information than they had anticipated. In September, the spacecraft observed a series of enormous explosions on the sun. The information transmitted back to Earth differed from scientists' expectations and provided new data on the solar atmosphere. It is hoped that this data will lead to a better understanding of the sun and similar celestial bodies.

Space agency officials are hopeful that Pioneer 10 will also aid in the technological development of future missions to the outer reaches of space. Like other scientific endeavors, the flight of Pioneer 10 will undoubtedly raise new questions about the planet Jupiter and the rest of our solar system before Pioneer 10 begins its endless journey through our vast galaxy.

JAMES C. FLETCHER
Administrator
National Aeronautics and Space Administration

Explorer Scouts stop erosion by lining the banks of a stream with stones.

YOUTH IN ECOLOGY

Butterfly and wild flower, mountain lion and caribou, blue whale and pelican, coral reef and prairie land—who shall speak for you? My grandchild may need to know you, to see and smell you, to hear and feel you, to be alive, bright and happy!

HUGH ILTIS

Ecology is the method by which some biologists study the world in which we live. It is a relatively new scientific discipline. In fact, ecology brings together several well-established sciences to solve special problems in the modern world. It is the job of the ecologist to learn as much as possible about plants and animals and their environment. The ecologist's study of environment must include physical, chemical, and biological facts about the places in which plants and animals live.

The word "naturalist" was once used to describe those biologists who recognized that some animals have a great influence on the life of other animals and plants, and that the climate and soil of a given place influence plants and animals. However, ecologists are concerned with the quality and quantity of these influences. By knowing these facts, they hope to be able to predict the outcome of any changes that occur in our world. For example, nuclear power-plants require large amounts of water to cool their reactors. This water is usually obtained from a river or a large lake. After being used, the water is returned to its source. By then, the water is several degrees warmer than it was to begin with. Ecologists have shown that even this small change reduces the amount of oxygen the water can hold and may destroy many aquatic organisms (organisms that live in the water). Not all ecologists work on problems directly concerned with pollution. However, their research uncovers the facts that must be known to solve some of the world's most serious environmental problems.

Good conservation is simply applied ecology. We live on a planet whose resources are finite: When they are used up, there are no more. It has taken a few billion years for life as we know it to evolve. This process of evolution has created an enormously complex system of living things, or an ecosystem. Although this system is constantly changing, most of the changes happen very slowly. Because there is only so much energy to be gained from sunlight and food, all organisms have special mechanisms and actions by which they make their living. If their special habitats or niches are seriously disturbed, or if their relations with other organisms are greatly altered, they become extinct. Three percent of the world's mammals have become extinct within historical times, and most of them have become extinct within the last 50 years.

Man is unique among living creatures because he can change his environment a great deal. He is the most adaptable of all large animals, for he uses tools and natural resources to build fantastic civilizations. In the process, however, man has almost entirely lost contact with the ecological world that existed on earth before his cultures developed. Man no longer simply occupies ecological habitats like other organisms: He makes them. Ecologists are learning that many of the changes man makes are harmful to plants and animals—including himself. Harmful changes to the environment are not unique to modern times. Farmers in ancient Greece cleared the land of forest to plant their crops, moving on to new areas when the fertility of the land decreased. The abandoned areas would then often be badly eroded by seasonal rainstorms. Grazing goats also helped decrease the forest area by destroying tree seedlings. With the cutting of the forest for firewood, for homes, and especially for ships, it was not too many

Teen-agers improve the health of a tree in a wildlife area by pruning dead limbs.

centuries before this great civilization began to weaken. This weakening was due partly to the loss of its most valuable resource, the forest. The Middle Ages had its pollution problems: The burning of soft coal and wood in the cities of northern Europe often resulted in severe air pollution.

But pollution problems have never been greater than they are today. Many problems are the result of the tremendous increase in the number of people on earth. The world's population is nearing 3,000,000,000 (billion). This means there will soon be about 44 people per square mile. The problem of supplying energy, food, shelter, and recreation for this huge number of people—and disposing of their wastes—is a major challenge for man. It was estimated that in 1967, $28,000,000 was spent collecting litter from the major highways of the United States; 5 years later this amount had nearly doubled. Industries using water discharge three to four times more waste than all the sewer systems in the United States.

First graders learn about soil by gathering samples and testing them.

Sixth graders check water runoff at an environmental site run by their school.

This is why one of the Great Lakes, Lake Erie, has become an open sewer, polluted and condemned for drinking as well as swimming. More than 1,000 communities still dump raw sewage directly into their rivers and streams.

The United States now enjoys relative prosperity. However, not all the effects of prosperity are good. Sulfur dioxide from cars, electric plants, and coal-burning factories irritates the respiratory tract and can damage the lungs. Americans make up 6 percent of the world's population. However, they use up 30 percent of the earth's total energy. While the population increases by 2,000,000 each year, the number of cars increases by twice that. Despite all precautions, there are still about 1,000 oil spills each year. Spills ruin beautiful sandy beaches and kill thousands of waterfowl by soaking their feathers and making them unable to hold body heat. Millions of acres of wildlife habitat are lost each year to housing and industrial developments and road building. The national forests of the country are under constant pressure from lumber and mining companies that would like to exploit their resources. In order to build 3,000,000 new houses each year for the expanding population, American builders will need 60 percent more lumber by 1978. Unless we learn to recycle, use substitutes, and simplify construction, lumber needs will continue to skyrocket. Today recycled paper saves 200,000,000 trees a year. This figure could be doubled with more cooperation from the American people.

Conservationists or environmental activists who will try to solve some of these problems are needed in every community. People of all ages will have to work together now for a better world. First, young people need to find out about ecological problems and to learn what projects other people have tried. Then they can decide what project they would like to undertake themselves.

LEARNING ABOUT THE ENVIRONMENT

One of the best ways to become informed about environmental issues is to start a clipping file. Collect articles from newspapers and magazines on one or more of the areas of environmental concern. Overpopulation, the shortage of natural resources, pollution, recycling, food additives, and litter are good examples. There is so much material available on most of these subjects that some sort of filing system will soon become necessary. The clipping file can be assembled by an individual or by members of a class or club. Once you decide on an environmental project, the clippings can be used to make effective materials for posters, scrapbooks, or other displays. Add to your files notes taken from TV or radio programs. Class or club members can monitor different news or talk shows, reporting important facts to the group.

In making your clipping file, you will soon realize that many of the issues requiring environmental action are very complicated, because different groups of people take different views on them. For example, you might collect material about a strip mine that conservationists fear will ruin a part of the country. They want to close down the mine because this method of taking the coal or metal ores out of the earth is destroying the countryside, leaving it completely useless for future generations. However, the owners of the mine believe that their method of working is much cheaper and faster than any other, and perhaps even safer for the workers than underground mining. The men who work at the strip mine do not want to see it closed, because they need their jobs to support their families. The men may not have the skills necessary for other jobs. Conflicts between what seems best for future generations and what seems best now for the people most closely involved are found in many of the controversies about environmental issues which are arising more and more frequently.

Another excellent way to become informed about ecological problems is to visit a power plant, a water treatment plant, a municipal dump, a mine, or a large factory. When you plan your trip, arrange to have someone from the plant give you as full a tour as possible. Ask his opinion on the controversial issues involved. Do as much reading as possible beforehand so that you can ask good questions. If you cannot arrange a visit, try to have an expert come to your group. Again, make sure that you have read up on the subject before the visitor comes.

Writing letters for information on environmental subjects is an excellent way to increase your knowledge. Perhaps letters could be substituted for a composition assignment in a language arts class one day. Ask your elected representatives for their stand on environmental bills that come before your state or federal government.

WHAT OTHER YOUNG PEOPLE HAVE DONE

During the 1930's and early 1940's, over 2,000,000 young men participated in a federal government project called the Civilian Conservation Corps (CCC). They lived in several thousand camps around the United States. They worked in state and national parks, building many of the roads, camping areas, and rustic buildings; planting trees; controlling erosion; and landscaping. This project was organized by the leading conservationists of that time. It gave work to many young men who might have been unemployed during the Depression years. But it did much more. It gave many of these young people a new outlook on life. It showed them how useful they could be. Most important of all, it taught

Boys from Becket Academy in Connecticut made an ecological study of the Connecticut River. Here they test water at an atomic power station in Vermont.

As part of a summer program called Becket Adventures, these Becket teenagers are attending an outdoor class on abuse of the environment.

them resourcefulness and a love for the peace and beauty of the countryside.

More recently a biology teacher in Delaware and his students conducted a door-to-door campaign to save nearby beaches from pollution and the destruction of their natural condition. As a direct result, previously planned sewage and industrial facilities were relocated, thus saving one of the few remaining natural sand dune areas on the east coast of the United States. The Delaware state government went on to enact the strongest state law to be enacted in the United States to control the use of coastal land.

Concerned students organized and carried out a nationwide program of environmental lectures, meetings, teach-ins and other activities on Earth Day, April 22, 1970. An estimated 20,000,000 participants across the United States observed Earth Day. As a result, many Americans learned more than they ever had before about environmental problems. They helped start a wide variety of environmental projects. Extensive coverage in the newspapers and on radio and television made the environment a familiar issue in the homes of virtually all Americans.

Students at La Sierra High School in Sacramento County, California, helped raise money for the down payment on a tract of land that adjoined their school and that they thought was worth saving. Although the down payment on the land was $5,000, they had such enthusiasm for the project that they were able to raise $12,000 by the deadline for the down payment. They went on to raise the $25,000 necessary to buy the land. Much of the credit for this project goes to Lori O'Dell, 15, who started the school ecology club and led a student delegation to the Sacramento County Planning Commission.

Geoffrey Mandel of New York City got together with six friends to start his environmental project. In addition to collecting bottles and cans for recycling, they also organized a school clean-up team. Armed with shovels, paper bags, and buckets of soapy water, the team spent one whole day cleaning up their street. They also planted flowers along several other streets. With the money raised from recycling, they had the school boiler repaired to cut down air pollution.

These California Cub Scouts are carrying paper they have collected for a recycling project.

HOW YOU CAN HELP

There are many valuable ways young people can become involved in ecology projects right now. Organization is important in getting things done. You should work toward forming an ecology committee or club with your friends and classmates. The more people involved, the more ideas you can explore and the more work you can do. Plan to meet at least once a week at first, and more often when your projects are under way. Elect a chairman or a president, and perhaps also a secretary-treasurer to handle any letter writing or financial matters.

Most groups find that an anti-litter campaign is a good place to begin because it gives them a chance to get results quickly. It proves both to the members of the group and to other people that they are serious about bettering their community. To focus attention on the problem of litter, the Boy Scouts and Girl Guides of Canada, along with an organization called Keep Canada Beautiful, have an annual litter chase. The object of this game is to see which team gathers the most litter in a

Members of Future Farmers of America are on a soil conservation field trip.

specified period of time. Your group might organize a morning hike called Unlitter-a-Mile. Some members might carry signs reading: "We Are Unlittering a Mile; Please Help Keep It Clean." See if local stores will provide bags or boxes, and arrange for trucks at the final pickup point. Planning an anti-litter campaign does not mean doing all the work. Most of all, it means trying to make other people more careful with their trash and more respectful of land and buildings so that everyone may enjoy them.

Once people in your school and your community have become more aware of their environment, and once you and your group have become used to working together on environmental projects, you will be ready to try a more ambitious activity. Young people in many towns and cities have worked successfully recycling waste materials. Young people can help run recycling centers, where glass, cans, paper, cardboard, and possibly organic materials such as leaves are collected for re-use. Demonstrations of composting organic wastes such as leaves would be a useful activity at recycling centers. Finished compost could be put in the bottom of the holes in which trees and shrubs are planted.

▸ OTHER USEFUL PROJECTS

Send for and pass out anti-pollution literature from door to door and to people along the street in cities and parks. Ask them to pass it on to a friend. Prepare and help run "Save the Environment" booths at fairs and sporting events. Pass out leaflets explaining why people must become involved in preserving their world. Draw up posters and charts to spotlight specific environmental problems such as overpopulation, pesticides, and air and water pollution, including the dumping of garbage in the ocean. Have a poster contest and hang the best ones in conspicuous places in the community. Plan a bicycle trail or bikeway in your town. Arrange a bike parade to publicize the new trail and try to get adults as well as young people to use bicycles or walk short distances. Investigate the extent of mass transportation facilities in your area. Encourage people to use buses, trains, or trolleys to cut down on automobile traffic.

People are a valuable part of the environment, and many of them do not eat a healthful or adequate diet. Help spread the word about healthful foods to your friends and parents. Start a campaign to get people to read the labels on the foods they buy so that they will learn what is really in the food they eat. Advise against the use of too much plastic and other packaging materials, and persuade people to buy beverages in returnable bottles only.

If you like animals and the out-of-doors, you could plan a series of exhibits showing how plants and animals depend upon one another. You could also show the importance of such animals as hawks, owls, bobcats, snakes, and skunks in ecology: They keep the numbers of mice, rabbits, and other animals within bounds. Plan hikes or campouts with your group—but with a difference. Make sure everyone on the outing understands the importance of leaving nature undisturbed. The delicate relationships between plants and animals are easily upset.

A very important aspect of conservation is the proper care of the soil. Become better acquainted with it. Have a soil conservationist talk to your group about what is being done in your area to take care of the soil. See about renting films, filmstrips, and slides dealing with conservation. Try to find out through simple experiments what types of soil absorb and hold water better than others. Compare soils containing organic matter, such as decayed leaves, sticks, manure, and hay, with soils containing little organic material. Arrange a trip to a farm or ranch in your area where good conservation practices are used. Ask the farmer or rancher about his use of the land and other resources. In your own backyard or in a garden notice how earthworms and other small animals benefit the soil. Gather lawn clippings and fallen leaves and use them as a mulch by placing them around the roots of flowers and shrubs to help hold moisture, keep the soil warm, and nourish soil organisms that fertilize the soil.

EVERYONE MUST HELP

Solving all of our ecological problems will require the work of many specialists in our society. Ecologists and conservationists cannot do the job by themselves. The work of engineers, architects, chemists, biologists, inventors, and many others will be needed if the world is to become a safer and more beautiful place for all living creatures. But you and your fellow conservationists must stay on the job, reminding others of the important work to be done. You must continue to carry the message of ecology to the public so that everyone will work toward a healthier environment and the better world that will flourish in it.

HAROLD R. HINDS
Manager
Maplevale Organic Farm

SOURCE MATERIAL

Schools. There are many excellent books and magazines available today that help teach an ecological approach to science. Ask your science teacher to write to the following address for the latest material on teaching ecology to your class: National Science Teachers Association, 1201 16th Street, N.W., Washington, D.C. 20036.

Summer Camps. Most summer camps include sessions of nature lore. Many also provide wilderness experiences, where young people spend a week or more hiking or canoeing in wilderness areas. There are also special science camps that stress ecology. These camps encourage projects studying and possibly solving pollution problems. For information about all kinds of camps write to the following: Camps Information Association, Room 2008, 1 Rockefeller Plaza, New York, N.Y. 10020; Advisory Council for Camps, Suite 704, 366 Madison Avenue, New York, N.Y. 10017.

Summer Vacations. Many state and national parks have guided walks, museum facilities, and evening lectures, talks, discussions, and demonstrations dealing with ecology and conservation. For information write to your state or provincial park services. For national parks in the United States write to these: Park Information, National Park Service, Dept. of the Interior, Washington, D.C. 20240; National Parks Association, 1701 18th Street, N.W., Washington, D.C. 20009.

Nature Centers. An increasing number of nature centers open every year in the United States. They are sometimes called environmental education centers. These centers sponsor programs and mount displays that attempt to explain the problems of man and his world. Many nature centers serve as collection points for recycling drives. They also offer guided walks and summer programs for young people. For more information about these centers write to Ecology Action Educational Institute, Box 3895, Modesto, California 95352.

Scouts and Other National Organizations. Many national organizations have discussions and launch projects aimed at solving pollution problems. Many offer special credits or awards for the study and application of good conservation practices. For information write to the following: National 4-H Foundation, 7100 Connecticut Avenue, Washington, D.C. 20009; National Grange, 1616 H Street, N.W., Washington, D.C. 20006; Boy Scouts of America, 1010 Vermont Avenue, N.W., Washington, D.C. 20005; Girl Scouts of America, 2000 L Street, N.W., Washington, D.C. 20036.

A Tasaday boy named Lobo is the champion tree climber in his native forest.

A STONE AGE PEOPLE

Just imagine what it would be like to find yourself set down in a remote forest among a group of cavemen living exactly the same way people lived thousands of years ago in the Stone Age. Impossible as it may seem, this is just what happened to a group of scientists in 1971.

The group was led by Manuel Elizalde, Jr., a sociologist; he is an adviser to Ferdinand Marcos, President of the Republic of the Philippines, and is the head of Panamin, an organization concerned with the protection of the many minority groups living in the Philippines. On June 7, Elizalde and a party of scientists landed their helicopter in one of the vast forested mountain areas of the interior of Mindanao, the second largest island of the Philippines. There they made their first contact with the Tasaday, a tribe of people living in complete isolation from the rest of the world.

The 24 Tasaday whom Elizalde and his colleagues found used only implements made of stone and of wood. They had no knowledge of how to grow food, and were completely unfamiliar with such cultivated plants as rice, corn, and tobacco. They had no cloth, nor did they know how to make it. And except for

The Tasaday are very skillful fishermen: They catch fish with their bare hands.

one recent visitor, they had never had any contact with outsiders.

The visitor was a man named Dafal, a member of the more advanced Manubo Blit tribe, which lives a long day's walk from the Tasaday. Dafal, a hunter and trapper, often roamed far from his home. During one trip in 1966, he came upon several strangers near a small stream. Dafal spoke to them in Manubo, which, though related to the language of the Tasaday, is nevertheless quite different. At first the Tasaday were frightened, but they did not run away. During the next few years, Dafal met the Tasaday several times, and, though he never saw their homes, he was able to make friends with these quiet, gentle people.

Dafal had many opportunities to observe the Tasaday closely. He watched them fashion crude stone axes for smashing open hard fruits and tree stems. Stone scrapers were the tools they used for making bamboo knives and containers for holding food and water. Until Dafal gave them bolos, long Philippine knives, they knew nothing of metal implements.

Dafal also introduced other devices, all of them advanced for Stone Age people. He gave the Tasaday bows for hunting, along with metal-tipped arrows and spears, but the Tasaday have made little use of these.

Many times Dafal watched the slow, tedious way the Tasaday make their fires. He saw them set a thin wooden rod into a wooden socket. Then one of them would spin the rod quickly back and forth between his hands. In time the rubbing of the rod in the socket pro-

The Tasaday are true cave people. The group above is gathered in the main cave where the Tasaday make their home. The men at left use a new press, which their friend Dafal helped them make. They use it to extract the starchy, nutritious pith (called *natak*) from palm logs.

duced enough heat to make a spark that set fire to some dried moss used as tinder.

The Tasaday do not grow food, hunt game, or domesticate animals. They live chiefly on wild yams, flowers, berries, and insect larvae. They are skillful at catching frogs, tadpoles, crabs, and small fish with their hands. The catch is wrapped in orchid leaves and cooked over a fire. Dafal taught the Tasaday to make animal traps. He also showed them how to extract the starch, called *natak,* from the cores of palm logs efficiently.

ELIZALDE'S VISIT

News of Dafal's discovery soon reached Manuel Elizalde. Plans for a scientific visit to the remote forest were finally made, and Dafal was included in the party.

Getting to the site by helicopter was a difficult task. There was no place for landing in the dense forest, so a group of men of the Tboli tribe was sent ahead on foot. They traveled for six days until they reached a spot not far from the caves of the Tasaday. As a precaution against unwelcome future intruders, no

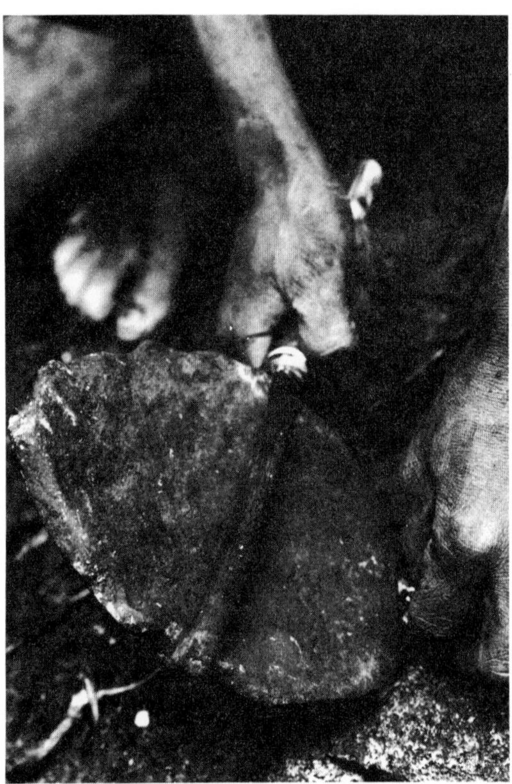

The most complicated Tasaday tool—a stone ax.

telltale clearing was made in the forest. Instead the Tboli built a large, nest-like platform of branches at the top of a 75-foot tree. One by one the explorers jumped from the hovering helicopter onto the unsteady platform. Balayem, a young Tasaday, met the visitors and guided them to the home of his people.

The caves of the Tasaday are in densely forested mountains at an altitude of 4,000 feet. Most of the group lives in one great cave about 15 feet high and 50 feet deep. When the Tasaday saw the strange men approaching, they stood shyly at the mouth of the cave, looking down at the visitors. But before too long they became smiling and friendly.

Since no outsider knows their language, it was difficult to communicate with the Tasaday. Igna, a woman of the Manubo Blit tribe and a member of the exploratory party, was able to understand some of what they said. Igna translated into Tboli. Then May Tuan, a leader of the Tboli tribe, translated into English or Tagalog, the official language of the Philippines. The visitors were fascinated by what they heard and saw.

The Stone Age people call themselves Tasaday after the name of a nearby high mountain. Although they have had no direct contact with other people, they said that at times they had observed hunters in the forest. They had also seen the houses of other people.

The Tasaday seemed anxious to avoid talking about any neighbors they might have. Elizalde believes there are several other small groups of forest people even more isolated than the Tasaday.

The scientific expedition learned much about these remote forest people, but many questions still remain unanswered. Where did this tiny isolated group come from? Who were their ancestors? One possible explanation is that the Tasaday were originally people of the Manubo Blit tribe. At some time during the last 40 or 50 years, they fled from their homes to escape a plague that swept through the Manubo land. Ever since then they have lived in their isolated state. But this theory leaves much to be explained.

Manuel Elizalde thinks that a second explanation might be nearer the truth. Perhaps 500 to 1,000 years ago other tribes split away from the Tasaday's Stone Age culture. These tribes gradually developed more advanced cultures. According to this theory, today's Tasaday are the last people to have kept the original culture of the region.

Six families make up the group of 24 Tasaday the scientists saw. Orphans and widows and widowers without children live with one or another of the six families as if they were truly a part of it. There seems to be no one person who is the leader of the group.

The scientists were puzzled by the reluctance of the Tasaday to talk about their neighbors. One reason may be their fear of disease brought from the outside. Some of them remember an epidemic that struck their group some time earlier.

The Tasaday have good reason for fearing "outside" diseases. Isolated groups like the Tasaday do not develop immunities to common diseases. A stranger might bring in germs that would sweep through the group with deadly effect.

Disease is only one of the problems faced

These fruits, vegetables, and small creatures are what the Tasaday eat.

by the newly discovered isolated group. Anthropologists know that a small primitive group has a hard time surviving as a people after it has been discovered. Its culture may disappear very quickly as some of the members of the group leave their homes to work on farms or live in villages.

Sometimes the land of the primitive group is destroyed, leaving them without a place where they can follow the old ways. Manuel Elizalde had known of the existence of the Tasaday for 2 years before he went to visit them. But because of his fears of what might happen to them when they were exposed to modern civilization, he went to see them only when he learned of threats to their existence.

Danger to the Tasaday took two forms. First, several large lumber companies were preparing to cut logging roads through the forests near their homes. The second threat came from slash-and-burn farmers. These farmers clear an area by cutting it over and burning it. Then they grow crops on the land for a few years. When the land becomes unproductive, they move on to new ground.

To protect the forests of the Tasaday, Elizalde had first the task of proving that people actually lived there. Then he asked President Marcos to set aside 50,000 acres of the mountain forest for the Tasaday and the neighboring Manubo Blit. In 1972, to protect the land of these people, the President ordered this done.

Saving their home will not save the Tasaday from great changes in their way of living. They have now seen a relatively large number of outside people, and have seen many of the tempting inventions that make modern life easier and more pleasant. Changes are almost sure to come.

But the hope is that the changes will be made because this is the wish of the Tasaday, and that the changes will come only when the Tasaday want them to.

LEO SCHNEIDER
Science Editor, *New Book of Knowledge*

TELEVISION

Television is the most important source of entertainment for great numbers of people all over the earth. Once considered a wild dream of overimaginative scientists, television is today a part of daily life. It is not only a source of entertainment, but it is also a major source of news and information, as well as a valuable tool for science, education, and industry.

Television makes it possible to show a lesson, given in one small classroom, to thousands of students at once. Television allows workers to watch over radioactive materials or dangerous machinery from a safe distance. Television cameras in satellites provide pictures of the earth's cloud cover, while space probes send closeup television pictures of the faraway planets.

"Television" comes from two words meaning "to see from afar." Seeing anything, whether far off or nearby, requires light. So, to understand how television works, we begin with light. You see a lighted electric bulb because the bulb gives off light that strikes your eyes. You see this page because light striking the page is reflected to your eyes.

Light also forms the scenes you see on the television screen. But it is not the light of the original scene. First, a television camera changes the light of the scene into currents of electricity. Then a transmitter changes the currents into radio waves. These waves reach your television set. The set first changes the waves into electrical currents, then it changes the currents into light that forms the images you see on the screen.

What makes the "ghosts" on your TV screen?
Ghosts, or double images, appear on your TV screen when the energy from the transmitter to your receiver is divided. Part of the wave travels by a direct route to your receiver. But the other part, deflected by an obstruction, travels a longer path and arrives a few microseconds later. The lateness of the arrival creates a second image slightly to the right of the first. Ghosts are not so apt to be a problem in open country as they are in cities, where there are many steel buildings, bridges, and other obstructions.

TAKING THE PICTURE

Television signals begin with a television camera. Like an ordinary camera, the television camera has lenses that concentrate light to form images of objects.

Usually several kinds of lenses are used. They are attached to a revolving disk, or turret, at the front of the camera. The turret makes it easy to switch quickly from one lens to another, to make objects appear closeup or faraway. The camera may also have a zoom lens. The cameraman adjusts the zoom lens to make it seem that the camera is moving toward an object or away from it, although neither the camera nor the object moves.

In an ordinary camera, light coming through the lens forms an image on a light-sensitive chemical coating the film. In the television camera the image is formed on a screen near the front of the tube. The screen is coated with a thin layer of a chemical called lead oxide. (The Latin word for "lead" is *plumbum.*) Because the screen contains a lead compound, the tube was given the name Plumbicon®.

Electricity can pass through many substances. Such substances are said to be **conductors** of electricity. As a conductor, lead oxide behaves in an unusual way. It is a better conductor in bright light than in dim light.

Let's suppose that the television camera is aimed at a dancer whose costume is partly light and partly dark. The camera's lens projects an image of the dancer onto the lead oxide surface of the screen. Part of the surface is covered by the image of the light portion of the costume. This part of the surface conducts a large current of electricity. But the part of the surface showing the dark portion of the costume conducts only a little electricity. Thus the lead oxide provides a way of changing the light and dark areas of an image into currents of electricity of various strengths.

The electricity comes from an **electron gun** at the back of the tube. There is a wire filament in the gun, like the filament that can be seen glowing in an electric bulb of

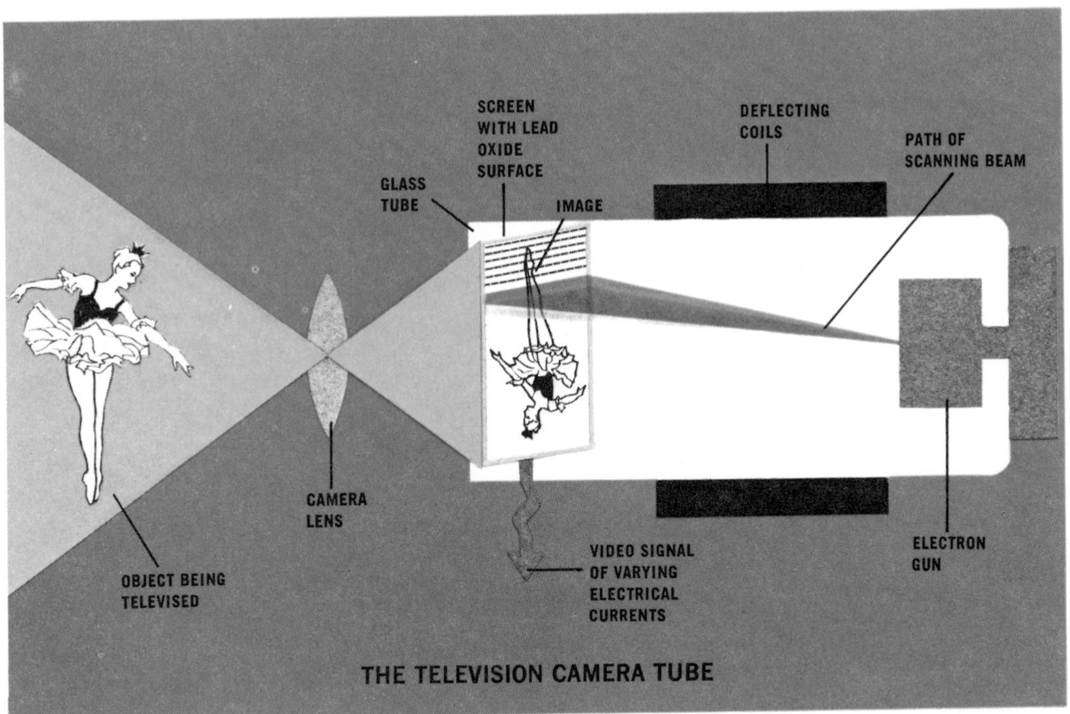

THE TELEVISION CAMERA TUBE

clear glass. Like all atoms, the atoms in the filament are made up of protons, electrons, and other particles. A current of electricity passes through the filament, heating it to a very high temperature. The heat knocks millions of electrons out of the filament every second.

The freed electrons are forced into a very narrow beam and shot toward the front of the tube. On the way the beam of electrons passes a series of **deflecting coils** that surround the tube. One set of coils forces the beam to sweep back and forth, from left to right, thousands of times each second. Another set of coils forces the beam to move down slowly and up quickly, in a regular pattern. The beam is aimed first at the upper left corner of the lead oxide surface. It sweeps across the top of the surface. Then the beam flicks back to the left and slightly lower, and sweeps, or **scans**, a new line across the surface. The beam moves much as your eyes do when you read, but thousands of times faster. Like your eyes absorbing the contents of the page line by line, the beam scans the image on the surface, line by line. In order to scan the whole image the beam sweeps back and forth 525 times. When it has finished scanning the whole image, the beam flicks back to the top and starts to scan again. This action is repeated so that 30 complete pictures are obtained every second. If there is motion in the scene that is being televised, each image is slightly different from the one before it and the one following it. The viewer at his television set is presented with 30 different pictures each second. The human eye is unable to detect such rapid changes. Instead of 30 pictures per second, the eye sees what appears to be a continuous moving picture.

The electron gun fires the same number of electrons toward each spot on the screen. Imagine that you can see one tiny spot where the image on the screen is bright. Many electrons from the beam can flow into the screen at that spot. As we saw, lead oxide is a good conductor in good light. The electrons that flow into the screen leave the glass tube through wires. In a spot where only dim light from the image falls, only a few electrons flow out of the tube.

A flow of electrons through a conductor such as lead oxide, or a wire, forms an elec-

What is "snow"?

"Snow" on a television set is a flurry of tiny specks, some bright, some dark, that cover the picture's fine details. It is sometimes the result of a picture signal that is too weak. The picture signal becomes mixed with random noise currents, which appear as the "snow." There is no way to get the noise current out of the picture. If "snow" is to be avoided, the picture current must be kept strong. This can best be done by using a properly designed outdoor antenna.

tric current. The current that flows out of the camera tube varies in strength. The strong and weak currents correspond to the light and dark areas scanned by the beam. The currents are the electrical representation of the image on the screen. These currents form the **video signal**.

The sound, or **audio signal**, of a television program must also be transmitted. Microphones are set up at the scene that is to be televised. They change sound waves into varying electrical currents. The currents are amplified; then they are transmitted, along with the video signal.

▶ SENDING THE PICTURE

To show a picture on its screen, the television receiver must scan in perfect step with the camera tube that sent the video signal. To make this happen an extra signal, called the **synchronizing pulse**, is added to the video signal. The pulse orders the receiver to begin scanning each new line at exactly the right instant.

The combined video, audio, and pulse signals are amplified more than 1,000,000 times. Then the signals are sent along wires to an antenna, which may be high up on a tall building or on a high tower built especially for broadcasting. The signals leave the antenna in the form of radio waves, which spread out in all directions at the speed of light, 186,000 miles per second.

Radio waves differ in **frequency**—that is, in the number of waves that spread out past a given place in one second. Waves used for television transmission are grouped in two bands. Channels 2 to 13 are in the first band. They use **VHF** (very high frequency) waves. These waves have frequencies (also called **cycles per second**) of about 54,000,000 to 216,000,000. **UHF** (ultrahigh frequency) waves make up the second band. They go up to 1,000,000,000 (billion) cycles per second and are used for Channels 14 to 83. Each station is assigned a numbered channel and a particular frequency it must use. The station's engineers must be careful to stay within their assigned frequency. The use of different frequencies for stations in the same area makes it possible to send different programs without having interference between stations. Radio waves weaken with distance, so two stations several hundred miles apart can use the same frequency without interference.

A television station may provide a satisfactory picture for a distance of only 50 miles or so from its antenna. But many stations can be linked in a network, making it possible for people all over a large country to watch a particular program at the same time.

One kind of network is set up by using towers about 30 miles apart. The signal is carried from one tower to the next by short radio waves, called **microwaves**. The signal is amplified in each tower before it is sent on. Networks are also set up with **coaxial cables** as the link. This specially designed type of cable carries television signals a long distance with little weakening.

Some communities have poor reception or none at all. Distance may be the reason or mountains may block the signals. Tall steel buildings reflect radio waves, and the reflected waves may also cause poor reception.

Community Antenna Television (CATV), also called Cable TV, provides good reception in such areas. A large antenna is set up on a high building or a mountain, where it can receive signals from a great distance. The signals may be amplified. They are fed into coaxial cables. The cables are connected to the homes of viewers who pay for the CATV service.

Artificial satellites are used to carry television around the world. The first transatlantic television broadcast was made in 1962. Telstar I, in orbit 3,000 miles above the earth, received, amplified, and sent back the signals to earth. Today internationally owned Intelsat satellites provide worldwide television.

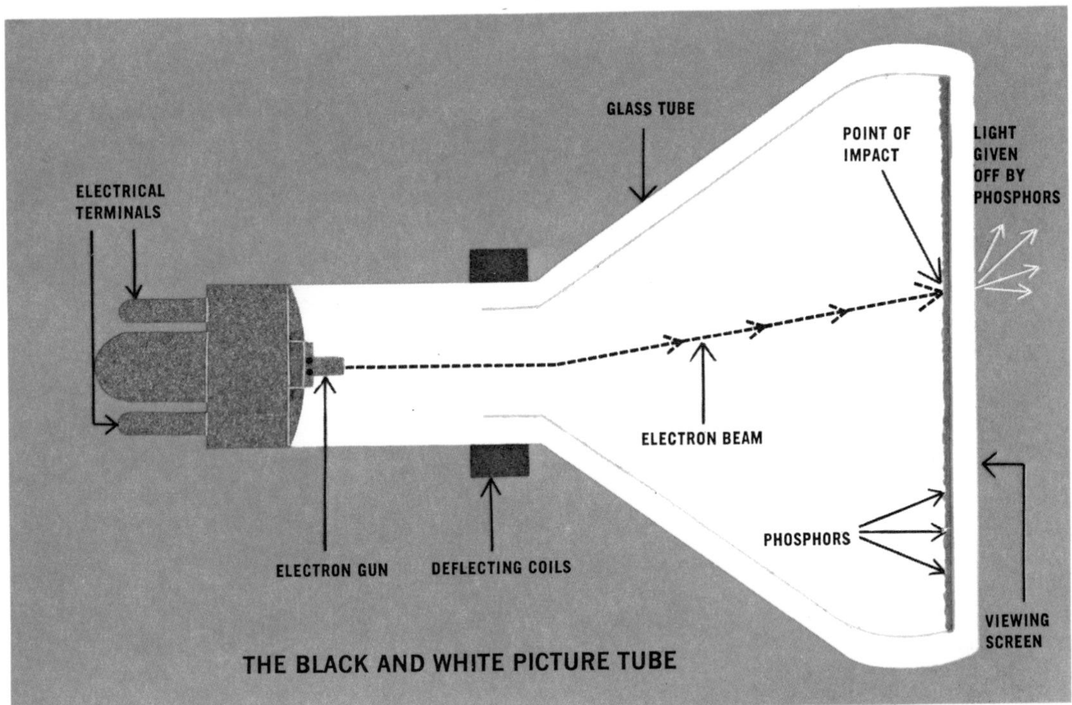

THE BLACK AND WHITE PICTURE TUBE

RECEIVING THE PICTURE

When you watch television, you are looking at the front end of a glass picture tube. The picture tube and the camera tube are alike in some ways. Each tube has an electron gun at the back, to provide a narrow beam of electrons. And each tube has a set of deflecting coils to control the scanning movements of the electron beam.

We saw that the scene viewed by the camera tube is scanned line by line, and turned into variable electric currents. The currents, in turn, are changed to variable radio waves.

The television receiver reverses the work done by the camera tube and the transmitter. In a series of steps the receiver turns the radio waves into light to re-create the scene that was transmitted. The incoming radio waves are first changed to weak electric currents in an antenna connected to the receiver. The receiver amplifies the currents, which carry three kinds of information.

First, there is the sound, or audio, signal. The receiver separates this signal from the others, amplifies it again, and feeds it into a loudspeaker. The loudspeaker changes electric currents into sound.

Second, there is the synchronizing pulse signal that was added in the studio. These pulses control the electron beam in the picture tube, so that the beam scans the front of the tube exactly in time with the scanning beam in the camera tube.

Third, there are the variable currents corresponding to the light and dark parts of the image. These currents are fed into the beam of electrons, so that its strength varies in the same way as the strength of the currents.

The front of the picture tube, on the inside, is coated with **phosphors**. These are substances that glow when they are struck by the electrons in the rapidly scanning electron beam. When many electrons strike a point on the screen, a tiny bright spot glows there. The glow lasts only a fraction of a second. At a point where only a few electrons strike, a dim spot results. The bright and dim spots correspond to the light and dark areas of the scene in the studio, so the scene is re-created on the screen. Look closely at a photograph in this book. It is made up of thousands of tiny dots. From a distance, the dots blur to form a picture.

The light and dark dots on the television screen also blur to form a picture.

▶ SENDING COLOR TELEVISION

To understand how color television works, you must know how colors are produced. In painting, the primary colors are red, blue, and yellow. Any color can be obtained by mixing the proper amounts of the primary colors.

When colored light is used, as in color television, the primary colors are red, blue, and green. They can be mixed to give any other color. In a color television program, light from the scene enters the camera. Special mirrors and filters in the camera separate the light into the three primary colors.

Each beam of colored light enters a separate camera tube. The red beam forms an image of its part of the scene on a light-sensitive layer of metal in the same way an image is formed in a black-and-white television camera tube. The green and blue beams similarly form images, each for its part of the scene.

Within each of the three tubes, an electron beam scans the image, turning it into a variable electric current. The current is changed to radio waves that are transmitted. In some methods of transmission, a fourth tube in the camera is used for black-and-white. There are also other methods for sending black-and-white out along with color, so that both color sets and black-and-white sets can receive the program. The signals in a color broadcast are complex, for in addition to the set of signals for black-and-white, there are three sets of signals for the three primary colors.

▶ RECEIVING COLOR TELEVISION

Color television cameras use three camera tubes, but a color-receiving set needs only one picture tube. However, color tubes are much more complicated devices than the tubes used for black-and-white reception. The color tube has three electron guns, one for each primary color. The front of the color tube has three kinds of phosphors. One kind glows red, one kind glows green, and the third kind glows blue, when struck by electrons. Each bit of phosphor is in the form of a tiny dot. The dots are arranged in clusters of three, with each cluster having a red, a green, and a blue phosphor dot.

A mask perforated by many holes is set just behind the phosphor dots. The holes are arranged in such a way that a dot of a given

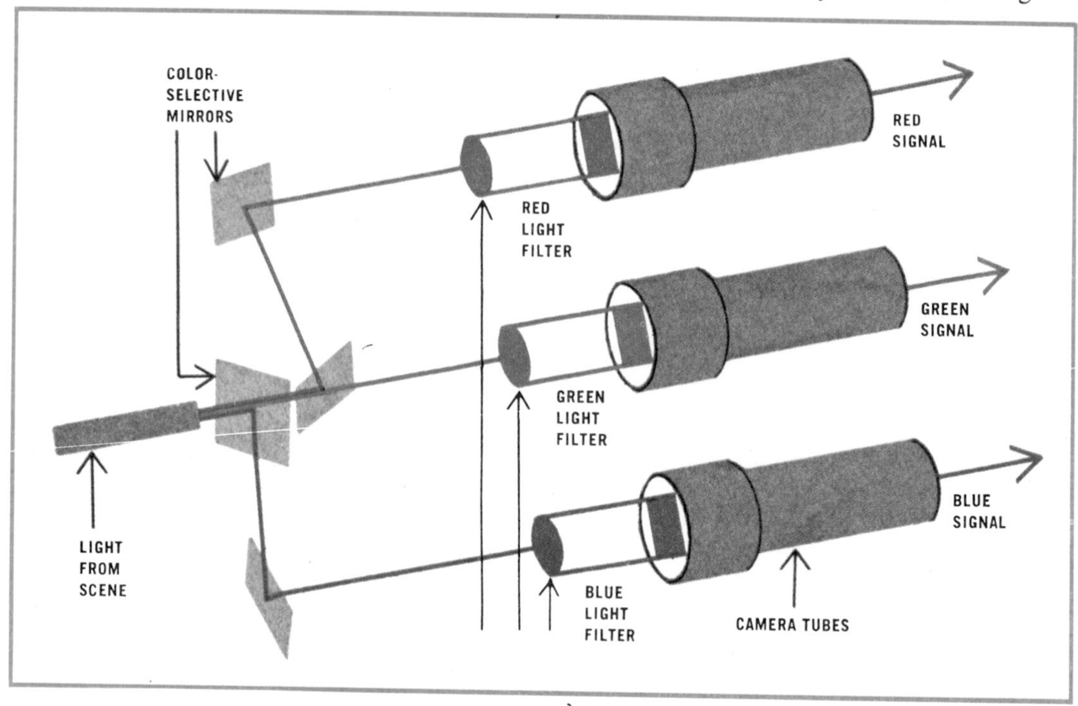

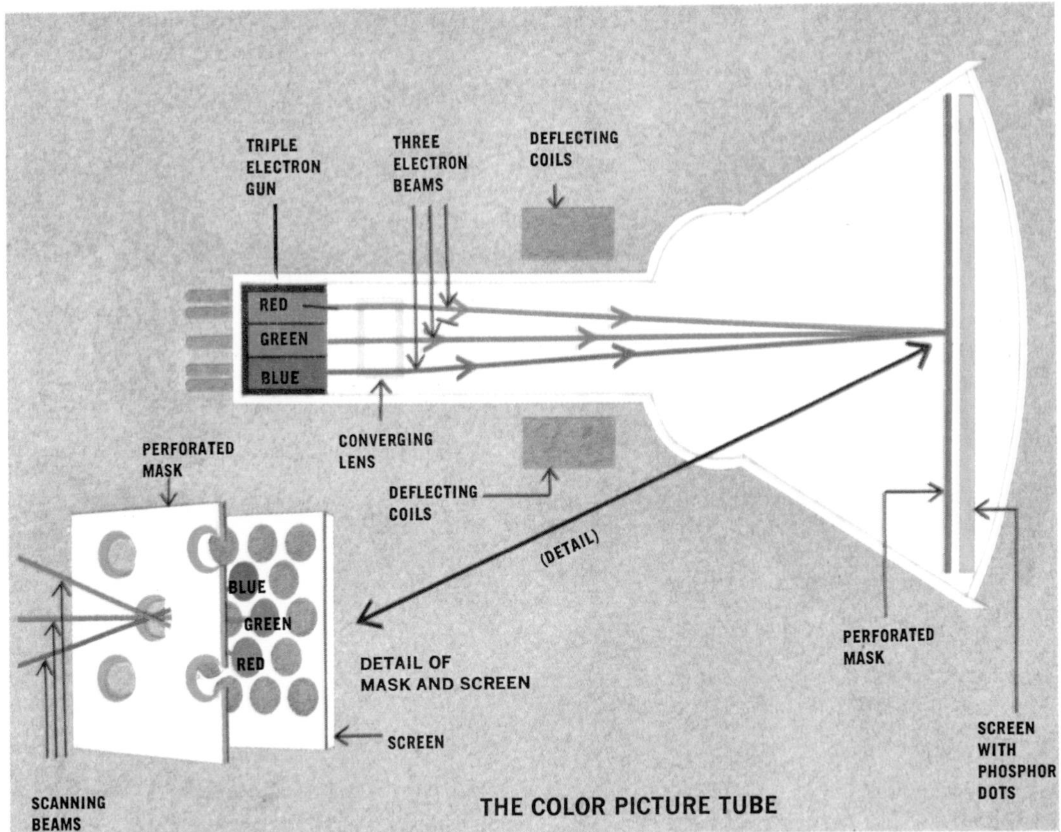

THE COLOR PICTURE TUBE

color is struck only by electrons from its own beam, and no other. For example, the only electrons that strike the dots of red phosphor are electrons from the beam that carries the red signal.

All three beams scan at the same time, so there is actually a red picture, a blue picture, and a green picture on the screen at the same time. The strength of each primary color at a particular spot varies with the strength of the signals from each gun. The dots are very close together. The viewer is several feet away, so his eyes see the mixture of primary colors as the whole range of colors that were in the original scene.

THE DEVELOPMENT OF TELEVISION

Television is based largely on devices that were developed for use in radio broadcasting. One of the most important of these was the vacuum tube, invented in 1906 by Lee De Forest (1873–1961). Various modifications of the vacuum tube were used for the basic work of radio broadcasting, in which radio waves must be produced, amplified, modulated (modified), and detected.

Vacuum tubes have been largely replaced by devices called transistors, which do the same jobs. Transistors have several very important advantages over vacuum tubes. They take up much less space than the tubes. Transistors also use far less electrical energy, and they produce far less waste heat.

Today scanning is electronically controlled, but the early scanning devices were mechanical. The picture to be transmitted was scanned by a revolving disk pierced with a series of small holes. Pictures produced by mechanical scanning were lacking in detail. Also, in action pictures the disk had to spin rapidly, and not much light got through the holes.

Today people all over the world can see how other people look and live. Foreign cultures and institutions can be known directly rather than merely reported on. In less than 50 years television has developed into a worldwide communications tool with infinite uses.

RICHARD E. PUTMAN
Consumer Electronics Division
General Electric Company

ANIMAL WORLD

Eastern screech owls in the World of Darkness at the Bronx Zoo.

What do you call an animal whose mother is a zebra and whose father is a Sardinian donkey? It's a zebroid. This baby zebroid was born in Germany.

ANIMALS IN THE NEWS

James Franciscus and Pax as they appeared in the television series "Longstreet." Pax was the winner of the 1972 Patsy Award for the best animal actor in a television series.

The oldest footprints ever found (*below*) were discovered preserved in rock in Australia. The *Ichthyostega*, an amphibian 3 feet long (imagined by an artist, *above*) may have left the prints 350,000,000 years ago.

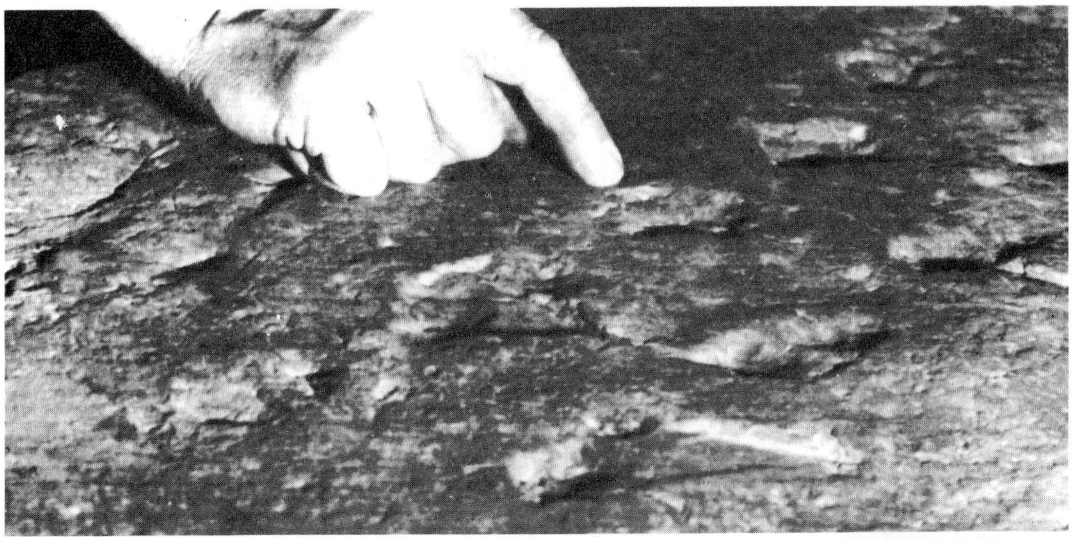

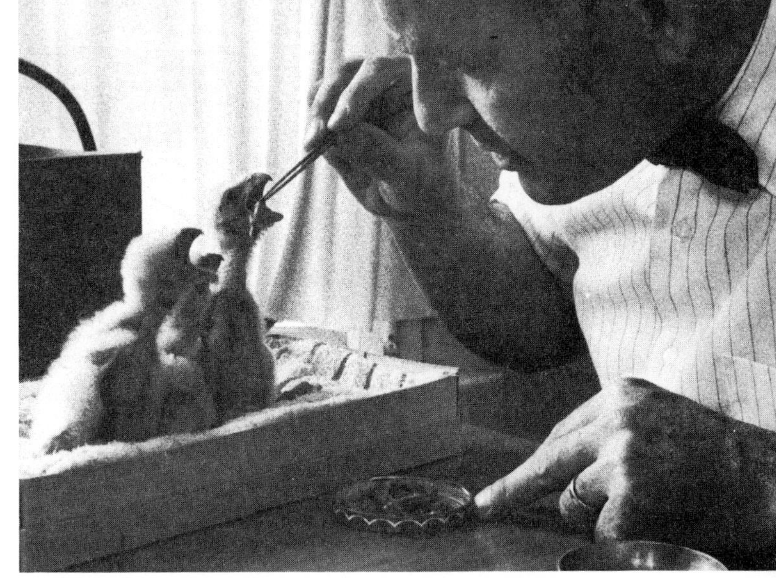

Red, White, and Blue, three baby falcons, open wide for their dinner, fed to them from an eyedropper. The birds represent the second successful attempt by Dr. Heinz Meng, a N.Y. State ornithologist, to breed falcons in captivity. His work offers hope that other endangered birds may be bred in captivity and saved.

This handsome pair of dachshunds are obviously anxious to make friends.

IT'S FUN TO HAVE A PET

What is it that makes us stop on the street and bend down to talk to the kitten we see rubbing its back against a mailbox? The answer may be a very simple one. The kitten is small and furry, and perhaps it looks lost. We want to touch it. But it might also be said that, by the attention we give the kitten, we are trying to establish a link betweeen our own world of man and the much wider world of animals. Keeping a pet, whatever else it gives us in the way of pleasure and companionship, is a way of having, close at hand, a reminder of the animal kingdom.

Now an elephant is a pretty obvious reminder, but most of us would have trouble housing one. (How do you hide an elephant from the landlord?) And although there are people who keep pet boa constrictors, most of us, when the subject of pets arises, think of two animals. We think of those two animals who have proved themselves to be, over the centuries, man's most reliable friends, and the most readily invited to share his home—the dog and the cat.

Much has been written on the relative merits of dogs and cats, and for every claim, a protest or counter-claim can be heard. Dog lovers hold that dogs are less independent than cats. ("Not true!" the cat lover answers.) And they claim that the dog is the more obedient animal. Here, most cat fanciers are forced to agree. Yet there are cats who come running—

An Abyssinian kitten's pedigree has little effect on his curiosity.

even waking from a deep sleep—when they are called, and there are dogs who merely raise their eyebrows and sigh when they hear their names.

If it is true that dogs are better companions because they always make their presence felt, it is also true that they demand greater attention from their master. They are generally less willing than cats are to be left alone for long periods, and must be walked at regular intervals if they are not allowed outdoors on their own.

The cat, on the other hand, is the perfect house animal, delighted never to set paw to pavement so long as it is assured of an exercise post and a well-kept sandbox. Yet the cat's very adaptability, stemming from its small size and its independent nature, condemns it in the eyes of those who desire in their pet an active member of the family. "How many cats do you know who play baseball?" "How many are noted for their love of long and strenuous romps in the woods?" Few, if any, we must admit, although you will occasionally hear stories about a cat who makes the effort. One case in point is that of a household I know in which there were both a cat and a dog. When the pets' owner would set off to the woods with the dog, the cat—a black, long-haired male—would follow his owner and the dog into the woods, always lagging 50 yards behind them and trying their patience, until the dog (a beagle), ignoring both his master and the cat, would shoot off in pursuit of his nose.

The black cat solved the hiking problem himself. When he grew tired, he would climb a tree and wait, comfortably perched, until the dog and his owner returned. (The cat also found his perch in the tree a good vantage point for watching the comings and goings of

No matter what their size, poodles have charm.

German shepherds almost always look noble.

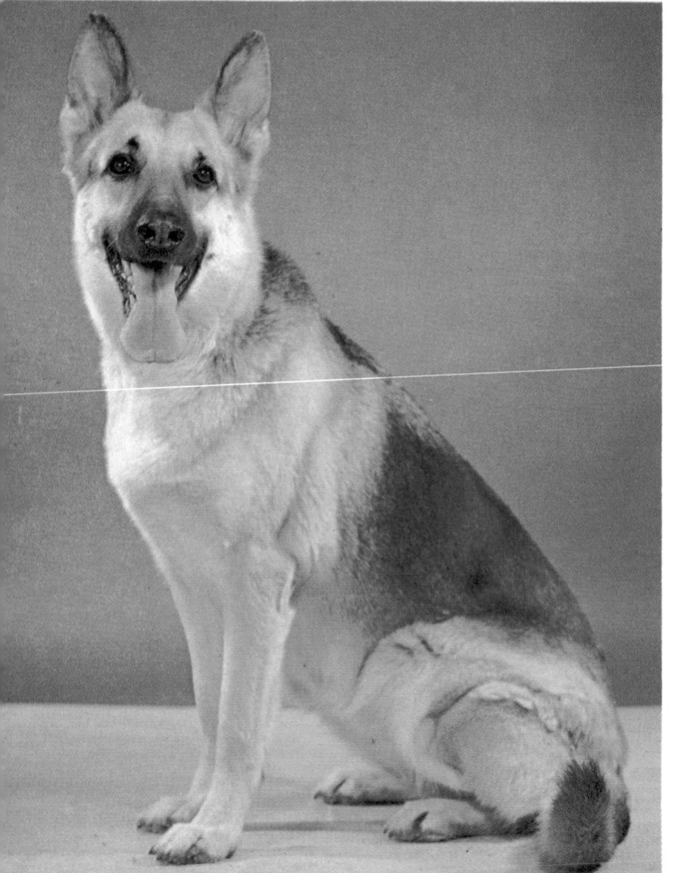

birds and chipmunks.) On walks when the dog and his owner preferred to come home by a different route, the cat would ride the entire distance on the owner's shoulder, the brush of his tail making a warm scarf for his master on a sharp November day.

The arguments in favor of either animal are endless, and when the advocates of dog and cat have had their say, the final choice is usually made for real, personal, and emotional —not sensible—"reasons." We love the dog for his great reliance upon us. We love the way he repays our care with absolute loyalty and ready displays of affection. We especially love him for his open, forthright nature; and for all these fine qualities, we gladly overlook those other characteristics that sometimes make him more of a burden than the cat.

If we love the dog because he is so open and direct, we love the cat because he is not. The cat's sleek panther grace and his tendency to be secretive and aloof suggest to us a world more remote, less familiar, than the dog's. We love the cat's silence and stealth.

Many people, refusing to choose one or the other, choose both. That is by far the best way.

OWNING A DOG

If you decide you want a dog, you will have no trouble finding one to suit your taste. A vast variety of breeds, sizes, and shapes is available. The Chihuahua you hold trembling in the palm of your hand, and the St. Bernard who can almost carry you on his back are both domestic dogs. The American Kennel Club recognizes 116 different breeds of dogs. Some of them are not generally popular now, and you only see them in dog shows. Pets in the United States—especially dogs—have been as subject to fashion as the length of a woman's skirt or the width of a man's necktie. Forty years ago, the wirehaired fox terrier was the most popular dog in the country. According to the most recent figures of the American Kennel Club, the poodle remains, as it has remained for the last several years, the most popular breed of dog. Rivaling the poodle are the German shepherd, the beagle, and the dachshund.

The poodle has lived in so many countries for so long that no one is sure where it came from originally. Some experts claim that it was originally developed as a water retriever in Germany, where it is called the *Pudel,* from *pudeln,* meaning to splash in water. But this highly intelligent animal has also been traditionally considered the national dog of France, where it can often be seen in circuses, performing complicated tricks. The American Kennel Club recognizes three sizes in the breed: the *standard* poodle, which stands over 15 inches at the shoulder; the *miniature,* standing under 15 but over 10; and the *toy,* 10 inches or under. All three classifications are exhibited in their familiar elegant clip, although many people find them even more charming when they are shaggy and unclipped.

The sturdy German shepherd is a work dog. It was developed over the centuries from the old herding and farm dogs of northern Europe. The shepherd is often used in police work and in assisting the blind because he combines the ability to undergo and retain special training with a calm, unexcitable nature. There are other breeds that are highly intelligent, and others that have well-controlled nerves, but none, specialists claim, in which these two qualities are so nicely combined.

The ideal shepherd is muscular, deep-chested, and long rather than tall. He usually has an attentive, fearless expression.

The beagle is another story. His expression is not fearless like the shepherd's, his demeanor not elegant like the poodle's. But his floppy ears and soft, pleading eyes make him irresistible. There is a charming theory that claims that the beagle got its name from an Old French word, *beegueulle,* which might be loosely translated as "loud-mouth." He does indeed have a big voice for a dog no larger than a miniature poodle.

The beagle is short in the leg and high in the tail, and usually has his nose to the ground. For he is a hound that hunts by smell. Other hounds, the greyhound for example, hunt by sight, and are endowed with the speed necessary for pursuing and trapping distant quarry. By comparison, the lovable beagle is a plodder.

The dachshund was formerly used for hunting badgers. (*Dachs* is German for "badger," and *Hund* for "dog.") He combines the attributes of most hounds, in that he hunts with his nose, with those of the terriers, who follow their prey into the earth. (*Terre,* while we're at it, is the French word for "earth," which is how terriers get their name.) An earlier German dachshund was larger and sturdier than the breed so widely known in the United States today. This American version—measuring 7 to 10 inches at the shoulder—although originally intended as a hunting dog, makes an ideal apartment dweller because its short legs get the maximum exercise from the minimum mileage. Some people also appreciate the fact that the dachshund's short, sleek coat is naturally well-groomed and leaves no hair on clothing or furniture.

This young beagle is dreaming of squirrels.

OWNING A CAT

If it is a cat you want and you are undecided which breed would suit you best, consider some of the most popular. They are among the favorites, according to the Cat Fanciers' Association, the largest organization of cat clubs, breeders, and exhibitors in the United States.

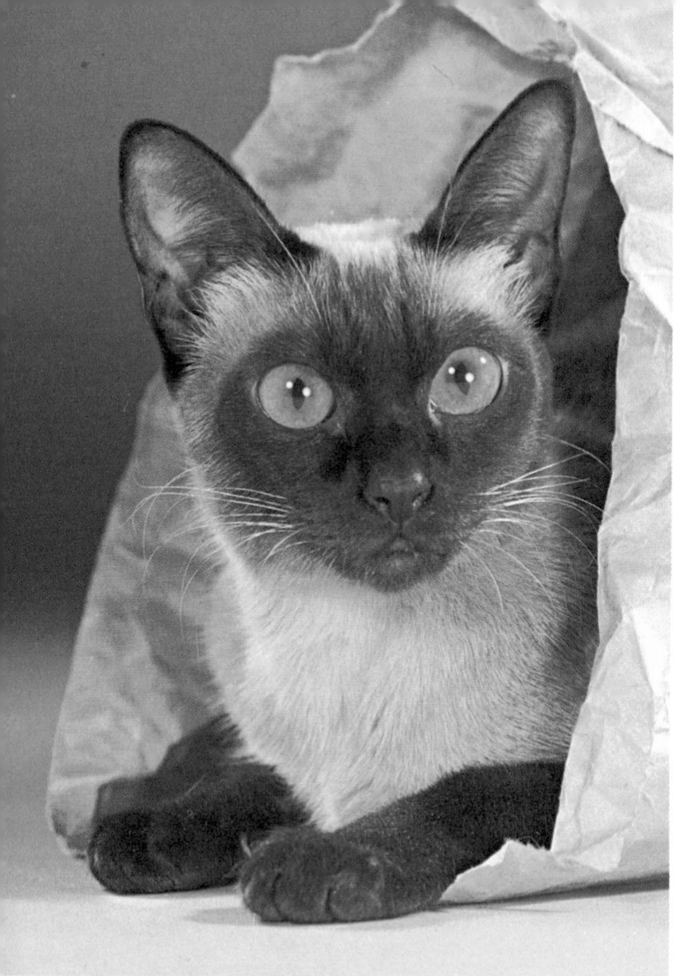

Even a seal point Siamese enjoys a paper bag.

A Persian is elegant to the tips of his ears.

The Siamese, of all the purebred cats, has for a number of years held first place. It is a two-tone cat with a light tan body and "points" of a different color. The seal point's face, ears, paws, and tail are black-brown. There are also blue point, chocolate point, lilac point, and the less common red point Siamese. Kittens are nearly white at birth, and their points grow dark as they mature. Siamese are long-legged, move with majestic feline grace, and have slanting oriental eyes that are blue.

The Abyssinian, or "Aby," cat is undoubtedly the choice for people who like an animal that is not too far removed from its wild forebears. Recognized for just over a hundred years, this breed is a strongly muscled, fast-moving, cunning cat with a reputation for being, of all the breeds, the most difficult to discipline. It has the distinction of being the sacred cat of ancient Egypt. (At least, that is what the specialists claim.) If you study the shape of its body—the muscular back, slim legs and small paws, the wedge-shaped head with its broad but tapering ears—you will see how much it resembles the cat statues of antiquity. As to coloration, the Abyssinian is at first glance rather undistinguished. His coat seems brown, but on closer inspection we see that it is "ticked"; that is, each hair is banded with, in this case, three colors: black, brown, and white.

If to the graceful Siamese and the fast-moving Abyssinian you prefer a cat that is short in the leg, broad in the shoulder, deep in the chest, square-jawed, massive-headed, and rather short-tailed, you will find the Persian to your taste. His frame, however, is not his most remarkable aspect. The Persian is prized for his luxuriant coat of thick, glossy hair that stands straight out from the body. This breed comes in nearly every color, even "silver."

The Persian must not be confused with the Angora, whose features are less bulldog-like, and whose long, very silky hair lies flat against the body. Angora lovers insist that this is a separate breed, which takes its name from Ankara (or Angora), the capital of Turkey, where it originated. Others say it is simply an imperfect specimen of the Persian. The Cat Fanciers' Association ignores the Angora, and

A young calico who is leggy and spirited.

recognizes the Persian as the standard long-hair breed.

The fourth breed, the purists will tell you, is not a breed at all. It has no pedigree, no history. Yet it is older than memory. This is the plain old cat, the alley cat, the most widely kept and widely loved of cats. He is also the most obliging of cats, since he comes in every conceivable color and pattern. There is the tabby, or tiger-striped cat, of different colors. There is the tuxedo tom—an essentially black cat all tricked out in white mask, white vest and bow tie, and four white gloves, looking like a dapper gentleman out for an evening at the opera. (But we know better.) Then there are the parti-colored cats: the tortoise-shell and the calico. Most parti-colored cats are female, the males being very rare and sterile. In the tortoiseshell, the red, cream, and black are mixed together, while in the calico the other colors, in separate patches, are set off by white.

The great popularity of the alley cat has led to its recognition by the Cat Fanciers' Association, which now designates it officially as the "Domestic Shorthair." It is not surprising that in a democracy, all cats, regardless of ancestry or length of tail, should receive equal respect. What is surprising is the airs some alley cats have suddenly assumed.

It is not seldom that pets give their owners the impression that it is they (the pets) who tolerate the owners, not vice versa. A glance at us over their shoulder as they leave the room, or the quizzical look accompanied with a tilt of the head seem to suggest that perhaps they have been reading some authoritative little account of the relative merits of different sorts of humans.

That kitten who rubs his back against the mailbox, if he finds you tolerable, may invite himself home to supper.

Richard Tedeschi
University of Massachusetts (Amherst)

BIRDS AND NIGHT CREATURES

What did the zoo keeper say to the hummingbird as he set it loose in a man-made rain forest with a waterfall 40 feet high?

"Make yourself at home."

And what did he say to the curl-crested aracari toucan as he offered it a salad of carrots, meat, eggs, cottage cheese, rice, raisins, fruits, vitamins, crushed limestone, and chicken mash?

Again the message was: "Hope you'll feel at home here."

That's the message of zoo directors today all over the world. The scientists who plan zoos and run them are making an effort to house birds and other animals in settings as much like their natural ones as possible. The idea is to encourage the wild creatures in zoos to live and act as if they were in their very own familiar part of the rain forest or the jungle or the outback.

For one thing, it's more fun for the people who visit zoos to see birds and animals as they would live in their native habitat, or environment. Second, it's a lot more instructive. Visitors don't just see one homesick pair of redheaded Peruvian manakins in a cage. They see the manakins in a replica of their home in the South American treetops, with a lot of their relatives and some of their colorful neighbors. (The quetzals, for example, and the paradise tanagers often fly by.)

Scientists who study birds and animals in zoos can also learn a lot more about their subjects if the subjects are courting, nesting, and behaving generally as they would in their natural settings.

In the long run, too, this new kind of zoo exhibit may help preserve and protect the wild creatures of the world. Many boys and girls who grow up in cities may never have an opportunity to see wildlife in its natural setting. A zoo exhibit that carefully reproduces nature may be a great awakening for many young people. They will see rocks, trees, plants, animals, and even insects, all as they are in the wild.

A feeling for the beauty of the natural world is an important first step. It can lead in time to an awareness of the need to preserve wildlife and wild places. And this awareness can lead to a willingness to work—and to vote—in the interests of conservation.

Thus, there is really no doubt in anyone's mind about the value of the new type of zoo exhibit. But the practical aspects of planning and constructing these exhibits are a real exercise in problem-solving.

The two newest buildings at the New York Zoological Park (Bronx Zoo) are imaginative answers to the challenge. One of the buildings is the Lila Acheson Wallace World of Birds, which opened to the public in June, 1972. The other building is the World of Darkness, which was designed to house nocturnal creatures (those that are active in darkness, rather than in daylight).

THE WORLD OF BIRDS

The planning and building of the World of Birds took more than 6 years and $3,500,000. William G. Conway, General Director and Curator of Ornithology of the Bronx Zoo, and a team from the zoo worked closely with Morris Ketchum, Jr., and Associates, architects.

The result is a cluster of large connecting cylinders of concrete block, with skylight roofs. The cylinders are of different heights, and each one of the skylights is angled to permit the greatest amount of sunlight to enter the building.

Extending like wings from the body of the building are two ramps of reinforced concrete. One ramp leads visitors from ground level to the second floor, where they can see the birds at treetop level. The second ramp is an exit ramp that returns visitors from the building to the entrance plaza. Traffic goes in one direction, and there are no stairs to climb.

Within the building there are more than 500 individual birds from all over the world. They represent more than 200 species and subspecies. The birds range in type from ground dwellers to residents of the treetops. Their natural habitats range from arid scrubland to tropical rain forest.

The Lila Acheson Wallace World of Birds, newest building at the Bronx Zoo, exhibits more than 500 birds in settings like their own natural habitats.

Visitors can walk through the rain forest with its dramatic waterfall.

The Rain Forest

The birds are presented in 25 different groups, or habitats. Many of them are open-fronted; they are not glass- or screen-enclosed. The largest and most dramatic of these is the rain forest. A room 70 feet long and 50 feet high houses about 100 birds common to the rain forests of the Western Hemisphere. There are hummingbirds, woodpeckers, thrushes, tanagers, trogons, barbets, and many other birds from the wilds of tropical America.

The habitat is heavily planted with palm and rubber trees and flowering vines. Tree trunks serve as perches for the birds.

A major feature of the exhibit is a large waterfall. Hummingbirds flash in and out of the water as it tumbles down the face of a cliff 40 feet high into a pool below. The cliff looks like real rock, but it is actually made of cement and fiber glass. A crew of workers took ladders 30 feet tall to a section of the Palisades in New Jersey. They brushed 12 layers of latex rubber and then a layer of burlap onto the rock face. From this giant rubber mold they cast the cliff for the rain forest. The cliff is stained to look like rock, and plants are rooted in pockets in the cliff face.

A viewing bridge carries visitors right into the display while birds fly freely around them. There is no glass or wire between birds and visitors.

To complete the atmosphere of a rain forest, a thunderstorm crashes through the exhibit every day. Rain pours out of shower nozzles; thunder booms through loudspeakers; and lightning is produced by strobe lights.

Other Major Habitats

A viewing bridge carries visitors right into a second large area: the African jungle. At least 50 jungle birds, including touracos, sun-

The toucan is at home in the treetops of a South American forest setting.

birds, and tropical starlings, live in a faithful reproduction of a jungle, with its thick tangle of vegetation. A huge man-made tree covers one whole side of the exhibit. The tree, 50 feet tall, is made of fiber glass and cork placed over a steel frame. In its branches there are hollows and platforms for nesting places.

Another habitat reproduces a New England forest scene. Many of the familiar birds of the northeastern United States are here. They include warblers, thrushes, cardinals, Baltimore orioles, thrashers, and ruby-throated hummingbirds.

Trunks of swamp cypress trees, festooned with Spanish moss, add realism to a two-level exhibit of birds from a swamp environment. From the lower-level viewing area, stilts, black rails, and other ground birds can be seen, while from the upper-level viewing area songbirds and flight birds can be seen.

Desert shrubs planted around a small pool suggest the natural habitat of a group of birds of the arid scrubland. All of them were brought to the zoo from East Africa. There are buff-crowned whydahs, blue-breasted grenadier waxbills, hemipodes, quail finches, larks, and sunbirds.

The behavior of some of these birds is of special interest. The whydah, for example, doesn't build a nest of its own. The female simply lays her eggs in the nest of the waxbill. The waxbill incubates the whydah's eggs until they hatch, then raises the whydah's chicks.

The tiny male hemipodes also play an unusual role. After the females lay their eggs, the males incubate the eggs and raise the young.

The Treetops, a group of five exhibits arranged in a large semicircle, is designed to give visitors a special treetop view of communities of birds. One of the exhibits, called East of the Andes, is a scene of life high in the trees of a

A visitor to the World of Birds may see the male manakin dance for the female.

The hornbill of Southeast Asia is a large bird with a wingspan of 5 feet.

South American forest. Toucans, with their huge orange bills; trogons; cotingas; woodhewers; and tinamous make their homes here.

At home in the African Treetops are Ross's touracos, with their bright head plumage; violet-backed starlings; and lilac-breasted rollers.

In another Treetops setting, visitors have an opportunity to see hornbills from Southeast Asia. These birds, with their large hornlike bills, are Old World relatives of the New World toucans. Hornbills have a wingspan of 5 feet and weigh from 4 to 6 pounds. The female hornbill walls herself inside a hole in a tree with her eggs. The zoo has provided its hornbills with a nest hole, in the hope that they will breed.

Other exhibits at the World of Birds show some of the ways male birds court females. Male manakins, for example, clear a space in the forest by stripping the leaves from shrubs. Then the male birds do a rapid dance, jumping back and forth among the stems of the shrubs, and making popping and whirring noises as they move. The females, hidden in the bushes nearby, look on. If one of them is attracted by the dance, she moves into the cleared area and selects a male. Visitors may actually see the manakins' courtship dance. The most likely times are the morning and late afternoon.

Other exhibits show the way birds solve the problem of sheltering their eggs and their young. There are birds whose home is a platform in a tree, a hole in a stream bank, or a nest in a whole colony of nests.

Feeding the Feathered Multitude

Feeding all the birds that have come to live in the World of Birds is a continuing responsibility for zoo officials. Two keepers work full time in a well-equipped kitchen to prepare special diets for the birds.

Many of them are from tropical areas, and the foods they live on in the wild are not readily available. Substitute foods must be found and vitamins and minerals added so that the birds are well nourished. The brilliant colors of many birds fade if they do not receive the proper diet.

Ten basic diets are prepared from 50 different ingredients, and the birds are fed at least twice a day. Insect-eating birds are fed a special high-protein mix. Fruit-eating species need a variety of fresh fruits. Blueberries are added to the diet of the manakins, for example.

Most of the feeders are placed in trees, since most of the birds exhibited are tree dwellers. Hummingbirds, which feed on the wing, obtain their food from hanging tubular feeders. To replace their normal diet of nectar and small insects, the hummingbirds are fed a liquid mixture of honey, condensed milk, carrot juice, beef extract, vitamins, fruit flies, and protein powder.

Bright green sunbirds are part of a special Courtship and Plumage exhibit.

The World of Darkness at the Bronx Zoo houses nocturnal creatures.

THE WORLD OF DARKNESS

A low black building shaped like a horseshoe stands on a little knoll in the Bronx Zoo. The building, known as the World of Darkness, is another answer to the challenge of exhibiting animals in settings that are like their own natural settings.

The mammals, birds, reptiles, and amphibians in the World of Darkness are all nocturnal. Their activity cycles conform to the hours of twilight and darkness. Inside the World of Darkness, outdoor settings are reproduced and day is turned into night so that visitors can observe the night creatures as they go about their normal activities.

Zoos all over the world have had night animals in their collections for a long time. But exhibiting these animals has been a problem. As Bronx Zoo Director Conway put it: "The Zoo visitor, peering into a darkened exhibit, usually saw a lump of fur described by the sign in front of the cage as strange and curious looking."

The Bronx Zoo has changed the day-night

The flying squirrel is wide-awake at night.

One setting combines a cave, the home of bats and toads, and a forest.

A swamp, complete with alligators, is re-created in the World of Darkness.

A kit fox is at home in a setting that reproduces a desert arroyo.

activity cycle of its nocturnal creatures by lighting the exhibit areas with high-intensity white light at night, and using low-level, often red, light during daytime hours. The reason for using red light is that red is practically invisible to nocturnal animals.

It took 7 years to plan and complete the World of Darkness. The $750,000 building, which opened in 1969, was designed by Morris Ketchum, Jr., and Associates.

Visitors all walk in one direction through the semicircular building, passing through three major display halls in which there are nearly 300 creatures in more than 30 exhibit areas.

The Forest at Night

The first of the three major halls is The Forest at Night. Exhibits in it include a display of owls and other scenes of night creatures in the treetops. Tree snakes, owl monkeys, and lorises from Asia are shown.

The sounds of a frog chorus rise from a nearby swamp. The sounds are taped, and the tall cypress trees in the swamp are made of fiber glass. But the alligators floating quietly in the water are real, and so are the skunks and raccoons on the shore behind them.

Wings in the Night

The second hall, Wings in the Night, presents birds such as owls and frogmouths, and mammals such as flying squirrels and bats. The main display shows fisherman bats swooping back and forth over a long, shallow pond, trying to scoop up fish with their claws.

Electronic equipment brings into man's hearing range the ultrahigh-frequency sounds the bats make as they swoop. Bats find their prey in the dark by a system called echoloca-

The eyes of the leopard cat gleam in the forest after dark.

tion. It is their own kind of sonar. They send out signals—a series of high-pitched squeaks—and they use the echoes of these signals to guide them in the dark.

Refuge Underground

The last hall, Refuge Underground, displays nocturnal creatures in their homes in burrows, crevices, and caves. The burrows and caves are lighted with red light. In a cutaway section of an underground tunnel, badgers can be seen, while aboveground an aardvark moves about in the man-made African night.

A model of a North American cave shows bats clustered on the roof, and salamanders and blind cave fish in the pool below.

In a setting that reproduces a small desert arroyo, the visitor can see foxes, armadillos, lizards, pack rats, and snakes in their shelters.

The last exhibit combines a tropical cave and a portion of the rain forest outside. The cave, copied mainly from settings in Trinidad, is complete with stalactites dripping water, and stalagmites on the cave floor. The cave is home to several species of bats and toads.

A stream runs through it and out into the rain forest beyond. Sloths hang from branches of the trees in the forest, and bats fly about. Pacas and agoutis, both rodents of South and Central America, and tinamous, which are game birds, can be seen along the forest floor.

The tour completed, the visitor steps once again into the world of daylight. He may never visit the treetop world of the South American forest or see a tropical cave or a desert arroyo. But he will take with him from the World of Birds and the World of Darkness a memory of all these settings, and of the creatures that live in them.

DOMINIC

Dominic was a lively one, always up to something. One day, more restless than usual, he decided there wasn't enough going on in his own neighborhood to satisfy his need for adventure. He just had to get away.

He owned an assortment of hats which he liked to wear, not for warmth or for shade or to shield him from rain, but for their various effects—rakish, dashing, solemn, or martial. He packed them, together with his precious piccolo and a few other things, in a large bandanna which he tied to the end of a stick so it could be carried easily over a shoulder.

Too impatient to dash around saying goodbye to everyone, he hammered this note to his door: "Dear Friends, I am leaving in

rather a hurry to see more of the world, so I have no time to say goodbye to you individually. I embrace you all and sniff you with love. I don't know when I'll be back. But back I will be. Dominic."

He locked the door, buried the key, and left home to seek his fortune—that is, to look for whatever it was that was going to happen to him out there in the unknown world.

He took the highroad going east so he could greet the sunrise as soon as it arrived, and also the nightfall. But he didn't travel in a straight line. He was forever leaving the road, coming back to it and leaving it again, investigating the source of every smell and sound, every sight that intrigued him. Nothing escaped his ardent attention.

On the second day of his journey, he reached a fork in the road and he wondered whether to go the way that veered off to the left or the one that curved over to the right. He would have been happy to go both ways at once. Since that was impossible, he flipped a coin—heads for the left, tails for the right. It fell on tails, so he chased his own tail three times around and took the road that curved over to the right.

By and by, there was an exceptional smell, one he had never encountered before, and hurrying toward it, as he always hurried toward every development, he came to another fork in the road, and there a witch-alligator stood, resting on a cane and looking as if she had been expecting him.

Dominic had never seen a witch-alligator. Though all smells engaged his interest, he wasn't sure he liked her particular one, and

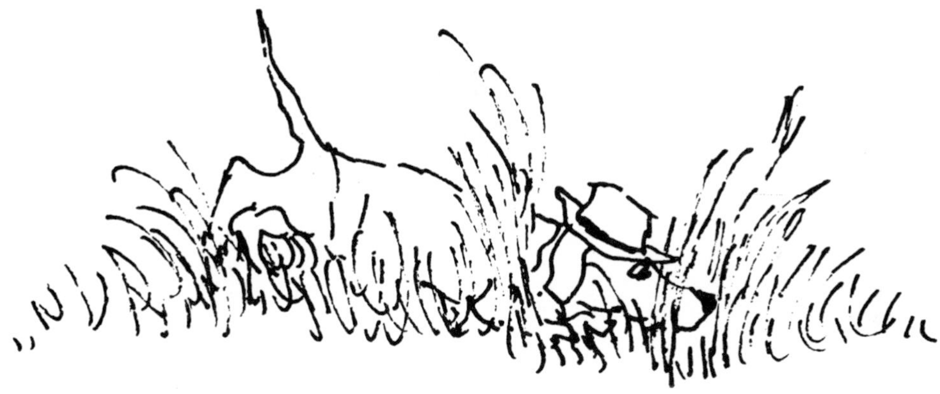

it seemed to him that she had many more teeth than were necessary for any ordinary dental purpose. Still, he greeted her in his usual high-spirited way: "Good morning! Happy day to us all!"

"Good morning to you," said the witch. "Do you know where you're going?"

"Not at all," Dominic said with a laugh. "I'm going wherever my fortune tells me to go."

"And would you like to know your fortune?" the witch asked, adjusting the fringes on her shawl. "I can see the future just as clearly as I see the present and more clearly than I can recall the past. For twenty-five cents I'll reveal your immediate prospects—

what is in store for you during the next few days. For half a dollar I'll describe the next full year of your life. For a dollar you can have your complete history, unexpurgated, from now to the finish."

Dominic thought a moment. Curious as he was about everything, especially everything concerning himself, he preferred to do his own learning. "I'm certainly interested in my fortune," he said. "Yet I think it would be much more fun to find out what happens when it happens. I like to be taken by surprise."

"Well," said the witch, "I know everything that's going to happen to you." Then she remarked that Dominic was unusually wise for so young a dog and offered him a bit of information. "I hope you don't mind if I tell you this much," she said. "That road there on the right goes nowhere. There's not a bit of magic up that road, no adventure, no surprise, nothing to discover or wonder at. Even the scenery is humdrum. You'd soon grow much too introspective. You'd take to daydreaming and tail-twiddling, get absent-minded and lazy, forget where you are and what you're about, sleep more than one should, and be wretchedly bored. Furthermore, after a

while, you'd reach a dead end and you'd have to come all that dreary way back to right here where we're standing now, only it wouldn't be now, it would be some woefully wasted time later.

"Now this road, the one on the left," she said, her heavy eyes glowing, "this road keeps right on going, as far as anyone cares to go, and if you take it, believe me, you'll never find yourself wondering what you might have missed by not taking the other. Up this road, which looks the same at the beginning, but is really ever so different, things will happen that you never could have guessed at—marvelous, unbelievable things. Up this way is where adventure is. I'm pretty sure I know which way you'll go." And she smiled, exposing all eighty teeth.

Dominic feverishly opened his big, polka-dotted bandanna, pulled out some sardines, and gave them to the witch, who consumed them in a gulp. He thanked her for her good advice and went hightailing it up the road to the left, the road to adventure.

an excerpt from *Dominic*
by WILLIAM STEIG

LIVING HISTORY

The Netherlands' Madurodam, the smallest city in the world.

Young people enjoy a visit to the *Wavertree*, flagship of the Seaport fleet.

SOUTH STREET SEAPORT

A new museum is being built in New York City. It is not at all an ordinary museum. It is called the South Street Seaport Museum, and it is so different from ordinary museums that the unusual things about it require an explanation.

Imagine these facts. The South Street Seaport Museum will cover, when it is finished, an area on the New York waterfront about as big as the famous—and enormous—Louvre museum in Paris. Some 750,000 people a year already visit South Street, although it is far from complete. When it is completed, it will include a historic five-block area, backing up five piers on the East River that will berth a collection of 12 historic ships. The museum complex will eventually include 20 restaurants, 100 apartments, 200 shops, and will occupy the 80 buildings encompassed in the restoration area. Visiting sailing ships and scientific vessels will be encouraged to put in at the South Street docks. There will never be turnstiles or admission charges to the overall South Street area, although admissions will be charged to some specific exhibits. Above all the Seaport Museum will not be a traditional museum *for* people. It will be a new kind of museum *by* and *of* people.

The South Street Seaport Museum will be a living museum within the city's historic harbor area. South Street was the street where the stately clipper ships tied up in the mid-19th century. It was the area that famous writers about the sea—men like Herman Melville—knew. It is an area that kept many of its old buildings over the decades because the city's famous Fulton Fish Market was located there. When plans for moving the fish market out of the Fulton Street area began to be discussed, it became obvious to lovers of maritime history that action was needed to save what was left of the old South Street.

Schermerhorn Row, along Fulton Street, site of the headquarters of the Seaport.

HOW IT BEGAN

It all began in the mid-1960's when a man named Peter Stanford, a sailing-ship scholar, decided to do something about the area around the old Fulton Fish Market. It included five blocks of sad old buildings. Countless students of architecture and of history had looked at them wistfully, hoping that someone would try to save them. The buildings were in the Federal style of architecture of the early 19th century. They were built of brick, were three or four stories tall, and had distinctive high, steep-pitched roofs—at least those did that hadn't been altered at one time or another. Particularly important were the group of buildings on lower Fulton Street known as Schermerhorn Row. Grass actually grew on the roofs of some of these buildings. Their windows were broken; their old brick walls sagged outward; and rain dripped from the top stories down through into the cellars. But their basic beauty and classic style showed through.

Stanford and his wife walked down Fulton Street to the spot where the old Fulton Street Ferry slip had been—where boats in Walt Whitman's day had left for Brooklyn. They roamed up and down South Street, looking at the grand old buildings that had housed spice merchants, ship chandleries, saloons, tugboat offices, clipper-ship offices—all the enterprises that had been so important in the era of the beautiful and graceful clipper ships that had docked along South Street in the 19th century. They imagined the bowsprits of ships extending once more over the same wonderful old South Street. They imagined barrels of provisions and other cargo stacked on the wharves. And so the idea of South Street Seaport Museum was born, in 1967.

BUILDING A NEW MUSEUM

Peter Stanford talked to many important people about a Seaport Museum. He and his wife found a dilapidated storefront at 16 Fulton Street. They rented it and put up a sign: "South Street Museum." They cleaned out the accumulated junk of years and whitewashed the walls. It was tough, dirty, and hard work. Friends began to help.

The bulletin board at South Street Seaport announces the schedule of summer musical events.

From the very beginning, it was decided that the Seaport Museum would not be an ordinary museum, with finely polished model cases, with "hands off" signs, with uniformed guards everywhere. Even at this early stage, the philosophy of the new Seaport was made clear. It was clear in the series of delightful walking tours of the area that were instituted in the very beginning. Before the 16 Fulton Street storefront had more than minimal displays, the South Street Seaport Museum idea came alive to thousands of people through such tours. The tours were organized to take advantage of the historic points of interest in the downtown area around the original Seaport Museum storefront. Every tour ended with a plea for members, for "Friends of South Street." In a short time, there were more than 1,000 Friends, who would contribute a minimum of $1 a year. Now there are approximately 20,000 Friends of South Street.

▸THE SEAPORT TAKES SHAPE

A small cardboard model of Schermerhorn Row and of Pier 16 with a couple of ships was the beginning. It was the end point of all the early walking tours and the center of interest when people came for evening seminars in such subjects as nautical knot tying, navigation, and piloting.

The basic idea of the Seaport was to combine a big public and a specialized public. South Street would appeal to many kinds of people: big groups of tourists with a general interest in the area, and special-interest groups. There would be countless events for huge crowds and other sessions for small groups. These groups have come to include, among others, the Maritime Collectors Club (specialists in stamps featuring ships), the Brooklyn Ship Lore and Model Club, the World Ship Society, the Steamship Historical Society, the Marine Society, the Council of American Master Mariners, and the Veteran Wireless Operators Association.

Not least among the "other groups" were groups of young people. From the very beginning, young people have been a vital part of the life of the Seaport. Young people have become Friends of South Street, have helped scrape paint off the decks of ships being restored, and have otherwise participated in the various activities of the Seaport. There have been folk-song concerts and rock concerts for young people, puppet shows, and children's theater in the Seaport buildings, on the docks, and aboard ship. School groups, youth groups, young people's organizations of all kinds, have come to the Seaport. The Seaport is as much for young people as it is for their parents.

There were doubters who did not believe that South Street could be saved. Although efforts were made to see just how much the owners of Schermerhorn Row would sell for, very little serious progress was made along this line because the amounts of money involved were so tremendous. Most people continued to take the whole project with a grain of salt. It was, thus far, entirely privately sponsored, and there was no real money yet. And then it happened—the thing many people had feared from the beginning. A real estate firm bought Schermerhorn Row and announced that it would be torn down for con-

Visitors to the Seaport Museum enjoy an outdoor pop concert.

struction of a new office building. After 6 months of negotiation, the firm that had bought Schermerhorn Row decided to help the Seaport and save the old buildings. New York City helped too. The city's Landmarks Commission declared the area a Landmark of New York.

Almost overnight, the Seaport was changed from a dream into a reality. It was then decided that the Seaport would need more land than just Schermerhorn Row. Ten million dollars was borrowed and the Seaport gained control of four other blocks in the area. These blocks plus Schermerhorn Row included 80 historic buildings.

The Seaport officials wanted the public to know exactly what the restoration would look like. A beautiful and elaborate model of the restored area and of the ships was built and displayed in the museum. The amazing foresight of this planning was illustrated in late 1972 when the 340-foot-long square-rigger *Moshulu* arrived at South Street to become the Seaport's eighth historic ship. The *Moshulu* had been included in the model of the Seaport built 4 years earlier, although Seaport officials had no idea at that time how she would be acquired. Built in 1904, the *Moshulu* lay for years in Amsterdam, relatively well preserved and of interest to many of the world's maritime museums looking for new exhibits. The *Moshulu* had been the winner of the last great race by merchant ships under sail carrying cargoes of grain. (The race was run from Australia to England.) The *Moshulu* was famous as an example of the finest in late sailing-ship design. She will be restored fully by the Seaport.

THE GREAT COLLECTION

The Seaport Museum began its collection of ships long before it had the staff to maintain them or to restore them for public view. This, like the idea of sponsoring public events, has been a vital part of Seaport philosophy from the earliest days of 16 Fulton Street.

Historic Brooklyn Bridge is the backdrop for the South Street Seaport Museum.

The Mayor's Cup Race, a Seaport event.

Bring in the ships and let them be seen. Bring historic vessels to the Seaport and put them at the piers, even before money is on hand to restore them. Create a fleet of old craft and, in so doing, stimulate the enthusiasm, the membership, and the foundation support that will eventually pay for their restoration.

Let us run down the fleet as it stands. There is the fishing schooner *Lettie G. Howard*. Built in 1893 at Essex, Massachusetts, this 75-foot craft had been in continuous service, earning her living up to a year before she was bought for the Seaport. She immediately attracted a group of enthusiastic volunteers who restored and cared for her. She has served as a Committee Boat for the annual Mayor's Cup Schooner Race. In 1972 she was towed up the Hudson and around into the Harlem River to be queen of a festival. In a 4-day period, some 18,000 people swarmed aboard her. This trip emphasizes the desire of the Seaport to be a living museum, to move its ships, and to participate in events away from the Seaport area. It is hoped that the Seaport will one day have Erie Canal barges on display along South Street. They were often towed into port in the mid-19th century. The canal barges could also be towed along the inland waterways of the East as floating museums.

The *Ambrose Light Vessel* (better known as the *Ambrose Lightship*), built in 1907, was another early unit in the Seaport's fleet. For many years, the *Ambrose* marked the entrance to the channel for big ships coming into New York Harbor. For more than 50 years every major liner coming to New York passed the *Ambrose* and saw her welcome light. The *Ambrose* and the *Lettie G. Howard* have pictorial displays aboard and both may be boarded.

The little tug *Mathilda,* once owned by the McAllister Brothers tugboat company, was built in 1899 and is a gem of the Seaport collection. She is not yet ready for the public but will eventually be restored and her engines put back into commission so that she can be used for Seaport work.

The flagship of the Seaport fleet is the *Wavertree.* Built in 1894 in Southampton, England, she is of iron construction and thus will be easier to maintain than most major museum ships, which are built of wood or steel. She is a queen that sailed every sea. Restoration work on her is going ahead slowly. When the restoration is complete, she will be one of the great historic tourist attractions of the United States. Her Captain's Cabin and the small sleeping cabins next to it are in a remarkable state of preservation considering how long she lay in Buenos Aires Harbor as a sand barge. Her poop deck, with its original wheel, is especially fascinating. Many a youngster has already stood in the Captain's Cabin listening wide-eyed to stories about the old ship.

The ferryboat *Hart,* built in 1925 and used on the Governors Island run in New York Harbor for years, is another "living museum" piece. The *Hart* is being used to train young men as marine hands. Rebuilt under the direction of a dedicated group of volunteers, she is on the frontier of Seaport community service work.

The *Pioneer,* built in 1885 at Marcus Hook, Pennsylvania, has been the Seaport Museum's most advanced social experiment. Rebuilt to perfection and given to the Seaport early in 1971, the *Pioneer* has been successfully used for two summers to help rehabilitate young drug addicts. *Pioneer* has made more than a dozen cruises, each of 2 weeks' duration. On each cruise, there have been 15 young people aboard.

On view—a figurehead from an old sailing ship.

The two most recent arrivals at the Seaport Museum are the *Moshulu* and the *Alexander Hamilton.* The *Alexander Hamilton* was a Hudson River Day Line paddle-wheeler, the last of her kind. Both ships will be part of an important gift-shop, bar, restaurant complex projected for Pier 16.

The Bicentennial celebration of the United States in 1976 has given a new goal to the Seaport Museum. A major part of the five-block restoration is to be finished in time for the 1976 ceremonies. A combination of help from New York State, New York City, and the federal government will be necessary to fund the building- and ship-restoration work necessary to make the Seaport Museum ready in 4 years. But most important of all will be the enthusiasm and support of the people who visit the Seaport—the people for whom it was created.

FRANK O. BRAYNARD
Program Director
South Street Seaport Museum

DAYS OF SAIL

At the turn of the century, around 1900, a photographer named Thomas W. Kennedy went down to South Street and took pictures of the waterfront. He knew that the day of sail—of the proud ships drawn up along South Street—was passing very quickly and that these photographs would have to be a record as well as works of art. The people involved with South Street Seaport are trying to bring back some of what was lost on South Street. They hope that one day the beautiful forest of masts and rigging that you see in these photographs may rise once more above the old docks at the foot of Fulton Street.

Like many good photographs, these exceptional shots by Thomas Kennedy truly capture the way things were long ago. When you look at them you can almost hear the sound of the horses' hooves and of the wagon wheels as they clatter along the cobbled streets, bringing supplies and cargo to the ships. You can almost hear the call of sailors to their shipmates as they come down South Street in their round-brimmed merchant seamen's hats. And you can almost imagine yourself a child aboard one of the canalboats drawn up near South Street, warmed by the heat of the potbellied stove in the cabin, secure in your bunk, and going to sleep to the mysterious sounds of the river lapping against the wooden hull of your boat.

The big, steel-hulled Scottish merchantman *Cambusdoon* was a new ship, built in 1895.

A canalboat moored near South Street is both home and place of business to this big family. They may well have come to the city with a cargo from upstate.

A drayman delivers coal to the bark *Charles Loring* of New York, built in 1878.

An American square-rigger lies at the foot of Maiden Lane, docked at Pier 19.

A seaman saunters down South Street, past two foreign merchantmen berthed at Old Slip.

THE SHIPS OF SOUTH STREET

A banner on the paddle-wheeler *Alexander Hamilton* welcomes visitors to South Street.

The South Street Seaport Museum has already started its collection of ships. There are sailing ships and ships from the days of steam. The piers along South Street are beginning to take on new life as restoration work begins on some ships and maintenance work on others. Preparations are made for new arrivals. The ships of South Street are not quaint old hulks; they are alive. A pot-bellied stove heats a cabin on the *Wavertree,* the *Ambrose* still smells of the fuel oil that powered her engines, children run around the deck of the *Lettie G. Howard,* a waterfront cat sits reflectively on a pier and watches the activity. Even chipping off old paint aboard the *Wavertree,* a small step among many that will restore her to all her tall-masted, full-rigged glory, becomes an exciting and vital adventure on the Street of Ships.

The *Ambrose Lightship* (built in 1907), her beacon light high on a mast, her warning bell still on deck, once helped ships navigate the waters off New York.

The iron-hulled *Wavertree*, now being restored, was launched in 1885, one of the last of the great sailing ships. She was wrecked off Cape Horn in 1910.

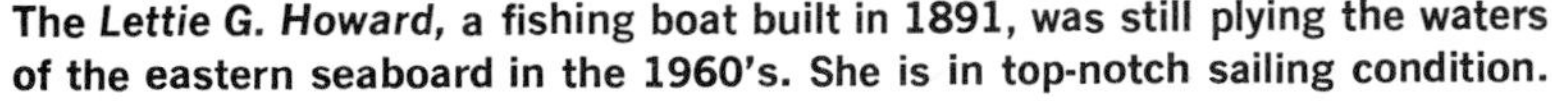

The *Lettie G. Howard*, a fishing boat built in 1891, was still plying the waters of the eastern seaboard in the 1960's. She is in top-notch sailing condition.

YESTERDAY'S TOYS

When I was sick and lay abed,
I had two pillows at my head,
And all my toys beside me lay
To keep me happy all the day.

Robert Louis Stevenson

Toys open the door to a world of fun and make-believe. Their appeal is never-ending, and every generation has its favorites. Visitors to the New-York Historical Society had a chance to see some of the favorite toys of the past in an exhibition called "Two Hundred Years of Toys in America." The collection spanned the 200 years from the early 18th century through the early 20th.

The exhibition included elegantly dressed dolls with leather trunks of clothes; miniature tea sets of fine English china; dollhouse furniture upholstered in damask; regiments of lead and wooden soldiers; hand-carved animals; tin banks that looked like gingerbread cottages; and horse-drawn fire engines, trolley cars, and wagons.

DOLLS

Dolls are stars in any collection of toys, and in this exhibit there was a superstar—the oldest and finest doll owned by the New-York Historical Society. She is a jointed wooden doll and was probably made in Germany in the late 18th century. Her features are painted, and her dark eyes are of glass. She wears a dress of gauzy green silk trimmed at the wrists with beige lace. The bodice is decorated with green and pink ribbons, and over the dress there is an apron of embroidered organdy.

Another display consisted of a group of cardboard cutout dolls, painted in watercolor. Some of these dolls were shown at household tasks. One woman was making apple turnovers, another kneading dough in a trough,

Charming cutout dolls illustrate the pursuits of proper 19th-century ladies.

and still another was seated, beating batter with a spoon in a wooden bowl. In a different setting, the cardboard dolls were shown in the drawing room—playing musical instruments, painting, and doing needlework.

One of the most elaborate of the dolls was a French fashion doll, bought in 1867 for a little girl named Alice Weekes, who named her doll Hortense Abbott Weekes. Hortense is a Parisian lady about 18 inches tall. Her head is of bisque (unglazed china), her arms and legs of wood, and her body of cloth. Hortense was shown in an elegant beige silk dress. Her blond hair, twisted up in a topknot, was crowned with a tiara of red and white stones.

In her trunk and all around Hortense were more of her French fashions. These included a muff of brown and white feathers, an ivory-handled silk parasol, and a leather box of kid gloves. Inside her tiny red-leather sewing box were gilt scissors, a miniature thimble, and brass and ivory opera glasses barely half an inch long.

But not all the dolls were as well dressed as Hortense. One was an early 19th century English peddler doll. Hanging from a string around her neck was a large basket loaded with her wares: pincushions, ribbons, and laces.

Two of the simplest and most appealing of all the dolls were a little old man and a little old woman with wrinkled faces, painted on the pointed ends of hazelnuts.

▶ MINIATURE DISHES AND FURNITURE

Doll dishes and furniture were every bit as elaborate as the dolls themselves—some of the miniature tea sets were actually made of the finest china of the day.

Displayed on the open shelves of a 19th-century cupboard almost 2 feet high was an entire collection of pewter dishes: plates, bowls, cups, and sugar bowl and creamer. There were also tiny china molds, a fluted cake pan, tall amber glasses with handles, and even a tiny metal candlesnuffer.

A number of room settings in the collection displayed miniature furniture, ranging from a formal drawing room to a country kitchen. The furniture in the formal room was of light wood with gold metal appliqué and rose damask upholstery.

Wooden soldiers guard a fine patchwork quilt.

There was also a collection of 19th-century beaded furniture: a canopy bed 6 inches high, armchairs, and a settee. Beads of bright colors were worked in geometric designs on a white background.

One room setting looked like a cozy, comfortable farm kitchen. The simple furniture was all of wood painted barn red and trimmed in yellow.

▶ TOY SOLDIERS

Toy soldiers, wooden or lead, were arranged in the exhibit in row upon orderly row: foot soldiers, some with guns on their shoulders and some with bayonets raised; drummers; flag bearers; and mounted troops.

The hand-carved wooden soldiers were ramrod straight in their tall black hats, scarlet jackets, and white trousers. Many of these were made by mountain craftsmen of Italy and Switzerland, who have passed on their art from one generation to another.

Wooden toys of the 19th century. The wooden horse is a typical toy on wheels.

▶ TOYS ON WHEELS

It is easy to imagine children of the 19th century kneeling by the hour to play with the wagons and fire engines in the collection. One special piece of fire-fighting equipment was drawn by three horses—a white one flanked by two black ones. The white fire engine, at least 2 feet long, carried two black ladders. There was even a big brass bell for the driver, a fireman in red with a red cap, to clang as he drove.

One especially appealing toy on wheels was a tin milk wagon, painted green, with the words "Pure Milk" and a picture of a cow painted in gold on the side. The wagon was pulled by a prancing yellow horse.

In the 19th century, people traveled about New York City in horse-drawn trolley cars. The exhibit included a yellow-roofed red trolley marked "Broadway Car Line." The windows were all open, and there was a platform in front and one at the rear so that passengers could step on and off.

At one time people who lived on farms and in remote communities depended on peddlers who went from place to place with household wares. One of the outstanding toys of the collection was a miniature replica of a peddler's wagon. The brightly painted wooden wagon was over a foot tall and more than 2 feet long. From the sides of the wagon hung dozens of items—everything the old peddler sold: tiny pots and pans, cups and plates, teapots and sugar bowls, rolls of fabric, candlesticks, pewter tankards, cookie cutters, scissors, funnels, and flatirons.

▶ CIRCUS TOYS

In the middle of the 19th century the traveling circuses of central Europe began to visit the United States. In almost no time, the circus became a national institution, and toys were made for all the children who loved the circus.

One display in the exhibition was filled with circus toys. There was a red bandwagon of cast iron, with gold wheels. In the wagon, which was drawn by two white horses, were six band members in blue uniforms and gold caps.

Nearby were the ball-jointed wooden animals and clowns from Albert Schoenhut's "Humpty Dumpty Circus." The Humpty Dumpty Circus, introduced in 1910, quickly became one of the most popular toys of the period.

SUNDAY TOYS

Sunday is a day of peace and rest. In earlier centuries parents felt that this day was one for quiet learning through quiet play. Especially learning the simple and steady truths of the Bible. Special toys were reserved for this day. Most popular, for many generations, was Noah's ark.

The Noah's ark on display was a sturdy vessel of dark wood, with old Noah and his faithful wife standing on the deck. Nearby, carved figures of their sons, Shem, Ham, and Japheth, stood with their wives. And on the roof of the ark perched the dark raven, who would later be sent out to look for land. In front of the ark, the animals waited, two by two, to go on board. There were more than 100 of these small animals: birds, cats, dogs, and familiar farm animals; then the more exotic beasts of the jungle—monkeys, lions, camels, elephants, and tigers.

There's a lot to be learned from the toys of the past, and a lot of fun to be had just looking at them.

Birds and a pig (*above*), intriguing games (*left*), and barnyard scene (*below*) with chickens, figures churning, and a farmer's wife in gingham. Children of the past had a world of fun on their nursery floors.

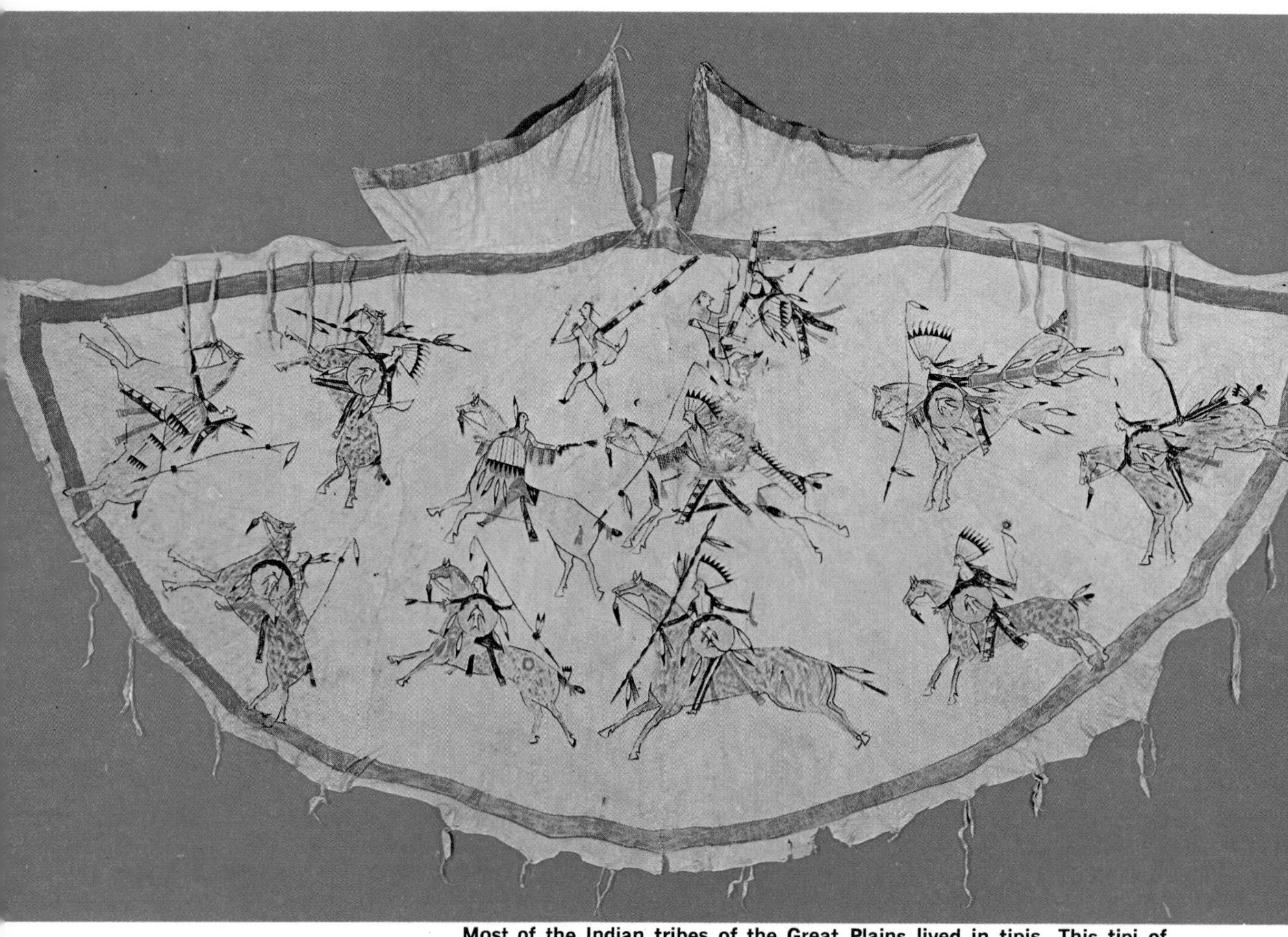

Most of the Indian tribes of the Great Plains lived in tipis. This tipi of painted buckskin is typical of those used by the Brulé Sioux Indians.

CULTURE OF THE NORTH AMERICAN INDIANS

Indian beginnings in North America may well date back 40,000 or more years. The first Americans, hunters and gatherers, moved slowly over the Bering Land Bridge, north of the Brooks Range, and journeyed south by way of the Mackenzie River. On the Great Plains, 12,000 years ago, the Indian people called the Old Bison Hunters were making kills using beautifully grooved flint points that and now called Folsom points by archeologists. In the Great Basin, among the then freshwater lakes, the people called the Old Basket Makers caught their fish and captured wildfowl. In their cave-homes, they made mats and fine baskets from reeds, and sandals. In the oak groves of southern California, the Old Millers, who were village dwellers, shelled, pounded, and crushed the acorn, and gathered seeds, roots, and berries, which were the basic foods they ate.

A FARMING REVOLUTION

For centuries, perhaps, life among the first Americans changed little. But nearly 10,000 years ago the lush grass of the Great Plains began to recede. The freshwater lakes in the Great Basin began to dry up. Indians began to move south into Mexico and beyond. Small settlements were made in Tamaulipas and in the Tehuacán Valley of Puebla, where many food plants were available. The Indians were to learn the secrets of the plants. Before long—between 7000 and 5500 B.C.—they were already planting pumpkins, gourds, runner beans, chili peppers, avocados, and the amaranth in small fields. Later maize (Indian corn), squash, lima beans, and other crops were added. No longer would the Indian in Tamaulipas or Puebla be solely a hunter or gatherer; he was now also a farmer.

Farming produced many changes among the Indians. It forced them, for the most part, to stay in one place. They no longer moved freely over the landscape. They became much concerned with time and the seasons—and with religious ceremonies that would bring the rain and good crops. There were new roles for the men—priests, warriors, traders—as well as for the women—the farmers. Farming further compelled the Indians to organize their lives in different ways.

Nor did the idea of farming remain in Mexico. It spread north to the pueblos and later into the American Southeast and Northeast. It had created a revolution in Indian life.

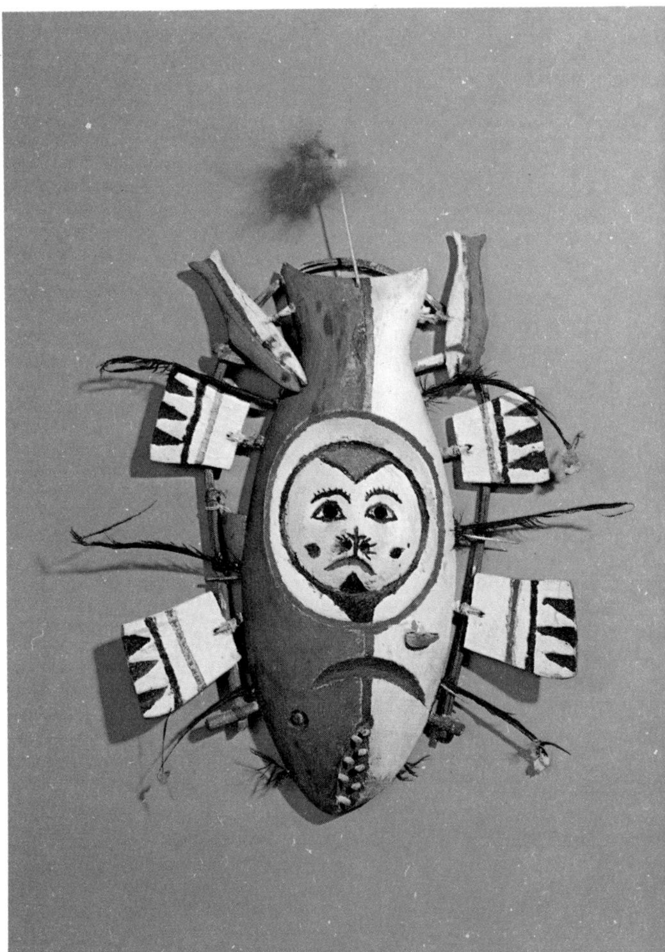

This Eskimo spirit mask reflects the importance of fish in the lives of the northern hunters.

AT THE TIME OF THE COMING OF THE EUROPEANS

But farming was by no means the only way in which Indians supported themselves. Only the Indians in the southern and eastern portions of North America were primarily farmers. The Indians east and west of Hudson Bay were not farmers at all. They were primarily caribou hunters. On the Great Plains, the descendants of the Old Bison Hunters hunted the American bison and antelope; only on the eastern fringes of the region was farming known. In the dry Great Basin, Indian peoples gathered seeds and pine nuts and grasshoppers in season. They also hunted small game. In California, too, the Indians were primarily gatherers. On the Pacific Coast from northern California to Alaska, salmon fishing, rather than farming, was the most important work of the people. At the time of the coming of the European, therefore, American Indian food-getting practices had become diversified. And it should be remembered, too, that there were differences among the Indians in language, in history, in religion, in housing and clothing, in arts and crafts, in medicine, in methods of making war, in education—even in personality. The Indians clearly were not one people; they had become many. It will help, in trying to understand how diverse the Indian cultures of North America were, to look more closely at specific tribes representing basic types of Indian culture.

NAVAJO BLANKETS

During the 1800's, the Navajo Indians wore blankets of varying styles and patterns. The "eye-dazzler" pattern (opposite page) is from the 1880's.

The Navajo sense of color and design is evident in this "chief pattern."

A diamond motif was common in "chief pattern" blankets of the 1880's.

Ornate designs and the color red are typical of blankets of the "serape style."

These hand-carved Hopi Indian dolls represent supernatural beings (kachinas).

HOPI KACHINA DOLLS

Kachinas may be good or evil or comic, as in the case of these Mudhead clowns.

The Owl kachina doll represents a kindly spirit.

Another benevolent kachina is the Squirrel.

This Hopi kachina doll is called Flower.

Some kachinas, such as this Whipper, are feared.

▸ NAVAJO

The Navajo, for example, wandered into the Dinetah (north central New Mexico), the "land of the people," perhaps as late as the 15th century. They were primarily hunters and gatherers. To sustain life they often raided the nearby Pueblos and before long were borrowing many of their ways. It was from the Pueblos that the Navajo learned the art of farming. Later Pueblo contacts also taught the Navajo much about weaving and pottery making, about the use of sand paintings, masks, and altars, and about the fascinating spirit world represented by the artfully made kachina dolls of the Hopi (which the Navajo learned to make too). The system of clans into which the Navajo were divided probably derived from the Pueblos. So, too, did the Navajo origin myth.

During the 18th century the Navajo continued their raids. They raided the Pueblos and the Spanish settlements. From the Spaniards they got horses, cattle, sheep, and goats. And taking their newfound wealth, the Navajo abandoned the old Dinetah and moved west into northwestern New Mexico and northeastern Arizona.

Their dwellings (the forked-pole hogans), their ceremonial lodges, dance grounds, and sheep corrals were scattered in isolated areas across the barren landscape. Where water was available the Navajo planted maize, beans, squash, and watermelons. The men were farmers; the women and children looked after the goats and sheep.

But there was no peace, not even in this isolated land. Navajo warriors battled the Spanish, the Mexicans, and after 1848, the Americans. In 1852, Fort Defiance was planted in the Navajo country. The Navajo raids increased. Finally the decision was made to end the raids forever. Kit Carson was sent into the Navajo country to round up the Indians. In the never-to-be-forgotten "Long Walk"—300 miles—the Navajo were forced to journey to the Bosque Redondo reservation on the Pecos River. Only after a 4-year stay were they (8,000 strong) permitted to return to their homeland.

They rebuilt their lives. They began to farm again. Work in silver and turquoise became important. They made fine rings, pendants, and bracelets. Navajo women poured out their souls in the rugmaking art. Blues and reds, rain and clouds, lightning, mountains.

But all was not well with the Navajo. For their numbers began to increase. In 1900 there were 30,000 Navajo; in 1930, 40,000. The new Dinetah was an overpopulated land. The government recommended stock reduction. The Navajo wavered. They found it difficult to change their old ways.

On the Navajo reservation today, however, change is coming rapidly. There are now over 100,000 Navajo. Money from oil, coal, natural gas, and uranium found on tribal land is helping to support the people. New schools, roads, and hospitals are being built. The new Rough Rock Community High School—an outstanding example of the new advances among the Navajo—is now open.

▸ HAIDA

The Haida lived in a lush forest environment surrounded by water that teemed with sea mammals and fish: the Queen Charlotte Islands off the coast of British Columbia. Expert fishermen, the Haida brought in huge catches of halibut, cod, and salmon. They caught the sea otter. They hunted the deer and caribou. The Haida were in fact quite well-off—quite rich.

Their houses were permanent gable-roofed dwellings fashioned from cedar planks. A totem pole stood in front of the house. At the time of the coming of the Europeans to their country in 1774, the Haida lived in 34 villages, all facing the sea.

So wealthy were the Haida that they developed a class system that included nobles, commoners, and slaves. Everyone in Haida society had a place and function.

The summer months were spent in fishing and sea hunting, whereas the winter months were given over to feasting, dancing, and art. Haida noblemen exhibited their wealth by giving away their material goods: their canoes, totem poles, and fine fish catches. The religious ceremonies of the Haida were called potlatches. They were designed to keep continuity with the Haida past, and to keep the Haida people alive and together.

In their spare time the Haida men worked in wood. They constructed war and family

An elaborate mask of painted wood and fiber, made by the Kwakiutl Indians of the Canadian coast and used in the ceremonies of their secret societies.

canoes; they made dishes and storage boxes, weapons, rattles, and dance masks. The women made boxes, mats, and various containers from the inner bark of the cedar and from cattail fibers. Spruce roots were woven into hats and baskets.

The European and American fur traders burst on the Haida villages in the late 18th century. They brought metal goods, firearms, beads, trinkets, and rum. With metal tools purchased in trade from the Europeans, the Haida were thus able to pursue further their work in wood. Their canoes could be built with less effort. Their totem poles could be made larger, more elaborate.

But the fur traders also brought disease, and the Haida population declined sharply. Nor did the missionaries help the Haida preserve their culture. They forbade them to practice many of their old customs, including the potlatch.

The Haida villages were continually reduced in number. White man's houses replaced those with the old gable roofs. The villages were reduced to two, Masset and Skidegate.

Since 1920 there has been little on the landscape to remind one of the old Haida way of life. True, many of the Haida continued to rely upon the fishing or canning industry for their livelihood. True, the houses continued to face the sea as of old. And true, too, in 1969 a 40-foot totem pole was carved at Masset to remind the Haida of their old glories. But even the casual visitor is well aware that the old ways are no more.

INDIAN POTTERY

This black clay bowl was made by Cherokees from North Carolina in 1966.

A pre-Columbian water jar found in Louisiana. It dates from between 1250 and 1500 A.D.

This ancient three-legged water jug was made by Indians living in what is now Arkansas.

Apache Indians fashioned this black clay bowl centuries before the arrival of Columbus.

An example of modern Indian art, this ceremonial pot was made by a Pueblo Indian in 1920.

The Iroquois Indians of central New York lived in longhouses. These rectangular dwellings were made of a framework of poles covered with bark.

▸ IROQUOIS

The Iroquois were dwellers of the northern forest. Their villages were set up in the Finger Lakes area of central New York. The Seneca, Cayuga, Onondaga, Oneida, and Mohawk made up the original League of the Iroquois (sometimes called "The Longhouse"), a powerful confederacy. They were later joined by the Tuscarora to form the Six Nations.

In the fields near the villages, the Iroquois women planted maize, squash, and beans—they called these vital crops "the Three Sisters." They also raised tobacco, melons, and sunflowers. While the women cared for the fields, the men hunted bear and deer, fished, and frequently waged war.

Despite the crash of war clubs, there was much time for creativity. Iroquois men took pride in making elm bark canoes, the clubs they used in war, and pipes. Members of the False Face Society—healers all—took special pride in carving basswood masks, the false faces, made so ugly that they would frighten off the evil spirits. There was time for song and storytelling. Nor were the women idle. In the winter months, they spent much time preparing wampum strings and belts. They made clay pots with rounded bottoms, narrow necks, and projecting rims. They decorated their clothing with porcupine quills and vegetable fibers.

The arrival of the Europeans in North America brought many changes to the Iroquois. Dutch and English firearms, purchased by the Indians, brought destruction to their enemies. The Iroquois annihilated the Huron. Their war parties fought the French and many Indian tribes in large areas of eastern North America. Missionaries arrived. The Indians turned to the European traders for

The open dwellings of the Seminole Indians of Florida reflect the warm climate in which they lived.

liquor, axes, hoes, and kettles. They adopted European dress. Even the wampum, once so carefully made from carefully chosen shells, was produced in European wampum factories and distributed to the Indians.

There was a reaction, of course. Handsome Lake, a Seneca, was told in a vision (1799) that the Great Spirit deplored the use of liquor. The Iroquois, he preached, must be careful not to imitate the ways of the white man. They must grow their own food. They must be good men and women. Handsome Lake became the prophet of the New Religion. It is to this very day an important force in Iroquois life.

The Iroquois still live in central New York, and in Canada on the banks of the St. Lawrence and Grand rivers. They have recently revived their old pottery-making arts. Ten Mohawks on the Grand River reserve started

The Ojibway, or Chippewa, Indians of the eastern forests lived in dome-shaped wigwams.

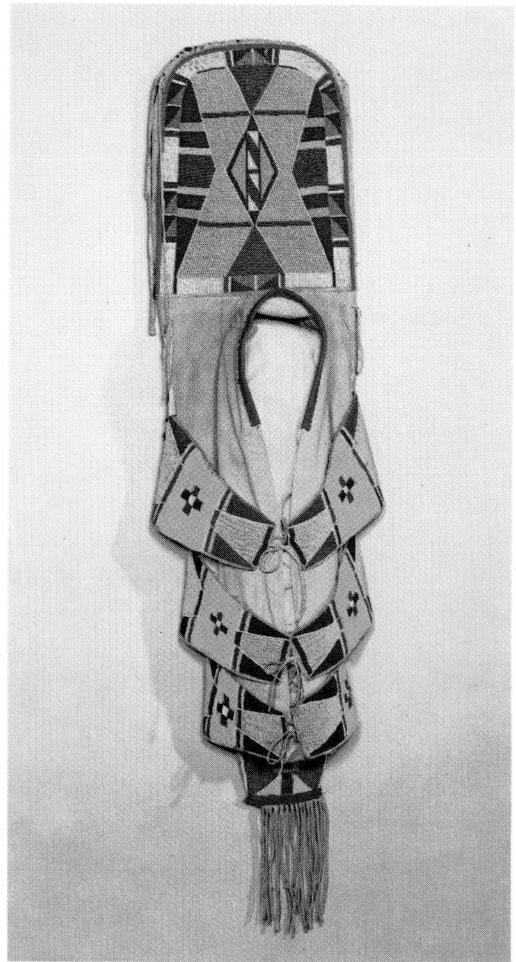

Beaded leather cradleboards, strapped to an Indian mother's back, were used to carry infants.

the revival when, in 1963, they went to work using local clays, old techniques, and old designs.

CROW

Indians had lived on the Great Plains since the days of the Old Bison Hunters. But their numbers were few. In the 16th and 17th centuries it was very difficult to bring down the American bison. It was difficult to approach the herds to make the kills. But that was all changed when the horse arrived on the Great Plains in the 18th century. Brought north from Mexico by the Spaniards, horses finally reached the Shoshone in the Great Basin and the Nez Percé in Oregon and Idaho. They eventually were traded to the tribes of the Plains.

To take advantage of the new wealth in horses, many tribes moved to the Plains from all points of the compass. The Comanche moved to the Plains from Utah and Colorado; the Pawnee moved north from the Southeast. The Sioux moved west from Minnesota, the Crow from the Missouri and Knife rivers.

The Crow became a typical Plains people. Their homeland was the country between the lower Yellowstone River and the Wind River Range. They moved with the bison. When the bison congregated in herds in the summer, the Crow congregated too. Their handsome four-poled tipis were set up in a camp circle. From it, on horseback, they launched their attack, riding round and round the perplexed bison, making the kills. In winter, when the great herds of bison scattered, the Crow scattered too.

Hunting and fighting were the most important activities of the Crow male. Life, after all, depended on his success as a hunter and a warrior. The Crow female, on the other hand, cared for the children; made, set up, and dismantled the tipi; and prepared the bison meat for eating. She also made the parfleche, or rawhide container, in which quantities of food could be stored. She was responsible for packing the dog or horse travois for passage over the grassland. Only when time permitted could she indulge in her favorite art: decorating the bison skins with porcupine quills.

But the hunting life was soon to pass. In 1868, by the terms of the Fort Laramie Treaty, the Crow were granted their reservation lands in Montana. By 1888 the bison were no more; the hunting days were over. No longer was there a need for tipi, for parfleche, for travois. Life for the Crow was to change considerably.

Today the Crow still occupy their reservation lands. In 1961 the United States Government paid the tribe $9,000,000 for lands that it had ceded in the 19th century. The money was used to improve Crow housing, to buy land that had previously been sold to whites, and to buy cattle. In 1963 the Crow were awarded $2,000,000 to compensate for the lands taken for construction of the Yellowtail Dam and Reservoir.

Indian art is not always traditional in form. Oscar Howe, a Sioux Indian, expresses the modern Indian experience in his *Sioux Eagle Dancer.*

NEW THEMES

Today nearly half of North America's Indians continue to live on reservations or reserves. And Indian opinion is in favor of retaining them. Yet there has been a steady movement—particularly of young people—to the cities. Poverty and unemployment have spurred the movement. But adaptions to city life have not been easy.

Indians normally move into the central business district. After they live there for a time, they move to outer fringes of the city, and then to the suburbs. The old tribal patterns tend to become lost in the process. Many Indians are assimilated into the larger, white society; many, of course, are not. For there is a growing trend among Indian urban dwellers to keep their Indian identity.

Reservation life is also changing rapidly. Much money is being spent, for example, on much-needed education. More and more funds are being spent on home building and home improvements. Small industries are being established. Tourism is being developed.

And the Indian—conscious of his identity, his past, his present, his future—is beginning to make the decisions that will influence his own life. He is saying more, writing more, and painting more. He is likely to introduce a new breadth into the whole American spirit.

DANIEL JACOBSON
Author, *Great Indian Tribes*

THE PLANT FROM THE GODS

When you think of corn, the chances are that you think of a delicious ear of corn on the cob. Perhaps you also think of corn bread, corn syrup, or hominy grits. But did you know that corn also goes into many other products? Corn is used in things as different as candy and medicine, baking powder and explosives, plastics and chicken feed.

The American Indians were the first people to know about corn. By the time the first European explorers reached the New World, Indian farmers were growing corn from the Atlantic Coast west to the Rocky Mountains, from South America to Canada. Corn was the most important food crop for most Indian peoples, and they had many stories about how corn came into the world.

One of the best known of these stories was told by the Ojibway Indians, who lived in the beautiful, wild country by Lake Superior. The hero of this story was a young boy named Wunzh, a member of the Ojibway tribe.

Long, long ago, so the story runs, the Ojibways lived entirely by hunting and fishing. They did not know about farming. When the hunting and fishing were good, the people lived well. When animals and fish were scarce, they starved.

Wunzh's father was a kind, good man, but he was not clever at hunting or fishing. His family went hungry most of the time, for the father hardly ever brought home enough to eat.

When Wunzh was at the age of becoming a young man, he went out to a lonely place in the forest, far from his village. He spent several days there alone, fasting and praying. If he followed the rituals correctly, a spirit would visit him in a dream. This spirit would be his friend and protector for the rest of his life.

All the boys of Wunzh's tribe went through this ceremony. It was part of becoming a man. Most of them prayed that their guardian spirits would help them to become famous hunters or mighty warriors. But Wunzh did not care much about glory for himself. More than anything else, he wanted to help his people, to keep them from going hungry when the hunting was bad. How wonderful it would be, he thought, if people could eat plants as well as animals!

Wunzh fasted for one day, two days, three days. By the morning of the fourth day, he was so weak from hunger that he could not get up from his bed of animal skins. But he made up his mind not to give in. He would take no food until he had found his guardian spirit. Suddenly, he saw a handsome young man coming down toward him out of the sky.

The young man was dressed in fine clothes of yellow and green.

Waving green plumes crowned his head. Surely, thought Wunzh, this must be the guardian spirit I have been waiting for.

The young man commanded Wunzh to get up and wrestle with him. Weak as he was, Wunzh obeyed. They wrestled long and hard, until Wunzh fell to the ground exhausted. Then the spirit (for that was what he was) said, "It is enough for one day, my friend. I will come again." He smiled at Wunzh and disappeared into the sky.

Twice more the spirit came and wrestled with Wunzh. Finally he said, "The Great Spirit, who made the world and everything that is in it, has granted your prayer. Tomorrow we must wrestle for one last time, and you will beat me. Then you must strip off my clothes and throw me down on the ground. Where I fall, make the earth soft, and clear away all the roots and weeds. Bury me in that spot. Come back now and then to see whether I have come back to life, and be careful not to let grass or weeds grow on my grave."

The next day, all went as the spirit had foretold. Wunzh defeated him easily. When he had carried out all the spirit's instructions, he went home to his family, but he said nothing to them about what had happened. A guardian spirit's words were magic and must be kept secret.

Wunzh took good care of the grave of his spirit friend. He came back often to pull up all the grass and weeds that tried to grow there. One day, he saw what seemed to be the green plumes of his spirit's headdress poking their tips out of the ground. Each time he came back, they were taller.

At the end of the summer, Wunzh took his father to the place in the forest where he had buried his spirit friend. There in the clearing stood a tall, graceful plant, as tall as a man. Waving plumes crowned the plant, like the plumes of the spirit's headdress. Its broad, green leaves and the golden ears of corn it held looked like the clothes the spirit had worn.

"This is my friend," said Wunzh to his father. "It is the friend of all mankind. It is *Mon-daw-min* (corn, in the Ojibway language). The Great Spirit has sent this plant to feed us. No longer need we go hungry when the hunting is bad. As long as we take good care of this gift of corn, the ground itself will give us a living."

Wunzh took an ear of corn from the plant, and stripped off the husk, just as he had stripped the clothes from his spirit friend. Then he picked the other ears, and the whole family joined in a feast of freshly roasted corn.

That is how corn came into the world, according to the Ojibway legend. Other tribes had different stories, but they all agreed that corn had come from the gods.

an excerpt from *The Story of Corn*
by PETER LIMBURG

Guardsmen pass in review during Queen's Birthday Parade (Trooping the Colour).

THE QUEEN'S GUARDS

Every year in June thousands of Londoners and visiting tourists turn out to watch a unique military spectacle called Trooping the Colour. The stirring ceremony, held in honor of the British monarch's birthday, features the elite Horse and Foot Guards regiments that serve as the Queen's personal bodyguard. Actually, Queen Elizabeth's birthday is in April, but because the weather is usually better in June, the official celebration is held then.

On the appointed day the seven regiments of the Queen's Guards salute the British monarch with a dazzling display of military pomp. Queen Elizabeth is there to review the Guardsmen in person. She is dressed for the occasion in the uniform of the regiment selected to troop its color—an old military custom in which the regimental flag (or color) is marched down the line of troops.

The Queen's Birthday Parade, as it is officially called, is a brilliant pageant. Describing the event, one commentator wrote: "No other country presents such a spectacular military parade. The scarlet tunics, the waving plumes, the glistening breastplates of the Horse Guards, the perfect grooming of the mounts, and above all, the precision of the drill make it an unforgettable experience."

Last year, however, a solemn note was added. On May 28, 1972, a few days before the parade, the Duke of Windsor died. The Duke, who was Queen Elizabeth's uncle, had been King Edward VIII for 11 months in 1936. But in December of that year he gave up the throne to marry Wallis Simpson, an American woman. The British Government opposed the marriage because Mrs. Simpson was a divorcée and a commoner. Rather than give up the woman he loved, King Edward surrendered the crown and became the Duke of Windsor.

As a mark of respect for her late uncle the Queen wore a black armband on her uniform tunic during the parade. The 1972 ceremony began with a long roll of muffled drums; the drums were draped in black. A minute of silence followed, and then a bagpiper played a mournful tune in memory of the Duke. Normally, the bells of Westminster Abbey are rung after the ceremony is over. But last year they were silent as a further tribute to the former British monarch.

Trooping the Colour is an old tradition, dating back to 1755. But it is just one of the many official duties of the 8,000-man Household Division, which consists of five regiments of Foot Guards and two of Horse Guards. These famed Guardsmen have protected Britain's kings and queens for over 300 years.

THE CHANGING OF THE GUARD

This year, as in the past, hundreds of thousands of visitors will come to London from all parts of the world. Many of them will go to Buckingham Palace, the monarch's residence, to see the Changing of the Guard. It is one of Europe's most popular tourist attractions, and the best-known ceremony involving the Queen's Guards.

The Changing of the Guard, or guard mounting, takes place nearly every morning. It begins shortly after 11 A.M., when the Old Guard (the unit of Guards on duty) forms up in the main courtyard of Buckingham Palace. A few minutes later, to the accompaniment of fifes and drums, another detachment of the

Queen Elizabeth receives a salute from scarlet-coated Foot Guards in front of Buckingham Palace.

The Changing of the Guard at Buckingham Palace.

The Life Guards on duty at Horse Guards, Whitehall.

Old Guard arrives from nearby St. James's Palace.

Then, at exactly 11:30, the New Guard parades into the courtyard. This is the highlight of the ceremony for the spectators who crowd around the palace. A 50-piece regimental band heads the line of march. Following close behind is a detachment of rifle-bearing Guardsmen in their familiar black bearskin hats, scarlet tunics, and blue trousers. Cameras click at a furious pace as excited tourists strain for a good view of the Guardsmen.

During the next half hour the Old and New Guards change places. Sentries are posted, and the orders of the day are read to them. In the background, the band plays a selection of military marches and popular tunes. The five Foot Guards regiments—the Grenadier, Coldstream, Scots, Irish, and Welsh Guards—take turns mounting guard at Buckingham Palace. Depending upon which regiment is on duty that day, there may be extra bits of color. For example, the Scots Guards have a contingent of bagpipers as well as a brass band; the Irish Guards march with their Irish wolfhound mascot, Fionn.

At five minutes past noon, the Changing of the Guard comes to an end. With a final flourish, the Old Guard marches back to barracks, leaving the New Guard to take over the duties of providing sentries for Buckingham and St. James's Palace.

Horse Guards on Parade

While the Foot Guards are performing at Buckingham Palace, another Changing of the Guard takes place at Whitehall—a cluster of government buildings on the site of the former royal palace. This guard is provided by one of the Household Division's two cavalry regiments—either the Life Guards or the Blues and Royals. Both regiments have mounted squadrons for ceremonial purposes. Their full-

Troopers of the Blues and Royals ride through traffic in central London.

dress uniform includes a plumed helmet, metal breastplate, and black boots reaching over the knee. The Life Guards have red tunics and white plumes; the Blues and Royals wear blue tunics and red plumes.

Daily at 11 A.M. a mounted detachment from one of the two regiments holds a brief ceremony in the front yard of Horse Guards, Whitehall. This building is the headquarters of the Household Division. Mounted Guards are on duty there between 10 A.M. and 4 P.M. every day.

Guardsmen are also posted at the Tower of London, where the Crown Jewels are kept, and at the Bank of England. A battalion of Foot Guards is stationed at Windsor Castle, which is used as a summer residence by the royal family. The Household Division also provides guards of honor for visiting dignitaries and special events. On official state occasions, such as the opening of Parliament, the Foot Guards line the streets and a mounted unit of the Horse Guards escorts the royal coach.

The first Guards regiments were formed in 1660, during the reign of King Charles II. His personal bodyguard consisted of the mounted Life Guards and the Grenadier and the Coldstream regiments of Foot Guards. In 1686 a regiment of Scots Guards was added. Another cavalry regiment, the Royal Horse Guards (now the Blues and Royals), joined the Household troops in 1820. In 1900, Queen Victoria authorized the organization of the Irish Guards, and 15 years later, during World War I, the Welsh Guards were formed. As a result of these additions all the major parts of the British Isles—England, Wales, Scotland, and Ireland—are represented by a Guards regiment.

Many tourists think that the Queen's Guards are only parade soldiers, strictly for show. Actually the Guards are crack fighting troops. These elite soldiers have fought in

Pipe Major Gilvin of the Scots Guards plays a traditional tune on his bagpipe.

The Ceremony of the Keys at the Tower of London.

every one of Britain's major wars since the 17th century.

▶ OFF TO THE WARS

The Guards first saw action 300 years ago, in 1672, during a war against the Dutch. In the 18th century, the Guards fought under the Duke of Marlborough, one of Britain's greatest generals, at the battles of Blenheim and Malplaquet. They also distinguished themselves at the Battle of Fontenoy in 1745. Guardsmen were among the troops sent to the American colonies during the War of Independence. They were with Lord Cornwallis when he surrendered to General George Washington at Yorktown in 1781.

Throughout the Napoleonic Wars, the Guards were in the thick of the fighting. They had one of their proudest moments at the Battle of Waterloo, in 1815. A force of 2,000 British troops, including the Grenadier, Coldstream, and Scots Guards, defended one of the key points—the Château of Hougomont—

against 30,000 French troops. After the battle the Duke of Wellington wrote that "the success of the Battle of Waterloo turned on the closing of the gates at Hougomont."

Guardsmen later fought in the Crimean War, the Boer War, and various colonial wars in Africa and the Middle East. In World War I, they went into action at Mons, Ypres, and many other important battles. They were at Dunkirk in World War II, and also served in the North African and Italian campaigns. The Guards Armored Division was part of the invading force that landed at Normandy, France, in 1944. The Guards fought side by side with American troops, including the famed 82nd Airborne Division.

QUEEN ELIZABETH'S KEYS

Although the Guards have not fought in a major war since 1945, they maintain combat readiness. More than half of the Household Division is stationed overseas, while the remainder attends to ceremonial functions at home. Most ceremonies take place during the day. But there is an interesting one that occurs every evening at 10 P.M. At that time the Chief Warder of the Tower of London locks the gates to this historic British fortress. It is his last official act of the day as head of the Yeoman Warders, "Beefeaters," who serve as watchmen and guides at the Tower.

While darkness shrouds the battlements of the former royal residence and prison, the Chief Warder quietly makes his rounds. The only sound is the tramp of marching feet, for the Chief Warder is accompanied by four Foot Guardsmen.

After locking the gates, the Chief Warder and his escort march briskly back to the guardroom. Suddenly there is a shouted command to halt. A sentry challenges them, and the following exchange takes place:

Sentry: "Halt, who comes there?"
Chief Warder: "The Keys."
Sentry: "Whose keys?"
Chief Warder: "Queen Elizabeth's Keys."
Sentry: "Pass, Queen Elizabeth's Keys, all's well."

Then the Guardsmen smartly present arms. The Chief Warder raises his hat in salute and calls out, "God preserve Queen Elizabeth!"

"Amen," reply the Guardsmen.

Guardsman at St. James's Palace.

WHERE AND WHEN TO SEE THE GUARDS

Buckingham Palace: The Changing of the Guard takes place at 11:30 every morning. The Old Guard forms at 11:07 in the main courtyard. While the guard is changed, a regimental band provides musical background.

St. James's Palace: St. James's detachment of the Guards forms up at 11:00 A.M. before marching to Buckingham Palace. Returns at 12:10 and holds short dismissal ceremony.

Horse Guards, Whitehall: Guard mounting takes place at 11 A.M. (10 A.M. Sundays). There is a dismounted parade and inspection at 4 P.M.

The Tower of London: Guard Mounting is held at 12 noon. The Ceremony of the Keys occurs at 10 P.M. (A special ticket of admission is needed for the Ceremony of the Keys.)

Another day has come to an end at the Tower of London. The Crown Jewels rest safely in their glass-encased vaults, protected by one of the finest military units anywhere in the world—the Queen's Guards.

HENRY I. KURTZ
Associate Editor, *Lands and Peoples*

Two "giants" peer over the roofs of miniature houses and shops. This style of architecture is typical of parts of the Netherlands.

THE SMALLEST CITY IN THE WORLD

Spread out over 5 acres of grassy parkland lies the smallest city in the world. A doll-sized community where houses, windmills, automobiles, and canals are 1/25 life size, it is Madurodam, the famous miniature city in the Netherlands.

Madurodam has often been called "Holland in a nutshell." For it contains, in miniature, the Netherlands' most important buildings, historic sites, and industrial facilities. A vivid reflection of the Netherlands, Madurodam represents the growth of a typical Dutch town—from A.D. 1000 to the present. The visitor can actually see how the Dutch people lived and worked during various periods in their history.

The little city, where buildings are only about 3 feet tall, is a gem of planning. Architects, engineers, town planners, and historians donated their time and knowledge so that the construction would be perfectly executed.

But Madurodam is more than just a tourist attraction, for it has a political life too. Its municipal council, made up of teen-agers, administers city affairs. It has its own flag and anthem. And its mayor is Her Royal Highness Crown Princess Beatrix!

Let's pretend we are visiting the Netherlands and are on a walking tour of Madurodam. We will begin in its oldest section, at the castle of Voordensteyn. Dating back to the

The Village of Starpenheuvel: it is a replica of a quiet, rural village that may be found tucked away anywhere in the Netherlands.

A water sports center, in miniature.

11th century, it looks as if it had been lifted from the pages of a fairy tale.

Close to the castle is a little square that goes back to the 13th century. Let's walk a bit closer and find out how the Dutch lived then. They had everything they needed within a very small area. The church, the bakery, the brewery, and the infirmary are all clustered close together. And nearby are the simple homes of the townspeople.

We continue to walk along, and, as we do, time passes and centuries come and go. We soon find ourselves strolling through the Dutch world of the 18th century. The little town has greatly expanded. We pause before the town gates and admire the line and shape of their fine archway. A short distance from the archway is the Great Church, which seems to stand and guard the town. It is an exact copy, built to scale, of famous St. Nicholas Abbey in the town of Middelburg.

We walk along and turn a corner, and in a flash the town has exploded into a modern, bustling city of the 20th century. Roads have become four-lane highways with cars and buses speeding along. Small shops have changed into large department stores. And there are schools, hospitals, parks, rows of apartment houses, and even an open-air theater.

We can see the gleam of railroad tracks and then the dark, sleek trains moving along them with ease and speed. The Madurodam railway system is in operation from morning to night and it demands constant maintenance attention. The tracks, 2½ inches wide, have more than 45,000 crossties.

The long-drawn-out sound of a boat whistle calls us to the harbor of Madurodam. Here are the luxurious passenger ships and the heavy-looking freighters busy sailing to and from the port. Cranes hoist their heavy loads onto the wharves; and dredges are busily working to keep the harbor from silting up. Loaded barges move along the rippled water and into the quiet of the canals.

And at Madurodam's national airport, tiny "jet" planes are continually coming in for a landing or departing for destinations unknown.

The gay sounds of an amusement park catch our attention. We stand and watch the Ferris wheels and the merry-go-rounds, and listen to an organ-grinder cranking out a sadly beautiful tune.

It is now dusk and the lights of the tiny city go on. There are more than 46,000 of these little lights, and they shine through the windows of the houses and other buildings. The ships in the harbor switch on their lights, and atop the airport tower the beacon begins to sweep through the oncoming night.

The neon lights on the little stores flicker on and off in pleasant rhythm. We stand amid the glow of this fairyland city, enjoying its gentle beauty and charm, and then finally we slowly turn to leave.

A LIVING MONUMENT

The story of the creation of Madurodam is a sad but inspiring one. The story tells of a young man, a youth full of hope and plans and high promise. He was named George John Lionel Maduro, and he was a student at Leiden University. He had come from Curaçao in the Dutch West Indies to finish his studies and become a lawyer. But this was at the time of World War II, and George Maduro threw himself into that struggle. During the bitter days of May, 1940, when Germany invaded the Netherlands, Lieutenant Maduro and his men fought valiantly. But he was taken prisoner. He managed to escape but was caught when he tried to rescue a fellow soldier. George Maduro, who was Jewish, was sent to Dachau concentration camp, where he died in 1945. After his death, he was awarded the Military Cross of the Order of William, which is the Netherlands' highest distinction for courage, judgment, and loyalty.

George Maduro's parents wished to do something to honor their son and the other young men who had fought and died with him. First they thought of building a monument of stone, but they were persuaded that a living monument would be better. And it was mainly through their gifts, followed by gifts from industry and business firms, that the city of Madurodam came into being.

Madurodam is truly a living monument; it benefits thousands, as all profits go to a sanatorium for Dutch university students. Since 1952, when it was established, more than 18,000,000 people have come to visit this monument, the smallest city in the world.

A Dutch polder—land reclaimed from a body of water. At one time windmills pumped the water out of the polder.

FUN TO READ

An illustration from *One Fine Day*, by Nonny Hogrogian, winner of the 1972 Caldecott Medal.

THE MOST DISHONEST THING

I remember the anger and the fury. But most of all I remember the heartbreak. And I don't think that, to the end of my days, I will forget it. No, I don't think I will.

It all goes back to the day of the game, the big game for the state championship. I remember the excitement that ran through the whole town. It was the first time in years that we were going to have a chance at the championship. Somehow, I don't know how it came about, we suddenly had a great football team. And I was the quarterback.

We were all set to go from our hometown to the state capital, when it happened. Mr. Jonas came to the school building—we were all waiting for the special bus—and he motioned to Charlie Rand. The two went off to one side and spoke seriously together. Then they called me over.

"You can't go along with us, Ed," Charlie Rand said.

I just looked at them. First at the long, lean figure of Mr. Jonas and then at the hard face of the coach.

"You're ineligible."

And that's about all I remember. I know that they said a lot of other things, and that both were furious with "the old battle-ax," as they called her. But I do remember standing after the bus left and just looking past the school building and out over the bare wheat fields that stretched as far as I could see, under a cold autumn sky. Then I saw some crows take off, the hard sun glinting off their backs.

I'm a big fellow, and even today my muscles are tough and hard from all the work I used to do helping Dad and my older brothers on the farm. And I tell you, if she were not a woman, I would've gone right down to her— But she was a woman.

I walked down the dusty, quiet main street. I saw Jim Pritchard standing outside his hardware store, and he motioned me over.

"What're you doing here?"

"Nothing."

"That's what I mean."

"Miss Cardin flunked me. Can't play."

We both turned and looked down, where the street sort of trailed off and the houses grew farther and farther apart. Way out there, on the rise of a little hill, was the Cardin place.

"I'd like to burn it down," he said.

I didn't say anything.

"She sits there alone in that big house and she rules the town."

"The school, you mean," I said bitterly.

"They should've put her out to pasture years ago."

Then we talked a bit more and I walked away. All I could think

of was what I was going to say to my brothers and to my father. They had already left to drive out to the capital, and they didn't know.

"There will be some big football scouts down at the game, Ed," my brother had said. "And you'll get your chance to show 'em what you got. You sure will."

"Yes, he sure will," my father had said.

In the afternoon I sat in the living room and listened to the game on the radio. The team lost badly, and the announcer kept saying that they missed their quarterback. When he said that, I felt worse.

The autumn evening came on fast. I was sitting by myself in the dark. Suddenly I got up, left the house, and started walking up the road until I came to the turn that led to the Cardin place. I stood in front of the house.

There was a light on in one of the front windows of the big frame house. I knew Miss Cardin would be sitting near the light, reading. Somehow that made me even more furious. I stooped over and picked up a rock from the road and threw it as hard as I could at the window. The glass shattered.

And then everything was quiet again. Far in the distance I could hear the lowing of the cows on the Smith farm, a thin and mournful sound.

"Edward?"

I looked up to the porch, and there she was. She was a slight woman, with her grey hair pulled back tightly from her face. It made her face all the more severe looking.

At first I didn't speak. "Why did you do it?" I finally said.

And then I picked up another stone from the road and threw it at the next window. When it broke, I saw her shiver as if the stone had hit her.

"Call the sheriff," I said, "and get me put away."

She looked at me, and then she turned and went into the house. I just stayed there, out on the road, and didn't move. I don't know why, but I didn't move. Then she came back on the porch. In her hand were some sheets of paper.

"Come up, Edward," she said.

I went up the wooden steps slowly, my eyes on the sheets of paper.

"It's your exam."

Then she held it out to me, and I saw written in red ink on the top the number 95. I took the top paper from her and read the mark again and then looked at her.

"That's your mark," she said. "The mark you deserved. I lied to Mr. Jonas. You didn't fail the test. I know how hard you tried these past weeks. I know it. I know how much you didn't want to fail."

I really had tried. She used to say to me, "All you do is think football." And she was right. "You're going to throw away everything for football. And you have so much in you, Edward. So much."

And then I heard her say, as if she were reading my thoughts, "You'd get a football scholarship, and that would be the end of you. It would, Edward. That's why I did what I did. I tried to kill your chances. I kept you out of the big game."

And then she said, "Take the exam and show it to Mr. Jonas. I will never walk into the school again."

She turned away and stood looking at the smashed windows. "You had every right to do what you did. You see, this is the most dishonest thing I have ever done in my whole life—in forty years of teaching, forty years, Edward."

I turned because she had begun to cry. I turned and went down the wooden steps and out to the road. I never once looked back at her.

a stort story by JAY BENNETT

Two runaway slaves escape their pursuers by hiding deep in a swamp.

A RAILROAD UNDERGROUND

"Come along, quick! The manstealers have got Jimmy!"

Cries echoed along the streets of the black community. The Reverend William Mitchell heard doors banging, women crying, feet pounding past on the dirt road beyond his yard. And now they'd caught Jimmy? The capture of runaway slaves was not unusual in southern Ohio in the early 1840's, but Jimmy had escaped from slavery so long ago that Mitchell had nearly forgotten that Jimmy was not a free Negro like himself.

"Go comfort Jimmy's wife. I've got to help them," he told Mrs. Mitchell, and ran out to join the rapidly swelling crowd.

In a few minutes some 200 men were racing across the fields like a swarm of angry bees. Three miles from town, they caught sight of Jimmy. Roped to a horse, he was being dragged along, stumbling and struggling, behind three mounted men. Jimmy heard his friends behind him and beckoned desperately to them to hurry.

Now the slave catchers held a hurried conference. Although they were on horseback and the pursuers were on foot, they could not outrun the mob without dragging Jimmy to death—and so losing a valuable piece of property. The leader's knife flashed as he leaned to cut the rope, and the three galloped off, leaving Jimmy gasping on the ground.

"How'd they get you?" Mitchell asked, helping Jimmy to his feet.

After he had caught his breath, Jimmy tried to tell them. "Somebody turned me in for the $100 reward," he said. "The manstealers just walked into my shop and slung a rope around my neck and hauled me off." Manstealers, or slave catchers, were men who made a living by hiring out their services to anybody who would pay them to seize runaway slaves who had escaped from the South, and take them back to their Southern owners.

Jimmy's neighbors picked him up and took him home in triumph on their shoulders. For him it was a permanent escape: the slave catchers did not try to come after him again. For the black minister, William Mitchell, it was the beginning of his role in the powerful resistance movement that people were beginning to call the Underground Railroad.

RUNNING THE RAILROAD

Nearly 20 years later, in his book, *The Underground Railroad* (published in England in 1860), Mitchell recorded the most popular legend of how the Railroad got its name. People said that a Kentucky slaveholder, pursuing his slave to the Ohio River and then losing all trace of him in Ohio, exclaimed, "Those damned Abolitionists must have a railroad under the ground to carry off our slaves!"

Of course it was not a real railroad. It was more like a network of homes where anti-slavery people sheltered fugitives and helped them get to the next sanctuary. But when these people heard the term, they happily adopted it as a fit label for their operation. Homes that hid runaways were called "stations," and their owners were called "stationmasters" or "agents." "Conductors" were people who guided fugitives from one station to the next.

If agents had to send written messages to each other, the messages had to be coded, so that even if they went astray and were read by the police, they would not be understood. One actual letter cited by historians read: "By tomorrow's mail you will receive two volumes of *The Irrepressible Conflict*." (*The Irrepressible Conflict* was a well-known book that predicted trouble between slave states and free states.) Conductors and agents had special signals to announce their presence—the hooting of an owl or a secret combination of knocks. They had passwords. To the question, "Who's there?" one password answer was, "A friend with friends."

Two manstealers try to drag a free black man off to sell him into slavery.

Like all Underground Railroad agents, Mitchell knew that he was breaking the law. However, he believed that the law he broke, the Fugitive Slave Law, was evil, and that his conscience required him to defy it. Although all Northern states had abolished slavery by 1804, the Fugitive Slave Law of 1793 demanded that runaway slaves in free states be returned to their owners in the South, where slavery was legal. After the War of 1812, news of Canada as a "land of freedom," where slaves could not legally be recaptured, began to filter to the South.

The number of runaway slaves increased. In the North, abolitionists—people who wanted to abolish slavery at all costs—grew more numerous. More and more of them committed themselves to active roles in the Underground Railroad. In Ohio, which was the only state that lay between Canada and the slave state of Kentucky, the network was well established by the 1830's. Similar webs spread across Delaware, Pennsylvania, Indiana, and into New York and the New England states.

During the 1840's the trickle of fugitives grew to a torrent. Aroused by the constant loss of their "property," angry Southerners pushed through Congress the harsher Fugitive Slave Law of 1850, which provided that anyone who helped runaway slaves could be fined $1,000 and jailed for six months. Far from discouraging abolitionists, the law infuriated them and made new converts to their cause. Traffic on the Railroad increased. At the height of its activity, it may have carried 2,000 blacks a year to freedom.

▸ STATIONS AND STATIONMASTERS

What kind of man or woman would become a self-proclaimed outlaw in the cause of the Underground Railroad? There were Quakers, Wesleyan Methodists, Scotch Covenanters, Presbyterians, and free black men and women of many faiths. Among the Quakers, Thomas Garrett of Delaware and Levi Coffin of Indiana were leaders in the freedom conspiracy. Levi Coffin, in fact, was given the honorary title of "President of the Underground Railroad." Some, like the Presbyterian minister John Rankin, of Ripley, Ohio, were Southern whites who, for religious reasons, could not accept slavery. Therefore, they moved to free states and devoted their lives to befriending runaway slaves. Some of the workers on the Railroad were escaped slaves themselves. Josiah Henson, Harriet Tubman, and Frederick Douglass were included in this brave group. Their activities were particularly dangerous because they constantly risked recapture.

An Underground Railroad stationmaster led an adventurous, exhausting, exciting life. He was never off duty. At any hour of the day or night a desperate runaway might knock at his door. He might have to feed as many as 20 hungry black runaways at dinnertime, at his own expense. Some nights he rose at 3 A.M. to harness his wagon, hide his shivering charges under bales of hay, and drive 15 miles or more through a snowstorm to the next station. If he was caught he could be jailed or ruined financially. In spite of these hazards there were probably about 1,540 stations in Ohio alone by the 1850's; and at least as many in the other free states.

William Mitchell had personal reasons for undertaking such hazards. Although, as the freeborn son of a black father and an Indian mother, he could not legally be enslaved, he had been orphaned at the age of 9 and apprenticed to a slaveholder. In his youth he had learned about the miseries of slavery from firsthand experience. Later he became a minister, moved to Ohio, and devoted himself to helping end the evils he had witnessed.

Mitchell's station was in southern Ohio, to the north of the station of a man named John Rankin. Rankin, who was also a minister, had a house on a hill overlooking the Ohio River. The river was the frontier between the slave state of Kentucky and the free state of Ohio. When the river was frozen, it could be crossed easily. Runaways on the Kentucky side of the river could see Rankin's lighted windows like a beacon, calling them to freedom.

One chilly night, Rankin took in a shivering young black woman named Mary, with her small son in her arms. She told a harrowing tale of being tracked to the edge of the river by men with baying hounds, only to find that the ice was thin and already beginning to break up. But she had no choice. She had to get across somehow. With freezing water rushing around her ankles and ice cracking under her feet at every step, she finally managed to reach the Ohio shore. As she was crawling up the steep banks, her pur-

Harriet Tubman was the fearless guide of many runaways.

suers on the Kentucky side reached the river. Luck was with her, however: just then the ice broke loose, and great chunks went roaring downstream. No one could follow her.

William Mitchell heard the story from Mary herself the following night, when he accepted her from Rankin and drove her 10 miles north to the next station. Millions of Americans later thrilled to the episode based on Mary's escape, "Eliza crossing the ice," in the popular novel *Uncle Tom's Cabin,* by Harriet Beecher Stowe (published in 1852). Harriet Beecher Stowe's home in Cincinnati was a station on the same network that included Mitchell and Rankin; she thus had plenty of opportunity to gather material from firsthand accounts.

A DANGEROUS ROUTE

Slaves had to be desperate to undertake the dangers and hardships of escape attempts. But they were growing increasingly so in the years 1840–60, because the economy of the South was changing in ways that made slavery an even harsher way of life. Eli

Whitney's new cotton gin made huge plantations profitable; and the opening of rich "Black Belt" farmlands in Mississippi and Louisiana meant that slaves were frequently "sold down the river" to frontier plantations, where conditions were more brutal.

Most runaways had no guide and of course no map. They took only what they could carry wrapped in a shawl or bandanna—a few provisions and any money that they had managed to save. They traveled under cover of darkness, always moving toward the North Star. They even had a song about it, still sung today—"Follow the Drinking Gourd," meaning the Big Dipper in the northern sky. If clouds covered the stars, they examined moss on tree trunks, which grows more thickly to the north.

By day they hid in the woods or under haystacks. If they were lucky, they burrowed in under a pile of corn, which supplied food as well as shelter. In winter, when it was hard to live off the land, starvation might drive them to knocking at farm doors. That was dangerous, even if the runaways had some money to pay for food, for they could easily be recaptured by someone who wanted the reward.

▸ HAPPIER JOURNEYS AND CLEVER TRICKS

Underground Railroad adventures were not always grim. Some even had their comical side. A man named Jack, for instance, had run away and left his girl friend behind. Missing her badly and having no good way to get news of her, he went to a fortune-teller. Naturally he had to tell the fortune-teller what to look for in the cards. In the process he revealed quite a bit of his own story. The fortune-teller assured him he would soon see his girl again. Then, the moment he left, she hurried off to the sheriff and claimed her $100 for giving news of a fugitive. Jack was promptly arrested and hauled off to jail.

On the day of his trial, the courthouse was jammed with noisy demonstrators protesting against his arrest. After a while a technical question came up, and both lawyers approached the bench to argue with the judge. The prisoner, with the sheriff, was standing near the door. Close behind him were the people who had come to see the trial, both black and white, most of whom were on Jack's side.

Suddenly, while the sheriff was looking the other way, a friend of Mitchell's put his hat on Jack's head. Jack took the hint, bowed down to the floor, and crawled out on his hands and knees between the legs of the people. Nobody seemed to notice him.

When the sheriff discovered that his prisoner was gone, he began shouting "Catch him!" In the uproar that followed, everyone rushed for the door. Some people were eager to catch Jack and claim a reward. But most of them were trying to cause as much confusion as possible to cover his escape.

The law held the sheriff responsible for his prisoner. If Jack

The dogs of a slave catcher trap a fleeing runaway up a tree.

was not recaptured, the sheriff would be fined $1,000 for letting Jack get away. The sheriff offered to pay that much to anyone who would bring him back. No one claimed the money. The next day, Sunday, the Reverend Mr. Mitchell dressed Jack in a lady's gown and brought him to church, where the congregation took up a collection for his safe passage to Canada.

Hiding runaways in stations was not the only part of the operation that required great skill. Conducting passengers from one station to the next, through country where they might be seen by "property-minded" Northerners, was also hazardous. Sometimes runaways were put in boxes and shipped as freight by rail or by boat. Conductors built special drawers, compartments, or false bottoms into their wagons where passengers could hide.

Fugitives were often concealed under loads of hay or garden produce. Certain conductors were businessmen with legitimate reasons for making frequent shipments. James Torrence, of Northwood, Ohio, was an exporter who shipped grain and feathers regularly to Sandusky, Ohio, a Great Lake port 120 miles away. The shipments were then put on a boat to Canada. Thus, fugitives who traveled in Torrence's bed of feathers were saved a great deal of time and risk.

In the late 1850's, when real railroad lines had been built

throughout the North, runaway slaves were sometimes put in the charge of real railroad conductors, who helped them ride free to Canada. Light-skinned runaways often passed for white on the trains; disguises served others.

When midwestern passengers reached Detroit, Sandusky, Green Bay, and other Great Lake ports, they were put in the hands of ferryboat captains known to be sympathetic to runaways. Fugitives often broke into a frenzy of cheering and praying when the boats pulled away from shore, and they knew they were finally safe. Certain captains who sailed seacoast routes between Southern and Northern cities also engaged in carrying this kind of "freedom freight."

While white Underground Railroad agents risked jail, black ones risked their lives. Ex-slaves like Frederick Douglass and Harriet Tubman, who were so active on the Railroad, could be captured and sent back to slavery at any moment. Far from trying to be inconspicuous, Douglass ran an anti-slavery newspaper, lectured widely, and manned a busy station on the Railroad.

The blacks who risked the most were those who slipped back into the South to act as conductors for other blacks. It is estimated that by 1860, 500 ex-slaves were infiltrating Southern states and guiding runaways out. Some of their names are lost. We do not know the name of the elderly black woman who left an Underground Railroad station against the advice of the stationmaster and returned to the South to bring out her children and grandchildren. Other, better-known conductors, like Josiah Henson and Harriet Tubman, helped write one of the most glorious chapters in black history. Harriet Tubman suffered from an illness that caused her to lose consciousness at unexpected moments. Nevertheless, after escaping to the North in 1849, she made the perilous journey into the South 19 times, successfully guiding parties of fugitives to Northern stations. These people were bitterly hated in the South, and re-enslavement was not the worst thing that could happen to them. They could be beaten and killed.

Mitchell knew one of these intrepid black conductors, John Mason. Mason claimed he had delivered 1,300 runaways altogether. By his own count, Mitchell knew that Mason had brought 265 fugitives to his station alone over a 19-month period. But John Mason ventured back into Kentucky once too often.

One day while he and his four charges were hiding under a stack of Indian corn, gnawing away at the hardened kernels, they heard the sound of hounds baying in the distance. It meant that the dogs had picked up their scent and were on their trail. They were still 50 miles from the Ohio frontier, and now they were about to be cornered.

They debated whether to run for it, seeking a stream to wash away the scent of their tracks and confuse the dogs. But the baying was too close now. There wasn't time for that.

"We'll have to make a stand right here, fight them," Mason said. "We can do it—there are five of us."

But not all slaves were heroes. Like human beings anywhere, some were incredibly brave, others were weak. When these slaves saw their owner coming, they were so conditioned from childhood to fear the white man that they could not resist.

Mason fought fiercely, but had to fight alone. He defied the white men, shouting, "Shoot me now, I won't live in slavery." But his captors broke both his arms and beat him to the ground. He was sold down the river to New Orleans, marked as a dangerous slave, to be heavily guarded.

When Mitchell heard of his friend's capture, he sadly concluded that Mason would have to be counted among the casualties of the Underground Railroad. But exactly one year, five months, and twenty days later, to his amazement, Mitchell received a letter from John Mason. And it was postmarked Hamilton, Ontario, Canada.

It was the unbreakable spirit of people like John Mason that fueled the Underground Railroad and made it a powerful weapon of the anti-slavery struggle. The great struggle was won when President Abraham Lincoln issued the Emancipation Proclamation, officially freeing all the slaves in the Confederacy, in 1863.

a historical adventure by ELISABETH MARGO

Henry Brown, shown at center in this cartoon, mailed himself to freedom.

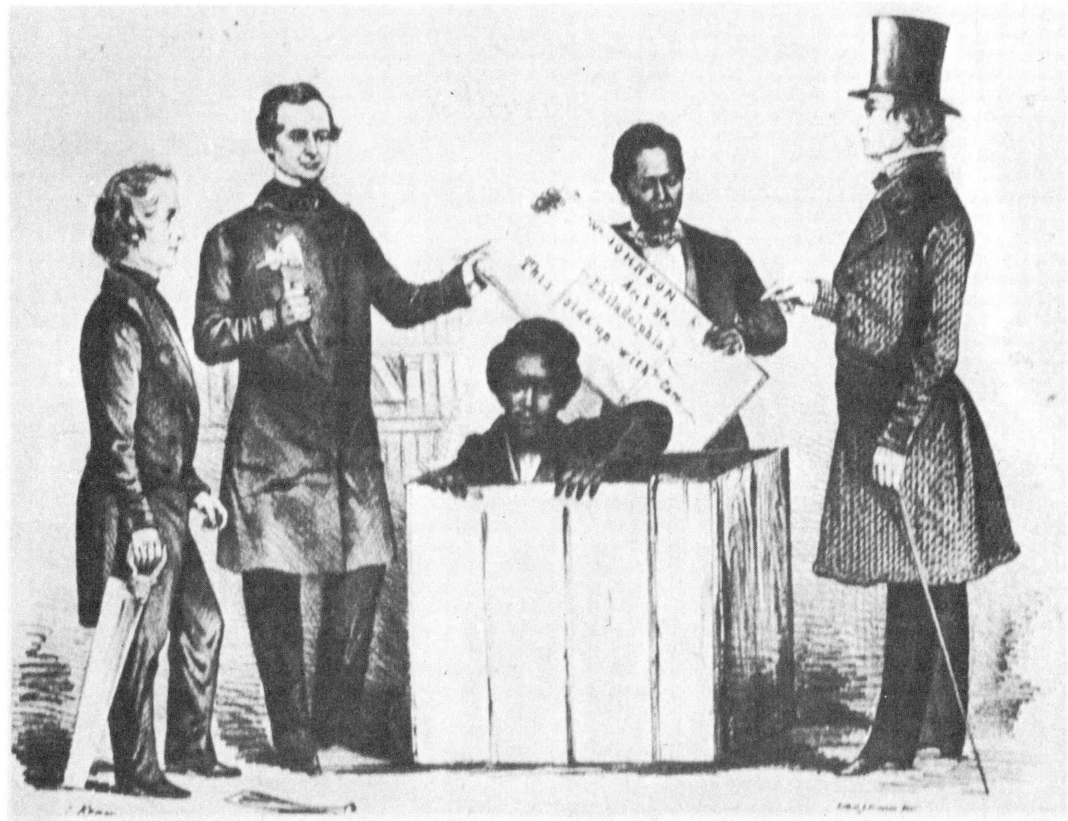

POETRY

Miss Quiss!
Look at this!
A pocketful of
Licorice!
You may have some
If you wish,
But every stick will
Cost a kiss.

Penny candy
Sugar hearts
Oranges &
Lemon tarts,

Ask me where my
Money goes?
To buy my sweetheart
Fancy clothes.

OWLS

We were speaking of owls.
The porch light was out as
We stood beside the spruce
Tree listening to the throat
Sounds circling around us.
"They are lost," said the
Older one and thought of a
Lighthouse to guide them.

"But it is the dark they like,"
I said, and the younger boy
Moved closer. Food was next,
And all the mice took cover.
So did the young one. And then,
As they moved from tree to tree,
Their soft feathers layered like
Leaves at night, they gave a
Farewell call, louder than the
Others.

With eyes bigger than moons, the
Young one asked, "Just how big
Did you say they were?"

MATTHEW HAD A MONSTER

Matthew had a monster who used
To visit him when he was asleep.
He was big.
He refused to take a bath.
He pulled flowers out of the garden.
He made big noises,
And he liked to pinch.

But Matthew didn't mind.
He knew you weren't afraid of monsters.
Instead,
You were the BOSS!

So, he walked up to the big, dirty,
Flower-pulling, loud, pinching monster,
And he puffed up his chest
To seem very tall.

"Keep clean!" he said, and he handed him
The soap he had not used before bed.

"Leave the flowers alone!" he said as he
Stepped on his mother's garden.

"You are not polite!" he said. He had
To shout a bit.

"And keep your hands to yourself!" he
Finally said as he pushed the monster
Right out of his dream.

poems by ROSAMOND DAUER

THE FLOWERS

All the names I know from nurse:
Gardener's garters, Shepherd's purse,
Bachelor's buttons, Lady's smock,
And the Lady Hollyhock.

Fairy places, fairy things,
Fairy woods where the wild bee wings,
Tiny trees for tiny dames—
These must all be fairy names!

Tiny woods below whose boughs
Shady fairies weave a house;
Tiny tree-tops, rose or thyme,
Where the braver fairies climb!

Fair are grown-up people's trees,
But the fairest woods are these;
Where, if I were not so tall,
I should live for good and all.

by Robert Louis Stevenson

EXCITING PICTURE BOOKS

A bushy-tailed fox steals some milk, and because of this has his tail cut off. And like any reasonable fox, he wants his tail back. That is what this book is all about. It all happens in a forest, one fine day. An old woman is gathering wood, and the fox sees her pail of milk near a tree. As he is very thirsty, he drinks the milk and pays the penalty. Now, in order to get his tail back, the poor fox must give the old woman her milk back.

This is not so easy a task as it might seem. The sad fox goes to a cow and asks for milk. But the cow asks for grass. So the fox goes to a field and asks the field for grass. The field, in turn, demands that the fox bring it some water. The fox goes to a stream, and the stream says, "Bring me a jug." He comes to a maiden who will give him a jug if he will find her blue bead. And so his quest goes on and on, until . . . yes, the fox does finally get his tail back!

Let your imagination soar as free as a bird; think about what would happen if all the seas were one sea . . . and if all the trees were one tree, and if all the axes were one ax, and if all the men were one man. The bold and colorful etchings illustrating this charming nursery rhyme will stimulate your imagination to soar to great heights. For you will find that this one huge man will take this one huge ax and chop down this one huge tree. And that tree will fall into the one huge sea—and what a splish-splash that is going to be!

IF ALL THE SEAS

WERE ONE SEA

ETCHINGS BY JANINA DOMANSKA

Moja, tau, nne, tano, mbili—these may sound like strange words. But they are not at all strange to the 45,000,000 people in the eastern part of Africa who speak Swahili. Swahili is spoken over such a vast geographical area that many have come to think of it as a unifying language among Africa's different countries and cultures.

Tom Feelings and his wife Muriel lived in Africa for more than two years. Mrs. Feelings taught in a high school in Kampala, the capital of Uganda, and the couple learned to speak Swahili. When they returned to the United States, they wrote *Moja Means One*. Their dedication reads, "To all Black children living in the Western Hemisphere, hoping you will one day ,speak the language—in Africa." However, all children will love this book. The simple text and impressive illustrations combine to give the reader a vivid account of life in eastern Africa. And best of all, you will learn to count from one to ten in Swahili.

Hildilid just doesn't like the night, and so she goes about trying to get rid of it. Who is Hildilid? Well, she is an old woman who lives alone with her wolfhound in the hills of Hexnam. Where is Hexnam? Somehow, in this clever and humorous story, we never find out. And in a way this makes the tale even more delightful.

Hildilid wants to get rid of night once and for all so that the sun will always shine on her hut. So she cuts a few twigs to make a broom and then sets to work, determined to sweep the night right out of her hut and out of the hills of Hexnam. But she fails in her attempt. Hildilid then tries to wash away the night, and then to stuff it into a great sack. She even tries to boil away the night in a huge caldron, while her faithful wolfhound sits by her side. But even that fails. Then, in desperation and anger, she tries to tie up the night. But the night refuses to be tied up. So Hildilid tucks the night into her straw bed; of course, the night jumps right out of the bed. In the end Hildilid gives up and goes to sleep. And so she is fast asleep when the golden sun rises over Hexnam, and the night is finally gone.

THE JOURNAL OF ONE DAVEY WYATT

I figured the worst thing ever happened to me was they uncovered gold over there in California. That whole business just went ripping across the country like a haunting. All of a sudden that's all everybody's thinking got twisted around and the only thing they would talk about; even more than crops or weather. Here was I, two thousand miles from the event and everybody was talking about it just like it was something that had happened in our own hereabouts of Elroyd, Iowa.

That was the scary part of it, I'll confide: something happening two thousand miles off in a place I knew punk about, coming right in and taking my life up by the scruff just like a March wind comes in from nowhere and wings things around and sends them off. Now, if things that happen two thousand miles off can come along and grab you up, what's the good of you ever building a fence or raising a calf or even heading out to spend the day fishing? It ain't for me, I'll tell. I like to know where I'm going to finish a day up at when I start it off.

Another thing: I don't reckon California would ever have got as all in a rattle by anything that took place in Elroyd, Iowa, and believe me, we've had some real skin-shakers, like the day Hummon's barn burned down and the time Drunk Jack pulled a pistol and shot away three of his toes. We once had the church steeple knocked off by a shot of lightning and the day my Uncle Matthew shot a bear in his backyard was the most considerable day in the life of lots of people.

But this business of gold was its own thunder and its own lightning. Growed men talked about it like it was something of a religious nature. They said the gold was lying about in California big as rocks and there for the picking. Why was it so special then? I asked. But nobody had an ear for common sense. After all, I was just a whip of fifteen and what did I know?

And then the gold fever—which was what they called it, just like it was something you'd check in to the doctor with—come to our house. Pa started in to talking on it and he and Ma sat at the kitchen table looking at each other and talking gold and California and other such things. I made believe not to listen, because I believed that if you don't let a thing get inside your head it can't ever be true. And if it can't ever be true then it can't ever happen. That was how I tried to work against it but it was harder than sweeping bees with a broom because I could feel myself hearing it and it getting bigger and bigger inside my head.

Then the next thing I knew Pa was talking to some of the men in

town about wagons and supplies and west-goin' trails and such things as that, things that a man who wants to spend the summer working his farm don't never think about. Then one day a fellow came rolling up to the front door in a buggy and gets out and Pa comes out and meets him and they shake hands. This fellow was dressed up neat as a flag, with a vest like a checkerboard spread across his belly and a suit of black broadcloth that shined bright in the seat.

I watched Pa and the stranger walk into the field and Pa stood there tall and lifted one of his long, strong arms and begun pointing, swinging his finger slow across the stand of cedar way out and then slow across again, like he used to do when I was just a little whipper asking him to show me what was ours. Then he went into the barn with the stranger, then to the house.

When I peeped in through the window there they was in the kitchen looking at some pieces of paper. Then the stranger stood up and shook hands with Pa solemn as a preacher, then with Ma, and then he went out. I watched him come out of the house, pleased with himself all right, get into his buggy, rustle the reins a little bit and drive off. I never wish hard luck on strangers, but I come close with that one.

I went into the yard and sat down under the old oak tree where it was always cool. It was a warm day in May all right, with the sun steady and bright yellow, the sky clean blue as far as it went. I just sat there dumb as a stone. Something was happening. I knew that much. Things was too quiet for something not to be happening. Happenings always begin in the quiet, then unhappen in a lot of noise.

I looked at the house and already it begun to look different to me. That fellow with the fancy vest had changed it just by putting his shoe leather inside of it. I looked around at the other few houses that I could see, where I had friends, and got the thought that if those fellows would've come by they wouldn't know my name anymore.

Then here was Pa, coming out the back door and taking his long, slow strides across the grass toward me. I drew up my knees and put my arms around them and looked up at him. He moved about a bit up there so's to block the sun and I wouldn't have to squint. Pa was real tall all right, one of the tallest men in Elroyd, Iowa. They used to say in town that when it begun to rain Martin Wyatt was the first to know about it. He had a narrow beard that come down from his ears, run the sides of his face and made a little point a couple inches under his chin. I was going to sprout me one just like it someday, when my hairs got manful enough. He was wearing a flat-crowned hat back on his head and had his sleeves rolled to the elbow.

"Davy," he said, "we're going to California."

Yes, I knew that. I didn't know it just on the button, but I knew something real bad was in the batter and the worst thing could only have been what he just said. That was the tallest, widest, deepest and hottest bad that could be. The bad might just as well be the worst, and that's what it was. I figure take the worst first and then the rest can't but find improvement. I got my way of looking at things.

"Who's goin'?" I asked, just in case.

He smiled.

"Why, the four of us," he said. "You, me, your Ma and your sister."

I moved my head up and down like a regular know-it-all.

"I just sold the farm," he said.

"He didn't look like no farmer to me."

"He's going to let it to somebody. Anyway, that's his business."

"The house too?" I asked.

"The whole shebang," Pa said. "Flies and all."

I looked down and bit my lip. Pa seen.

"I needed the money," he said "to buy a couple span of oxen and a good wagon and supplies. Do you know how long we're going to be on the trail?"

"No sir."

"Four months, maybe more. It's going to be great fun," he said. He said it like he was trying to cheer me.

I looked up at him.

"Why?" I asked. "Why we got to go to California?"

Now he got down on the grass and sat next to me.

"Davey," he said, "this is 1850 and the world is changing. It's changing shape, tone, sound—everything."

"That's right true," I said. But my heart wasn't in it.

"Change means change, it's as simple as that. And it's healthy. It brings good things. You can't take advantage of those things that are changing if you stand still in one spot."

"Why don't we jus' hold on and let the change come to us?"

"Because," Pa said, "if you do that, if you wait for that to happen, why, by the time the change reaches you the change has already changed and there's already a new one coming. You understand that, boy?"

"I reckon so," I said. But I wished he had writ it on paper so's I could study it and get the real hang of it.

"Now, when I was a boy your age my Pa brought us out here from the east because the change was here, the opportunity was here, and you see we've done real fine. Now the new things are happening in California. Bigger opportunities are there. A better life. That's worth going after, don't you think?"

"But suppose it ain't better?" I asked.

"I hear tell it's better," he said. "People are moving that way. Lots of people. Why, thousands of them! The government favors it, too. They say we've got to go out there and stake it. It's important."

"You gonna dig for gold?"

"I might," he said. "But that isn't the only thing out there. I tell you, Davey, there's lots of new and important things for a man to do in California. I've been thinking on it for months and I've concluded it's the right thing to do."

He was all excited about it, I could tell. It was in his voice and in his eyes.

"Can I take Billy?" I asked.

He smiled at me.

"Billy's a good strong pony," he said. "He'll do fine."

"And we're gonna live in a wagon for four months?"

"That's right. We're going to go across plains and deserts and rivers and over mountains and see such places you never dreamed of. I've been listening to men who've done it. The tales they tell, Davey, well, you'll just have to see the truth of it all with your own eyes."

Well, I thought, maybe it wasn't going to be such a bad thing after all. But still, I was going to hold my opinion till I'd seen for myself.

an excerpt from *The Journal of One Davey Wyatt*
by DONALD HONIG

FUN TO MAKE AND DO

You can make it: a needlepoint hanging entitled *Nature's Panorama.*

STAMP COLLECTING

In 1972, interest in the hobby of stamp collecting, or philately, grew more than ever before. Stamp clubs all over the world increased in number; stamp exhibitions broke all previous attendance records; and publications devoted to the subject of stamp collecting enrolled greater numbers of new subscribers. Along with the increase in the number of collectors, the nations of the world stepped up their stamp output.

Many of the new countries—such as Bangladesh (formerly East Pakistan)—issued stamps for the first time. The total number of stamp-issuing nations may actually have decreased from previous years, however. In 1971 the six Trucial States (sheikhdoms on the Persian Gulf) joined together as one nation, called the United Arab Emirates. In 1972 the country decided to issue stamps for the entire group instead of for each individual member.

As in the past, some nations turned to their own history for subjects of stamp issues. Other nations drew upon local scenes, nature, art, literature, and current events. The United States released many new stamps during 1972. The most unusual of them were issued at Cape Hatteras National Seashore in North Carolina. The complete design, picturing the seashore, covers four perforated 2-cent stamps. The United States also issued a series of jumbo-size 8-cent stamps picturing the fur seal, the cardinal, the brown pelican, and the bighorn sheep. Still another U.S. issue was an interesting depiction of Mark Twain's well-known character Tom Sawyer.

Among the stamps issued by Canada during the year were four 15-cent stamps commemorating the four earth-science conferences, held in Toronto and Montreal; and the first two of a series of 20 stamps on the Canadian Plains Indians.

Greece released seven stamps devoted to its historic monasteries and churches; Britain honored the silver wedding anniversary of Queen Elizabeth II and Prince Philip; Qatar issued a multicolored series of eight stamps showing its native birds; and the People's Republic of China released six stamps showing scenes from the Peking opera *Taking Tiger Mountain by Strategy*.

NEW STAMPS OF 1972

United States

Qatar

Canada

Iceland

Greece

A TOPICAL STAMP COLLECTION OF FAIRY TALES AND FABLES

A series of stamps telling the story of Little Red Riding Hood.

The Magic Carpet

Hansel and Gretel

Snow White

A Czech Fable

Thumbelina

Puss in Boots

Narcissus

A Korean Fable

The Grafenberg Treasure

The Arabian Nights

The Tortoise and the Hare

The Tinderbox

West Germany: four stamps, together showing the Munich Olympic grounds.

Countless nations honored the 1972 Olympics with new stamp issues. The commemoratives released by West Germany, the host country for the Summer Games, were the most extensive: there were not only individual stamps but also souvenir sheets. One sheet, a striking novelty, shows a bird's-eye view of the Olympic grounds; it is so well produced that each building, no matter how small, can be clearly seen. The United States issued four stamps, commemorating the Winter and Summer Games. The multicolored stamps all have the theme "man in motion." Czechoslovakia, France, and Yugoslavia, as well as Japan, the host nation, were among the countries that issued stamps saluting the Winter Games at Sapporo.

The World Chess Championship, pitting Bobby Fischer of the United States against Boris Spassky of the Soviet Union, was honored by a 15-krónur stamp of a chessboard, issued by Iceland, where the match took place.

Stamps issued by the United Nations continued to be popular. The UN Postal Administration released four single-color stamps. The issue commemorated the UN Conference on the Human Environment that was held in Stockholm, Sweden, in 1972.

Literature has always been a popular subject for stamps. One especially appealing topical stamp collection depicts fairy tales and fables. Many countries have issued such stamps, showing stories known to their own children, and sometimes to children all over the world. Hans Christian Andersen has been honored on the stamps of Denmark, his native country, and the Grimm Brothers have been shown on the stamps of Germany, their birthplace. West Germany has probably issued more stamps with legendary characters than any other nation in the world. One set of West German stamps tells the full story of Little Red Riding Hood, with scenes of Red Riding Hood's departure from home, meeting the wolf, the wolf in her grandmother's bed, and the arrival of the woodcutter.

HERMAN HERST, JR.
Author, *Fun and Profit in Stamp Collecting*

A GAME OF ECOLOGY

The game of ecology found on the following pages will take you and up to three of your friends on an imaginary journey around the United States by way of various outstanding wilderness areas. On the way, you may get some ideas on how you yourself can help preserve our environment.

To play the game, you will need a pair of **dice,** 20 **index cards,** a different colored **button** for each player, and a **score sheet.** The object of the game is for a player, by moving his button the exact number of boxes shown on the dice, to try to land in the wilderness areas (marked 1 through 10) and gather as many points as possible before returning to the box marked Home. He gets 100 points for each wilderness area, but he must land in it exactly. If he is three jumps away from an area and the dice come up more than three, he overshoots the area, fails to score, and must go on.

Some of the boxes are marked **Draw O** or **Draw X.** When a player lands on one of these, he must draw a card from a pile of O and X cards laid facedown on the playing table, and do whatever the card he draws tells him. Before you play, prepare the cards. Instructions are given below.

A player may go around the board as many times as necessary and take whatever route will give him the most points. Each time he lands directly on a wilderness area he gets 100 points. The first player to score 1,500 points wins the game.

The **Draw Cards** are prepared by taking ten index cards and placing a large O on the back of each and then ten more index cards, placing an X on the back. The O cards are reward cards; the X cards are penalty cards. On the front of the appropriate cards, first the O's, then the X's, write one of the instructions from the list below:

O Card Instructions:

"You found a littered campsite and cleaned it up. Move to nearest wilderness area."

"You passed through a city and persuaded a homeowner not to burn his raked leaves in the gutter. You get 50 points."

"You wrote to your congressman protesting the pollution of your favorite river. Go ahead 10 jumps. Take 50 points."

"You persuaded your Scout pack to clean up the banks of a nearby river. Go ahead to next wilderness area."

"A car passed and its driver threw trash out of the window. You picked it up. Advance 10 jumps and collect 100 points for any wilderness area you pass through."

"You painted a poster for your class ecology contest. It won first prize. Go to nearest wilderness area for 100 points."

"When rain threatened a farmer's hay crop, you stopped to help him get it into the barn. Go to next wilderness area."

"Your dad's motorboat leaked oil. You talked him into getting an electric outboard motor. Take 100 points."

"You read a book on ecology. Advance to next wilderness area."

"You persuaded a relative to join a conservation club. You get 50 points."

X Card Instructions:

"You carelessly threw a candy bar wrapper away. Lose one turn."

"You chopped down a growing tree to make a tent pole. Lose one turn and 50 points."

"You saw a smokestack belching out black smoke but did not telephone the local smog-control agency. Lose one turn."

"You carelessly left your last campfire smouldering. Lose 50 points."

"You failed to boil the water from the old well you drank out of. If you survive, lose one turn."

"You picked up a wild bear cub you found and this made its mother charge you. Lose one turn."

"You washed your socks with a high-phosphate detergent. That helped pollute a lake. Lose one turn."

"You added a butterfly to your collection. Lose 50 points."

"You broke up a beaver dam. Lose one turn and 50 points."

"You tore flowers out by the roots. Lose one turn and 50 points."

After the Draw Cards are prepared, they should be placed in separate piles, one for the O's and one for X's, facedown. When a player draws a card from either pile, he replaces it in that pile and reshuffles.

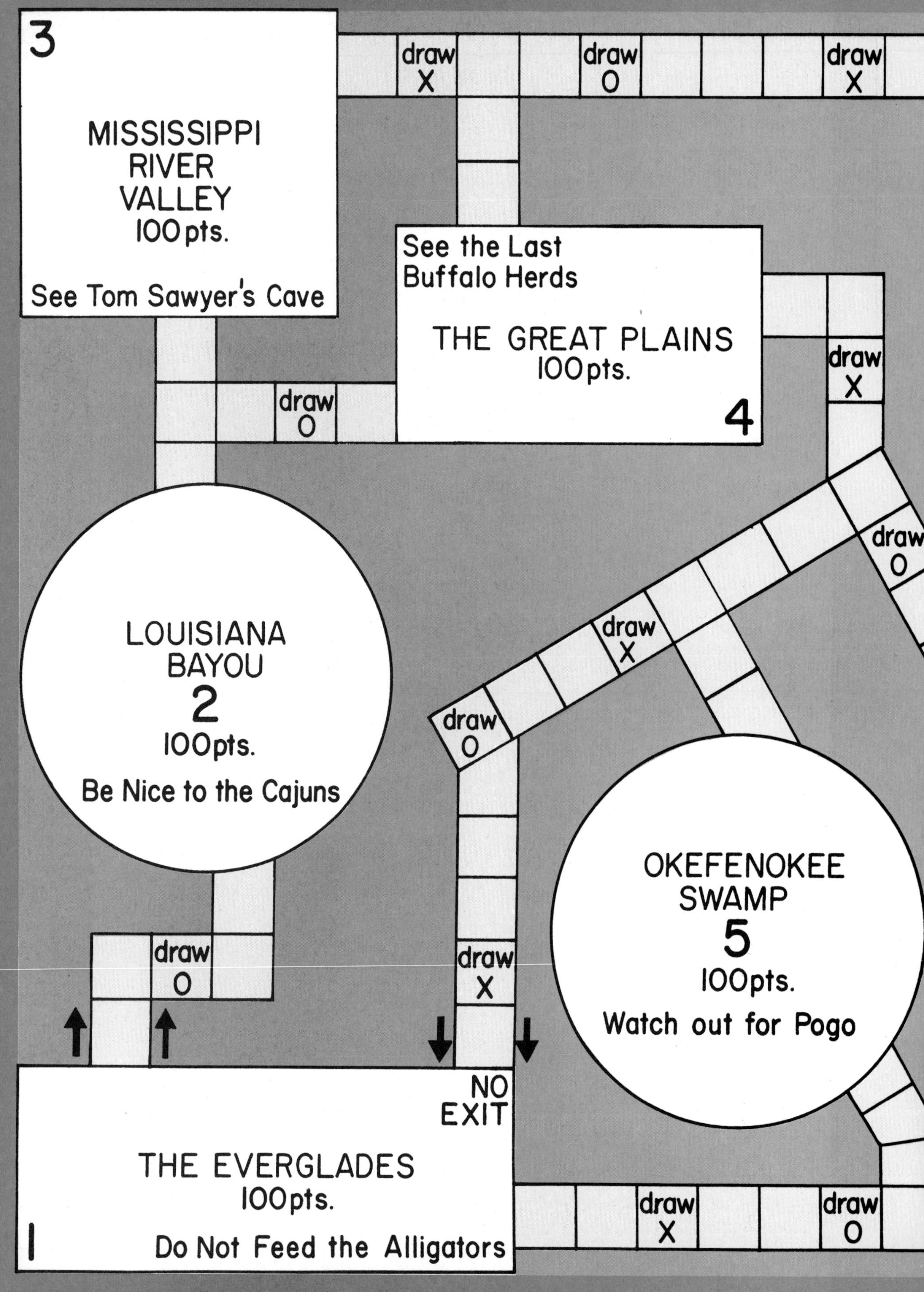
3
MISSISSIPPI RIVER VALLEY
100 pts.
See Tom Sawyer's Cave
draw X
draw O
draw X
See the Last Buffalo Herds
THE GREAT PLAINS
100 pts.
4
draw O
draw X
draw O
LOUISIANA BAYOU
2
100pts.
Be Nice to the Cajuns
draw X
draw O
draw O
draw X
OKEFENOKEE SWAMP
5
100pts.
Watch out for Pogo
NO EXIT
THE EVERGLADES
100pts.
1
Do Not Feed the Alligators
draw X
draw O

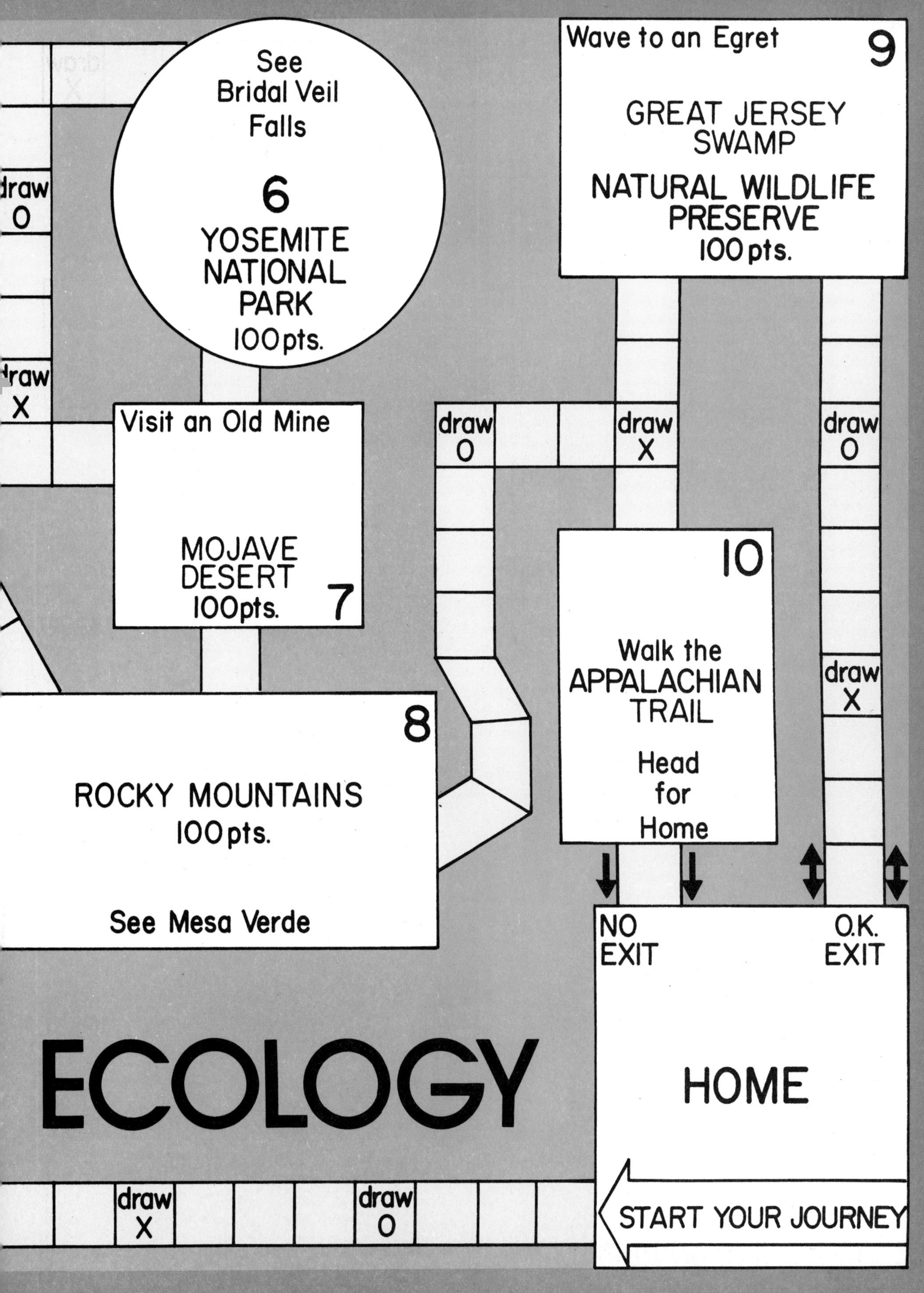
See
Bridal Veil
Falls
6
YOSEMITE
NATIONAL
PARK
100 pts.
draw
O
draw
X
Wave to an Egret
9
GREAT JERSEY
SWAMP
NATURAL WILDLIFE
PRESERVE
100 pts.
Visit an Old Mine
MOJAVE
DESERT
100pts.
7
draw
O
draw
X
draw
O
10
Walk the
APPALACHIAN
TRAIL
Head
for
Home
draw
X
8
ROCKY MOUNTAINS
100 pts.
See Mesa Verde
NO
EXIT
O.K.
EXIT
ECOLOGY
HOME
draw
X
draw
O
START YOUR JOURNEY

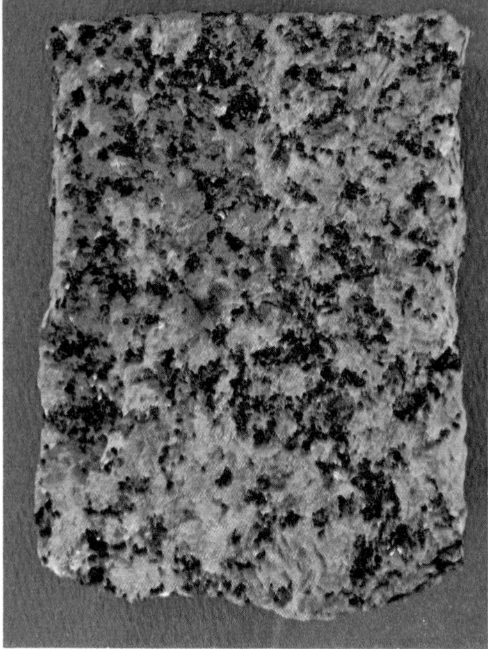

Granite from Minnesota might become part of a great building or a monument to a national hero. Granite is a hard, durable building material.

Basalt is rock that was once molten lava. If you find a piece of basalt, it could mean there was once an active volcano near the spot where you picked it up. Basalt is used in building roads.

Anthracite (hard) coal from the mines of Pennsylvania has a mysterious sheen in addition to being one of the world's most useful and valuable fuels.

Limestone from Pennsylvania—and other places too—is made from the shells of millions of tiny sea creatures. It is among the most valuable of rocks and essential to builders.

TREASURES UNDERFOOT

There are few collections that are easier to start than collections of rocks and minerals. They are literally all around you, wherever you look. Look down at the ground and pick up an interesting rock or mineral: you may well have started a lifetime hobby.

Since there are so many rocks and minerals readily available to collectors, you may want to begin by deciding what special kind of rock or mineral collection you would like to have. Your collection could be based on as simple an idea as beauty. Many rocks and minerals lying in a vacant lot, for instance, are very beautiful when you pick them up and really look at them for the first time. Or you might choose to make a collection of minerals that are especially useful to man—and many of them are necessary to man's life on earth. Or you might want to make a collection of the basic rocks on which your town or city is built. Whatever plan you choose, there is a world of interest in rocks and minerals.

Marble from Georgia (and from the other marble-producing states) might find its way into a sculptor's studio and become a beautiful statue, or it might become part of a building.

Gray slate from Pennsylvania might find its way into your front walk or fireplace hearth. Or it might end up as the flat stone you toss in the game that is sometimes called "hopscotch."

Red sandstone like this piece from New York was used in many American cities in the 19th century in the construction of houses and other buildings we now call "brownstones."

Asbestos from Canada (and other places) has become one of the most valuable minerals man has. The insulation in the walls of your house that keeps out the cold may be asbestos.

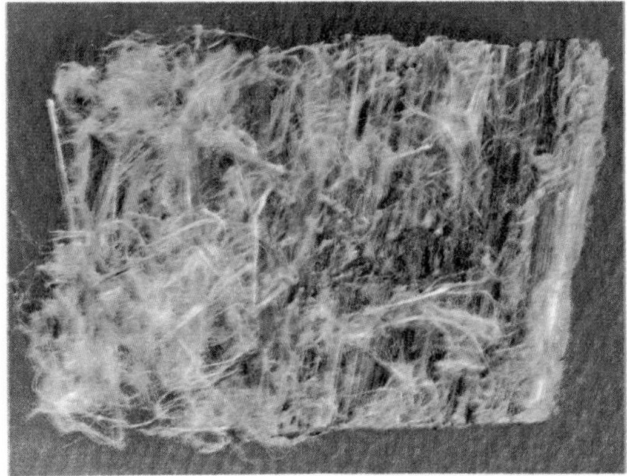

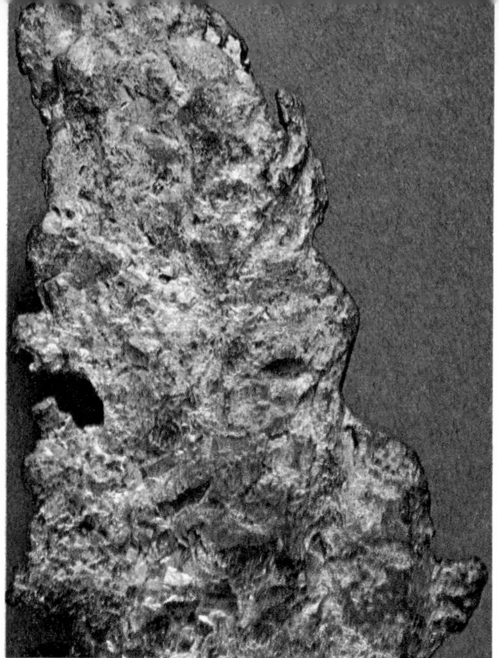

Copper ore has a distinctive color, just as copper does when it is made into pots and pans. Man has known about copper for a long time.

Gold like this, called placer gold, was the treasure sought by the forty-niners in California. Pieces of gold were found in the sand of stream beds and drew thousands west.

Lodestone is nature's own magnet. This piece is attracting iron filings. In ancient times, people were sure there was magic in the lodestone.

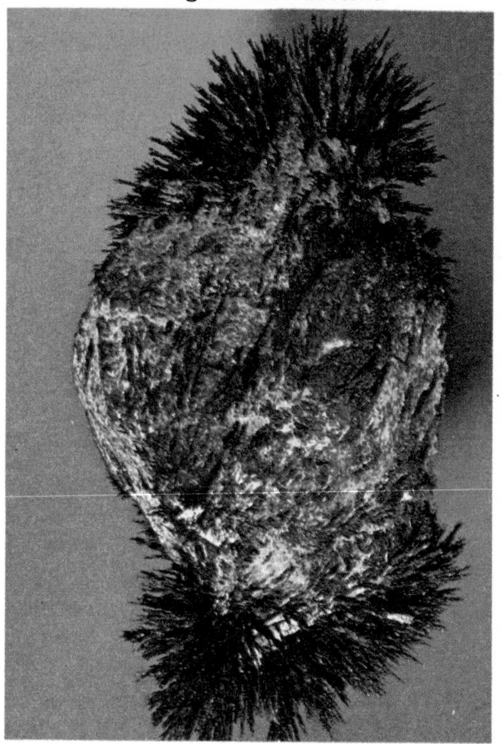

Graphite is something you use every day—if you go to school. Although we speak of "lead pencils," we really mean graphite pencils. This mineral is soft and makes very visible lines.

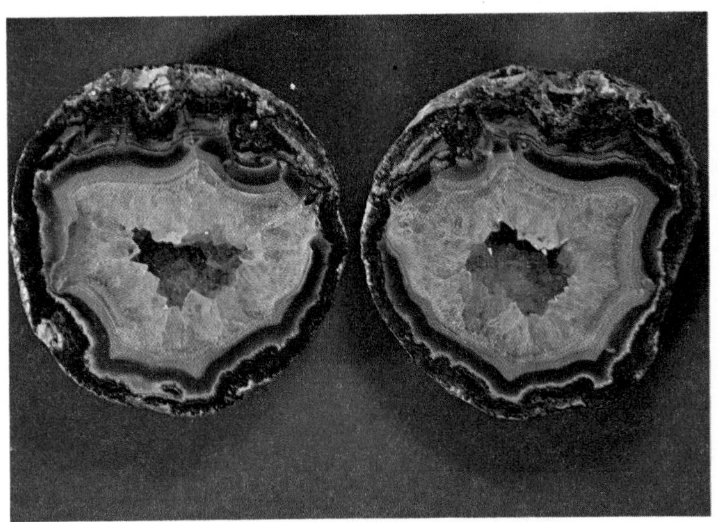

Quartz geodes like this pair from Mexico are among the most popular finds of mineral collectors. A geode is like an egg made of rock. Crack it open and find a mineral inside.

Sulfur is a mineral, but it is not a metal. It is valuable, for it is used in industry and in making the paper on which this book is printed.

Silver is a rather dull gray before polishing. But it takes on its familiar shiny look very easily. It is the "other metal" prospectors went west to find in the 19th century.

Pyrite is a tricky mineral. In fact, it is called "fool's gold" because it looks something like gold ore—if you are very anxious to get rich.

FUN WITH HANDICRAFTS

Have you ever made a hat from folded paper? Or pressed flowers you picked on a walk? Perhaps you once made a mask for Halloween, or some ornaments for a Christmas tree. If you have done any of these things, or have ever made anything with your hands, you have learned a craft. Crafts are fun to do, and they enable us to make our own original creations.

Today, when so many of the products we use in everyday life are manufactured, handcrafted items are valued because they seem very special. Also, many people are discovering that it is a great pleasure to make things instead of buying them in a store. For this

Ferns, driftwood, and pressed flowers are all naturecraft materials. Look outdoors for more.

reason, a large number of craft shops and departments in larger stores sell all kinds of craft materials and provide instruction to those who want to learn crafts. In addition, books and magazines teach crafts to grown-ups and young people alike. Boys and girls also learn crafts from each other, from their Scout leaders, and from their teachers in school.

USE YOUR IMAGINATION

Anything at all can be used as a craft material, for the most important ingredient in a craft project is imagination. Although craft shops offer many interesting materials to work with, some crafts can be enjoyed with little or no expense. One of these, called **naturecraft,** uses materials found out of doors, such as shells, flowers, rocks, driftwood, seeds, leaves, straw, cornhusks, and many others. An imaginative craftsman can turn the most ordinary natural materials into something beautiful or useful, such as jewelry, dolls, or lamps.

Scrapcraft is another craft that doesn't require much in the way of purchased materials. Instead of simply throwing away old cans, plastic bottles, or egg cartons, use them for a craft project. Imagine jewelry made from flip tops, dolls from plastic bottles, or a lamp from old egg cartons! If they are well made, no one will guess that these things were once cast-offs. Like naturecraft, scrapcraft depends very much upon the imagination of the crafter, and there are hundreds of things that can be made from junk. This is a kind of "recycling," and it is not only fun but helps to fight pollution as well. Sometimes scrapcraft is called "ecologycraft."

Naturecraft and scrapcraft help us to find art and enjoyment all around us. Another way we can do this is in the craft of making **rubbings.** Rubbings are easy to do. All you need is a piece of paper and a crayon. The paper is taped over something that has a raised or impressed design on it. It could be a coin or a manhole cover. The crayon is rubbed lightly back and forth over the paper until the design underneath appears on the paper. Like naturecraft and scrapcraft, rubbings may be made from things found everywhere. Some rubbings are very beautiful and can be found framed and hung in people's homes.

Fun with scrapcraft. Above: Giant eggs made by covering balloons with newspaper, doilies, or lace. Below: Animals made from plastic bottles and paper cups, covered with papier-mâché.

A band of witches, flying in formation, can add just the right note of witchcraft to a Halloween party. And this mobile of acorn-faced ladies, in bright kerchiefs and capes, is cheerful enough to fly through your room at any season. The mobile combines **scrapcraft** and **naturecraft.**

To make a mobile of your own, you will need some scraps of fabric and some natural materials. For each witch cut a semicircle from construction paper. Spread glue on the paper and press it on the wrong side of a piece of fabric. Cut around the construction paper. Form into a cone shape, glue into place, and you have a witch's cape.

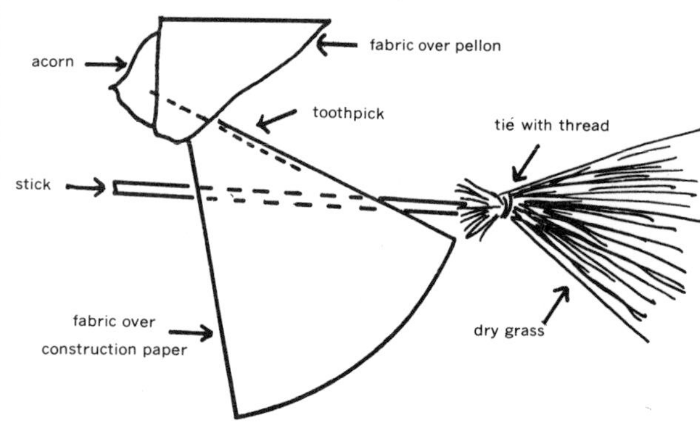

For the head, push a toothpick into an acorn. Slip the toothpick into the cone and with cellophane tape, tape the toothpick against the side of the cone. For the kerchief, cut a triangle from stiff cloth (Pellon) and glue it onto a piece of fabric. Cut around the stiff cloth. Glue along the longest edge of the triangle and place around the acorn.

For the broom, push a thin twig about 4 inches long through holes under the witch's chin and through the center back. Tie a tuft of dry grass onto the end of the twig.

The design of the mobile is up to you. In the illustration, the witches hang on thread from the ends of a twig. You can use a similarly shaped rod of almost any material.

Needlepoint is more than a hobby—it's almost a national pastime. Belts (*left*) and a pillow (*right*) are two of the useful and beautiful items that can be done in needlepoint. If you like, you can make up your own design.

AT A CRAFT SHOP

If you visit a craft shop, you will discover that it is possible to buy materials to make almost anything. In earlier times people made their own candles and soap, dyed and wove fabrics, braided or hooked rugs—basically because there was no other way to have the things they needed. Today we regard these activities as hobbies and pursue them for the pleasure of doing them. Some of the most popular crafts are candlemaking, macramé (knot tying), découpage (decorating with paper cutouts), needlecraft, ceramics, beading, batik, and tie-dye. Practically all the crafts that we know today come to us from the past: there are very few really new crafts, but old ones are continually being rediscovered.

Needlecraft has always been well known, but in 1972 large numbers of people took it up as a hobby. **Needlepoint,** one kind of needlecraft, has become especially popular among young people. In needlepoint, a canvas backing is entirely covered with stitches of thread or yarn. Naturally, various colors are used to create designs, and the stitches themselves can be varied to form different patterns and textures. A piece of needlepoint can be worked using only one stitch, or it can have several different types of stitches in it.

There are many needlepoint kits available that offer canvas with the design already printed on it and enough yarn to cover it with needlepoint. Working from one of these kits is an excellent way to learn needlepoint, but, once you have learned, it is even more enjoyable to make up your own design and stitch it in the colors of your choice. This way, a piece of needlepoint becomes very much like an original painting.

Needlepoint can be used to decorate various items: pillow covers, belts, straps, eyeglass cases, vests, chair covers, and purses. The most popular crafts today are those that, like needlepoint, can be useful as well as beautiful; for every time something handcrafted is worn or used, the pleasure of having made it is renewed.

SYBIL C. HARP
Editor, *Creative Crafts* Magazine

RIDDLES AND PUZZLES

RIDDLE ME THIS!

What is shaped like a box, has no feet, and runs up and down? *An elevator.*

What belongs to you, but is used more by others? *Your name.*

What pet is found in most automobiles? *Car-pet.*

What does a duck do when it flies upside down? *Quacks up.*

What has a tongue but can't talk? *A shoe.*

What do frogs have that no other animal has? *Baby frogs.*

What did the tie say to the hat? *You go ahead and I'll hang around.*

On which side does the leopard have the most spots? *The outside.*

What did the porcupine say when he bumped into a cactus? *Is that you, mother?*

Why does a giraffe eat so little? *He makes a little go a long way.*

If an apple a day keeps the doctor away, what does an onion do? *Keeps everyone away.*

The Wonder of Words

You have often heard people speak of "**UNCLE SAM**" when they were really talking about the United States of America. As everyone knows, the term is a nickname that stands for the United States.

The term **UNCLE SAM** came about during the War of 1812. At that time, supplies of meat intended for the armies in upper New York state passed through Troy, New York. The local inspector Samuel Wilson was called **UNCLE SAM** by local officials, co-workers and friends.

As Wilson dealt with crate after crate of material, each stamped "US," meaning United States property, it became a common joke to pretend it stood for **UNCLE SAM**. Somehow everyone started using the nickname. In 1913 a New York Post editorial referred to the United States as **UNCLE SAM**. The nickname is still used today. We even know what this make-believe uncle looks like!

ICY WORDS

by Roberta Fairall

Polar Bear would like to entICE you to find the words which end in ICE. The definitions below should suffICE. You can do it in a trICE.

ANSWERS:

1. Mice; 2. Rice; 3. Nice; 4. Spice; 5. Price; 6. Slice; 7. Twice; 8. Office; 9. Police; 10. Novice; 11. Splice; 12. Advice; 13. Chalice; 14. Service; 15. Justice.

HIDDEN PICTURE

Spring is here! This young lady is looking at all the blooming flowers, but she has lost some things. Can you help her find them? They are: an umbrella; purse; a comb; an apron; a tube of lipstick; a glove; a hat; and a pair of glasses.

Guessing Games

WORD HUNTING

Let's go word hunting. There are enough letters in each picture on the right side to spell the name of the matching picture on the left side. Spell each word on the right. Then take out some of its letters, and spell the word on the left. Happy hunting!

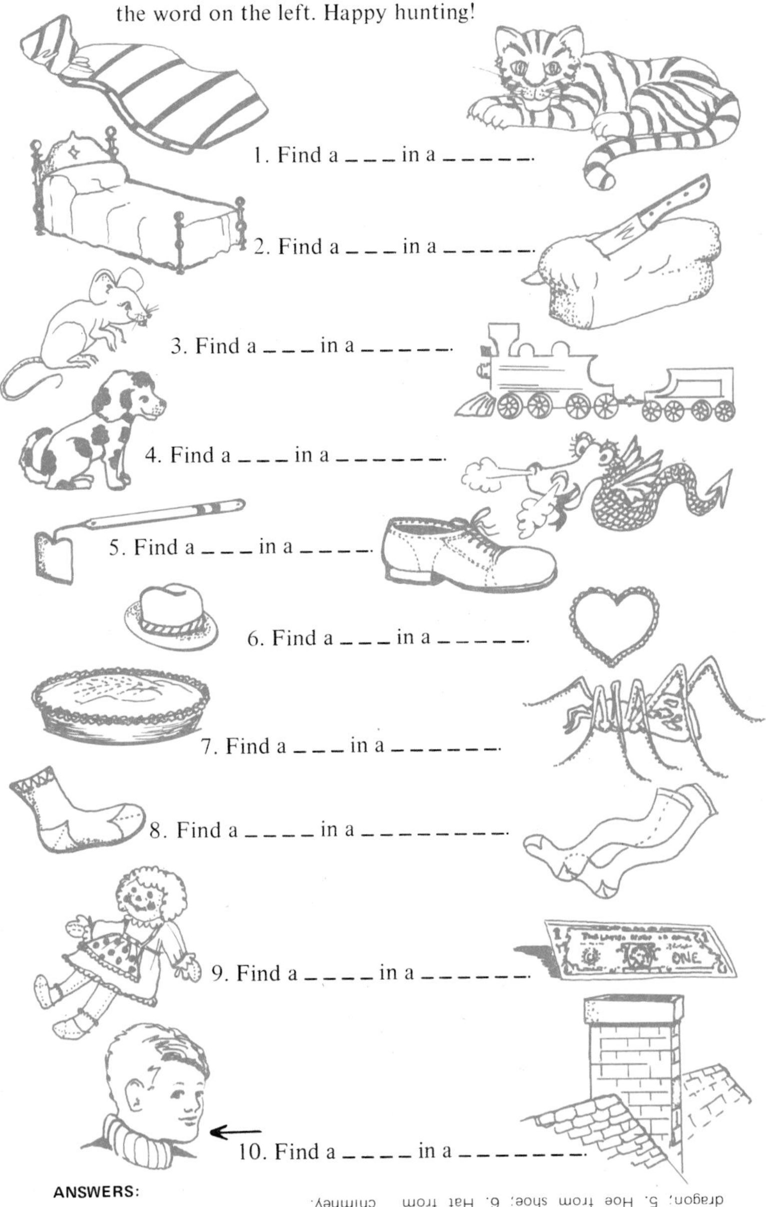

ANSWERS:

1. Tie from tiger; 2. Bed from bread; 3. Rat from train; 4. Dog from dragon; 5. Hoe from shoe; 6. Hat from heart; 7. Pie from spider; 8. Sock from stocking; 9. Doll from dollar; 10. Chin from chimney.

COIN COLLECTING

The year 1972 was an exciting one for coin collectors. Interest among young people, as well as among beginning collectors of all ages, was given a boost with the introduction of a new set of coin albums. These albums are keyed to current United States coins, which people often collect by looking through pocket change. They provide the proper housing for sets of coins of the past decade. Collections of this kind can be completed without the purchase of expensive rare coins. The albums have stimulated activity among those who prefer to start their coin collection without spending a lot of money.

New coin albums for young and adult collectors.

The Philadelphia Mint accidentally provided the public with a coin that would be a perfect specimen to go into the new albums. Early in the year, double-die cents were discovered among the millions of 1972-dated pennies coming from the mint's production lines. Here, for the first time in years, was a real "treasure" that could be found in pocket change. The coin can be easily spotted by its ghostly double image. The date on the face of these specimens has a second impression above and slightly to the right of the primary impression. The mistake can also be clearly

Look for this double-die coin in pocket change.

seen in the motto "In God We Trust." Here the letters are nearly doubled and widely separated. Time alone will tell how valuable the 1972 double-die penny will become. But many collectors are aware that a similar piece, dating from 1955, is now valued at $350.

At the other end of the scale from the "pocket change" collection is the continuing interest in rare coins. Prices for these special coins continue to rise. During 1972 two of the top United States coins, the 1913 Liberty nickel and the 1804 silver dollar, were sold for a total of $180,000.

Always of special interest to the collector are the many imaginative souvenir pieces and circulating coins issued each year, honoring people or events. Among the most topical coins issued in 1972 were six silver 10-mark pieces released by West Germany to commemorate the Munich Summer Games of the 1972 Olympics. The largest and heaviest solid silver piece was issued by Panama during the year. The 20-balboa denomination bears the likeness of Simón Bolívar, the Latin-American liberator. And the Cayman Islands, a British crown colony, marked its first coinage system by issuing four pieces.

On July 4, the American Revolution Bi-

Silver Olympic coins released by West Germany.

centennial Commission issued its first official national medal in honor of the 200th birthday of the United States, to be celebrated in 1976. The bronze medal bears a portrait of George Washington on the face side; on the other side are symbols of the events that led to the Revolutionary War. This souvenir for collectors is in the form of a stamp-medal combination. The medal comes enclosed in an envelope bearing the special 1972 postage stamp bicentennial issue.

During the 1972 election year, the hobby of coin collecting found its way into the national political scene. Presidential candidate George McGovern announced that if elected, he would see to it that a gold coin be struck in 1976 as part of the observance of the nation's bicentennial. Although this announcement did not lead to a similar one from the President, the Republican platform did include a call for lifting the provisions against American ownership of gold in all forms.

The collecting of world gold coin issues is still severely restricted because of federal regulations. In 1972, however, one banned coin, a 1955 30-peso gold piece of the Dominican Republic, was removed from the restricted list.

Collectors of United States paper money experienced another good year, with the issuing of two note series. The first bears the signature of Romana Acosta Bañuelos, who became treasurer of the United States on December 17, 1971. The second bears the signature of George P. Shultz, who succeeded John B. Connally as secretary of the treasury on June 12, 1972.

. . . in honor of 200th birthday of the U.S. . . .

Several important events relating to United States mints and the coin collector took place during the year. In June a group of young collectors were guests of Tricia Nixon Cox, the President's elder daughter, at a White House reception. The occasion was the publication of a special booklet prepared by the United States Mint. The booklet tells the story of the history and heritage of the nation's coins.

Tricia Nixon Cox was hostess at a special White House reception for young coin collectors.

On March 23 the old San Francisco Mint was saved from the wrecker's ball. President Nixon conveyed ownership of the building back to the United States Mint for the building's restoration and development. It will eventually serve as the headquarters of the collector service division, and as an educational and historical museum. The museum will focus on the history of the San Francisco Mint and the role it played in the development of California and the West.

And, as the year drew to a close, the coin-collecting community was eagerly awaiting the sale of the government's hoard of scarce silver dollars from the historic Carson City Mint. These coins, about 3,000,000 in all, were made between 1878 and 1891. The offering, being called The Great Silver Sale, brings to mind the theme of the 1972 National Coin Week: "Coins Are Forever."

CLIFFORD MISHLER
Coins Magazine and *Numismatic News*

YOUTH IN THE NEWS

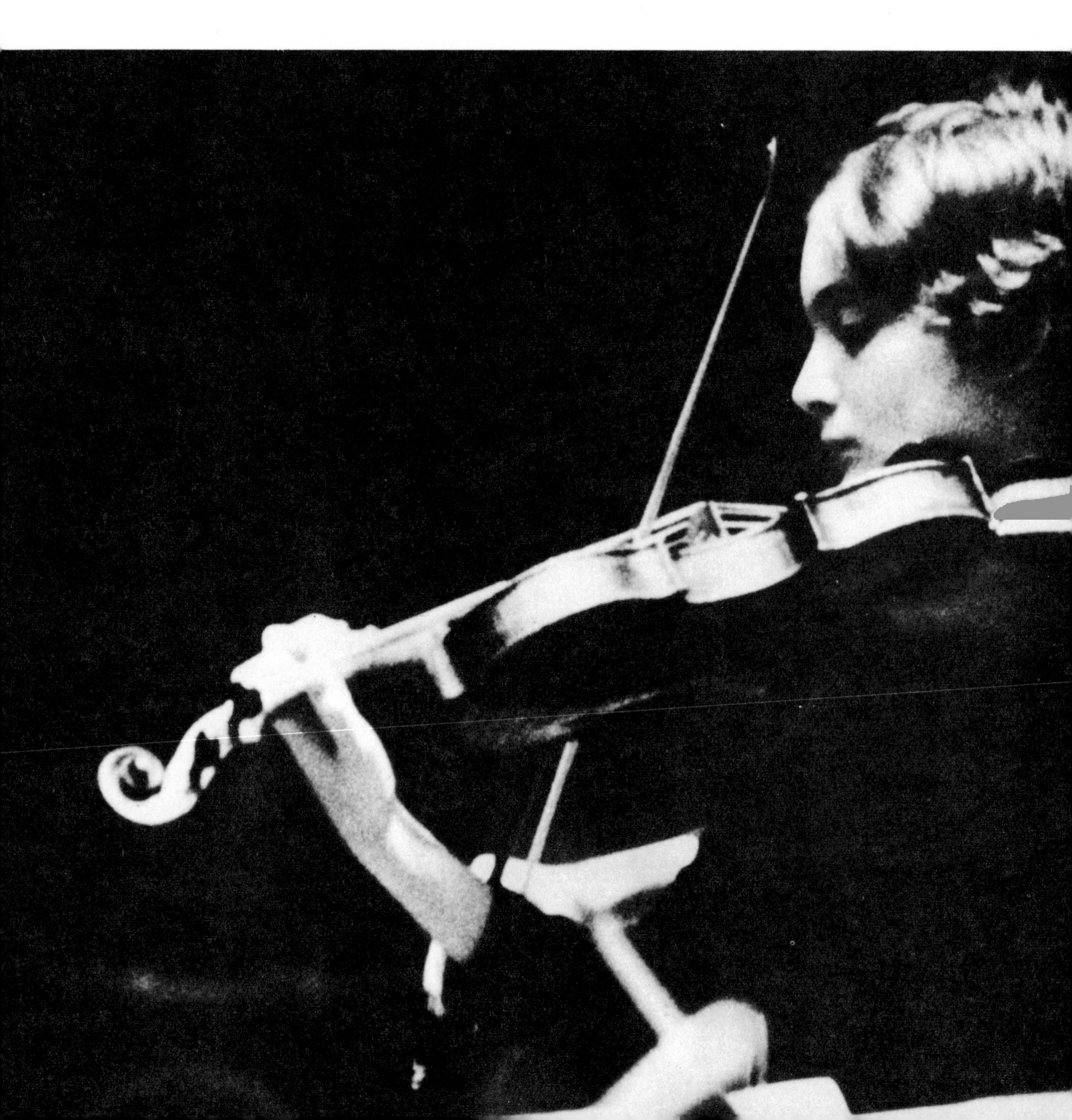

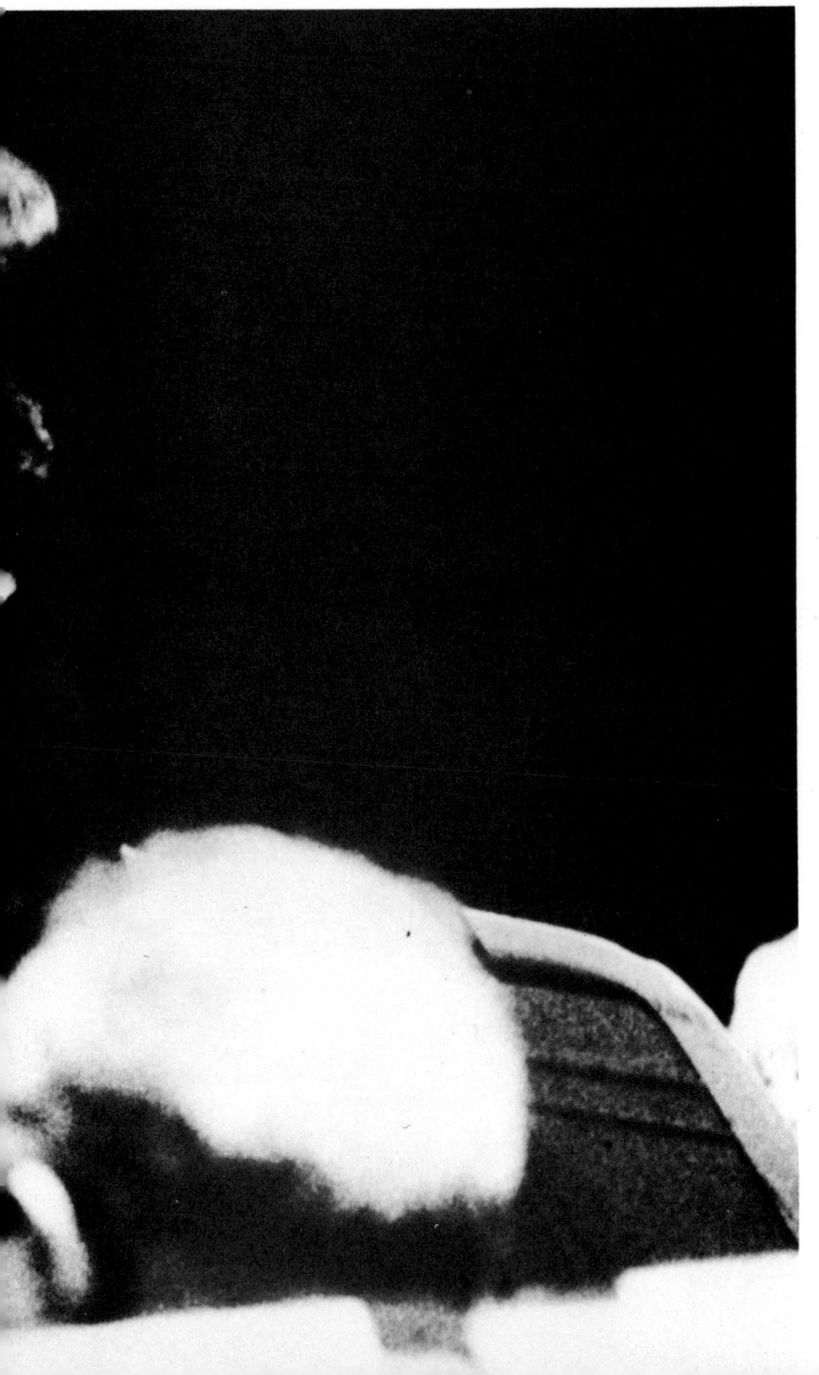

Lilit Gampel, 12-year-old Los Angeles violinist, won high praise from critics for her performances with the Boston Pops and New York Philharmonic orchestras. Her violin is three quarters standard size.

Adam Klein, 11, sang the role of Yniold, a young boy, in the Metropolitan Opera Company's *Pelléas et Mélisande*, by Debussy. Previously, adult sopranos had sung the part at the Metropolitan.

Jigme Singye Wangchuk at 16 became king of Bhutan, after his father's death in July.

Samantha Cox, 6, of Australia, is on her way to fame as an artist. She has been winning one competition after another. Her medium is ordinary house paint, and she uses a brush an inch wide.

Miss American Teen-Ager of 1972 is Carla Tevault, 17, of Indiana.

Winners of the 31st Westinghouse Science Talent Search, seated left to right: Susan E. Landau, 17; Nina F. Tabachnik, 16; Tony G. Horowitz, 17, all of New York. Behind them are Westinghouse vice-president Robert L. Wells, left, and Dr. Glenn T. Seaborg, Nobel Prize winner in chemistry.

David Cassidy in concert.

DAVID CASSIDY, TEENLAND'S IDOL

To the pre-teen and early teen-age set, he's the biggest idol since Bobby Sherman and The Monkees. Teenland's current heartthrob, TV, concert, and recording superstar, David Bruce Cassidy was born on April 12, 1950, in New York City. When David was 5, his parents, actress-singer Evelyn Ward and actor Jack Cassidy, were divorced. But their show-business background had its effect on young David. At a very early age he decided that he was going to be an actor.

David began studying the guitar while he was attending school in Los Angeles, California, where he had moved with his mother. At her urging, he completed high school before going to work with the Los Angeles Theatre Group. After an appearance in the Group's production of *And So to Bed,* David left California for New York and the bright lights of Broadway. He attended acting classes and supported himself by working in the mailroom of a textile company.

His first big theatrical break came in 1969 when he got a part in Allan Sherman's Broadway production, *The Fig Leaves Are Falling.* Although David received good notices, the musical did not, and it closed after 2 days.

More determined than ever to pursue an acting career, David returned to Hollywood, where he appeared on several television shows. These dramatic roles proved to be the turning point in his career. Viewers who saw him on such TV programs as "Marcus Welby, M.D.," "Bonanza," and "Medical Center" flooded the stations with fan mail.

In 1970 David tried out for and won the role of 16-year-old Keith Partridge on the new television series "The Partridge Family." At the time of his audition, the producers did not know that David could sing. They were also unaware that Shirley Jones, who was to play his mother on the show, was actually his real-life stepmother.

With "The Partridge Family" series a television hit, David turned his attention to making records. His first disc single, "I Think I Love You," sold an unbelievable 3,500,000 copies shortly after its release, earning David his first Gold Record. (It has since racked up sales of over 5,000,000 copies.) Both "Cherish" and "Doesn't Somebody Want to Be Wanted," two other singles, passed the million mark in sales and brought David two more Gold Records. *The Partridge Family* album has sold well enough to earn two Gold Records, while *Up to Date,* another album, did extremely well on the charts.

His handsome, dimpled face, sea green eyes, and boyish smile have won David Cassidy quite a following. In 1972, to give his millions of fans a closer look at their idol, David's manager and producers booked a nationwide personal-appearance tour. The concerts were often sold out weeks, and sometimes months, in advance.

In an effort to explain David's popularity, his manager, Jim Flood, says that David has a "positive sexual quality, a youthful, clean-cut look that is threatening neither physically nor emotionally to young girls." But David says: "I like to think that my fans go for my music rather than my face because that's what I'm all about." Whatever it is, David is one of the music industry's most popular stars.

MARK SPITZ, SUPERSTAR

As the starter's gun sounded in Munich's swimming hall, the 22-year-old American with the Omar Sharif mustache dived into the pool. Like a sleek marlin, Mark Spitz plunged in and out of the water as he took a commanding lead in the 200-meter butterfly event of the 1972 Olympics. The other swimmers never had a chance. Just over 2 minutes later, Spitz streaked home to win the first of his gold medals.

During the next few days, the handsome, 6-foot Californian started his own gold rush. By the end of the week he had won seven gold medals—a record unequaled in the history of modern Olympic competition.

The glory Spitz won at the 1972 Olympics was a far cry from the humiliation he had suffered 4 years earlier at the Mexico City Olympics. Then he had been an awkward adolescent of 18, who had cockily predicted he would win six gold medals. In fact, he failed to win even one in individual competition. He came away with only two golds, both in relay events.

Four years had made a difference. The new Mark Spitz was a poised and confident young man who said little and did much.

Mark Andrew Spitz was born in Modesto, California, on February 10, 1950. Two years later, his family moved to Honolulu, Hawaii. At famed Waikiki Beach, Mark first learned to swim. Later, when the family moved back to California, his father encouraged him to take up the sport on a competitive basis. Soon Mark was setting records at junior league meets. At the Pan-American Games in 1967, Mark splashed his way to five gold medals. But then came his poor showing at Mexico City in 1968. It was a big letdown for Mark, and he dropped out of the swimming scene for a while.

In 1969 he enrolled at the University of Indiana as a pre-dental student. There he was taken in tow by James Counsilman, one of the country's top collegiate swimming coaches. The two developed a close personal friendship. Mark was soon back in top form and led Indiana to three straight NCAA championships. Having regained his confidence, Mark looked forward to the Munich Olympics.

There, on his first day of competition, Mark won the 200-meter butterfly and—later that day—the 400-meter freestyle relay. On the following day he captured his third gold medal, in the 200-meter freestyle. After a day of rest the swimming champ went on to win the 100-meter butterfly and the 800-meter freestyle relay. In a 4-day period he had won five gold medals, tying a record established by the Italian fencer Nedo Nadi in 1920. But Spitz wasn't through. He swam to victory in the 100-meter freestyle and the 400-meter medley relay. With an incredible tally of seven gold medals in seven tries, Mark became the superhero of the 1972 Olympics.

After the games, Mark announced his retirement from swimming competition. Although he has been offered film contracts and other business opportunities, the young athlete says he intends to continue his dental studies. "I might drop out of school for a while to do some things," he told newsmen, "and then go back to learning how to be a dentist."

Mark Spitz, 22-year-old U.S. super-swimmer, holds 5 of his 7 Olympic gold medals.

An array of fascinating puppets, large and small, made by the Puppetry Class.

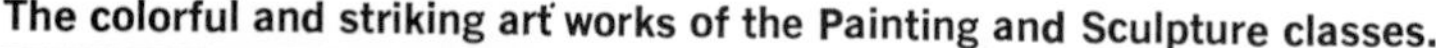

The colorful and striking art works of the Painting and Sculpture classes.

YOUNG ARTISTS

A special exhibition, entitled A Year with Children, was held in New York's Guggenheim Museum in 1972. The show was composed of art works created by children from public and non-public schools, in a program sponsored by the New York City Board of Education, the New York State Council on the Arts, and various museums and foundations.

The program was designed to improve learning skills of children performing below grade level in reading and mathematics. The basic idea is that cultural exposure and the development of artistic skills lead to improved performance in everyday schoolwork.

More than 300 specially selected young people, none of whom had manifested any previous artistic talent, took part in the year-long program. Thirteen different workshop areas were offered to them. One afternoon a week was given over to interesting field trips. The young people visited art galleries, artists' studios, and museums, and went to dance recitals and to the theater.

The exhibition held at the end of the program was a dramatic display of the work of the participants. There were colorful paintings of flowers, landscapes, and city scenes. There were imaginative collages and life-size puppets. Sculpture, both abstract and figurative, and portraits were featured, as well as a large photography display.

The exciting exhibition attracted many visitors. It offered striking proof that the more young people are exposed to the world around them, the more imaginative their own artistic expression becomes.

A bold painting by 11-year-old Earl Addison.

An unusual collage by the Mixed-Media Class.

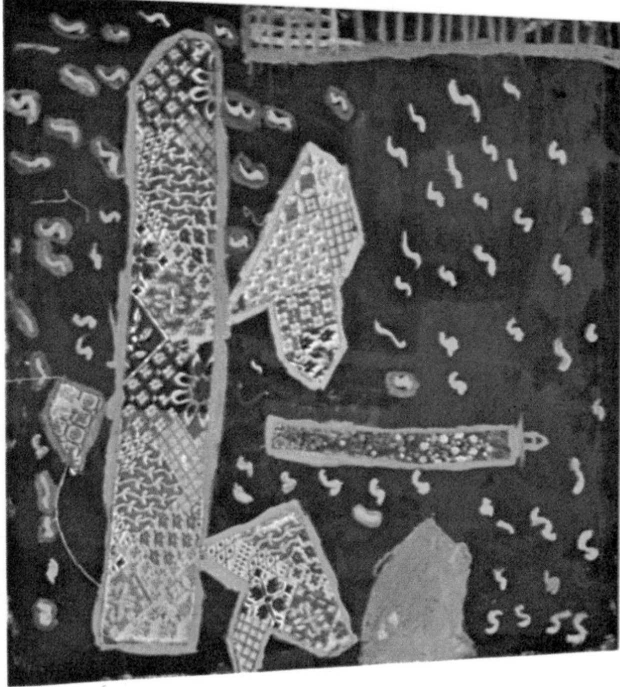

Twelve-year-old Colleen Buddo created this lovely collage.

The Animation Film Class worked together to devise this lively auto.

CLOWNS, CLOWNS, CLOWNS!
Right: A painting by 13-year-old Charles Swhing. Below: An Animation Film Class project. Below right: A puppet by 12-year-old Hugh Whylie.

BOY SCOUTS OF AMERICA

In 1969 the Boy Scouts of America began a program called BOYPOWER '76. Its purpose is to bring into Scouting at least one third of all American boys from 8 to 17 years of age. The program will end in 1976, when it is hoped that membership in the Boy Scouts will reach more than 6,500,000.

In 1972 the Scouts made strides toward achieving this goal. One approach was to add semiprofessional workers to many local Scouting units. These workers are being used in Scout programs involving boys in rural poverty areas and city ghettos. In another project, they are helping, to bring expanded service to American Indian boys. Semiprofessionals were also employed for work in public housing areas; they are helping to bring about a greater use of Scouting programs in public housing units.

Project SOAR (*S*ave *O*ur *A*merican *R*esources) was highlighted by Keep America Beautiful Day, April 29, 1972. Approximately 4,000,000 Scouts and leaders were joined by representatives of other organizations in a nationwide drive against litter. They collected over 1,000,000 tons of rubbish. Any material considered suitable for recycling was sent to reclamation centers. Because of this success,

The Boy Scouts of America at their 31st Annual Dawn Patrol Breakfast, held in New York City. Vice-President Spiro Agnew was one of the speakers.

another anti-litter day is being planned, for April 28, 1973.

Exploring, which welcomes young men and women 15 through 20 years of age, is the fastest growing Boy Scout program. The activities of the Exploring program are selected and conducted by young people who are primarily interested in learning about careers. Some 2,700 members and representatives of local Explorer posts elected national officers during the Exploring Congress held in Washington, D.C., on April 12–16, 1972. Participation of Scout members gave them a meaningful voice in national decisions affecting the 400,000 young adults involved in this program. These decisions and the results of discussions were published in *Exploring,* the program's national magazine.

More than 2,000 Explorers took part in the 1972 Explorer Olympics, held at Fort Collins, Colorado, on June 25–30. Athletic competition was conducted in co-operation with the United States Olympic Committee. The 75 young adults on the three winning teams were part of the official United States delegation to the Youth Village of the 1972 Olympics, held in Munich, Germany.

In 1971 the Boy Scouts of America launched Operation REACH, a youth action plan aimed at preventing drug abuse. This program was greatly expanded in 1972. In addition to fighting drug addiction, the plan makes it possible for young people to help one another find positive alternatives that would make drug use unnecessary.

The 4,000,000-acre Maine-Matagamon Wilderness Base in northwest Maine grew in popularity in 1972. New trails were opened and base camps were established to accommodate the great numbers of Scouts who traveled to the Maine National High Adventure Area.

In a break with tradition, the Boy Scouts of America introduced a brand-new handbook during the year. The title has been changed from *Boy Scouts of America Handbook* to *Scout Handbook,* and the contents have been significantly revised. Emphasis is placed on today's world. The updated handbook is more city-oriented and deals with the complex problems that a youngster must face and solve. When the Scout handbook was first published in 1911, it stressed the outdoor life, for the young adult faced a much simpler and more rural world. The past 70 years, however, have brought many changes. The Boy Scouts of America, through their new programs, projects, and handbook, recognize this fact and are making every effort to move in a positive manner to fulfill their responsibilities to today's youth.

Boy Scouts shoot the White Water Rapids at the Scout Wilderness Base in Maine.

ALDEN G. BARBER
Chief Scout Executive, Boy Scouts of America

Camp Fire recently opened its doors to young men. A new member, Peter Hoover of Minneapolis, Minn., instructs young Camp Fire Girls in nature lore.

CAMP FIRE GIRLS

The Camp Fire Girls held their Quadrennial Meeting in Seattle, Washington, in November, 1971. At that time, the delegates reaffirmed their determination to "do something" to help shape the future of the Camp Fire organization and the future of young people. Discussions were held on the important issues of the day. Two topics of major importance were the long-range goals of the Camp Fire Girls and the rapidly changing social trends of the 1970's. The actions taken by the Camp Fire organization during 1972 illustrate its recognition of the various issues and challenges facing young girls and boys. In major policy changes, Camp Fire has shown its willingness to try new approaches in helping to guide young people in today's world.

The most surprising development of the Quadrennial Meeting was the decision by Camp Fire's National Council to permit boys of high school age to join the national organization. According to Gwen Harper, Director of Program Development, this bold move is in line with current trends toward more casual and informal education directly connected with daily living experiences. "Young people are freer to see each other as friends, rather than simply as potential dates." In addition to the new co-ed program, group leadership is now also open to men.

The National Council also voted to give Camp Fire members of high school age an opportunity to exercise a greater amount of leadership. A resolution was passed permitting high school students to become leaders of groups at younger age levels. To qualify as a group leader, a young girl or boy must meet certain requirements and attend a leadership laboratory.

The Camp Fire organization did not limit its new program activities to Club units in the United States. In Puerto Rico, efforts were intensified during 1972 to assist local communities in organizing Camp Fire groups. Spanish-language materials were prepared for helping Puerto Rican Camp Fire officials provide needed services for their communities.

New program booklets for Discovery Club members (young people of junior high school age) were published in 1972. This is part of Camp Fire's continuing expansion and revision of program materials. The project was begun in 1971 when new booklets for Horizon Club members (girls and boys of high school age) were issued. Booklets for the two youngest age groups are scheduled for publication in 1973. These new program booklets encourage the members and officers of the Club to work together in creating timely and exciting projects. The new materials strongly emphasize individual exploration, personal development, and issues of social concern.

LESLIE VERTER
Camp Fire Girls, Inc.

An adult volunteer advises a young Boys' Club member in a shop class.

BOYS' CLUBS OF AMERICA

In an effort to provide Boys' Club services to millions of young men throughout the country, the Boys' Clubs of America added a record-breaking 75 new Clubs to their roster during 1972. With this accomplishment, two historic milestones were reached by the 112-year-old national youth-guidance organization: the dedication of the 1,000th Boys' Club, and the enrollment of the 1,000,000th member. Both of these achievements were attained a full 3 years ahead of schedule. The 10-year goal of "1,000 Boys' Clubs for 1,000,000 Boys" had been established in 1965 in memory of the late President Herbert Hoover. Mr. Hoover had served for 28 years as board chairman of the Boys' Clubs.

Despite the record pace at which the Boys' Clubs of America grew throughout the year, making them the nation's fastest-growing youth organization, the quantity and quality of their services were in no way diminished. After careful examination of the organization's programs, the directors of the Boys' Clubs agreed that the rapid expansion enabled the Clubs to serve more young men.

Many of the activities undertaken by the Boys' Clubs in 1972 reflected both the expanded membership rolls and the changing times. A need for more specialized services was recognized, and the Boys' Clubs placed particular emphasis on giving a greater voice to young people. While the Boys' Clubs have always given their members this recognition, an increased tempo was very much in evidence during 1972.

For example, it was decided to provide more meaningful programs for all age levels, and especially for older boys. With this in mind, a series of pilot discussions on human relations was held at many of the larger city Clubs. These meetings produced timely suggestions from the teen-age members present. Some of the recommendations included more Club involvement with parents, and the establishment of "boy councils" to provide exchange programs between inner-city and suburban youths. It was also suggested that the Clubs become sounding boards for the problems of the community and that more inter-Club and inter-community "rap sessions" be held.

In 1972, the 66th annual Boys' Clubs Convention was held in Washington, D.C. A record attendance of more than 1,500 Boys' Club leaders representing 49 states, Canada, Puerto Rico, and England was recorded.

The administrative leadership of the organization changed hands in 1972. William R. Bricker, who has been associated with Boys' Clubs since he was a young member, assumed control as national director of Boys' Clubs of America.

E. J. STAPLETON
Boys' Clubs of America

DOING YOUR OWN THING

Members of the various youth organizations throughout the United States are encouraged to develop their own special interests. The prevailing theme is "do your own thing"—whether it be machinery or music, arts or athletics, writing or wiring.

Electrically inclined? Fine. Young men—and women, too—learn how to make and repair lamps, or wire the latest electrical gadget. If sports is your thing, you're always in season. There's baseball, football, leaping hurdles, or an intense game of chess to keep your mind and body busy and fit. Practice your swimming and you might end up with a few gold medals at the next Olympic Games.

Fashion is in the news the year round. Girls with an interest in sewing are urged to pick up a needle and thread and plan a new wardrobe for themselves.

And doing your own thing with a saw, some nails, and wood can lead to rewarding results. Try doing your thing; you'll enjoy it!

Boys' Clubs of America: a young Tom Edison.

Future Farmers of America attend a class in agricultural electrification.

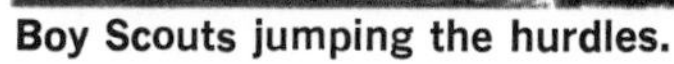

Boy Scouts jumping the hurdles.

Girl Scouts learn about careers in fashion.

A 4-H Club adult volunteer helps a young member with his carpentry project.

GIRL SCOUTS OF THE U.S.A.

By 1972, more than 32,000,000 girls between the ages of 7 and 17 had repeated the words of the Girl Scout Promise: "On my honor, I will try to do my duty to God and my country; to help other people at all times; to obey the Girl Scout Laws." This pledge is a link that binds together Girl Scouts past and present. They have learned ideals of character and patriotism while enjoying a program of work, play, and companionship. They have been taught how to protect their health, to practice useful skills, and to become good members of their communities. Their motto, "Be prepared," and their slogan, "Do a good turn daily," have served to help girls develop self-reliance, self-control, and an eagerness to help others.

A Girl Scout grinds bottles for recycling.

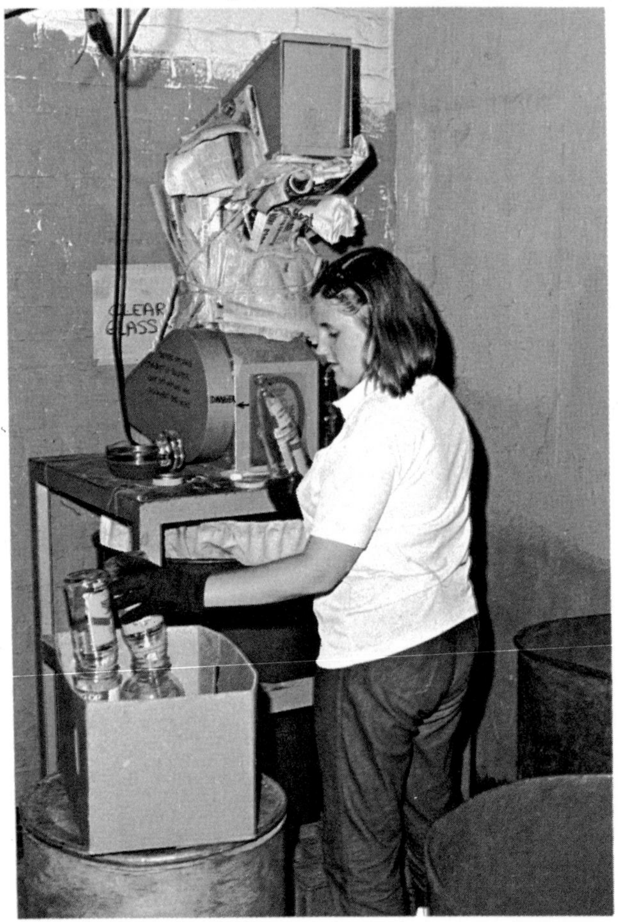

Since its beginnings 61 years ago, the Girl Scout organization has seen many changes. Each year, new programs and projects are planned to keep pace with the rapidly changing times and to give the Girl Scouts an ever-increasing awareness of the world in which they live.

In 1972 the Girl Scouts of the U.S.A. placed particular emphasis on "inspiring each girl to develop her own values and sense of worth as an individual." A program was designed to provide activities and opportunities that would help girls learn to make decisions and to develop the skills and attitudes needed for becoming happy, resourceful adults.

The Girl Scout National Council held their 1972 convention in Dallas, Texas, in October. More than 360 Senior Girl Scouts (ages 14 through 17) were selected by their respective councils to attend the conference. The primary objective of the meeting was to set the course of Girl Scouting for the next 3 years.

Two major projects—ACTION 70 and ECO–ACTION—continued to receive attention in 1972. ACTION 70, a nationwide program to eliminate prejudice and foster greater human understanding, was given top priority. Girl Scouts throughout the country joined with minority groups in an effort to solve present-day problems and pressures. The Girl Scouts worked with youngsters from ghetto and rural areas, children of migrant workers, physically or mentally handicapped persons, and the elderly.

Girl Scouts also continued their work in projects to improve the environment. Through their ECO–ACTION program, they engaged in thousands of ecological projects. The girls helped to build vest-pocket parks, playscapes, and nature trails, and to establish environmental learning centers in many cities throughout the United States. They worked with the Soil Conservation Service, the Fish and Wildlife Service, and the National Park Service to discover, test, and follow sound environmental practices. Some Girl Scouts attended "Sur-

Girl Scout volunteers work for Project Headstart, a children's training program.

vival U," a workshop on ecological problems in a fast-changing environment, held at the University of Wisconsin.

In April, the Girl Scouts joined forces with the Boy Scouts in Keep America Beautiful Day. More than 1,000,000 tons of rubbish were removed from public places, and about 150,000 tons of material suitable for recycling were collected. In an effort to beautify the nation's parks and recreation areas, the Scouts planted more than 300,000 trees.

One of this decade's most serious problems is that of drug addiction. During 1972 the Girl Scouts were involved in many programs to prevent drug abuse. One such project brought an international award to a Senior Girl Scout troop in Oak Ridge, Tennessee. The girls in Troop Number 67 received the Walter Donald Ross trophy, given by the World Association of Girl Guides and Girl Scouts, for outstanding community service. This is the first time the coveted award has been presented to a U.S. Girl Scout troop.

International, national, and local events called "wider opportunities" proved to be the highlight of the year for some 4,000 Girl Scouts. These events gave the girls an opportunity to camp, backpack, hike, take bicycle trips, make archeological digs, ride horseback, visit national Girl Scout centers, and attend conferences. Some Scouts went abroad on exchange visits to member-countries of the World Association of Girl Guides and Girl Scouts.

Thousands of Girl Scout "camperships" were given during 1972 to boys and girls from families with limited incomes. As in years past, the DeWitt Wallace Reader's Digest Foundation Scholarship Fund awarded a special "campership." Through this special fund, 150 girls from various low-income areas visited Girl Scout National Center West, a 15,000-acre wilderness tract in Wyoming's Big Horn Basin.

RICHARD G. KNOX
Girl Scouts of the U.S.A.

4-H CLUBS

During 1972, nearly 5,000,000 4-H'ers worked and had fun together. These young people took part in activities best suited to their interests and environment: an instructional 4-H television series, day camps, special-interest courses, nutrition programs.

With the 1972 theme, A New Day—A New Way, 4-H'ers across the country were involved in projects that benefitted not only themselves but their community and other nations. The fastest growing of these programs is the 4-H nutrition program. More than 5,000,000 youths learned that it's fun and easy to choose a balanced diet no matter where you live. Along with better eating habits, they learned easy food preparation and food shopping skills.

Many 4-H activities have taken on an urban look. The garden or field crop project of the past has become a mini-garden in a window box or a backyard. 4-H'ers are learning to repair lawn mowers and manage money through yard maintenance projects. Other activities vary from karate to consumer education, and all emphasize the learn-by-doing technique.

Whether the 4-H'er lives in the city or the country, the environment and community are of great concern. Members are involved in soil conservation, wildlife protection, pollution control, and community beautification.

The National 4-H Conference was held in Washington, D.C., in April, 1972. The delegation made recommendations for future 4-H programs. In late November 1,600 4-H project winners attended the National 4-H Congress in Chicago. This annual event gives 4-H'ers and business people a chance to meet and discuss common problems.

E. DEAN VAUGHAN
Director, 4-H Programs

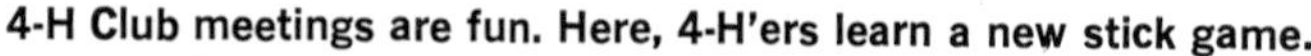

4-H Club meetings are fun. Here, 4-H'ers learn a new stick game.

Future Farmers of America test soil to see if it is suitable for growing plants.

FUTURE FARMERS OF AMERICA

Future Farmers of America was originally intended as a national organization for farm girls and boys who studied agriculture in high school. In recent years, however, the organization has expanded to include non-farm youths interested in farm-related careers. Many young people have shown an interest in agribusiness occupations, such as horticulture, agricultural sales, and food processing.

These widened horizons may be responsible for the nearly 3,000 new members who joined the organization during 1972. There are now more than 430,000 FFA members.

In 1972 the national FFA organization sought to increase membership and participation even further. Twenty-seven "Update" meetings were held across the nation. They were attended by FFA advisers, state education personnel, and teachers. The "Update" program emphasized the use of FFA as an instructional tool, and made advisers familiar with FFA performance objectives.

In 1972, six national FFA officers traveled to every state in the nation. During their journey, they visited FFA chapters and attended state FFA conventions. They met with leaders of government, business, and industry, and participated in the "Update" programs.

The 45th National FFA Convention was held in Kansas City, Missouri. Approximately 14,300 members and their guests attended. The theme of this year's meeting was "FFA Unites Youth with Opportunities." A highlight of the conference was a series of national competitions. Awards were presented to winners in six categories: dairy cattle, dairy products, livestock, meats, agricultural mechanics, and poultry.

Another highlight was the awards program. Dennis M. Smith, 18, of Park City, Kentucky, was named winner of the National Public Speaking Contest. His speech, "America's Greatest Industry, the Production of Waste," was on ecology. David Galley, 20, a dairy farmer from Garrettsville, New York, was named the Star Farmer of America. And Edward Higley, 19, a logger from Brattleboro, Vermont, was honored as the Star Agribusinessman of America.

A. Daniel Reuwee
Director of Information
Future Farmers of America

20th-century "pioneers" pitch an elaborate camp in the desert.

THE CAMPING BOOM

There was once a time when the word "camping" brought such simple things to mind as Boy Scouts and pup tents, unbearable backpacks stuffed with bulky cans of beans, and "Army-Navy" stores smelling of canvas. In those days few people but Boy Scouts went camping. Across the United States, park superintendents sometimes felt like wringing their hands in despair and loneliness. How the times have changed! Today, camping is not only a popular fad, it may well be on its way to replacing spectator sports as the greatest of all American pastimes.

Signs of a camping boom are everywhere: crowded parks, overused trails, and campsites that must be reserved two months in advance. The military surplus stores are being replaced by shops specializing in everything from freeze-dried foods to featherweight mountain tents. In fact, the manufacture and sale of camping equipment has become one of America's fastest-growing industries.

WHY CAMPING REVIVED

There are a number of reasons for the Americans' recent discovery of the great outdoors. Actually, it represents a re-discovery of a major part of America's cultural heritage. For deep inside every American there lingers a shadow of the long-gone pioneers. The difference is that modern Americans can face the forest and the mountain, not in fear, not as obstacles to be conquered, but with pride and respect, as places to be cherished and enjoyed.

The current popularity of camping may also represent a need that many people are experiencing now, especially young people: the need to get closer to the earth. In the 1960's the new interest in ecology and the need to fight pollution made people realize the importance to them of the natural beauty they ran the risk of losing. Problems in the big cities, which also began to be discussed frankly in the 1960's, made many city dwellers aware of the beauty and peace of the wilderness. For many reasons, Americans were beginning to look for an escape. What they began to seek, if only for a weekend, was the chance of experiencing life at a slower pace and in some natural setting. As a result, camping and the activities related to it—fishing, hiking, canoeing, nature photography—have increased more than tenfold in the past decade.

A camper finds solitude high in the mountains.

A sleeping bag provides comfort for the night.

KINDS OF CAMPING

Since the days of pup tents and canned beans, camping has taken many forms. There are many places to go and an enormous variety of equipment to take if you wish to. For the sake of simplifying the choices, let us consider three major categories of camping.

First, and perhaps most popular, is "camping with all the comforts of home." This kind of camping is completely dependent on the internal-combustion engine—on cars and campers and trailers—and what the engine can transport to the campsite. Next comes backpacking, which is dependent only on one's own muscles. Backpacking is rapidly developing into a culture of its very own and is very popular with young people. And finally there is specialty camping, which can range from a canoe trip to a cross-country ski tour. Each has its own delights and drawbacks.

If you have never spent a night in a tent or under the stars, you would do well to begin humbly, preferably in the backyard with rented or borrowed equipment. Too often, the beginning camper lays out a small fortune to buy elaborate equipment only to discover later that half of the purchases are unnecessary and the other half are unsuitable. The best idea is to buy little and try out as much of it as you can in advance.

Car camping, with at least some of the comforts of home, is the next step. In most parks where camping is permitted, sites accessible to vehicles are provided, having fireplaces, picnic tables, and even tent platforms. Here is where the beginner can really test borrowed equipment against future purchases. For example, if you expect to graduate to backpacking eventually, you could try sleeping out here in one of the lighter-weight, down-filled sleeping bags. If you prefer to sleep in the car, a less expensive, heavier, synthetic-fiber bag is fine. The same can be said for tents, of which there are a great many varieties. The camper who never expects to stray far from his car may ultimately want to purchase a family-size wall tent. The backpacker-in-training may find that a simple plastic tarp to make a shelter will be enough.

A mattress is a must for any kind of camping. Increasingly, the traditional air mattress is being replaced by the lightweight plastic or foam rubber pad. These range from the 6-inch-thick models designed for car camping to the ⅝-inch backpacker specials. A small camp stove is also essential; you can no longer depend on there being firewood at any campground. Your choice of a stove—like that of tents, sleeping bags, and mattresses—depends on what kind of camping you want to do in the long run.

The delights of car camping are obvious, particularly at mealtime. In a larder and an ice chest (since weight is no problem) you can store food for a very fine meal. But car camping does have its drawbacks. Even under the best of circumstances, it generally throws the camper close to other groups of campers. In fact, in some popular state and national parks, campgrounds have begun to resemble tent cities—crowded, noisy, with little chance to be alone.

Pseudo camping—that is, the occupation of campsites by trailers and other "live-in" vehicles—has also become popular with some people. In fact, a kind of chain reaction may be setting in. The "live-in" campers crowd the car campers, converting some of them into backpackers. As the ranks of the backpackers

Trailers, equipped with all the comforts of home, crowd America's camping sites.

Some campers prefer to "rough it" by pitching a tent in the woods.

Backpacking—a day well spent on the trail.

Time out for a hearty meal.

swell, some backpackers give up the crowded trail for more specialized methods of camping.

Even with trails getting more crowded, there is something about backpacking that cannot be matched by any other form of camping. With a pack on his back, a camper is totally independent, a free spirit, setting his own pace, at liberty to camp wherever he chooses. He is unburdened of the responsibility of looking after a car, a canoe, or a pack animal. Since the backpacker is a self-contained camper, he must take special care that he carries only what is absolutely essential.

In addition to the four items of equipment needed by any camper—sleeping bag, mattress, stove, and tarp or tent—the backpacker must concern himself with a choice of boots and pack as well. Tennis shoes may be acceptable for short hikes, but when you are walking 6 to 15 miles a day under a 35-pound load, over rough trails, lightweight boots that cover the ankle, with lug soles of rubber or neoprene, are far superior. Trail boots have become so fashionable, in fact, that some are now available at regular shoe stores. As for packs, the aluminum frame with a multipocket nylon bag is standard. Be sure it includes a waistband. By securing the load to the hips, it can help relieve tiring pressure on back and shoulder muscles.

The good backpacker always travels light. Extra clothing is for warmth and dryness, not fashion. In the food department, all bulky packaging is discarded at home, and foodstuffs are repackaged in polyethylene bags. Meals generally are planned around dehydrated or freeze-dried meats, soups, or starches. These days, a wide variety of dry foods are available at the supermarket. Heavy cans of beans are truly a thing of the past.

Traveling light is especially important in mountain terrain. A heavy pack can turn an otherwise easy ascent into an agony. But even a light pack is no substitute for physical conditioning. Before setting out on any trip, the wise backpacker makes sure he is in reasonably good physical shape.

Specialty camping generally requires less physical exertion than backpacking (though ski touring and canoe trips involving portages provide notable exceptions to that rule). By

Not even the cold winter snows discourage some campers.

the same token, the specialist must often make a greater financial investment in his sport, either by purchasing equipment (a canoe for example) or by joining one of the thousands of special outings conducted by professional guides, outfitters, clubs, and associations throughout the United States.

Specialty camping provides an endless variety of adventure: kayaking on whitewater rivers, rafting down the rapids of the wild Colorado between the soaring sandstone walls of the Grand Canyon, canoeing on the lakes and ponds of the North Woods, riding with pack animals into the alpine wilderness of the Rockies and the High Sierra, exploring the maze-like canyon lands of the desert Southwest in a four-wheel–drive vehicle, schussing away from the developed ski resort on a cross-country tour across unbroken snowfields. Although the basic techniques of camping may be appropriate in each case, you must master special skills to suit the occasion. It goes without saying that canoe campers must know how to paddle and portage a canoe, that pack trippers must learn how to care for their stock animals, and that ski tourers must know how to spend a safe and comfortable night in subfreezing temperature.

Boatsmen prepare for a camping expedition.

Camping means trying to bathe in a bucket . . .

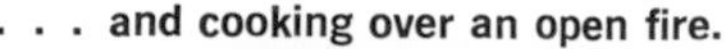

. . . and cooking over an open fire.

THE PRINCIPLES OF CAMPING

Regardless of the kind of trip you take, the principles of camping are pretty much the same from sea level to mountaintop.

(1) Avoid fatigue. Stop for the night with at least two hours of daylight remaining for setting up camp and preparing dinner. If you're planning to cook your first meal over an open fire, allow time for collecting the necessary dry firewood.

(2) Select a campsite that is secure from rock- or snowslides, heavy wind, and rising waters. A spot by a rushing stream may seem like an ideal campsite. But if it should rain heavily during your camping expedition, the stream may overflow its banks, causing great discomfort and inconvenience.

(3) Set a pot of water to boil on your stove. Or, if you are in country where there is an ample supply of dry, dead wood, get the pot boiling over a small cooking fire. Hot water will come in handy later. Do *not* make a roaring campfire. It is wasteful of firewood and difficult to cook over.

(4) Set up your shelter and prepare bed sites. Do *not* follow the advice of the old woodcraft books, which advocated bough beds. Cutting or breaking off live branches in our time can be considered nothing less than an ecological atrocity. (And besides, why boughs when you have a foam pad?)

(5) Try to complete your meal before dark, out of consideration for the person who must wash the dishes.

(6) Concentrate sanitary facilities in one area well removed from the water supply. As one handbook puts it, regarding the disposal of human waste: "Consider the ways of the cat: dig, and cover—everything."

(7) In breaking camp the next morning, be sure your fire is out. Drown it with water. Then drown it again. And again.

(8) Do not leave behind any garbage or litter. Do not bury or otherwise attempt to hide it. What you cannot burn you must carry out in your pack. The site must be left in as natural a condition as you found it. If someone has been there before you, chances are you can leave it looking *more* natural.

As the forests and mountains and shores and riverbanks of America are increasingly used by campers, there is an increasing need

Campers traveling by packtrain set up camp for the night.

for a new code of outdoor behavior. Too often, on the trail as well as in developed campgrounds, the rules of common courtesy are disregarded. Portable radios blare shrilly beyond midnight. Some campsites are illuminated until dawn by lanterns, whose unshielded glare penetrates the walls of nearby tents. The whine of motor scooters and snowmobiles intrudes on the wilderness. In the good old uncrowded days, a man outdoors could do almost anything he pleased, and often did. Today, he must consider his neighbors.

The contemporary camper has a final responsibility, but it is largely unacknowledged by many people who actively use and enjoy America's scenic resources. In their haste to pitch a tent beside some bubbling brook, these campers never pause to wonder why the brook still bubbles, or how the campground they are using has been protected from "development." They simply enjoy the presence of nature and pass on, as if brooks and forests and parks and wilderness, and all the wonderful places people go to camp, existed by accident. They fail to recognize that in America today parklands are established and protected by dedicated people, not by accident. And so the ultimate responsibility of the camper is the payment of his "dues." This does not mean actual fees. The dues in question are the camper's obligation to help preserve what he uses and to make sure that his country keeps enough land natural and wild that camping may go on for all the generations yet to come.

JOHN G. MITCHELL
Editor in Chief
Sierra Club Publications

WORLD OF SPORTS

The U.S. team proudly marches in the opening ceremonies of the Munich Olympics.

Hideki Takanda of Japan carries the Olympic torch up the steps of Makomanai Stadium, signaling the start of the Winter Games in Sapporo, Japan.

THE 1972 OLYMPIC GAMES

1972 was an Olympic year, and the first event was the festival of winter sports. The XI Olympic Winter Games were held in Sapporo, Japan, in February. The Japanese had worked for 5 years to build the necessary facilities for the youth of the world. In addition, accommodations had to be provided for several thousand journalists and television and radio personnel.

Sapporo was so proud of being the capital of the world of winter sport that it built a new subway, a larger airport, a city hall, and new highways. With the new sports facilities, these improvements will help the city for many generations to come.

Teams from 35 countries, numbering 1,300 athletes, participated in the Winter Games. But of the teams entered, 14 had fewer than six competitors. Although Olympic events should be universal, few of the 130 National Olympic Committees are seriously interested in winter sports. Baron de Coubertin, who revived the Olympic Games in 1896, was opposed to having Winter Games because, he said, there should be only one Olympic Games. And while the Winter Games have encouraged interest in healthful winter sports and recreation, many think they have served their purpose and should be discontinued.

However, the Winter Games in Sapporo can be considered a great success, and the Japanese were proud of the compliments they received from both participants and spectators. The general atmosphere in the city was a happy one, marked by the friendly hospitality extended to all visitors.

Russia's Irina Rodnina and Aleksei Ulanov won the gold medal in pairs figure skating.

Gustavo Thoeni of Italy races to a gold medal victory in the men's giant slalom.

THE WINTER WINNERS

The U.S. team had its greatest success in the speed skating events for women. In the 500-meter, Anne Henning, from Northbrook, Illinois, was victorious. She also placed third in the 1,000-meter. Dianne Holum, also from Northbrook, won the 1,500-meter race and came in second in the 3,000-meter.

Three of the four speed skating events for men—the 1,500-, the 5,000-, and the 10,000-meter races—were won by the Dutch skater Ard Schenk. But the 500-meter was taken by Erhard Keller, a West German skater.

The women's figure skating was won by Trixi Schuba, an Austrian, and the men's by Ondrej Nepela, from Czechoslovakia. U.S. figure skaters were very good in the spectacular freestyle, but lost out in the tiresome school figures. Both first and second places in the pairs skating were won by competitors from the Soviet Union. (The gold medals were won by Irina Rodnina and Aleksei Ulanov.)

One of the surprises of the Games was the showing of the young and inexperienced ice hockey team from the United States. It placed second, behind the Soviet team.

The highly rated French and Austrian Alpine ski teams failed to live up to expectations. The Swiss competitors, Bernhard Russi and Marie Thérèse Nadig, won the men's and women's downhill. Miss Nadig also won the giant slalom for women. Swiss participants took second and third in the giant slalom for men. And the four-man bobsledding race was captured by the Swiss quartet. Altogether, they were great days for the Swiss team.

In Nordic skiing the Japanese competitors, led by Yukio Kasaya, took all three medals in the 70-meter jump, to the great satisfaction of the Japanese spectators. In the 90-meter jump, however, the Japanese failed to show, and the victory unexpectedly went to a young Pole, Wojciech Fortuna. Most of the cross-country races were won by the Soviet Union.

Above: A translucent roof stretches across the three stadiums at Olympic Village in Munich. Below: Memorial services are held in the main Olympic stadium for the slain Israeli athletes.

THE SUMMER GAMES

The Summer Games of the XX Olympiad, held in Munich, West Germany, included more competitors (8,500) from more countries (121) than any previous Games. The Games began on August 26 with a sensational opening ceremony, the highlight of which was the arrival of the Olympic torch. On July 28 the torch had been lit in Olympia, Greece; it was then carried 3,500 miles by an international relay team of 5,976 runners. The final leg, ending in Munich's main stadium, was run by West Germany's Günter Zahn. With the torch, Zahn lit the Olympic flame, which burned day and night until the closing ceremonies on September 10.

Munich's main competition area was spectacularly designed. But the West Germans had planned the events themselves so that they would be held in a simple manner.

However, the Summer Games were marred by the horrible massacre of 11 members of the Israeli team by Arab terrorists. This was one of the penalties of the enormous success of the Games, which, with the tremendous international interest they attract (never before have 400,000,000 people watched and followed an event), offer an unequaled stage for publicity.

Another unhappy incident, and one that aroused much controversy, was the protest of black African sports leaders that led to the exclusion of the team from Rhodesia.

Water Sports

The sensation of the men's swimming events was Mark Spitz of the United States. He won seven gold medals and established new individual world records in four of the events. This was quite a feat, but it also indicated that some of the events were too much alike. In the next Games, some of these events will probably be eliminated.

Other new world records were set by Mike Burton, United States, in the 1,500-meter freestyle; John Hencken, United States, in the 200-meter breaststroke; Gunnar Larsson, Sweden, in the 200-meter individual medley; and Nobutaka Taguchi, Japan, in the 100-meter breaststroke. In fact, new world or Olympic records were set in most swimming events, indicating the progress being made in this fine sport.

An incident that aroused controversy was the disqualification of Rick DeMont, a young U.S. swimmer. He had won the 400-meter freestyle. However, he was stripped of his medal and barred from further competition after tests revealed the presence of a banned drug in his system. DeMont suffers from asthma and has been taking medicine for it since childhood. Apparently, the U.S. team doctors had not cleared the prescription with the Olympic medical committee. DeMont was the first gold medal winner in 60 years ordered to return the coveted prize.

As has been the case in recent Games, women's swimming was dominated by young girls from the United States. They set new records and were victorious in most events, except those in which the winner was the sensational young Australian star, Shane Gould. She placed first in the 200-meter and 400-meter freestyle and in the 200-meter medley—all with new world records.

In men's and women's diving, Vladimir Vasin of the Soviet Union and Micki King of the United States won the gold medals for their springboard dives. Klaus Dibiasi of Italy and Ulrika Knape of Sweden placed first in the platform events.

The so-called "wild water" canoe and kayak slalom events, staged in Augsburg, were on the Olympic program for the first time. They are spectacular events, but since they are difficult to arrange in a large city, they will probably not be on the program again. All four events were won by competitors from East Germany.

One of the most pleasing victories of the Games was scored by the eight oarsmen from New Zealand. This crew had previously defeated the finest crews in Europe for the European championship. (The crew members were all workers who had trained at night and on weekends. There was no money from their Federation for travel expenses. So the competitors themselves gathered the necessary funds to take them to Europe, where they won the championship over their highly rated competitors.) At the Olympic Games, this crew, true amateurs by all definitions, succeeded again in demonstrating their supremacy over the greatest oarsmen in the world. It was a very popular victory.

The U.S. swimmer Mark Spitz made Olympic history by winning an unprecedented 7 gold medals.

The yachting regatta, at Kiel, was probably the finest ever held. The U.S. competitor Harry Melges won in the Soling class. In two other classes, the Star and the Dragon, Australian boats won. The other yachting events were won by a variety of countries.

Basketball

The Soviet and the U.S. teams qualified for the final in basketball. The Soviet team was in front most of the time until the last few minutes of play, when the United States forged ahead by one point. The Russians, trying to call time-out as the final buzzer sounded, were given an additional few seconds. When that time was up, it seemed that the U.S. team had won. Spectators came onto the floor, and confusion reigned on the court. Then an Olympic official announced that there were still 3 seconds left to play. During the 3 seconds the Soviet team scored a basket and, presumably, won the game. There was a protest, however, by the U.S. team because it was claimed that the Olympic official had interfered by overruling the official scorer.

So, after winning every Olympic basketball game since 1936, the United States did not get the gold medal in 1972. (It refused to accept the second-place silver medal.) The U.S. Olympic Committee registered a protest, which has yet to be considered.

Kipchoge Keino of Kenya won a gold medal in the Steeplechase event.

Finland's Lasse Viren, leading all his competitors, goes on to win the 10,000-meter run.

Wolfgang Nordwig of East Germany clears the bar at 18 feet ½ inch in the pole vault competition.

Track and Field

United States athletes won many men's track and field events, including the 400-meter and 800-meter runs, the long jump, and the 110-meter hurdles. For the first time in 64 years a U.S. athlete, Frank Shorter, won the marathon.

However, this area of Olympic competition is no longer dominated by U.S. athletes. Valery Borzov of the Soviet Union won the 100- and 200-meter dashes. The track and field events also resulted in the welcome reappearance of Finnish athletes on the victory stand. Finland had been the master of distance racing for 25 years before World War II, and, for the first time since the war, Finland again displayed its ability. The Finnish athlete Pekka Vasala won the 1,500-meter, and Lasse Viren won the 5,000-meter and set a new world record in the 10,000-meter run.

The most important athletic event, the strenuous decathlon, was won by Nikolai Avilov of the Soviet Union, who set a new world record. The pole vault was won by Wolfgang Nordwig of East Germany. (The United States lost the pole vault for the first time, probably because of an argument over the type of pole to be used.)

Track and field for women was monopolized by the girls from East and West Germany. But in the difficult pentathlon, Mary Peters from Britain was the victor.

Gymnastics

In the basic sport of gymnastics, requiring great self-discipline, all the women's events were won by competitors from either East Germany or the Soviet Union. But the star of the gymnastic events was petite Olga Korbut, a 17-year-old girl from the Soviet Union. Her breathtaking agility captivated all spectators. Although Olga missed winning the all around title, she won gold medals in floor exercises and balance beam.

Gymnastics for men was monopolized by the Japanese, who generally outranked the rest of the field. They won four of the individual events and the team competition.

Other Competitions

In equestrian sport, the strenuous 3-day event was captured by Richard Mead of Britain, who led his team to victory. Equestrian sport is one of the few where women participate with men, and first and second places in the individual dressage were won by female competitors from West Germany and the Soviet Union. Graziano Mancinelli of Italy placed first in the individual jumping event. Both archery events, on the program for the first time, were won by competitors from the United States. Doreen Wilber won the women's championship, and John Williams the men's.

Russian gymnast Olga Korbut won two gold medals and the admiration of Olympic spectators.

Four new world records were set in the shooting competitions. They were set by John Writer of the United States, in the small-bore rifle, 3-position event; Ho Jun Li of North Korea, in the small-bore rifle, prone-position event; Lakov Zhelezniak of the Soviet Union, in the moving-target event; and Angelo Scalzone of Italy, in the trapshooting event.

The individual event of the modern pentathlon was won by András Balczo of Hungary. The Soviet Union won the team event.

The Japanese team won the men's volleyball tournament, defeating the East German team. But in an exciting game, the Japanese

WINTER GAMES—SAPPORO, JAPAN

Final Medal Standings

Nation	Gold	Silver	Bronze	Total
U.S.S.R.	8	5	3	16
East Germany	4	3	7	14
Switzerland	4	3	3	10
Netherlands	4	3	2	9
United States	3	2	3	8
West Germany	3	1	1	5
Norway	2	5	5	12
Italy	2	2	1	5
Austria	1	2	2	5
Sweden	1	1	2	4
Japan	1	1	1	3
Czechoslovakia	1	0	2	3
Spain	1	0	0	1
Poland	1	0	0	1
Finland	0	4	1	5
France	0	1	2	3
Canada	0	1	0	1

Owing to a first place tie, an extra gold medal was presented in place of a silver one.

lost the women's tournament to the Soviet Union.

In freestyle wrestling, U.S. wrestlers made an excellent record, winning three gold medals. Soviet wrestlers, however, won five golds. In Greco-Roman wrestling, not very popular in the United States, most of the medals went to Eastern European competitors from Bulgaria, Rumania, and the Soviet Union.

For the first time, U.S. lifters failed to score in weightlifting. Three of the events were won by Soviet lifters, and three by Bulgarians. The rest of the medals were widely scattered.

In boxing, the Cubans racked up three gold medals, one silver, and one bronze. Amateur boxing is no longer a college sport and has lost much of its popularity in the United States.

The Games of the XX Olympiad were truly exciting and can be considered a great success. This international gathering of athletes of all races, religions, and political affiliations holds out the promise of a happier and more peaceful future.

AVERY BRUNDAGE
President
International Olympic Committee

SUMMER GAMES—MUNICH, WEST GERMANY

Final Medal Standings

Nation	Gold	Silver	Bronze	Total
U.S.S.R.	50	27	22	99
United States	33	31	30	94
East Germany	20	23	23	66
West Germany	13	11	16	40
Japan	13	8	8	29
Australia	8	7	2	17
Poland	7	5	9	21
Hungary	6	13	16	35
Bulgaria	6	10	5	21
Italy	5	3	10	18
Sweden	4	6	6	16
Britain	4	5	9	18
Rumania	3	6	7	16
Cuba	3	1	4	8
Finland	3	1	4	8
Netherlands	3	1	1	5
France	2	4	7	13
Czechoslovakia	2	4	2	8
Kenya	2	3	4	9
Yugoslavia	2	1	2	5
Norway	2	1	1	4
North Korea	1	1	3	5
New Zealand	1	1	1	3
Uganda	1	1	0	2
Denmark	1	0	0	1
Switzerland	0	3	0	3
Canada	0	2	3	5
Belgium	0	2	1	3
Iran	0	2	1	3
Greece	0	2	0	2
Mongolia	0	2	0	2
Austria	0	1	2	3
Colombia	0	1	2	3
Argentina	0	1	0	1
Lebanon	0	1	0	1
Mexico	0	1	0	1
Pakistan	0	1	0	1
South Korea	0	1	0	1
Tunisia	0	1	0	1
Turkey	0	1	0	1
Brazil	0	0	2	2
Ethiopia	0	0	2	2
Spain	0	0	2	2
Ghana	0	0	1	1
India	0	0	1	1
Jamaica	0	0	1	1
Niger	0	0	1	1
Nigeria	0	0	1	1

Rowers straining at the oars: Claudia Gotting, Munich. Age 7.

PAINTBOX OLYMPICS

For months before the Olympic Summer Games began, the city of Munich, Germany, was all bustle and building. Even schoolchildren played a part in the preparations. The city held an art contest, called the Paintbox Olympics, inviting German children to enter paintings showing what they thought the Games would be like. Nearly 6,000 entries were judged by age group, and winners were awarded gold, silver, and bronze medals.

Basketball: Rudolf Piesker, Munich. Age 13.

Gymnastics: Fred Brefka, Bremen. Age 14.

1972 OLYMPIC GOLD MEDAL WINNERS

WINTER GAMES—SAPPORO, JAPAN

SPORT	EVENT	WINNER
Biathlon	Individual	Magnar Solberg, Norway
	Relay	U.S.S.R.
Bobsledding	Two Man	West Germany
	Four Man	Switzerland
Hockey	Team	U.S.S.R.
Luge	Men's Singles	Wolfgang Scheidel, East Germany
	Men's Doubles	Italy and East Germany (tie)
	Women's Singles	Anna Marie Muller, East Germany
Skiing, Alpine	Men's Downhill	Bernhard Russi, Switzerland
	Men's Giant Slalom	Gustavo Thoeni, Italy
	Men's Special Slalom	Francisco Fernández Ochoa, Spain
	Women's Downhill	Marie Thérèse Nadig, Switzerland
	Women's Giant Slalom	Marie Thérèse Nadig, Switzerland
	Women's Special Slalom	Barbara Cochran, U.S.
Skiing, Nordic	Men's 15-kilometer Cross-Country	Sven-Ake Lundback, Sweden
	Men's 30-kilometer Cross-Country	Vyacheslav Vedenin, U.S.S.R.
	Men's 50-kilometer Cross-Country	Paal Tyldum, Norway
	Men's 40-kilometer Cross-Country Relay	U.S.S.R.
	Men's Combined	Ulrich Wehling, East Germany
	Men's 70-meter Jump	Yukio Kasaya, Japan
	Men's 90-meter Jump	Wojciech Fortuna, Poland
	Women's 5-kilometer Cross-Country	Galina Koulakova, U.S.S.R.
	Women's 10-kilometer Cross-Country	Galina Koulakova, U.S.S.R.
	Women's 15-kilometer Cross-Country Relay	U.S.S.R.
Figure Skating	Men's Singles	Ondrej Nepela, Czechoslovakia
	Women's Singles	Beatrix Schuba, Austria
	Pairs	Irina Rodnina/Aleksei Ulanov, U.S.S.R.
Speed Skating	Men's 500-meter	Erhard Keller, West Germany
	Men's 1,500-meter	Ard Schenk, Netherlands
	Men's 5,000-meter	Ard Schenk, Netherlands
	Men's 10,000-meter	Ard Schenk, Netherlands
	Women's 500-meter	Anne Henning, U.S.
	Women's 1,000-meter	Monika Pflug, West Germany
	Women's 1,500-meter	Dianne Holum, U.S.
	Women's 3,000-meter	Stien Baas-Kaiser, Netherlands

SUMMER GAMES—MUNICH, WEST GERMANY

SPORT	EVENT	WINNER
Archery	Men	John Williams, U.S.
	Women	Doreen Wilber, U.S.
Basketball	Team	U.S.S.R.
Boxing	Light Flyweight	György Gedo, Hungary
	Flyweight	Gheorghi Kostadinov, Bulgaria
	Bantamweight	Orlando Martínez, Cuba
	Featherweight	Boris Kousnetsov, U.S.S.R.
	Lightweight	Jan Szczepanski, Poland
	Light Welterweight	Ray Seales, U.S.
	Welterweight	Emilio Correa, Cuba
	Light Middleweight	Dieter Kottysch, West Germany
	Middleweight	Vyacheslav Lemechev, U.S.S.R.
	Light Heavyweight	Mate Parlov, Yugoslavia
	Heavyweight	Teófilo Stevenson, Cuba
Canoeing, Men	Canadian Singles	Ivan Patzaichin, Rumania

SUMMER GAMES—MUNICH, WEST GERMANY (CONT.)

SPORT	EVENT	WINNER
Canoeing, Men (cont.)	Canadian Slalom	Reinhard Eiben, East Germany
	Canadian Doubles Slalom	East Germany
	Canadian Pairs	U.S.S.R.
	Kayak Singles	Aleksandr Shaparenko, U.S.S.R.
	Kayak Slalom	Siegbert Horn, East Germany
	Kayak Pairs	U.S.S.R.
	Kayak Fours	U.S.S.R.
Canoeing, Women	Kayak Singles	Yulia Ryabchinskaya, U.S.S.R.
	Kayak Slalom	Angelika Bahmann, East Germany
	Kayak Pairs	U.S.S.R.
Cycling	1,000-meter Time Trial	Niels Fredborg, Denmark
	Sprint	Daniel Morelon, France
	Individual Pursuit	Knut Knudsen, Norway
	Road Race	Hennie Kuiper, Netherlands
	Team Pursuit	West Germany
	Tandem	U.S.S.R.
	100-kilometer Time Trial	U.S.S.R.
Equestrian	Individual 3-day Event	Richard Meade, Britain
	Team 3-day Event	Britain
	Individual Dressage	Liselott Linsenhoff, West Germany
	Dressage Grand Prix	U.S.S.R.
	Individual Jumping	Graziano Mancinelli, Italy
	Team Jumping	West Germany
Fencing, Men	Foil	Witold Woyda, Poland
	Team Foil	Poland
	Saber	Viktor Sidiak, U.S.S.R.
	Team Saber	Italy
	Epee	Csaba Fenyvesi, Hungary
	Team Epee	Hungary
Fencing, Women	Foil	Antonella Lonzo Rogno, Italy
	Team Foil	U.S.S.R.
Field Hockey	Team	West Germany
Gymnastics, Men	Team	Japan
	All Around	Swao Kato, Japan
	Floor Exercises	Nikolai Andrianov, U.S.S.R.
	Side Horse	Viktor Klimenko, U.S.S.R.
	Rings	Akinori Nakayama, Japan
	Long Horse	Klaus Koeste, East Germany
	Parallel Bars	Swao Kato, Japan
	Horizontal Bar	Mitsuo Tsukahara, Japan
Gymnastics, Women	Team	U.S.S.R.
	All Around	Ludmila Tourischeva, U.S.S.R.
	Long Horse	Karin Janz, East Germany
	Uneven Bars	Karin Janz, East Germany
	Balance Beam	Olga Korbut, U.S.S.R.
	Floor Exercises	Olga Korbut, U.S.S.R.
Handball	Team	Yugoslavia
Judo	Lightweight	Takao Kawaguchi, Japan
	Welterweight	Toyokazu Nomura, Japan
	Middleweight	Shinobu Sekine, Japan
	Light Heavyweight	Shota Chochoshvili, U.S.S.R.
	Heavyweight	Willem Ruska, Netherlands
	Open Class	Willem Ruska, Netherlands
Pentathlon, Modern	Individual	András Balczo, Hungary
	Team	U.S.S.R.
Rowing	Singles Sculls	Yuri Malishev, U.S.S.R.
	Double Sculls	U.S.S.R.
	Coxless Pair	East Germany
	Coxed Pair	East Germany
	Coxless Fours	East Germany

SUMMER GAMES—MUNICH, WEST GERMANY (CONT.)

SPORT	EVENT	WINNER
Rowing (cont.)	Coxed Fours	West Germany
	Eights	New Zealand
Shooting	Free Rifle	Lones Wigger, U.S.
	Small-Bore Rifle, 3 positions	John Writer, U.S.
	Small-Bore Rifle, prone	Ho Jun Li, North Korea
	Free Pistol	Ragnar Skanaker, Sweden
	Rapid-Fire Pistol	Józef Zapedzki, Poland
	Moving Target	Lakov Zhelezniak, U.S.S.R.
	Trap	Angelo Scalzone, Italy
	Skeet	Konrad Wirnhier, West Germany
Soccer	Team	Poland
Swimming, Men	100-meter Freestyle	Mark Spitz, U.S.
	200-meter Freestyle	Mark Spitz, U.S.
	400-meter Freestyle	Brad Cooper, Australia
	1,500-meter Freestyle	Mike Burton, U.S.
	100-meter Breaststroke	Nobutaka Taguchi, Japan
	200-meter Breaststroke	John Hencken, U.S.
	100-meter Butterfly	Mark Spitz, U.S.
	200-meter Butterfly	Mark Spitz, U.S.
	100-meter Backstroke	Roland Matthes, East Germany
	200-meter Backstroke	Roland Matthes, East Germany
	200-meter Individual Medley	Gunnar Larsson, Sweden
	400-meter Individual Medley	Gunnar Larsson, Sweden
	400-meter Freestyle Relay	U.S.
	800-meter Freestyle Relay	U.S.
	400-meter Medley	U.S.
	Springboard Dive	Vladimir Vasin, U.S.S.R.
	Platform Dive	Klaus Dibiasi, Italy
Swimming, Women	100-meter Freestyle	Sandra Neilson, U.S.
	200-meter Freestyle	Shane Gould, Australia
	400-meter Freestyle	Shane Gould, Australia
	800-meter Freestyle	Keena Rothhammer, U.S.
	100-meter Breaststroke	Cathy Carr, U.S.
	200-meter Breaststroke	Beverly Whitfield, Australia
	100-meter Butterfly	Mayumi Aoki, Japan
	200-meter Butterfly	Karen Moe, U.S.
	100-meter Backstroke	Melissa Belote, U.S.
	200-meter Backstroke	Melissa Belote, U.S.
	200-meter Medley	Shane Gould, Australia
	400-meter Medley	Gail Neall, Australia
	400-meter Medley Relay	U.S.
	400-meter Freestyle Relay	U.S.
	Springboard Dive	Micki King, U.S.
	Platform Dive	Ulrika Knape, Sweden
Track and Field, Men	100-meter Dash	Valery Borzov, U.S.S.R.
	200-meter Dash	Valery Borzov, U.S.S.R.
	400-meter Relay	U.S.
	400-meter Run	Vince Matthews, U.S.
	800-meter Run	Dave Wottle, U.S.
	1,500-meter Run	Pekka Vasala, Finland
	1,600-meter Relay	Kenya
	5,000-meter Run	Lasse Viren, Finland
	10,000-meter Run	Lasse Viren, Finland
	Marathon	Frank Shorter, U.S.
	110-meter Hurdles	Rod Milburn, U.S.
	400-meter Hurdles	John Akii-Bua, Uganda
	3,000-meter Steeplechase	Kipchoge Keino, Kenya
	High Jump	Yuri Tarmak, U.S.S.R.
	Long Jump	Randy Williams, U.S.
	Triple Jump	Viktor Saneyev, U.S.S.R.

SUMMER GAMES—MUNICH, WEST GERMANY (CONT.)

SPORT	EVENT	WINNER
Track and Field, Men (cont.)	Pole Vault	Wolfgang Nordwig, East Germany
	Shot Put	Wladyslaw Komar, Poland
	Discus Throw	Ludwik Danek, Czechoslovakia
	Hammer Throw	Anatoly Bondarchuk, U.S.S.R.
	Javelin Throw	Klaus Wolfermann, West Germany
	Decathlon	Nikolai Avilov, U.S.S.R.
	20-kilometer Walk	Peter Frenkel, East Germany
	50-kilometer Walk	Bernd Kannenberg, West Germany
Track and Field, Women	100-meter Dash	Renete Stecher, East Germany
	200-meter Dash	Renete Stecher, East Germany
	400-meter Relay	West Germany
	400-meter Dash	Monika Zehrt, East Germany
	800-meter Run	Hildegard Falck, West Germany
	1,500-meter Run	Ludmila Bragina, U.S.S.R.
	1,600-meter Relay	East Germany
	100-meter Hurdles	Annelie Ehrhardt, East Germany
	High Jump	Ulrika Meyfarth, West Germany
	Long Jump	Heidemarie Rosendahl, West Germany
	Shot Put	Nadezhda Chizhova, U.S.S.R.
	Discus Throw	Faina Melnik, U.S.S.R.
	Javelin	Ruth Fuchs, East Germany
	Pentathlon	Mary Peters, Britain
Volleyball	Men	Japan
	Women	U.S.S.R.
Water Polo	Team	U.S.S.R.
Weightlifting	Flyweight	Zygmunt Smalcerz, Poland
	Bantamweight	Imre Földi, Hungary
	Featherweight	Norai Nurikian, Bulgaria
	Lightweight	Mukharbi Kirzhinov, U.S.S.R.
	Middleweight	Yordan Bikov, Bulgaria
	Light Heavyweight	Leif Jenssen, Norway
	Middle Heavyweight	Andon Nikolv, Bulgaria
	Heavyweight	Yan Talts, U.S.S.R.
	Super Heavyweight	Vasily Alekseyev, U.S.S.R.
Wrestling, Freestyle	Paperweight	Roman Dmitriev, U.S.S.R.
	Flyweight	Kymomi Kato, Japan
	Bantamweight	Hideaki Yanagida, Japan
	Featherweight	Zaga Abdulbekov, U.S.S.R.
	Lightweight	Dan Gable, U.S.
	Welterweight	Wayne Wells, U.S.
	Middleweight	Levan Tediashvili, U.S.S.R.
	Light Heavyweight	Ben Peterson, U.S.
	Heavyweight	Ivan Yarygin, U.S.S.R.
	Super Heavyweight	Aleksandr Medved, U.S.S.R.
Wrestling, Greco-Roman	Paperweight	Gheorghe Berceanu, Rumania
	Flyweight	Petar Kirov, Bulgaria
	Bantamweight	Rustem Kazakov, U.S.S.R.
	Featherweight	Gheorghi Markov, Bulgaria
	Lightweight	Shamil Khisamutdinov, U.S.S.R.
	Welterweight	Vitezslav Macha, Czechoslovakia
	Middleweight	Csaba Hegebus, Hungary
	Light Heavyweight	Valery Rezantsev, U.S.S.R.
	Heavyweight	Nicolai Martinescu, Rumania
	Super Heavyweight	Anatoly Roshin, U.S.S.R.
Yachting	Soling	Harry Melges, U.S.
	Dragon	John Bruce Cueno, Australia
	Star	David Forbes, Australia
	Flying Dutchman	Rodney Pattison, Britain
	Tempest	Valentin Mankin, U.S.S.R.
	Finn	Serge Maury, France

AUTO RACING

WORLD DRIVING FORMULA I CHAMPIONSHIPS

Grand Prix	Driver
Argentina	Jackie Stewart, Scotland
South Africa	Denis Hulme, New Zealand
Spain	Emerson Fittipaldi, Brazil
Belgium	Emerson Fittipaldi
Monaco	Jean-Pierre Beltoise, France
France	Jackie Stewart
Great Britain	Emerson Fittipaldi
Germany	Jacky Ickx, Belgium
Austria	Emerson Fittipaldi
Italy	Emerson Fittipaldi
Canada	Jackie Stewart
United States	Jackie Stewart

World Driving Champion: Emerson Fittipaldi

OTHER CHAMPIONSHIPS

NASCAR Grand National Champion: Richard Petty, United States

SCCA Canadian-American Challenge Cup: George Follmer, United States

USAC Champion: Joe Leonard, United States

Indianapolis 500: Mark Donohue, United States

Emerson Fittipaldi is triumphant after winning the British Grand Prix. World driving champion of 1972, Fittipaldi won 5 Formula I races.

Fittipaldi rounds a curve on the wet and slippery track at the Monaco Grand Prix.

Cincinnati's Johnny Bench tags Oakland runner to end 5th World Series game.

BASEBALL

The Oakland Athletics were uniquely dressed in Kelly green, Fort Knox gold, and wedding gown white, and they wore moustaches and long hair. But they also were capable of playing baseball. They proved it by finishing with a five and a half game margin in the American League West; by defeating the Detroit Tigers in the playoff for the league title; and by conquering the powerful Cincinnati Reds in the World Series.

Pitching, supplied by the starting hurlers Jim "Catfish" Hunter, Ken Holtzman, and John "Blue Moon" Odom, with relief aid from Rollie Fingers and Vida Blue, was the dominant factor through the long summer, the playoff, and the series.

For the first time since the leagues were divided into six-club divisions, the two post-season competitions were decided in exciting, five-game sets. The Athletics outlasted the

Steve Carlton of the Philadelphia Phillies in action against the New York Mets. Carlton, a southpaw, won the 1972 Cy Young award for being the best pitcher in the National League.

Detroit Tigers, and the Reds eliminated the Pittsburgh Pirates, who had won the 1971 World Series over Baltimore. (The Orioles, after three consecutive American League pennants, fell into third place in the Eastern division.)

1972 WORLD SERIES RESULTS

		R	H	E	Winning/Losing Pitcher
1	Oakland	3	4	0	Holtzman
	Cincinnati	2	7	0	Nolan
2	Oakland	2	9	1	Hunter
	Cincinnati	1	6	0	Grimsley
3	Cincinnati	1	4	2	Billingham
	Oakland	0	3	2	Odom
4	Oakland	3	10	1	Fingers
	Cincinnati	2	7	1	Carroll
5	Cincinnati	5	8	0	Grimsley
	Oakland	4	7	2	Fingers
6	Cincinnati	8	10	0	Grimsley
	Oakland	1	7	1	Blue
7	Oakland	3	6	1	Hunter
	Cincinnati	2	4	2	Borbon

The World Series provided similar suspense. The heavily favored Reds lost the first two games to the surprising Athletics. But they fought back for a 3–3 deadlock before Oakland won the decisive seventh engagement. Six of the seven games were decided by one run, and the improbable hero was a part-time catcher, Gene Tenace.

Tenace, who had a .225 batting average and hit only five home runs during the regular season, walloped four World Series homers. In doing so he tied a record shared by such celebrated sluggers of the past as Babe Ruth, Lou Gehrig, Duke Snider, and Hank Bauer. The pitching star for the Athletics was the reliever, Fingers, who appeared in six games and throttled the Reds on five occasions.

Rod Carew of the Minnesota Twins won the American League batting title for the second time, with a .318 average; and Dick Allen, transplanted from the Dodgers to the Chicago White Sox, was the home run leader with 37. Luis Tiant of the Red Sox had the lowest earned run average (1.91) among pitchers, to go with a 15–6 won-lost mark.

In the National League, Billy Williams of the Chicago Cubs paced the batsmen with .333. Johnny Bench of Cincinnati led the home run department with 40, and Steve Carlton of the Phillies paced the pitchers with a 1.97 ERA and a won-lost log of 27–10.

FINAL MAJOR LEAGUE STANDINGS

AMERICAN LEAGUE

Eastern Division

	W	L	Pct.	GB
Detroit	86	70	.551	
Boston	85	70	.548	½
Baltimore	80	74	.519	5
New York	79	76	.510	6½
Cleveland	72	84	.462	14
Milwaukee	65	91	.417	21

Western Division

	W	L	Pct.	GB
* Oakland	93	62	.600	
Chicago	87	67	.565	5½
Minnesota	77	77	.500	15½
Kansas City	76	78	.494	16½
California	75	80	.484	18
Texas	54	100	.351	38½

NATIONAL LEAGUE

Eastern Division

	W	L	Pct.	GB
Pittsburgh	96	59	.619	
Chicago	85	70	.548	11
New York	83	73	.532	13½
St. Louis	75	81	.481	21½
Montreal	70	86	.449	26½
Philadelphia	59	97	.378	37½

Western Division

	W	L	Pct.	GB
* Cincinnati	95	59	.617	
Houston	84	69	.549	10½
Los Angeles	85	70	.548	10½
Atlanta	70	84	.455	25
San Francisco	69	86	.445	26½
San Diego	58	95	.379	36½

* Pennant winners

MAJOR LEAGUE LEADERS

BATTING
(400 or more at bats)

AMERICAN LEAGUE

	G	AB	H	Pct.
Carew, Minnesota	142	535	170	.318
Piniella, Kansas City	151	574	179	.312
D. Allen, Chicago	148	506	156	.308
C. May, Chicago	148	523	161	.308
Rudi, Oakland	147	593	181	.305
Scheinblum, Kansas City	134	450	135	.300
Mayberry, Kansas City	149	503	150	.298
Fisk, Boston	131	457	134	.293
Otis, Kansas City	143	540	158	.293
Murcer, New York	153	585	171	.292

NATIONAL LEAGUE

	G	AB	H	Pct.
B. Williams, Chicago	150	574	191	.333
Garr, Atlanta	134	554	180	.325
Baker, Atlanta	127	446	143	.321
Cedeno, Houston	139	559	179	.320
Oliver, Pittsburgh	140	565	176	.312
Watson, Houston	147	549	171	.311
Brock, St. Louis	153	622	193	.310
Rose, Cincinnati	154	645	198	.307
Simmons, St. Louis	152	594	181	.305
Santo, Chicago	133	464	140	.302

PITCHING

	W	L	ERA
Tiant, Boston, AL	15	6	1.91
G. Perry, Cleveland, AL	24	16	1.92
Carlton, Philadelphia, NL	27	10	1.97
Nolan, Cincinnati, NL	15	5	1.99
Hunter, Oakland, AL	21	7	2.03
Palmer, Baltimore, AL	21	10	2.07
N. Ryan, California, AL	19	6	2.28
Lolich, Detroit, AL	22	14	2.50
Wood, Chicago, AL	24	17	2.53

HOME RUNS

	HR
Bench, Cincinnati, NL	40
Colbert, San Diego, NL	38
D. Allen, Chicago, AL	37
B. Williams, Chicago, NL	37
H. Aaron, Atlanta, NL	34
Stargell, Pittsburgh, NL	33
Murcer, New York, AL	33
Killebrew, Minnesota, AL	26
Epstein, Oakland, AL	26

LITTLE LEAGUE BASEBALL

A Latin-American player is out at the plate in a game between Puerto Rican and U.S. teams.

Backed by power hitting and strong pitching, Taiwan's team won the 26th annual Little League World Series. It was the second straight world championship for the Asian youngsters, who represent the Nationalist Republic of China.

International Little League competition in 1972 involved some 6,000 leagues in 31 countries. From these teams, the top eight were selected for the series playoffs held in Williamsport, Pennsylvania, in August. In the final game, Taiwan was pitted against an American team from Hammond, Indiana.

Taiwan blasted Hammond 6 to 0, with slugger Lin Hsing-jui contributing three hits, including a home run. Taiwan's pitcher Chen Chih-shun hurled a four-hit shutout.

The 1972 Little League Champions of the World: the team from Taiwan.

Wilt Chamberlain of the Lakers in action in final NBA championship game.

BASKETBALL

It was a year in which the professional Los Angeles Lakers, perennially second-place finishers, finally reached the top. And in collegiate competition the UCLA Bruins added a sixth consecutive championship.

During the previous decade, the Los Angeles Lakers had been the runner-up team seven times. Their triumph in the NBA playoffs was a soul-satisfying achievement for 35-year-old Wilt Chamberlain, 34-year-old Jerry West, and for the team's first-year coach, Bill Sharman, who had left the Utah Stars after leading them to the ABA title.

En route to a 69–13 record during the regular season, the Lakers broke seven major team marks. The team records included most victories in a season (69); longest winning streak in professional sports history (33); largest margin in the standings (63 points over Golden State); and all-time best winning percentage (.841). Chamberlain and West led in three of the five vital individual statistical categories. Chamberlain led in field-goal percentage and rebounds, West in assists.

In the playoffs, the Lakers defeated the Chicago Bulls, Milwaukee Bucks, and New York Knicks. Confronted by the defending champion Bucks with their great young center, Kareem Abdul-Jabbar, the Lakers lost the first game, then won four of the succeeding five. In the decisive sixth engagement, Milwaukee led by 10 points in the final period and still lost, as Chamberlain clearly outplayed Jabbar. Against the Knicks in the championship series, the Lakers were stunned by the effective New York offense in the opener, then swept the next four contests.

In the Western division of the ABA, the Indiana Pacers trailed the Utah Stars in the season standings. But they came to life in the playoffs, and swept through the Denver Rockets, the Utah Stars, and the New York Nets. It was the second ABA crown for Indiana in three years.

UCLA's Bill Walton leaps for ball in NCAA championship game against Florida State. UCLA won.

In providing their coach, John Wooden, with his eighth NCAA title in nine years, UCLA went undefeated through 30 games, extending its two-season streak to 45 consecutive triumphs. The outstanding performers were a 6-foot 11-inch sophomore, Bill Walton, and the lone senior on the squad, Henry Bibby. In the NCAA tournament final, UCLA defeated Florida State University, 81–76.

COLLEGE BASKETBALL

Conference	Winner
Atlantic Coast	North Carolina
Big Eight	Kansas State
Big Ten	Minnesota
Ivy League	Pennsylvania
Mid-American	Toledo
Missouri Valley	Louisville
Pacific Eight	UCLA
Southeastern	Kentucky
Southern	East Carolina
Southwest	Texas
West Coast Athletic	San Francisco
Western Athletic	Brigham Young
Yankee	Rhode Island

NCAA: UCLA

National Invitation Tournament: Maryland

FINAL NBA STANDINGS

EASTERN CONFERENCE

Atlantic Division

Team	W	L	Pct.
Boston	56	26	.683
New York	48	34	.585
Philadelphia	30	52	.366
Buffalo	22	60	.268

Central Division

	W	L	Pct.
Baltimore	38	44	.463
Atlanta	36	46	.439
Cincinnati	30	52	.366
Cleveland	23	59	.280

WESTERN CONFERENCE

Midwest Division

	W	L	Pct.
Milwaukee	63	19	.768
Chicago	57	25	.695
Phoenix	49	33	.598
Detroit	26	56	.317

Pacific Division

	W	L	Pct.
Los Angeles	69	13	.841
Golden State	51	31	.622
Seattle	47	35	.573
Houston	34	48	.415
Portland	18	64	.220

NBA Championship: Los Angeles

FINAL ABA STANDINGS

East Division

Team	W	L	Pct.
Kentucky	68	16	.810
Virginia	45	39	.536
New York	44	40	.524
Floridians	36	48	.429
Carolina	35	49	.417
Pittsburgh	25	59	.298

West Division

	W	L	Pct.
Utah	60	24	.714
Indiana	47	37	.560
Dallas	42	42	.500
Denver	34	50	.405
Memphis	26	58	.310

ABA Championship: Indiana

BOWLING

AMERICAN BOWLING CONGRESS CHAMPIONS

Classic Division

Singles	Teata Semiz
Doubles	Carmen Salvino/Barry Asher
Team	Basch Advertising (New York, N.Y.)
All Events	Teata Semiz

Regular Division

Singles	Bill Pointer
Doubles	Jerry Nutt/Bill Stanfield
Team	Hamm's Beer (Minneapolis, Minn.)
All Events	Mac Lowry

WOMEN'S INTERNATIONAL BOWLING CHAMPIONS

Open Division

Singles	D. D. Jacobson
Doubles	Judy Roberts/Betty Remmick
Team	Angeltown Creations (Placentia, Calif.)
All Events	Millie Martorella

BOXING

WORLD BOXING CHAMPIONS

Division	Champion
Heavyweight	Joe Frazier, U.S.
Light Heavyweight	Bob Foster, U.S.
Middleweight	Carlos Monzon, Argentina
Jr. Middleweight	Koichi Wajima, Japan
Welterweight	José Napoles, Mexico
Jr. Welterweight (disputed)	Bruno Arcari, Italy Alfonso Frazier, Panama
Lightweight (disputed)	Chango Carmona, Mexico Roberto Duran, Panama
Jr. Lightweight (disputed)	Ricardo Arrendondo, Mexico Ben Villaflor, Philippines
Featherweight (disputed)	Clemente Sánchez, Mexico Ernesto Marcel, Panama
Bantamweight	Enrique Pindar, Panama
Flyweight (disputed)	Venice Borkorsor, Thailand Masao Ohba, Japan

Panama's Roberto Duran (dark trunks) pins Scotland's Ken Buchanan to ropes in 11th round of world lightweight championship fight. Duran won the bout.

Best-in-show: Adamant James (*left*) at Westminster, and Maya Dancer at International.

DOG SHOWS

Poodles topped the list in total number of entries in major U.S. dog shows in 1972.

WESTMINSTER KENNEL CLUB

Best in Show	Ch. Chinoe's Adamant James
Hound	Ch. Reveille Re-Up, Basenji
Nonsporting	Ch. Tally Ho Tiffany, miniature poodle
Sporting	Ch. Chinoe's Adamant James, English springer spaniel
Terrier	Ch. Glamoor Gang Buster, Skye Terrier
Toy	Ch. Joanne-Chen's Maya Dancer, Maltese
Working	Ch. Nebriowa Miss Bobbi Sox, Pembroke Welsh corgi

INTERNATIONAL KENNEL CLUB

Best in Show	Ch. Joanne-Chen's Maya Dancer
Hound	Basil Rathbone II, basset
Nonsporting	Ch. Acadia Xaari, standard poodle
Sporting	Ch. Sagamore Toccoa, ascob cocker spaniel
Terrier	Ch. Urston Pimmoney E. Pedlar, West Highland white
Toy	Ch. Joanne-Chen's Maya Dancer, Maltese
Working	Ch. Kydor Cresta, Pembroke Welsh corgi

FOOTBALL

The National Football League's 1972 season was marked by several noteworthy achievements. The Miami Dolphins, winners of the Eastern Division title in the American Conference, went undefeated in the regular 14-game season. It was only the third time in the NFL's 52-year history that a team had accomplished this feat. The Chicago Bears were undefeated in 1934 and again in 1942. However, the Bears played only 13- and 11-game seasons respectively.

In the same conference, the Pittsburgh Steelers finished at the head of the Central Division—their first division title in four decades of existence. The other playoff spots in the American Conference were filled by the Oakland Raiders, victors in the Western Division, and the Cleveland Browns, runner-up to Pittsburgh.

In the National Conference, the Washington Redskins won the Eastern Division title with an 11–3 record. The Redskins topped the Dallas Cowboys, 1972 Super Bowl champions, but both teams qualified for the playoffs. For Washington, it was the first division championship in 30 years.

The Green Bay Packers, once a powerhouse in the NFL, recaptured some of their old glory. They won the Central Division title, dethroning the reigning Minnesota Vikings, who had held it for 4 years. The Western Division crown was captured by the San Francisco 49ers for the third straight year.

A perfect 11–0 record earned the University of Southern California the coveted MacArthur Bowl—awarded to the nation's best college football team. Nebraska, 1971's number one team, fell from the top spot. But it produced the two best individual players of the year: running back Johnny Rodgers, who won the Heisman Trophy, and Rich Glover, who received the Outland Trophy as the defensive star of the year.

Southern California's halfback Anthony Davis gave the season's most electrifying performance by scoring six touchdowns against Notre Dame—including runs of 96 and 97 yards. In postseason bowl games, USC routed Ohio State 42–17 in the Rose Bowl, while Nebraska smashed Notre Dame 40–6 in the Orange Bowl.

New York Jets running back John Riggins is stopped by Miami Dolphins "No-Name" defense led by middle linebacker Nick Buoniconti (Number 85).

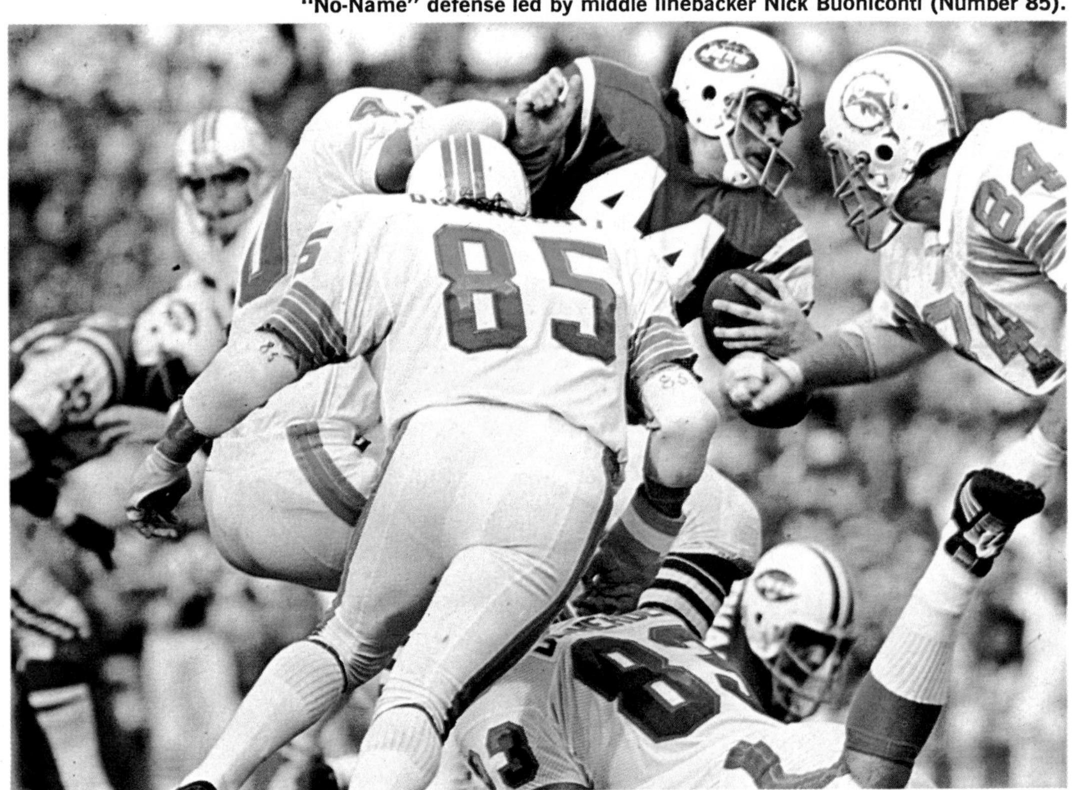

FINAL NFL STANDINGS

AMERICAN CONFERENCE

Eastern Division

Team	W	L	T	Pct.	PF	PA
Miami	14	0	0	1.000	385	171
N.Y. Jets	7	7	0	.500	367	324
Baltimore	5	9	0	.357	235	252
Buffalo	4	9	1	.321	257	377
New England	3	11	0	.214	192	446

Central Division

	W	L	T	Pct.	PF	PA
Pittsburgh	11	3	0	.786	343	175
Cleveland	10	4	0	.714	268	249
Cincinnati	8	6	0	.571	299	229
Houston	1	13	0	.071	164	380

Western Division

	W	L	T	Pct.	PF	PA
Oakland	10	3	1	.750	365	248
Kansas City	8	6	0	.571	287	254
Denver	5	9	0	.357	325	350
San Diego	4	9	1	.321	264	344

Conference Champion: Miami

NATIONAL CONFERENCE

Eastern Division

Team	W	L	T	Pct.	PF	PA
Washington	11	3	0	.786	336	218
Dallas	10	4	0	.714	319	240
N.Y. Giants	8	6	0	.571	331	247
St. Louis	4	9	1	.321	193	303
Philadelphia	2	11	1	.179	145	352

Central Division

	W	L	T	Pct.	PF	PA
Green Bay	10	4	0	.714	304	226
Detroit	8	5	1	.607	339	290
Minnesota	7	7	0	.500	301	252
Chicago	4	9	1	.321	225	275

Western Division

	W	L	T	Pct.	PF	PA
San Francisco	8	5	1	.607	353	249
Atlanta	7	7	0	.500	269	274
Los Angeles	6	7	1	.464	291	286
New Orleans	2	11	1	.179	215	361

Conference Champion: Washington

1973 Super Bowl Winner: Miami

COLLEGE FOOTBALL

Conference	Winner
Atlantic Coast	North Carolina
Big Eight	Oklahoma
Big Ten	Ohio State
Ivy League	Dartmouth
Mid-American	Kent State
Pacific Eight	Southern California
Southeastern	Alabama
Southern	East Carolina
Southwest	Texas
Western Athletic	Arizona State
Yankee	Massachusetts

Heisman Trophy: Johnny Rodgers, Nebraska

Heisman Trophy winner Johnny Rodgers, of the University of Nebraska, with his award.

Tailback Anthony Davis of the University of Southern California plunges through Notre Dame defenders to score a touchdown. USC won the game.

Larry Brown (*center*), Washington Redskins running back, fumbles the ball in a game with the Philadelphia Eagles. Ball was recovered by the Eagles.

GOLF

Jack Nicklaus failed to achieve the grand slam of golf in 1972, which means that the fabulous Ohio shotmaker is simply colossal, but not superman. In the spring, Nicklaus captured his fourth Masters title, with a three-stroke margin. And in June he conquered the tricky Pebble Beach course to gain his third U.S. Open title, likewise with an advantage of three shots.

That left the British Open and the PGA tournaments on the road to what an Englishman called "the impossible quadrilateral." The quest became a fruitless chase on the sand hills of Muirfield, Scotland, when Lee Trevino, with an unbelievable putting touch, finished one stroke ahead of Nicklaus. That made an anticlimax of the PGA event, which was won by Gary Player, as Nicklaus, troubled by a sore thumb, finished six strokes back.

Along the route, Nicklaus tied the late Bobby Jones, with 13 career victories in the world's major tournaments. He also accumulated over $320,000 in prize money toward the end of the year. This eclipsed his own high mark of $244,490 for a single campaign, established in 1971.

In women's competition, Mrs. Susie Maxwell Berning won the U.S. Women's Open championship, held at Mamaroneck, New York. Mrs. Berning captured the title by a narrow one-stroke margin over runners-up Kathy Ahern, Pam Barnett, and Judy Rankin. It was the second championship for Mrs. Berning, who had previously won it in 1968.

Jack Nicklaus in the 1972 Masters Tournament, which he won by a margin of three strokes.

PROFESSIONAL	
	Individual
Masters	Jack Nicklaus, U.S.
U.S. Open	Jack Nicklaus
Canadian Open	Gay Brewer, U.S.
British Open	Lee Trevino, U.S.
PGA	Gary Player, South Africa
World Series of Golf	Gary Player
U.S. Women's Open	Susie Maxwell Berning, U.S.
Ladies PGA	Kathy Ahern, U.S.
	Team
World Cup	Taiwan
AMATEUR	
	Individual
U.S. Amateur	Vinny Giles, U.S.
U.S. Women's Amateur	Mary Budke, U.S.
British Amateur	Trevor Homer, Britain
	Team
Curtis Cup	United States

HOCKEY

Bobby Orr skated with a damaged knee from midseason until the end of the playoff. But that didn't prevent him from collecting most of the National Hockey League's major individual trophies as he led the Boston Bruins to a Stanley Cup victory.

Orr captured the Norris Trophy as the league's best defenseman, the Hart Trophy as the most valuable player (MVP) during the regular season, and the Conn Smythe Trophy as the MVP in the playoffs.

FINAL NHL STANDINGS

East Division

Team	W	L	T	Pts.
Boston	54	13	11	119
New York	48	17	13	109
Montreal	46	16	16	108
Toronto	33	31	14	80
Detroit	33	35	10	76
Buffalo	16	43	19	51
Vancouver	20	50	8	48

West Division

	W	L	T	Pts.
Chicago	46	17	15	107
Minnesota	37	29	12	86
St. Louis	28	39	11	67
Pittsburgh	26	38	14	66
Philadelphia	26	38	14	66
California	21	39	18	60
Los Angeles	20	49	9	49

Stanley Cup: Boston

OUTSTANDING PLAYERS

Ross Trophy (scorer)	Phil Esposito, Boston
Calder Trophy (rookie)	Ken Dryden, Montreal
Vezina Trophy (goalie)	Tony Esposito and Gary Smith, Chicago
Hart Trophy (most valuable player)	Bobby Orr, Boston
Lady Byng Trophy (sportsmanship)	Jean Ratelle, New York
Norris Trophy (defenseman)	Bobby Orr
Conn Smythe Trophy (Stanley Cup play)	Bobby Orr

Rangers surround Bobby Orr in Stanley Cup game.

With a won-lost record of 54–13, the Bruins easily captured the Eastern division title. In post-season competition, they eliminated Toronto, 4 games to 1, and St. Louis, 4–0, before conquering the New York Rangers, 4–2, in the decisive series for the Stanley Cup. The defending champion Montreal Canadiens had been ousted by the Rangers, 4–2.

Phil Esposito, who won the Art Ross Trophy as the leading scorer, was Orr's chief collaborator in the success of the Bruins. There were also notable contributions in the playoffs by the Boston goalies, Ed Johnston and Gerry Cheevers. In the cup final, Cheevers blanked the Rangers, 3–0. An appearance in the championship series was a rare distinction for the Rangers, who haven't won the cup since 1940, but there was still no champagne.

While the NHL was recognizing Ken Dryden, Jean Ratelle, Tony Esposito, and Gary Smith as its star performers, the newly organized World Hockey Association was making inroads on the old league's talent. The prize catch by the WHA was Bobby Hull of the Black Hawks. He was signed by Winnipeg under a contract that could total $2,750,000.

Riva Ridge, in the lead, racing to victory in the 98th Kentucky Derby.

HORSE RACING

HARNESS STAKES WINNERS

Race	Horse
Cane Futurity	Hilarious Way
Colonial Trot	Super Bowl
Dexter Cup Trot	Songcan
Hambletonian	Super Bowl
International Trot	Speedy Crown
Kentucky Futurity	Super Bowl
Little Brown Jug	Strike Out
Messenger Stakes	Silent Majority
Mother Goose Stakes	Wanda
Realization Pace	Albatross
Realization Trot	Speedy Crown
Yonkers Futurity	Super Bowl

THOROUGHBRED STAKES WINNERS

Race	Horse
Belmont Futurity	Secretariat
Belmont Stakes	Riva Ridge
Brooklyn Handicap	Key to the Mint
Flamingo Stakes	Hold Your Peace
Jockey Club Gold Cup	Autobiography
Kentucky Derby	Riva Ridge
Preakness	Bee Bee Bee
Suburban Handicap	Hitchcock
Travers	Key to the Mint
United Nations Handicap	Acclimatization
Wood Memorial	Upper Case
Woodward Stakes	Key to the Mint

ICE SKATING

FIGURE SKATING

United States Championships

Men	Ken Shelley
Women	Janet Lynn
Pairs	Jo Jo Starbuck/Ken Shelley
Dance	Judy Schwomeyer/James Sladky

World Championships

Men	Ondrej Nepela, Czechoslovakia
Women	Beatrix Schuba, Austria
Pairs	Irina Rodnina/Aleksei Ulanov, U.S.S.R.
Dance	Ludmila Pakhomova/Aleksandr Gorshkov, U.S.S.R.

SPEED SKATING

World Championships

Men	Ard Schenk, Netherlands
Women	Atte Keulen-Deelstra, Netherlands

Jo Jo Starbuck and Ken Shelley, winners of pairs in U.S. figure skating championships.

SKIING

WORLD CUP CHAMPIONSHIPS

Men	Gustavo Thoeni, Italy
Women	Annemarie Proell, Austria

U.S. ALPINE CHAMPIONSHIPS

	Men
Downhill	Steve Lathrop, U.S.
Giant Slalom	Jim Hunter, Canada
Slalom	Terry Palmer, U.S.
Combined	Steve Lathrop

	Women
Downhill	Stephanie Forrest, U.S.
Giant Slalom	Sandra Poulsen, U.S.
Slalom	Marilyn Cochran, U.S.
Combined	Stephanie Forrest

NCAA CHAMPIONSHIPS

Downhill	Otto Tschudi, University of Denver
Slalom	Mike Porcarelli, University of Colorado
Alpine Combined	Mike Porcarelli
Cross-Country	Stale Engen, University of Wyoming
Jumping	Odd Hammernes, University of New Hampshire
Team	University of Colorado

Mike Porcarelli, winner of Slalom and Alpine Combined events in NCAA skiing championships.

Melissa Belote swims to a 1972 world record.

SWIMMING

When Mark Spitz received the AAU's Sullivan Award as the nation's outstanding amateur athlete, in the spring of 1972, he hinted that he might retire from swimming competition to concentrate on his dentistry studies at the University of Indiana.

There was a slight delay in the inspection of molars while Spitz went to Munich and made the greatest splash in the history of the Olympic Games. Competing in four individual and three relay events, the 22-year-old Californian collected seven gold medals. On each occasion, he either set or participated in the establishment of a new world record. In 8 days, he competed 13 times, including trial heats, winning the 100 and 200 butterfly and the 100 and 200 freestyle. He was also on the victorious U.S. relay teams in the 400 and 800 freestyle and the 400 medley.

In no previous Olympic competition had anybody won seven gold medals or captured as many as four in individual events.

Aside from Spitz's achievements, the U.S. swimmers won 11 gold medals, nine of which were won by women. World records were set by Cathy Carr in the 100 breaststroke, Karen Moe in the 200 butterfly, Keena Rothhammer in the 800 freestyle, and Melissa Belote in the 200 backstroke.

WORLD SWIMMING RECORDS SET IN 1972

Event	Holder	Time
	Men	
100-meter freestyle	Mark Spitz, U.S.	0:51.22
200-meter freestyle	Mark Spitz, U.S.	1:52.78
400-meter freestyle	Kurt Krumpholtz, U.S.	4:00.11
800-meter freestyle	Brad Cooper, Australia	8:23.80
1,500-meter freestyle	Mike Burton, U.S.	15:52.58
100-meter breaststroke	Nobutaka Taguchi, Japan	1:04.94
200-meter breaststroke	John Hencken, U.S.	2:21.55
100-meter butterfly	Mark Spitz, U.S.	0:54.27
200-meter butterfly	Mark Spitz, U.S.	2:00.70
100-meter backstroke	Roland Matthes, East Germany	0:56.30
200-meter backstroke	Roland Matthes, East Germany	2:02.82
200-meter individual medley	Gunnar Larsson, Sweden	2:07.17
400-meter individual medley	Gary Hall, U.S.	4:30.81
	Women	
100-meter freestyle	Shane Gould, Australia	0:58.50
200-meter freestyle	Shane Gould, Australia	2:03.56
400-meter freestyle	Shane Gould, Australia	4:19.04
800-meter freestyle	Keena Rothhammer, U.S.	8:53.68
100-meter breaststroke	Cathy Carr, U.S.	1:13.58
100-meter butterfly	Mayumi Aoki, Japan	1:03.34
200-meter butterfly	Karen Moe, U.S.	2:15.57
200-meter backstroke	Melissa Belote, U.S.	2:19.19
200-meter individual medley	Shane Gould, Australia	2:23.07
400-meter individual medley	Gail Neall, Australia	5:02.97

TENNIS

Men's tennis competition during 1972 seemed to be a continuing battle between Stan Smith of the United States and Ilie Nastase of Rumania. They shared honors in the world's most important tournaments, Wimbledon and the U.S. Open. Smith captured the title in Britain, and Nastase was the winner at Forest Hills, Long Island.

After conquering Nastase in a blistering five-set match at Wimbledon, Smith failed to reach the final at Forest Hills. That tournament was marked by upsets. The Australian big three, Ken Rosewall, Rod Laver, and John Newcombe, bowed out in the early rounds; Smith was defeated by Arthur Ashe in the semifinals; and Nastase turned back Ashe in the championship match.

Smith was the star of the U.S. team's 3–2 victory in the Davis Cup Challenge Round at Bucharest. Smith won both of his single matches, over Nastase and Ion Tiriac, and teamed with Erik Van Dillen for a triumph in the vital doubles match.

On the money list Rosewall enjoyed spectacular success, winning the $50,000 purse in the World Championship Tennis tour in May. He had pocketed an identical amount in the same competition 5 months earlier.

Two young people, Evonne Goolagong of Australia and Chris Evert of Fort Lauderdale, Florida, were the glamorous figures on the women's circuit. But most of the glory and the cash went to the more experienced Billie Jean King. Mrs. King, a Californian, gained her fourth Wimbledon crown. She did so by defeating Evonne Goolagong, the defending titleholder, in the final. Mrs. King then went on to achieve her third U.S. Open triumph, without the loss of a set. Kerry Melville was Mrs. King's victim in the final.

Rumania's Ilie Nastase on his way to winning the men's singles title in the U.S. Open.

TOURNAMENT TENNIS

	U.S. Open	Wimbledon	Australian Open	French Open
Men's Singles	Ilie Nastase, Rumania	Stan Smith, U.S.	Ken Rosewall, Australia	Andrés Gimeno, Spain
Women's Singles	Billie Jean King, U.S.	Billie Jean King, U.S.	Virginia Wade, Britain	Billie Jean King, U.S.
Men's Doubles	Cliff Drysdale, South Africa Roger Taylor, Britain	Bob Hewitt, South Africa Frew McMillan, South Africa	Ken Rosewall, Australia Owen Davidson, Australia	Bob Hewitt, South Africa Frew McMillan, South Africa
Women's Doubles	Françoise Durr, France Betty Stove, Netherlands	Billie Jean King, U.S. Betty Stove, Netherlands	Helen Gourlay, Australia Kerry Harris, Australia	Billie Jean King, U.S. Betty Stove, Netherlands

Davis Cup Winner: United States

Chris Evert, the 17-year-old American tennis sensation (*left*), and Australia's 20-year-old Evonne Goolagong, during their 1972 match at Wimbledon. The two young girls are exciting players who have captured the public eye.

CHRIS EVERT

Chris Evert is the American counterpart of Evonne Goolagong, the young Australian tennis sensation. At 17 years of age, Chris is somewhat younger than Evonne. But between them, the two have added zest and glamor to the tennis circuit. When they were matched in a Cleveland tournament in July, 1972, a record tennis crowd (for Ohio) of 7,428 turned out. Chris, the pixie from Fort Lauderdale, Florida, won that one, reversing the result of their semifinal engagement at Wimbledon earlier in the summer. Both were upset in the U.S. Open tournament and did not get to play each other. The Forest Hills, Long Island, throngs were disappointed because they had anticipated another match between the two girls.

Tennis is a family affair for the Everts, James and Colette, and four of their five children: Chris; Jeanne, 14; and the boys, Drew, 18, and John, 11. The fifth is too young, but the other four participate in competition at various levels. Tennis is an interest that comes natural to them, since their father is a former tournament player and is the director of a Fort Lauderdale tennis club.

Chrissie, already the game's slender crown princess, told her father when she was 14, "I want to be the best tennis player in the world." She isn't too far from the goal, and her success stems from the rigid schedule of daily practice maintained in the Evert household.

EVONNE GOOLAGONG

On the tennis courts Evonne Goolagong does very well on her own. Socially or in a business discussion, she is protected by an unfailing shield, Vic Edwards. He is the tough, weather-beaten Australian tennis coach who plucked Evonne out of a remote area of their native land and led her to the ultimate in international competition, the Wimbledon championship, in 1971. She was then 19 years old.

Edwards directs the largest string of tennis schools in Australia. Another former Wimbledon titleholder, John Newcombe, learned the basics of tennis at one of Edwards' classes.

It was in one of his country schools that Edwards discovered Evonne, an 11-year-old aborigine with extraordinary potential.

"We judged her mainly on reflexes, ball sense, and timing," Edwards explained. "She was a natural athlete. It was easy to build strokes from there." Edwards brought Evonne to live in his home in Sydney, and three years later became her legal guardian.

Evonne is still close to her parents and visits them frequently. But as Edwards said, "Her life just isn't there any longer. She has lived a metropolitan, international life, and that's quite different from a country town, population 950." Nevertheless, Edwards feels a need to protect Evonne.

When Evonne does go off on her own, there's a 12-year-old sister, Janelle, "who could be as good or better than Evonne."

TRACK AND FIELD

Bob Seagren set a new world record in the pole vault by clearing the crossbar at 18 feet 5¾ inches during the Olympic trial competitions held in July at Eugene, Oregon.

WORLD TRACK AND FIELD RECORDS SET IN 1972

Event	Holder	Time, Distance, or Points
	Men	
880-yard run	Dave Wottle, U.S.	1:44.3
2-mile run	Lasse Viren, Finland	8:14.0
3-mile run	Emile Puttemans, Belgium	12:47.6
3,000-meter run	Emile Puttemans, Belgium	7:37.6
5,000-meter run	Emile Puttemans, Belgium	13:13.0
10,000-meter run	Lasse Viren, Finland	27:38.4
3,000-meter steeplechase	Anders Gaerderud, Sweden	8:20.8
400-meter hurdles	John Akii-Bua, Uganda	47.8
Triple Jump	Viktor Saneyev, U.S.S.R.	57′ 2¾″
Pole Vault	Bob Seagren, U.S.	18′ 5¾″
Javelin Throw	Janis Lusis, U.S.S.R.	307′ 9″
Decathlon	Nikolai Avilov, U.S.S.R.	8,454 pts.
	Women	
1,500-meter run	Ludmila Bragina, U.S.S.R.	4:01.4
3,000-meter run	Paola Pigni, Italy	9:09.0
High Jump	Jordanka Blagoyeva, Bulgaria	6′ 4¼″
Shot Put	Nadezhda Chizhova, U.S.S.R.	69′
Discus Throw	Argentina Menis, Rumania	220′ 10½″
Pentathlon	Mary Peters, Britain	4,801 pts.

One minute it's smooth sailing for this whitewater-boating enthusiast (*left*), and then—splash—his kayak flips over and he takes an unscheduled dip.

WHITEWATER BOATING

Danger is what lures people into white water. To run river rapids in fragile craft has become the favorite sport of thousands of Europeans and, more recently, of North Americans too. Tempting fate by rushing pell-mell over and around rocks and through twisting currents and waves can be the thrill of a lifetime.

Many people who try whitewater boating for fun become serious about it. They study under experts, practice, buy expensive equipment, and ride ever more difficult rapids. They become experts themselves and compete against each other, right up to the Olympics.

Whitewater-boating enthusiasts are not interested in long placid trips on calm waters. They actively seek the rough waters of rocky streams and rivers. When they find a challenging stretch of white water, they pit their strength and skill against it time after time. The Hiwassee River, near Chattanooga, Tennessee, for example, draws hundreds of rapids runners every weekend. Most of these enthusiasts travel 50 to 150 miles to get there.

Once only a midsummer sport, whitewater boating, like surfing, is now done all year long. Clad in a rubber wet suit, the whitewater paddler stays warm enough from his own exertions, wet or dry, even when there's snow on the ground.

▸TUBES AND RAFTS

The simplest vessel for running rapids is a large inner tube, the type used on the wheels of some trucks, tractors, and airplanes. A tube with a large center opening can be decked with roughly sewn canvas and covered with a cushion to prevent harsh contact with jagged rocks.

Tubes are not very maneuverable when paddling is done with the hands alone. A canoe paddle helps. Tubes are sometimes tied together in groups, so that, for example, parents who have taken their children along can keep track of them.

Rubber rafts of many kinds are used on rapids. A raft may be built to carry any number of riders, from 2 to 20 or more. Military surplus lifesaving rafts, originally carried aboard troop transports and military

A group of rafters prepare to embark on a journey down the Chattanooga River.

Rafts are hard to maneuver in tricky rapids.

aircraft, were once very popular for white-water boating. Rafts are now being built especially for running rapids or for float trips on rivers.

Most rubber rafts are about 3 to 7 yards long and roughly rectangular, although some have pointed bows. A rubber raft has a tough skin and does not deflate easily. The skin usually consists of four layers of nylon, six of neoprene, and one of Hypalon (a tough synthetic rubber). Special glue makes the joints particularly strong. If the skin is pierced, there is only a slow leak, which can be quickly repaired with a standard kit.

A rubber raft is usually inflated by using a bellows, a foot pump, or a carbon dioxide cartridge. The internal pressure is low—2 to 2½ pounds per square inch—so an air leak is never explosive. A raft usually has from two to five separate air compartments, but the whole raft can stay afloat even if only one compartment is inflated. Some rubber rafts have aluminum frames, to prevent them from wrapping around their occupants like a bun around a hamburger.

Rafts are also made with a solid deck, such as a sheet of plywood, supported by inner tubes, oil drums, or other flotation devices.

Running swirling river rapids in a canoe requires both courage and skill.

Because they are often too rigid and too deep, rafts of this kind tend to break up in rapids. They are really better used in calm waters.

CANOES AND KAYAKS

Before the interest in whitewater boating, canoeists usually chose to portage around rapids. However, expert canoeists have usually known how to run rapids when they had to. Canoeing in white water has now become a sport.

While the rafter may bumble down the river hit or miss, with little chance to choose his course or avoid obstacles, the canoeist can maneuver very well. However, his rigid craft can be pierced or dented by rocks, or smashed to pieces by water pressure if caught sideways in a current. Canoeing in white water requires real skill.

The Eskimo kayak was adopted by rapids runners because of its amazing maneuverability. Besides being pointed at both ends like a canoe, it is decked over to keep water out. When a kayaker is wearing his spray skirt—a waterproof apron fitted tightly around his waist and secured around the cowling of his cockpit with elastic—he can turn upside down in the water without flooding his boat.

In fact, the maneuverability of the kayak is so great that it's downright skittish to handle. But when skill has been developed, this is all to the good.

The modern kayak is no longer the skin boat of the Eskimo, nor the canvas boat developed from it. Kayaks are now often fashioned from fiber glass in molds by the vacuum process. There are many variations in kayak design. The bottom can be round, flat, or V-shaped. The deck can have a cowling around it or rounded corners. The cockpit can be centered or slightly fore or aft of center. The kayaker considers his craft an extension of his body. His kayak is built to fit him, with the seat the right size, the foot brace the right distance from the seat, and the pads of foam rubber properly placed under the foredeck so that he can brace his knees against them.

The foldboat, developed in Europe, was long the favorite craft for running rapids, but it is giving way to the kayak.

Many other kinds of boats can be used in rapids, depending on the depth of the water over the rocks. For instance, the rivermen of the Colorado prefer a wooden dory, with high stem and stern, like that used by fishermen on

Life preservers, rubber wet suits, and helmets may be worn by boaters, but dress varies.

the Grand Banks in the North Atlantic. On the Colorado, it is called a cataract boat.

EQUIPMENT

The kayaker generally uses a double-bladed paddle; the canoeist uses a single- or a double-bladed paddle (single-bladed paddles in a two-man canoe); and rafters either use paddles or have oars that are permanently attached to the raft. Paddles may have blades of metal or plywood, or they may be made of a single piece of wood. The latter kind are often reinforced with glass cloth. Blades are sometimes slightly curved at the ends or somewhat spoon-shaped for a stronger bite in the water. Because such blades twist in the water with certain strokes, however, many racers prefer simple, symmetrical blades.

Clothing for running rapids varies with both the climate and the difficulty of the rapids. On a very easy run, a bathing suit might be enough. Generally, however, a rafter should wear sneakers to protect his feet from sharp rocks when he has to jump overboard to dislodge the raft from an obstruction. A strong current can flip a raft over or fling the people off, in which case it is well to be wearing long trousers and shirt, as well as thermal underwear to soften the shock against the body and limbs. In cold weather, wool is the fabric that best preserves body heat. A rubber wet suit is also useful.

Good sense, and the law in many places, require the wearing of a life preserver, because swimming ability is of no use if one is knocked senseless. Kayakers and canoeists generally wear helmets. Rafters wear them, too, when rafting in particularly rough waters. The helmet should not interfere with hearing, because a rumbling noise is usually the first warning of rapids ahead.

GETTING STARTED

Over 600 raft trips are offered in the western United States each summer by organizations that provide equipment and instruction. More than 10,000 people float down the Colorado each summer. The Appalachians have fewer miles of rapids than the mountains of the West, but the sport is growing quickly wherever good rapids exist.

In addition to the commercial outfitters, there are networks of local, regional, and national clubs. A first trial of the rapids might be done on a rubber raft from any reliable outfitter. The person who is really interested should join the nearest club, in order to benefit from the experience of other whitewater sportsmen. The clubs run frequent weekend jaunts to whitewater rivers, and the old pros are glad to instruct novices.

Instruction is really needed for kayaking, because many unusual motions must be learned and practiced, such as leaning toward the outside on a turn and bracing oneself with the paddle downstream from the kayak. One must also learn the very special Duffek "hanging" stroke for fast tight turns, the technique of "ferrying" across fast water, and esquimautage. This means tipping over and then righting the kayak with a paddle stroke and a twist of the hips. Safety instruction is very important, since most of the serious accidents happen to novices.

RACING

Paddling skill cannot do much for the speed of a raft, so raft races are mostly for fun. In

1969 Larry Patrick, then a Georgia Tech student, organized the annual Ramblin' Raft Race on 9.2 miles of the Chattahoochee River near Atlanta, Georgia. The first race had 50 entries, and the 1972 race, 5,000. All imaginable types of rafts were entered. One raft, made of 175 inner tubes, had a crew of 65. In the "showboat" class there were rafts bearing gardens and trees, a piano, a Volkswagen, and a number of other odd things. Most of these exotic objects ended in the river after the heavy rafts broke up on the rocks. (The Volkswagen actually had a beaver living quite happily in the back seat by the time it was pulled out.)

It was in Europe that the running of rapids developed as a sport, and there also that racing began, over half a century ago. A major American event, the Arkansas River Race, in Colorado, was first run in 1949. It covers 25 miles of river, with several rapids. This type of race is called a downriver race.

A short race of concentrated difficulty is the slalom, named for the skiing event and similar to it. A tough rapid is selected, and is made tougher with 25 to 30 "gates"—pairs of poles suspended from wires above the river. Contestants must pass through these gates in the proper direction, without touching them. Racers run the rapids one at a time, racing against the clock and usually taking about 5 minutes.

For the 1972 Olympics, artificial rapids were built near Augsburg, Germany, at a cost of $4,000,000. Europeans usually win all the medals in slalom, so it was a surprise when Jamie McEwan, 20, of Silver Spring, Maryland, won the bronze medal in the Canadian Slalom.

THE ULTIMATE RAPIDS

Walt Blackadar, a physician, was long fascinated with the idea of running the horrible rapids of an impossible, impassable river, the Alsek, which runs from the Yukon across part of British Columbia to Alaska. In August, 1972, he did it, despite warnings from everyone who had seen the Alsek. He had himself and a kayak flown in, and made the 230-mile trip in about a week.

The Alsek flows through glaciers, so icebergs break off and float down the rapids.

A woman competitor makes her run in the Kayak Singles event at the 1972 Munich Olympics.

Turn Back Canyon is a 5-mile gorge with a 20-degree downgrade; it is only 30 feet wide in places, with banks 500 to 1,000 feet high. There are numerous waterfalls. There are "boiling pots" with water spouting as high as 20 feet. The current was so fast—35 to 40 miles per hour—that a house-sized rock had behind it a great hole rather than an eddy.

Blackadar's kayak was upside-down twice, but he managed to "roll up." He was slammed into a cliff and pinned there by the current. He hit icebergs in the water. A whirlpool caught his kayak, lifted it vertically, and whirled it around, dropping him upside-down. Part of his deck was torn out, so his kayak swamped, and it took him six tries to roll up again. His exultation at surviving such a trip can only be imagined. To cap the experience, he several times saw grizzly bears, standing 10 feet tall on the bank and roaring at him. Danger is what brings thrills to whitewater sport, and the novice must learn the ways of white water in order to get through it safely and enjoy its thrills.

ROBERT SCOTT MILNE
Society of American Travel Writers

Bikes dominate the scene today in big cities and small towns alike.

ALL ABOUT BIKES

Riding a bicycle, from the first wobbly trip around the block to the 100 miles a day of the experienced cyclist, is one of the great pleasures. It can give one a sense of daring and achievement, an escape from dullness. In the United States bicycling has reached a degree of popularity it has not enjoyed since cars took over the roads. There are 7,000,000 to 9,000,000 cyclists, young and old, riding in America today.

The popularity of cycling is part of the new interest in health and environment. Some years back Dr. Paul Dudley White began advising people to ride bikes daily because this exercise is especially good for the heart, circulation, and general health. Since he was President Eisenhower's doctor, people paid attention. Then, as more and more was heard about the growing pollution of our air and water, people began to view the bicycle as a partial answer to that problem, too.

Now you see many adults cycling to and from work on city streets. Unlike cars, bikes do not pour carbon monoxide and other impurities into the air we breathe; and the exercise fits nicely into the working day. As for country cycling, it "gets you close to nature." You can feel the air on your face and body, and smell grass, leaf mold, and sea.

EARLY BICYCLES

The first bicycle, built around 1696 by a Frenchman named Sivrac, had two wheels but no pedals and no steering mechanism. If you tipped to right or left, you fell; you could not steer in the direction of the tip to stay upright. Then, in 1816, Baron von Drais, a German, built another "walking machine." You straddled the machine and pushed with your feet, left, right, left, right, leaning your body against a padded bar. You steered the front wheel with a tiller, just as a sailboat is

The town turned out in 1881 to see off the Germantown [Pa.] Cycling Club.

steered, but from the "bow end" of the machine. In 1839 a Scot, Kirkpatrick MacMillan, put pedals on a bike. They were connected to the rear wheel by drive rods. In 1861, Pierre and Ernest Michaux, Frenchmen, put regular pedals on the axle of the front wheel, an arrangement like that of a modern tricycle.

In the 1870's and 1880's the front wheels of bikes got bigger and bigger, the rear ones smaller and smaller. Speed was the reason: the bigger the front wheel the farther you went with one revolution of the pedals. This high-wheel bike was called an "ordinary." It was tricky to mount and very likely to throw you forward over the front wheel. Around 1884 in England, J. K. Starley built the first practical "safety bicycle," the forerunner of the modern bike. It had two wheels of equal size; the pedals were on a chain wheel in the middle and were connected by a drive chain to the rear-wheel sprocket.

J. B. Dunlop, a veterinarian of Belfast, Ireland, made a set of air-filled canvas-and-rubber tires for his son's tricycle in 1888; they were the first pneumatic tires for any purpose. They made cycling faster and much more comfortable.

Then shiftable gears came into the picture. They were mechanical systems for shifting from "hard" pedaling for speed on the flat to "easy" pedaling for uphill work. The earliest gears were inside the rear hub, as many still are. But by 1906 a French manufacturer, Paul de Vivie, had put the first *dérailleur* on a bicycle. This external system eased the work of pedaling with each shift.

Shiftable gears don't make you go faster. They only make possible a choice between hard pedaling and easy pedaling as you go downhill, on a level, or uphill.

▸CYCLING ADVENTURES

In its long history, the bicycle has provided many kinds of adventure. Beginning with the walking machine invented by Baron von Drais, there has been bicycle racing: racing on closed tracks, on open roads, and even cross-country.

There is also a kind of racing whose object

The draisine was a bicycle built in 1816 by German Baron Karl von Drais.

In the late 1800's the bicycle built for two was considered dashing.

The ordinary of 1884 was all the rage among the kids on the block.

Today a 10-speed racing bike is near the top of the most wanted list.

School is out and boys and girls head for home with their bicycles.

Cyclists round the bend in an annual race in Brookline, Mass.

More and more city dwellers choose to ride bicycles to work.

is to match or surpass record maximum speeds: a bicycle follows behind a powered vehicle, such as a train or car, which "sucks" the bike and its rider along. In 1899 a New York policeman named Charles M. Murphy did a mile in 57 seconds, on a planked track, while riding behind a Long Island Railroad train. He went down in history as Mile-a-Minute-Murphy. In 1962, in Germany, a Frenchman, Jose Meiffret, hit 128 miles per hour for ⅝ of a mile (1 kilometer) on a specially reinforced bike behind a Mercedes Benz automobile.

Bicycle touring goes way back, too. Tom Stevens' 1884 round-the-world trip, from San Francisco to San Francisco, using boats when necessary, took place at a time when Indians were shooting arrows at western travelers. Stevens made that trip on an ordinary.

In the 1880's and 1890's there was a fad for coasting down Mount Washington, in New Hampshire, on ordinaries. It was a rough ride, with no stops except when you pitched forward onto the rocks. And hands and arms were left aching from using the hand brakes.

YOU AND YOUR BIKE

What sort of bike is best? If you are under 9 years of age, the sensible bike for you is one small enough to let you touch the ground with your toes as you sit in the saddle. For stopping or slowing down, it should have a coaster brake—the kind you apply by pedaling backwards. From age 9 to 14 you can best use a three-speed or five-speed bike with internal gears and hand brakes. At 14 and older you can ride a light-weight ten-speed, especially if you are an enthusiast and want to go on long bike tours. For once-in-a-while biking, the hardy, reliable English Racer with Sturmey Archer three-speed gear is the best buy. (The Racer is not a racer; that's just a name someone gave it long ago.)

The ten-speed bike is king now. Teen-age cyclists spend from $70 to over $400 for ten-speeds. At the lowest price they are a poor buy—too heavy, with inferior steel tubing and weak construction. An English Racer is a better buy in this range.

But ten-speeds are for good riders. Shifting the gears takes skill. Without toe clips the ten-speed is incomplete; they hold your toes on the pedals, allowing you to pull up as well as press down. Your seat should be set high, so that when your foot is on the down pedal your leg is nearly straight down.

Bicycling offers wonderful opportunities for fun—but there are some very real problems, too. Main highways and busy roads and streets are not safe to ride on; the smart cyclist uses back roads and quiet streets whenever he can. To make sure that car drivers can see them after dark, many cyclists strap little French lights on arms and legs, fasten reflecting tape or glass on the bike, and wear white clothing. Remember, safety is the thing.

Riding skill is important for safety. You should be able to slow down and speed up as needed, and to ride a straight line—not all over the road. You should try to see possible dangers ahead: the door of the parked car that may open in front of you, the storm drain in the road that can grab your front wheel and send you flying. You should also know the traffic laws as well as a licensed car driver.

Safety means a bike in good repair and equipped with good tires, brakes, and lights. Bicycles need frequent care and adjustment. The good cyclist learns to do much of this work himself; it saves time and money and it helps, on a long trip, to be able to fix your bike yourself. There are several good books on selecting and repairing a bike. These tell what tools you should have and how to make various repairs.

It's a good idea to belong to a bicycle club if you want to make many long trips. Such a group can advise you about routes and places to stay, and can arrange group trips suited to your cycling ability. American Youth Hostels, Inc., is the best-known group. Write them for information on cycle touring in the United States and around the world.

When you do get into real cycling you not only have the pleasure of biking but also the sense of belonging to a grown-up sports fraternity: biking is a sport you will be able to take part in all your life. It's a fact that some very young people and some very old ones can do their 100 miles a day as a matter of course. Very happy and healthy people they are, too.

HARVEY GARDNER
Managing Editor, Gold Medal Books

Boris Spassky (*left*) and Bobby Fischer during their championship chess match.

A CHAMPIONSHIP CHESS MATCH

The time was 2:47 in the afternoon of September 1, 1972. The place was Sports Hall in Reykjavik, Iceland—site of the 1972 world championship chess match. Twenty-nine-year-old Bobby Fischer, the United States chess wizard, had just walked onstage. Fischer, the challenger in the most highly publicized chess match ever held, was late as usual. His Russian opponent, Boris Spassky, the defending champion, was not even present.

As the gangling, six-foot-two Fischer arrived that afternoon, referee Lothar Schmid stepped forward to make an announcement. A hush fell over the capacity crowd of 2,500 chess enthusiasts.

"Ladies and gentlemen," Schmid began, "Mr. Spassky has resigned by telephone at 12:50." There was a burst of applause, then Schmid continued. "Mr. Fischer has won this game, No. 21, and he is the winner of the match."

Robert James Fischer, whose brilliant career as a chess player began at the age of 6, had fulfilled his own prophecy. He had become chess champion of the world—the first American to hold the title.

When Schmid finished his statement, the audience rose to salute the new king of chess with a standing ovation. While the steady, rhythmic applause built up to a roar, Fischer awkwardly nodded his thanks. Then he finished signing his score sheet, glanced shyly at the audience, and hurried offstage. Thus ended one of history's greatest chess duels. The final score was Fischer 12½, Spassky 8½.

"It was really the match of the century," referee Schmid said later. "It brought together the world's two strongest players. . . . Perhaps the quality of the play was not always the very best, but there always have been mistakes in championship matches. The interest in this match! Never, never in the history of chess has this been seen. This will never come again."

Indeed the interest in the match was tremendous. Chess players all over the world had heard of Bobby Fischer, the boy wonder of chess. They were awed by his remarkable record of victories over the strongest players. They were also astonished by the record purse of $125,000 (plus another $125,000, contributed by an English millionaire) that was to be shared by the players. (When Boris Spassky won the championship in 1969, he received only $1,400.) Thousands of chess fans flocked to Sports Hall to see the games. For the first time in international chess competition, arrangements were made for film and television coverage.

▸A HUMAN CHESS MACHINE

The major attraction of the match was the colorful and unpredictable young player from the United States. Bobby Fischer has been called everything from a spoiled brat and a poor sport to a mystery man and a chess machine. Throughout his career he has shunned publicity and actually seems frightened of the press. One newspaper described him as "stubborn, spoiled, petulant, demanding, suspicious—all but a recluse."

Many people were critical of Fischer's behavior during the match—which was marked by a never-ending list of demands, and occasional outbursts of bad temper. But even those who dislike him as a person admit that he is a true genius at the chessboard. Virtually all chess experts now agree that he is the strongest chess player in the world.

Born in Chicago in 1943, Bobby Fischer spent most of his early years in Brooklyn, New York. His parents were divorced when he was 2 years old, and his mother had to work to support the family. Bobby's older sister, Joan, took care of him during the day. To keep him amused, she bought various games at a local candy store. One day she brought home a $1 chess set and taught Bobby the moves. Fischer was only 6 at the time, but he quickly mastered the game.

In fact, he fell in love with chess. Soon he was reading every chess book he could get his hands on. At night, he slept with a chessboard by his bed. Within a few years he was playing at local chess clubs—beating his adult opponents. At 13 he was junior chess champion of the United States. A year later he became the youngest United States national champion in history. At 15 he was the world's youngest international grandmaster.

Followers of the game predicted that he would be world champion before his 21st birthday. But then Fischer ran into trouble. In the 1962 international playoffs he finished fourth behind three Russian grandmasters. Fischer angrily accused the Russians of cheating. He claimed that the Russian grandmasters played only for draws with each other so they could save their best efforts for him. The Russians went on to win the title—which they held from 1948 to 1972.

For the next few years, a bitter Fischer became the "ugly American" of the chess world. He stalked away from tournaments when his demands weren't met, behaved rudely, and finally went into semi-retirement. People began to think of him as a bright star that had flickered out.

But just when everyone had crossed him off the list of contenders for the championship, Fischer came storming back like a hurricane. To challenge the world champion, a player must win his way through a 3-year cycle of international tournaments. Fischer's record in these playoffs was nothing short of spectacular. Beginning in 1970, he mowed down international grandmasters like tenpins.

First he took on Mark Taimanov of the Soviet Union. Taimanov was shut out 6 to 0. Next came Bent Larsen of Denmark. He went

BOX SCORE OF CHAMPIONSHIP

Game	Number of Moves	Fischer	Spassky
1	56	0	1
2	*	0	1
3	41	1	0
4	45	½	½
5	27	1	0
6	41	1	0
7	49	½	½
8	37	1	0
9	29	½	½
10	56	1	0
11	31	0	1
12	55	½	½
13	74	1	0
14	40	½	½
15	43	½	½
16	60	½	½
17	45	½	½
18	47	½	½
19	40	½	½
20	54	½	½
21	40	1	0
Total		**12½**	**8½**

* Fischer forfeited the second game by failing to appear.

Between games, Bobby Fischer relaxes on a boat in waters off Iceland.

down to defeat by the same unbelievable score. Two straight shutouts in international grandmaster competition had never occurred before.

People began talking about Fischer's hypnotic power over other players. "There is some strange magnetic influence in Bobby," one Soviet grandmaster commented, "that spiritually wrecks his opponents." Fischer insists his wins are simply a matter of "making the best moves."

The Russian grandmaster Tigran Petrosian was the final man to stand between Fischer and world titleholder Boris Spassky. Fischer won the first game of that match, extending his victory streak in international competition to a record 20 games. He lost the second game, but bounced back to win the match by a score of 6½ to 2½—taking the last four games in a row.

A GENTLEMAN–PLAYER

And so the stage was set for the 1972 match between Fischer and Spassky. The two men had met once before in another international tournament. Spassky had won three of their five games, with the others ending in draws. Some people thought that the boastful Fischer—who had long claimed to be the world's best chess player—would finally meet his master. There were others, however, who believed that Fischer was unbeatable.

In contrast to the nervous, bad-tempered, and often arrogant Bobby Fischer, Boris Spassky is the ever-courteous gentleman. Soft-spoken and of an easygoing nature, Spassky described himself to one reporter as "a lazy Russian bear." Like Fischer, the 35-year-old Spassky comes from a home where the parents were divorced. He was also the youngest grandmaster of his time—at age 18.

There the similarity ends. Spassky is a settled family man, while Fischer is a bachelor and a loner. Spassky is a man of varied interests, including sports, the arts, and gourmet food. Fischer has only one interest—chess. Although he loves the game of chess, Spassky stated before the match: "I would be the happiest man alive if I were no longer world champion . . . I like to play chess for fun and not fame."

THE MATCH OF THE CENTURY

From the beginning, the Fischer-Spassky match ran into difficulties. First, there was the selection of a site acceptable to both men. After much haggling over money and other matters, Reykjavik, the capital of Iceland, was chosen.

The trouble did not end there, however.

Along a quiet stretch of rocky seashore, Boris Spassky practices a move.

The match was supposed to begin on July 2. Spassky was on hand 2 weeks before. Fischer kept delaying his arrival, demanding more money and other concessions. Some believed that the American was waging a war of nerves designed to upset the Russian champion. Finally, James D. Slater, a millionaire chess buff, offered to double the pot to $250,000, and Fischer came out of hiding.

There were other stormy moments during the match as a result of Fischer's constant demands. Among other things, the American challenger insisted on the removal of all television and motion-picture cameras, the use of a small private room for the games, and a chessboard with smaller squares.

In spite of Fischer's antics, the tournament continued. The match was scheduled for 24 games. The winner of a game received 1 point, while a draw gave each player ½ point. To keep his title, Spassky needed 12 points. Fischer had to score 12½ points to win the crown. Spassky moved to an early lead, beating Fischer in the first game, and winning the second by forfeit when the challenger—angry over the continued presence of television cameras—refused to show up. Rumors circulated that Fischer, down 0 to 2, might walk out on the match altogether.

Instead, Fischer made a dramatic comeback and quickly turned the tables. He won the third game decisively and fought to a draw in the fourth. The next six games showed Fischer at his best. He won four games and drew two. Now it was Spassky who found himself trailing badly—6½ to 3½. Like other grandmasters who had fallen before Fischer's driving attack, Spassky began to make careless mistakes. His playing became sluggish, and he seemed to have lost the will to win.

Nevertheless, Spassky was far from through. He fought on doggedly, winning the 11th game and playing much stronger chess after that. Of the ten games that followed, eight were draws. But Fischer pulled out two decisive victories in the 13th and 21st games, and the chess world had a new champion.

Bobby Fischer had ended 24 years of Russian supremacy in chess. More than that, he had put chess in the limelight and made it an important international sport. The games in Reykjavik captured the interest of millions of people around the world. Already there is talk of a Fischer-Spassky rematch with a purse of $500,000 or more.

As for Fischer, he took his triumph in stride. The day after the match he was asked how it felt to be world champion. He shrugged and replied matter-of-factly, "I've always felt I was the champion."

THE CHESS BOOM

In the wake of the 1972 championship chess match between Bobby Fischer and Boris Spassky, a wave of interest in the ancient game has swept across the United States. The "Bobby Boom," as some are calling it in honor of the eccentric American chess genius, has resulted in increased sales of chess sets and books, and a growing demand for chess lessons.

A happy chess-set manufacturer reported "Business is fantastic." His statement was echoed by booksellers and department-store managers from Los Angeles to New York. "Our chess books just sat on the shelves before the Fischer-Spassky tournament," one bookshop owner stated. "Then everything took off. They went from the slowest- to the fastest-moving items in the store in a matter of days."

Among the best sellers are such beginner's books as *Chess in 10 Easy Lessons* by American Grandmaster Larry Evans, and *Chess the Easy Way* by Reuben Fine, another grandmaster. More advanced players can match wits with Bobby Fischer by reading his book *My Sixty Memorable Games.* For those wishing to learn about the former Russian champion, there is *Boris Spassky* by Andrew Soltis.

Some stores anticipated the chess boom and got ready for it. A well-known New York department store bought up chess sets from all over the world in the months before the Fischer-Spassky tournament. They ranged from a $3.50 traveling chess set with small, magnetic pieces to a $200 deluxe outfit from Florence, Italy, featuring a calf-leather board and pieces made of antimony.

Business and entertainment promoters are also busily at work. An enterprising San Francisco man named Cyrus Weiss is trying to organize a professional chess league similar to those in football and other major sports. Teams would play a regular schedule, with the matches being televised. To make things

The Spassky-Fischer chess match had everyone playing chess. Here, two youngsters ponder the next move while playing chess at a community center.

more interesting, Weiss would like to use live chess pieces on a gigantic board. "We could fill an entire TV screen," he says, "by using pretty girls in symbolic hats to represent the pieces." Even with the present chess furor, the United States lags far behind other nations in enthusiasm for the game. There are an estimated 60,000,000 serious chess players around the world. The Soviet Union leads all other nations with a total of 4,000,000 registered players—as opposed to a mere 35,000 in the United States Chess Federation. Many Russian youths follow chess the way Americans follow football and baseball. Nearly half of the world's international grandmasters are Russian.

Chess is undoubtedly the most mentally challenging and taxing game. It requires absolute concentration and the ability to think many moves ahead. It is also physically wearing. During championship games, players have become so keyed up that they have fainted dead away. Others have suffered severe loss of weight in the course of a tournament. As former World Champion Tigran Petrosian has noted, "Chess may start out as an art or science, but in the end it is an athletic event."

To keep in shape physically, chess grandmasters are active in various sports. When preparing for an important match, Bobby Fischer plays tennis, swims, lifts weights, and rides an Exercycle. Boris Spassky's workout includes yoga, running, and swimming.

Chess is one of the world's oldest games. It was probably invented in India about A.D. 600. It was originally called the army game because the pieces represented military branches. For example, pawns were made to look like infantrymen, and knights were cavalrymen. In ancient India, chariots and elephants were included, but today they have been replaced by rooks and bishops.

Some of history's most noted statesmen, scientists, and writers were ardent chess players. Benjamin Franklin believed that playing chess was a good way to learn "foresight, circumspection, caution, and the habit of not being discouraged by our present state of affairs." Lenin, the Russian revolutionary leader, called chess "the gymnasium of the mind." The great scientist Albert Einstein thought the game could control a person to the point where it "holds its master in its bonds . . . and in some way shapes his spirit."

This unique Indian chess set dates from about 1830. The beautifully hand-carved figures are made of ivory, and the board of lacquered wood.

Whether the current American chess craze lasts remains to be seen. In the meantime, thousands of Americans are learning the difference between the Sicilian Defense and the Queen's Gambit Declined. At this very moment, some future Bobby Fischer may be practicing the basic moves with an inexpensive set of plastic chessmen. After all, that's how Fischer got his start at the age of 6—playing with a chess set bought at a neighborhood candy store in Brooklyn, New York.

The figures in this contemporary Polish chess set are depicted in traditional costumes.

Skip Brittle, one of America's best steeplechase jockeys, takes the lead.

STEEPLECHASE RACING

Steeplechase and hurdles racing are two of the most exciting forms of sports competition in the world. Anyone who has seen a steeplechase or hurdles race knows what truly unusual forms of horse racing they are. Anyone who has ever ridden a horse and jumped it over a ditch or barrier will get a familiar and odd feeling of excitement in the pit of his stomach as he watches the steeplechase jockeys take their mounts over a series of high, difficult jumps while racing at literally breakneck speeds.

Steeplechase and hurdles racing are two closely connected sports with somewhat different rules and practices. Basically, the same type of jockey races in both kinds of event. In steeplechase racing the horses usually run on a turf course, and the jumps they take are permanently positioned. In hurdles races, the hurdles or hedge barriers the horses must clear are movable and the track they are run on is often dirt. Since the movable barriers of hurdles racing are not so dangerous to horse and rider as the fixed barriers of steeplechase racing, the jockeys can take more chances. Hence, hurdles races are usually faster moving; they are also very dusty. The jockeys in both steeplechase and hurdles races usually wear goggles to protect their eyes. In hurdles races, goggles help combat the clouds of dust

The horses pound toward a jump in a steeplechase at Fair Hill, Maryland.

and flying branches from the hurdles. In steeplechase meets run over turf the horses also kick up clumps of grass and earth which spray up in the faces of the jockeys.

MORE THAN A SPORT

Sometimes a sport is more than a sport. Steeplechase and hurdles races grew popular in the 19th century in Ireland, England, France, and the United States among other places. That was a period when horses and horse breeding for a variety of purposes were matters of great importance. Horses were the most popular means of transportation. One of the ways horses were used was on the battlefield. In Europe and the United States, the armies still had cavalry units, and cavalrymen were well trained horsemen. They rode in great cavalry charges armed with heavy sabers. And when a man participated in a cavalry charge he had to meet every obstacle in his path as it came. Many of the men who began steeplechase racing were cavalrymen on leave or former cavalrymen. The furious dash over obstacles at high speed of the steeplechase competition was like a cavalry charge, and was one way for a military horseman to keep in practice when he was at home.

Steeplechase and hurdles racing, especially in Ireland, England, and the southeastern United States, also grew out of the popularity, in the 19th century, of fox hunting. The men in these countries who took up steeplechase racing were most often fox hunters in training for their next hunt, for the conditions of steeplechase racing were even more like those of the fox hunt than they were like those of the battlefield.

A close race at Deep River, North Carolina. Brittle (center) was winner.

Steeplechase and hurdles racing probably started very informally when farmers or country squires who raised horses would challenge a group of neighbors to a competition to see who was the best rider and who raised the best horses. The word "steeplechase" itself comes from the informal racecourse that would be set up by a group of friends and neighbors in the English countryside: They would lay out a course for their competition, using, as landmarks, the steeples of the churches in the towns of the area. The horsemen would all line up and start from the same spot and head for an agreed series of steeples, jumping all the hedges, ditches, gates, and fences in their path until they reached the final steeple in the course.

GREAT RACES

Steeplechase racing reached its peak of popularity in the late 19th century. However, it is still popular today. In France, there is a special horse racing season set aside for steeplechases. It still has great importance in Ireland and England, too. England's famous Grand National Steeplechase, run annually over the Aintree course in Liverpool, remains one of the world's major sporting events. It also has the reputation of being the most demanding and most dangerous of all the world's major steeplechase courses. Horses are brought to England from all over the world to compete in the Grand National.

In the United States, there are jump races held at a number of the major tracks in New

York State and in the horse and hunt country of Delaware, Maryland, Virginia, and eastern West Virginia. However, this exciting sport has declined in the United States in recent years and is not nearly so popular as it was in the 19th century. This may be due, in part, to the decline of fox hunting in the United States and the decline in the amount of available land on which to hunt. Americans are more familiar with the flat races run by thoroughbred race horses, and with harness racing.

DARING YOUNG MAN

One of the most outstanding steeplechase jockeys in the United States is a young man just out of college named Clay Brittle III. He is generally known as Skip. He is 24 years old and has been interested in horses all his life. He grew up in the great horse-raising country of Virginia. Skip Brittle began serious racing when he was still a teenager, riding in meets as a "gentleman jockey." (That means he competed as an amateur and was not paid.) In 1969 he began his career as a professional jockey, riding in major steeplechase events in the eastern United States. Even when he was in college, Skip Brittle was able to ride almost every day. (He went to a branch of the University of Virginia.)

When you read about most jockeys and see their pictures in newspapers, you have probably noticed that most of them are small men who weigh relatively little. In flat racing it is vital that the thoroughbred horse not be slowed down by the weight of his rider. Skip Brittle would never make a good flat-racing jockey because he is 6 feet tall, and he weighs about 150 pounds. But the horses used in steeplechase and hurdle races are usually sturdier than the slim thoroughbreds used in flat racing, which are bred for great speed. The horses used in steeplechases must be swift, but they are essentially hunters and they are bred, as a rule, for great stamina. It takes enormous amounts of strength and endurance for a horse to weather the multiple jumps of a steeplechase successfully. Steeplechase horses can, therefore, carry bigger riders, like Skip Brittle. And steeplechase riders must have the strength to control the horses in the most hazardous jumps.

Skip Brittle, wearing his bright racing silks, waits to mount up for a race in Pennsylvania.

Skip Brittle is not sure how long he wants to go on racing or how long the kind of racing he knows best will go in the United States. But it is certain that horses and riding are the greatest interests in his life. And anyone who has had the thrill of winning at the hard-riding, dangerous competition of steeplechase and hurdles racing would find it very hard to sit quietly behind a desk.

THE CREATIVE WORLD

Striking, life-size clown puppets, made by young pupils.

THROUGH MY EYES

When I was six years old, I wrote a play called *Murder on the Brooklyn Bridge.* It was a very bloody play. In fact it was so gruesome none of the neighborhood mothers would allow their children to appear in it. Without a cast, it could not be produced. No one saw my first work.

Today young people with creative ideas are not as likely to go unseen, unread, or unheard. They do not automatically hide out in the family attic to write their first novel, play, or book of poetry. They are more likely to borrow a neighbor's super 8 camera and make a film. A television show called "Through My Eyes," seen in many parts of the United States, gave a group of talented young filmmakers an unusual chance to have their works presented before a wide audience.

There are two major reasons for the great interest young people now have in filmmaking. First of all, most young Americans have grown up with television. They have most likely watched thousands of hours of it. Visual images—pictures—have become the most familiar kind of image to them. Second, film equipment has become simpler, lighter, and cheaper. It is now possible for young people to buy simple film equipment with money they have earned themselves. If they do need to borrow equipment from an adult, they are more likely to be successful than they would once have been. Adults, too, are using simpler and less expensive cameras. And there is a less important but still significant reason for the interest in filmmaking among young people: Film culture as a whole has become more acceptable and is discussed more seriously as a creative art.

But the young filmmaker of today does have one great problem. How does he get his

Douglas Brodoff (left) and Roger Calistro (right), both 16, won first prize in the NET film contest. Here they meet veteran film producer Otto Preminger.

film shown anywhere but in the family basement? With this question in mind, a man named Lee Polk—who was then director of programing for children at National Educational Television (NET)—proposed that NET run its own festival of children's films. Polk planned to set up his festival as a competition. Prizes would be awarded to three winners in each of two age groups—6 to 12, and 13 to 18. The winning films would then be seen as part of a nationally broadcast program. Basically, Polk had two goals. He wanted to show the best work being done in film by children and he wanted to encourage more children to make more films.

NATIONWIDE COMPETITION

In the fall of 1970, Polk and his associate producer began contacting noncommercial television stations that might wish to participate in the competition. About 100 stations agreed to take part. They used some of their program breaks to invite children to enter the competition. In many cases, the participating stations also held their own competitions before sending their selections of best films on to New York.

By February of 1971, NET had received the best local entries and the national phase of the competition began. A date early in May, 1971, was then set for broadcasting a 1-hour program. It was to be called "Through My Eyes." It was scheduled to be seen on 200 noncommercial stations around the country.

The first job at hand was that of narrowing down the number of films to be viewed by the judges. This was done over a period of several weeks in the screening rooms of NET. Then the judges themselves were asked to rule on the "best of the best." The judges were themselves an interesting group. They included Arthur Penn, a prominent film director; film critic Richard Schickel of *Life* magazine; John Culkin, director of the Center for Understanding Media; and two teen-age filmmakers named Rufus Seder and Kathy Ahern.

MANY THEMES

The films the judges saw were about such subjects as war, drugs, pollution, and the end of the world. In one film, a seemingly innocent snowball fight between two boys ended with both boys dead and two others jumping into camera range to take their places.

Little "Ingy"—short for Ingmar—was the symbol for National Educational Television's film competition for young people.

Not many of the films contained much to laugh about. It seems that young filmmakers are very much interested in treating serious subjects. One delightful exception was a film an 8-year-old boy made about his cat and her favorite sleeping place under the dining room table. It was a simple film with a sound track that did not always match the picture. Once, on the sound track, the young filmmaker (who was also the narrator) told the viewers, "Well, that's just about all"; then his cat reappeared, and he went on to say, "Well, that's just about it." But the film, despite its technical flaws, was real, funny, and warm because it was about something that mattered to the boy who made it.

Finally, the judges made their selections for the first-, second-, and third-best films in the two categories. Once the winners were chosen, the program called "Through My Eyes" was close to being born.

GETTING IT ALL TOGETHER

The job of the people who put together "Through My Eyes" may sound simple, but it really was not. First of all, it was decided to use more than just the six winning films on the program. Some very good films had not won prizes. Several of them deserved to be shown because of what they could teach the audience

A member of a teenage film club in New York City shoots a scene.

about making a film. The goal of the project was really not to conduct a national talent hunt to find the best young filmmaker in the United States. It was actually an effort to start a national festival of young people's films. The most the sponsors of the effort could hope for was that, if their jobs had been done well, the audience would be a little better prepared and a little more eager to make their own films.

The final decision was to show 13 films, in whole or in part, on the program. The films had to be arranged so that viewers would want to watch the entire program. Certain information about the films also had to be added to the program. And so the staff had to go back to the screening room—this time with stopwatches and note pads. The cuts had to be very carefully planned to show what was best, most important, and most rewarding in each film. Long hours of argument and compromise were involved.

Finally, a script for the program was written, grouping some of the winners into convenient categories such as "protest films" and "miniature documentaries." The funny moments in the films were balanced against the serious moments. In true theatrical fashion, the first-place winners were saved for the end of the program.

A good scriptwriter has to be a little like a good distance runner. He must know how he is doing on each lap. In the writer's case, he must know how many words he can fit between films. If you say too much between films, the audience is likely to forget it is watching a film program. If there are too few words, the audience lacks the basic information it needs about the films. What the script must do is keep the pace, remind the viewer of the theme of the program, and tell what is coming up next.

In the case of "Through My Eyes," the script was improved by the host of the program, David Steinberg. A young comedian who is interested in films, Steinberg added some of his own stories about his early experiences going to the movies. He managed to tell these stories without losing track of the script—which was being shown to him on a teleprompter.

In one frantic day, all of the elements of

Neighborhood boys consider the possibility of becoming filmmakers themselves.

"Through My Eyes" had to be made to fit together. These elements included the edited films, Steinberg's commentary, and his interviews with the senior winners. All of this had to be accomplished before the whole group was thrown out of the studio so that a crew could prepare the space for another, live show.

FINISHED PRODUCT

A few days later, the finished program was previewed, and the whole staff felt better. The winning film made a wonderful climax to the program. It was called *The Second Original Sin* and was made by Douglas Brodoff and Roger Calistro of Woodbridge, Connecticut. It was an animated film with wildly inventive drawings that lead us up to the "Wisdom Tree." There Adam, Eve, and the Serpent enact their familiar roles (Sin Number One). When Adam finishes eating the apple, he discards the core and pollution begins (Sin Number Two).

There were other fine moments in the program. There was a boy's view of a bicycle ride, using double images, slow motion technique, and music composed and recorded by the 16-year-old filmmaker, Michael Owens. There was a takeoff on Snoopy's adventures with the Red Baron—who was, in this case, called the Yellow Baron. The boys who made this film used fast-action techniques borrowed from silent films and made a plane themselves for re-creating a World War I air battle. There was a fish-eat-fish cartoon called *Seafood.* And there was the junior winner, called *Tom the Head,* about a bodiless head that wished it were something else, turned into a grape, and was eaten. The stated moral of the film: "Quit while you're a head."

It is possible for any young person to become a filmmaker overnight. See if there is a film club in your town. If there is—and many are being formed—they may be able to help you with the equipment and the know-how you need. If not, do it all yourself. Beg or borrow a camera and a tape recorder. Then go out and film your own story—whatever has visual interest and matters to you. "Through My Eyes" was just a step toward showing what young people can accomplish in films.

Gregory Vitiello
Senior Writer, Children's Television Workshop

Commedia dell'arte, with its strolling troupes, was an early form of street theater.

STREET THEATER

Have you ever looked—really looked—at the street you live on? A street is an exciting place, where beautiful, funny, and sometimes wonderful things happen every day. In some ways a street is like the stage of a theater, a place where people come and go and meet each other, and act out little pieces of the stories of their lives.

Every street has its own rhythm and its own music, and no two streets have exactly the same stories to tell. If you live in a small town, you probably know all the people who make up the day-to-day drama of your street. In large cities, where the rhythm of the streets is faster and constantly changes, the human drama becomes so rich that you could never watch it all, even if you kept your eyes open all day and all night.

In the past 10 years, large numbers of people across the United States suddenly began to notice that our streets are like the stage of a theater. The life that takes place on them can be as exciting as any play. And because our streets are also part of our homes, they are like theaters in another sense. They are places where we can relax, can play, and can enjoy entertainment. And so, during the past decade, a new kind of theater was born.

Hundreds of groups are now performing what has come to be known as "street theater." Often, this new theater is the work of professional acting companies who come into the neighborhood and perform their plays and their dances and songs in the street. But sometimes this new kind of theater comes from the street itself, from people who live in the community and want to share with each other the human drama of their own lives.

HOW STREET THEATER BEGAN

Street theater actually had its beginnings well over 2,000 years ago. As part of the religious ceremonies of ancient Greece, festivals were held in the streets. People thronged into the squares to celebrate the feast days of their gods. These festivals gave rise to the first dramas of the Western world, in which events in the lives of the heroes were portrayed.

In the Middle Ages the streets of Europe were theaters where dancers, jugglers, troubadors, and magicians brought their pretty tales and songs and their bags of tricks. In England the craft guilds used wagons to perform cycles of plays, called mystery plays, presenting stories from the Bible. The wagons rolled along, one behind the other, each equipped with a separate scene. A wagon would stop in front of a group of spectators, and when the actors had finished performing, the wagon would roll on to the next group.

A little later, in Italy, strolling troupes of actors traveled from town to town with their songs and stories in their heads, and their costumes and stage properties in huge sacks hung over their shoulders. This kind of performance was called *commedia dell'arte.*

STREET THEATER IN THE UNITED STATES

The United States developed its own version of traveling street theater in the 19th century. Before the railroad became a major form of transportation, many people got their theater entertainment from medicine shows. Salesmen used to carry their medicines and other wares from place to place in small wagons. When people gathered around to shop, these "medicine men" pulled little stages down from their wagons and put on a show for their customers, right there in the street.

Although modern methods of transportation have changed all this, the street theater movement of recent years is rediscovering many of the old methods. For example, the East River Players, a New York group, perform on simple raised platforms that are probably about the same size as the outdoor stages used centuries ago in the marketplaces of medieval Europe. Philadelphia's Society Hill Playhouse Street Theater performs its plays from the back of a small truck, while the Soul and Latin Theater, another New York group, has its stage on a truck whose rear door flaps down—just like that of the old medicine show wagons.

Simplicity is the standard for most of the traveling performers. Many troupes use variants of the Illinois Free Street Theater's fold-out trailer. The Phoenix Theater–Gordon Duffey Street Theater comes to town in a converted school bus with a fold-down stage. The New York Shakespeare Festival's Mobile Theater is more elaborate, with five trailers and hydraulically operated equipment. Other groups, such as the East Harlem Third World Revelationists, the various Everyman Companies across the country, and the East River Players of Harlem, use only the barest staging and no sound equipment at all.

Today street theater has become an important part of the life of many communities, and the movement is growing rapidly. Every summer, New York's Lincoln Center invites street theater groups from several states to perform. In the summer of 1972, 1,500 performers, from 30 groups, presented their own productions in a festival that lasted two full weeks.

Street theater in the United States began with the "medicine man" performing for his customers.

Opening day at Lincoln Center's 1972 street theater festival.

TWO KINDS OF STREET THEATER

Although people usually call all theater in the streets "street theater," the playing companies themselves make a distinction. They say that "mobile theater" refers to groups that come into a community from the outside, while "street theater" properly refers to groups that spring up within the community itself.

In many cases there is little difference between the two types of theater. But generally speaking, the mobile theaters bring to local neighborhoods plays and entertainment prepared and performed by professionals. The best example of this kind of company is the New York Shakespeare Festival's Mobile Theater. This group uses high-level professional actors from the Broadway and off-Broadway stage. It performs classic plays and uses very sophisticated equipment.

For example, the Mobile Theater toured the city's streets and playgrounds with a delightful version of Shakespeare's comedy *Two Gentlemen of Verona*. It was a colorful production with singing, dancing, and new dialogue that everyone could enjoy. When the Mobile Theater first started, its most popular production was its version of *Hamlet*. The production became known as "the black *Hamlet*" because the hero was played by a black actor who spoke his lines in the language of the ghetto.

As for "street theater" in the strict sense, countless smaller, less professional groups grew up out of their own home streets. Most of these groups began in the streets of large cities. Now they are found across the country. Philadelphia has its Society Hill Playhouse Street Theater. Boston has its Summerthing. Chicago has its Free Street Theater. Watts, in California, has its Douglass House Writers Workshop. And New York has so many different groups that it is hard to count them all.

This kind of theater is best understood if you think of it as "people's" theater—theater in which the people of the neighborhood take an active part. The actress Miriam Colón calls her Puerto Rican Traveling Theater company "community theater." "We have strong ties with the community," she says. "The theater has become a vital part of community life. Our audiences talk back to the actors, they advise

Philadelphia's Society Hill Playhouse performs from the back of a small truck.

the characters on stage, they touch them, they ask questions. They become part of the show."

The best example of theater that grew up in a community to serve its needs is César Chávez' Teatro Campesino in California. Chávez' group sprang up out of the union leader's efforts to reach and educate California's unorganized farm workers. The plays performed by this group all deal with hunger, low pay, poor working conditions, and the civil and human rights of farm workers. These are the problems of these people's lives, and the plays are all meant to teach the workers how to solve them.

In fact, education is the most important feature of many of the street theater productions. And in this respect, today's street theater is very close to the theater of the Middle Ages in Europe, when the Catholic Church used street theater to instruct people in the beliefs and practices of their religion.

In some cases the community people themselves help to write and produce the plays. Many plays, therefore, reflect the problems and concerns of the neighborhood. Through their plays, people are trying to talk to their neighbors, their friends, and their children and parents. They are trying to teach the people they care about to solve their own problems and to develop a feeling of pride in themselves.

Many of the street theaters that have sprung from the ghettos of large cities perform plays about drugs, discrimination, poverty, disease, poor living conditions—and about the pride that comes to people when they solve these problems. A favorite play of the Everyman Company of Brooklyn, called *The Blind Junkie,* is about a drug addict. And almost every street theater has one play like the Fulton Theater Company's *Heritage,* which teaches people of the ghetto that they have good reason to be proud of their ancestors and of themselves.

Every company, in fact, has at least one play that teaches people that their own street is beautiful.

MARILYN STASIO
Theater Critic
Cue Magazine

ART AND MACHINES

Art has always been a record of what people think about themselves and their world. Art objects or art experiences reveal what we know about ourselves. They also show us where we should look to know more about ourselves and our world.

Since the time of the Renaissance, almost 500 years ago, artists have been concerned with what science could tell them about our world. The artists of the Renaissance used the laws and discoveries of science to make their work reflect the life of the people of their time. For example, Leonardo da Vinci, the painter of the famous *Mona Lisa,* wanted to understand more about how the human body works. He thought this knowledge would help him express the new feelings that he and other Renaissance artists had about themselves and their society. Leonardo went to a skilled anatomist, a man who worked somewhat like a surgeon or a doctor would work today, to learn how the muscles, tendons, and bones of the human body function to control our movements. With what he learned from the anatomist, Leonardo was able to draw and paint the human body so well that he is still admired today as a great figure painter.

Modern artists are equally interested in learning new things about themselves and their world. They notice the effects that modern science has had upon the way all of us live. They see the way in which computers are being used to process the large amounts of information that our complicated society creates each day. It is apparent to modern artists that computers can contribute to art just as they contribute to business, medicine, space exploration, and many other fields. Computers are changing the ways in which we communicate with one another. Many artists now want to work with scientists and computer experts. They feel that if they do they can increase their understanding of what these great changes in the way people communicate mean to our daily lives. They also hope to gain a better understanding of what we think about ourselves.

To have machines—even complicated electronic computers—as the subject of art or closely connected with art is not a new thing. In the last 70 years, artists have produced work that shows man's position in relation to machines and how he uses them to further control the world in which he lives. In the last 10 years, artists have even sent their works to be made in factories so that they can use the most advanced techniques and materials to create art objects. In fact, it sometimes seems as if artists are competing with machines to see which can make the more beautiful, useful, or important objects.

THE COMPUTER AGE

In the computer, the artist sees the possibility of doing his work faster; and so he goes to the computer scientist, just as Leonardo went to the anatomist, to help him make new forms. The two men—artist and computer scientist—working together produce something that neither could have produced alone.

The Cybernetic Tower of Light, which is now being constructed in Paris, is an impressive example of what can happen when artists interested in technology work with engineers, architects, and computer specialists. Scheduled to be finished sometime in 1974, the tower will stand higher than the Eiffel Tower in Paris and will cost $40,000,000. The artist who conceived the project, Nicholas Schoffer, has been working with moving sculpture since 1950. In 1961 he designed a cybernetic tower over 300 feet high for the city of Liège, Belgium.

Schoffer wants his new tower to play an important part in the life of modern Paris. Beneath the tower there will be an underground cybernetic center with computers that will receive information about conditions in Paris such as weather, traffic volume on the streets, and noise levels. In response to the signals received from the city's environment, the computers will organize spectacular displays of light and sound from the tower's

An artist's model for the amazing Cybernetic Tower of Light, which will soon rise in Paris.

The Boston Public Gardens were filled with light and sound by PULSA in 1968.

The PULSA control system for their show at the Museum of Modern Art.

many lights, projectors, and mirrors. By looking at the light beamed into the night sky, people in the city will receive a visual impression of the energy of the city. Besides all of the electronic equipment, the 1,300-foot tower will have conference centers, theaters, restaurants, and observation decks where Parisians can relax and enjoy themselves.

As artists work with computers, they begin to think of the world in which we live in terms of the flow of messages and signals between people. These modern artists do not try to make objects; rather they try to design or make experiences that will help share the new way they understand their world. Seeing their work becomes a theatrical event: the people who have come to see the work play the part of spectators and actors at the same time.

A group of young artists and technicians called PULSA created a new kind of artistic experience for the Museum of Modern Art in New York City in 1970. In the garden of the museum, the PULSA group placed strobe lights, speakers, and infrared heaters. They also installed two television cameras and other

The beautiful and eerie lights of an environment show in New Haven.

equipment above the garden to monitor the movements of people and the amount of light and sound there. The cameras and the equipment sent the information they "saw" to a computer system, which was also placed near the garden. The computer processed the information so as to change the patterns of light, heat, and sound coming from the strobes, heaters, and speakers. As museum visitors walked through the garden, their movements helped to design or make the light and sound effects they saw around them.

An American artist named James Seawright designed a smaller environment-piece called *Electronic Peristyle.* In this piece, the viewer and the movements he makes influence what he sees and feels. *Electronic Peristyle* was first shown at the Kansas City Performing Arts Foundation. It consists of a circle 21 feet in diameter, surrounded by columns. When a person walks inside the circle, electronic sensory equipment transforms his movements into information. The information is fed into an electronic device that controls the patterns of sound, light, and wind that come from the

Heaters and light, sensors and sound fill the sculpture garden of the Museum of Modern Art.

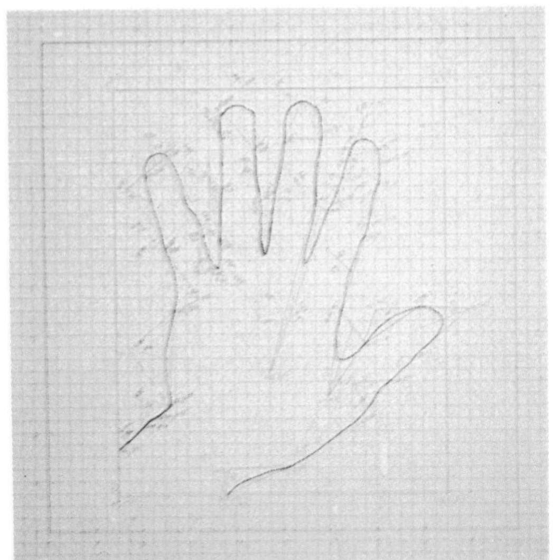

Artspeak drawing of a hand with coordinates plotted as they will be "told" to the computer.

This man is drawing on the CRT screen of a Graphic I Console with a light pen.

columns. By carefully watching the effects, the viewer can see how he has influenced what is going on. Although the piece is very complex, the artist himself admits that it is only a simple beginning. He has ideas for more "intelligent" systems, or pieces; these would be even more interesting.

ELECTRONIC DRAWING BOARD

The works that have been discussed so far are large and technical. It is also possible to use a computer to make drawings and designs that are similar to those an artist makes on his drawing board. But an artist would not be able to do them so fast as the computer. Special computer "languages" for special problems have been invented for doctors, engineers, or artists who want to use computers but do not want to learn the more complicated computer languages used by scientists.

Professor Jacob Schwartz at New York University has developed a language called Artspeak for artists. With it, artists can "speak" with the computer, using ordinary English words, and algebra. Artspeak is so simple to learn that children 10 and 12 years old have mastered it and produced their own computer art. The Artspeak picture included in this article is an artist's drawing of a hand. Each segment of the drawing has been plotted in terms of X and Y coordinates. (It is much like making a graph in algebra class.) These numbers will be used to tell the computer exactly where each part of the drawing of the hand is placed. Once the computer has been given the location of the original lines that make up the hand, it can be instructed to "move," to "mirror," to "reduce," or to "draw 100 times" so as to change the original drawing of the hand into new forms. There are many simple directions and commands possible in Artspeak. They are coded electrically on punched cards—the kind of card you may get with your telephone bill—and fed into the computer. The computer draws the image with its "hand," a mechanical line plotter, and returns the punched cards. Artspeak can also be used to make simple movies and to compose music. The only restriction or limit is that the process must be mathematically described for the computer.

The artist can work with the computer in a

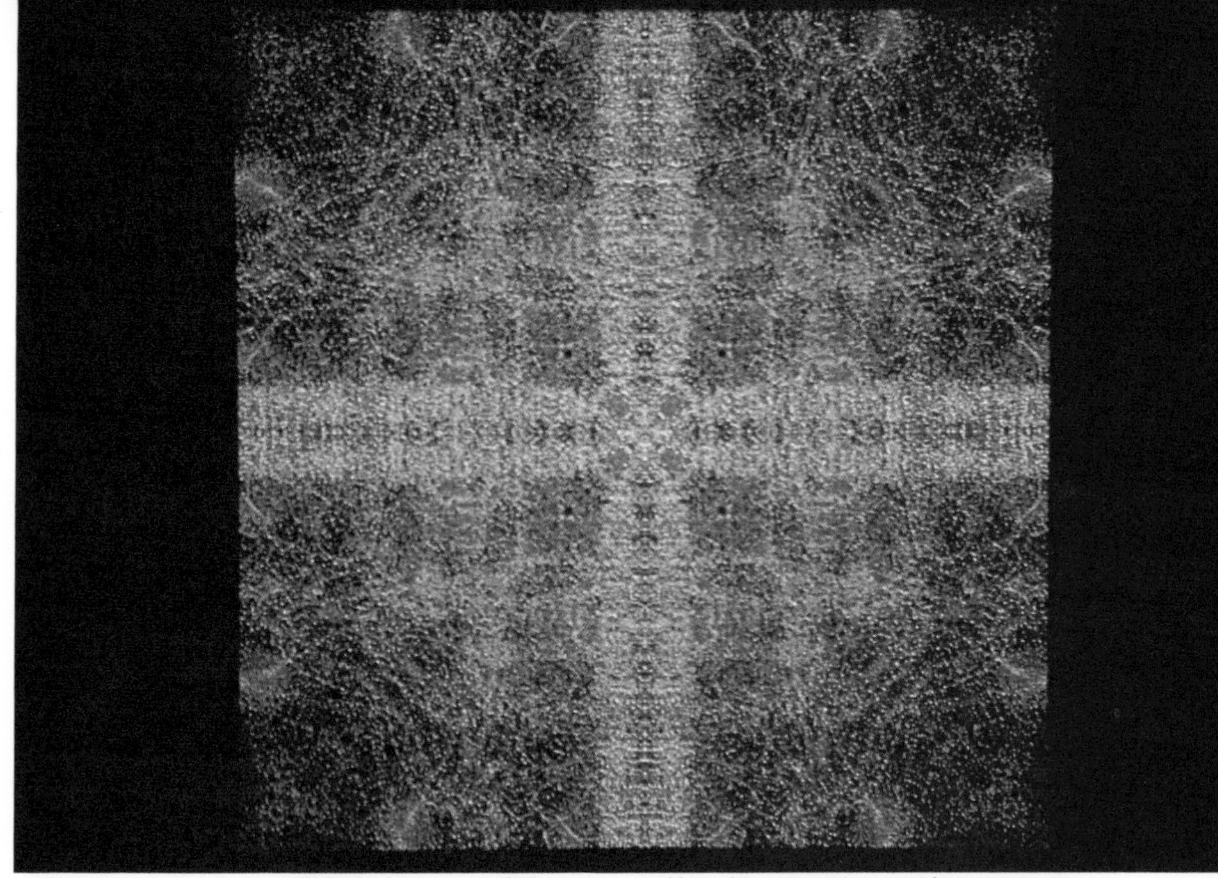

This design was made by a man working with patterns created by a computer.

more direct way by using a cathode-ray tube (CRT). The tube is a screen, similar to a television picture tube. The computer's answers to commands are instantly displayed on the CRT, and the artist can actually "talk" directly to the computer, using a light pen, rather than take the time to write programs and carry them through. If the artist wants to change some part of his drawing or design, he can see the effect of the changes on the CRT immediately.

Systems Development Corporation in California is working on a graphics system using a CRT that may allow artists to use a computer no matter where they are. The machine they are working on will resemble a typewriter. The "typewriter" will connect the programer—by telephone lines—with a computer far away. To talk with the computer the operator will simply write or draw on a Rand Tablet, an electronically treated writing surface, something like a magic slate. (The system will be able to read handwriting.) In a very few minutes, the reply will be flashed on a CRT screen.

Color graphics can be created by mounting a camera on the CRT. The image is created by using color filters and taking many exposures of the images shown on the screen. Movies can be made in much the same way if a motion-picture camera is installed. As the operator manipulates the image, he can command the computer to produce effects that resemble those used in conventional motion-picture camera operation.

These are just a few examples of the many ways in which the artist in the modern world of machines can make machines his finest tools. With machines, especially the computer, the artist is now able to make his art reflect the world around him in the most sensitive way possible. And computers make it possible for the viewer to enter into the work of art, experience it, and himself become a part of it and change it. With the aid of machines the artist and the viewer are able to enter into a creative—almost magical—partnership.

RICHARD KATHMANN
Co-director
Chicago River Spectacle Company

YOUNG PHOTOGRAPHERS

Do you like taking pictures? Are you talented with a camera? Then you may want to join the thousands of young photographers who submit their work each year to the Scholastic Photography Awards program. On these pages are some of the 1972 prize-winning photographs. All the entrants were students in grades 7 through 12 in the United States and Canada. The work submitted was in both color and black and white. The 1972 awards program, the 45th conducted by Scholastic Magazines, Inc., was sponsored for the 10th year by the Eastman Kodak Company. A committee of national judges selected 270 winners of college scholarship grants, cash prizes, and medallions of excellence.

"Up for the Winter," by Gemma Stravitsch, Huntington Station, N.Y. Age 13.

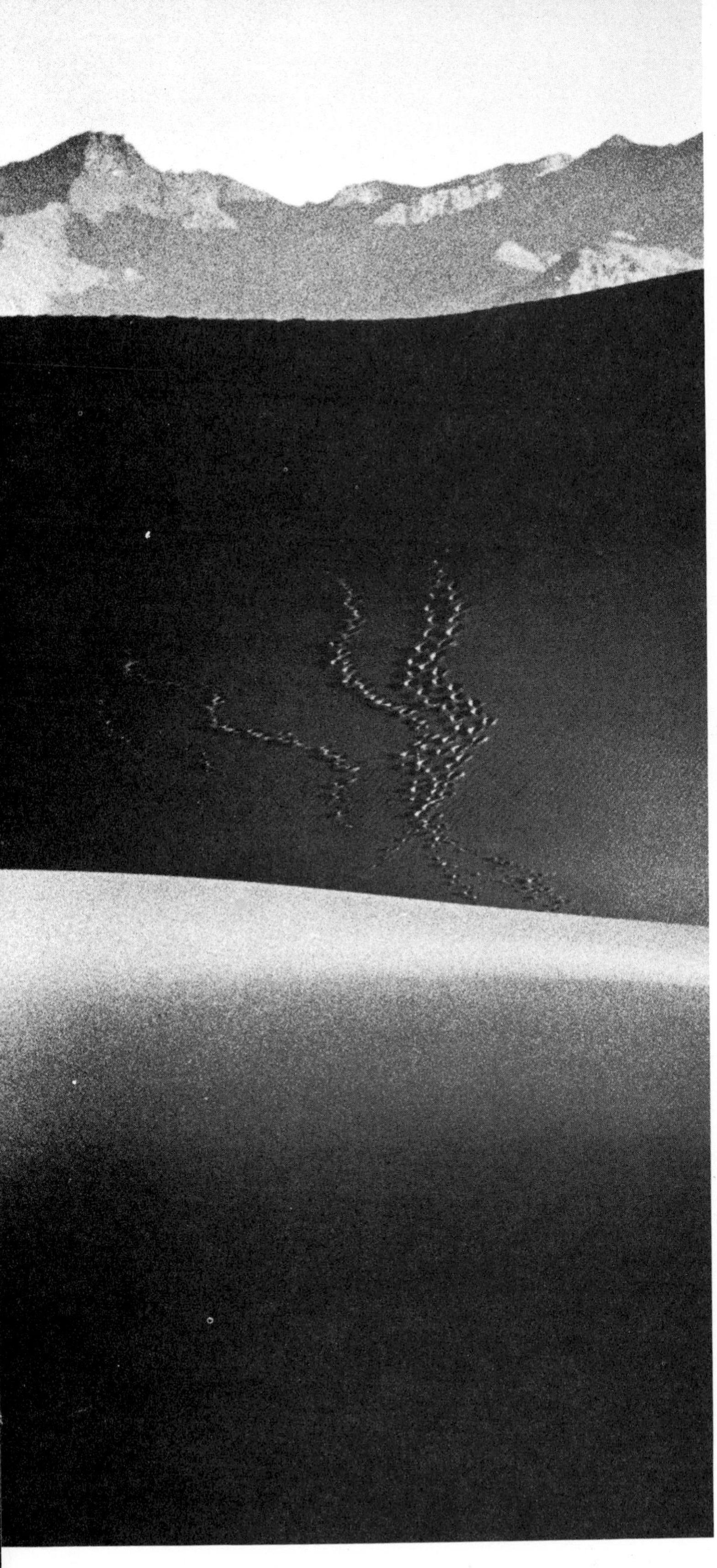

Above: "Spokes," by Randy Pearce, Upland, California. Age 13. Below: "Cyanotic Spruce," by John Owens, Bedford, Indiana. Age 16. Left: "Sand Dune Footstep," by Ron Contarsy, Reseda, California. Age 18.

Young concertgoers give all of their attention to Leonard Bernstein.

YOUNG PEOPLE'S CONCERTS

On a windy November afternoon 75 years ago, during a raging blizzard that blanketed New York with 10 inches of snow, a group of children flocked to an unusual concert at Carnegie Hall. Carnegie Hall was then the city's leading auditorium for concerts. They were going to attend a unique concert for young people. It was given under the direction of Frank Damrosch and marked the beginning of a bold experiment to help youngsters acquire a taste for good music. Some people thought that the idea would not work. "All children do *not* have a natural inclination toward music," wrote one skeptical critic soon afterward, "because a great many like the banjo and instruments of that kind and cannot be persuaded to like anything else."

IN THE BEGINNING

The concert began with the Austrian national anthem. This was because the melody was taken from a composition of Franz Joseph Haydn. Damrosch then proceeded to explain to his young listeners how the melody was put together. Many must have been surprised to learn that a composer had to deal with such elements as phrases, periods, sections, and harmonic design. Perhaps most of them thought that composers just made up tunes without any rules or plans and wrote them down.

In the second orchestral number, Mendelssohn's *Fingal's Cave Overture,* Damrosch introduced his audience to one of the larger musical forms. He explained how the three important themes were developed and contrasted. To interest the children more, Damrosch made up such a fascinating story to go with the music that he forgot to tell them that Fingal's Cave can really be found in a grotto off the west coast of Scotland. The last orchestral number on the program was Wagner's turbulent *Ride of the Valkyries.* To close the program a soprano named Emma Juch sang six songs, including "Little Boy Blue" by Ethelbert Nevin.

That concert was the first public lesson for children in America in what was then the very unpopular subject of what to listen for in music. The afternoon proved to be as instructive for many grown-ups as it was for children.

The concerts were so popular that they were continued. About 12 years later, Damrosch's younger brother, Walter, took over as conductor. Concerts for young people were soon being given by the leading orchestras of other American cities. Chicago heard them as early as 1903. Soon after the end of World War I, the orchestras of Cleveland and Boston began offering young people's concerts. Concerts in Philadelphia were also extended to the public schools. The idea of young people's concerts crossed the Atlantic in 1922. The first public concerts for children in England were started then.

A REGULAR SERIES

When the New York Philharmonic introduced a regular series of young people's concerts on January 26, 1924, the triple duties of conductor, pianist, and speaker were fulfilled by Ernest Schelling, much as a successor, Leonard Bernstein, would do many years later. By this time slides were used to help children learn the shape and mechanical details of musical instruments. In addition, slides of composers, diagrams of the orchestra, and illustrations of musical themes were shown.

Devoting his first concert to the orchestra's string section, Schelling showed how a violin was put together. He then explained the role of strings in the structure of a symphony. For the Chopin *Polonaise Militaire,* which followed, pictures were shown of the Polish dance on which the music was based. The cello came into its own with Saint-Saëns' *The Swan.* The children were also asked to join in singing the patriotic song "Columbia, the Gem of the Ocean," as the words were projected on a screen.

Carefully prepared program notes for the concerts were included in a notebook passed out to the children as they came in. It had space for their own notes and for their answers to a quiz on the music which the audience was given. At the end of the series, prizes were given for the best notebooks.

During the next 30 years a number of new things were introduced into the New York Philharmonic Young People's Concerts. A special series of concerts was added for children under 9. Performances by "surprise celebrities" became a regular feature at the senior concerts. Radio auditions for young soloists were held. There was also an annual contest for composers under 17. Prizes were awarded to the winners, and their compositions were played at the concerts. Schelling was succeeded as director by Rudolph Ganz. He was followed by Igor Buketoff and Wilfred Pelletier. Distinguished guest conductors made frequent appearances. Possibly the most popular was Leopold Stokowski, who was himself a pioneer in such concerts. Unafraid of some good-natured bedlam, he made one concert interesting by encouraging a game of "tag" in the aisles during a performance of the *Summer Day Suite* by the Russian composer Sergei Prokofiev.

NEW DIMENSIONS

Under the direction of Leonard Bernstein, the concerts were given a new format and an enormously expanded audience on January 18, 1958. They were seen for the first time on nationwide television. Written and narrated by Bernstein, many subsequent programs were devoted to gifted young performers. Several of the talented young musicians who first appeared on the program went on to achieve international fame. Other concerts honored such outstanding composers as Aaron Copland, Igor Stravinsky, and Dmitri Shostakovich. But the majority of concerts continued the basic purpose of explaining music and musical form—now with the help of the television camera.

Producing the four annual videotaped concerts seen all over the United States and, in

An assistant conductor named Mary Quach leads one of the concerts in the series.

In 1968 cellist Lawrence Foster, then 14, played with the New York Philharmonic, under assistant conductor Alois Springer.

The serious face of Leonard Bernstein (*above*) became familiar to children and adults all over the United States when the Young People's Concerts went on television. Steven and Martin Vann (*right*), twin brothers who were also duo-pianists, were among the many young soloists who played with the Philharmonic during Bernstein's long and successful career as director of the Young People's Concerts.

rebroadcasts, all over the world requires the skills of highly trained programing and engineering specialists. More than $1,000,000 worth of mobile color television equipment is also required. Many weeks of planning, arranging, and rehearsing are necessary before the broadcast itself.

The narration for the broadcasts is written by the conductor, who submits copies of the script to the director. At production meetings the script is discussed from many viewpoints, and changes are made where necessary. The script must be timed to the second with a stopwatch while the conductor reads it. Later, at rehearsals, all the music is timed this way.

Another very important job is studying the music and deciding which camera shots and angles are best for every part of the show. Closeups are often used when an instrument has an important solo passage. The director must choose the camera angles, framing, order, and pace of the shots. He must decide which shots will be used when several cameras are picking up various sections of the orchestra at the same time. Before the broadcast all these questions must be resolved. The camera shots and their continuity must be planned. And, finally, a shooting plan must be drawn up.

FROM THE CONTROL ROOMS

Because most concert halls do not have a control room for television broadcasting, all equipment used must be specially installed for the performance and dismantled afterward. Early in the morning of the day of the broadcast, two huge trucks (mobile units) pull up alongside the entrance to Philharmonic Hall in New York City, where the broadcasts originate. One truck houses the video control room. The other truck contains the generators and some other technical equipment. Technicians have been working through the night, laying cables; setting up lights; and moving in microphones, cameras, and other equipment. The installation of all electronic equipment is supervised by an engineer-in-charge. He checks carefully during the broadcast to make certain that everything is working properly. The audio engineer decides where to place the microphones.

Six color-television cameras are usually needed for a broadcast. Most television shows require only four. Two mobile cameras are onstage. Two cameras are placed in the audience and one is located in the film projection booth close to the ceiling. The remaining camera is hidden behind the orchestra, in the middle of the stage. The lens of this onstage camera projects through a special "porthole" and is used for direct head-on shots of the conductor. Each camera is manned by an expert cameraman. He wears a telephone headset for two-way communication with the director and associate director.

For the audio (sound) part of the concert, 23 microphones are set up onstage. In addition, a special microphone is pinned to the conductor's necktie for his explanations of the music under discussion.

The lighting director supervises the placement of the extra television lighting that he has designed. This is a complicated process. Television lights are strong, and members of the orchestra must not be blinded by the glare when they are playing. In addition to the full light onstage, there must be four or five brightly lit areas in the hall so that television viewers can see how the live audience is reacting to the concert.

Each broadcast has two stage managers. One oversees the entrances and exits of the performers. He is also responsible for placing chairs, music stands, and the piano, and for maintaining order onstage. The other stage manager supervises any cards, pictures, or other illustrative material used. Both stage managers give instructions to the stagehands who handle the equipment.

Unlike most television programs, the "Young People's Concerts" uses two separate control rooms, one for video (what is seen), and the other for audio. The video control room is in one of the trucks. The audio control room is located above the stage, on the right-hand side of the auditorium.

In the video control room, television screens, called "monitors," are set up. One monitor for each camera shows what picture that specific camera is "seeing." Other monitors show the picture that is being broadcast or relayed by underground cable to two videotape recorders, located a half mile away in the television network's own studios. The pro-

A very young man himself, the popular new conductor Michael Tilson Thomas took over the concert series in 1972.

ducer-director sits flanked by an associate director and a technical director. They are seated at a long table that faces one bank of monitors and is equipped with microphones and control buttons. The associate director relays the director's instructions to the cameramen. They move into position and focus on the picture requested. The technical director pushes the button that will put the right picture on the air when the director wants it.

Seated behind the directors are a production assistant and two assistants to the director. The production assistant is responsible primarily for clocking the exact time elapsed in each portion of the script and music. One of the assistants follows the script and the prompting device. This enables the director to return to the proper place in the score after viewing the monitors. The other assistant is responsible for the smooth operation of personnel, technical equipment, and schedules. In a darkened part of the video control room, engineers watch another bank of monitors to make certain that the best quality television signals are being transmitted.

In the audio control room, the audio engineer adjusts the controls that pick up the sound of the orchestra, soloists, audience response, and the conductor's voice. The music co-ordinator, a trained specialist in recording and sound balancing, sits next to the audio engineer, with whom he works.

In addition to the millions of people who have seen the more than 60 regular television broadcasts of the New York Philharmonic Young People's Concerts to date, the programs are seen by millions more through television rebroadcasts in foreign countries, and are seen by millions of students in classrooms. In 1972 the young conductor Michael Tilson Thomas took over the series. There is little doubt that Thomas' forthcoming concerts will again prove the success of the "bold experiment" that began on that snowy afternoon 75 years ago. And there is little doubt that the young people's concerts that were started in many other cities will also continue with great success.

JOEL HONIG
Contributor to *Opera News*

CHANGING: A NEW SONG

"Changing" is a new song. It is not likely that you have heard it before unless you just happened to be strolling past the composer's window while he was writing it. It is a song in the folk-rock tradition, and it was written especially for young people. It will soon appear in a new songbook. Try to play it on your piano. If you do not play the piano, try to pick it out on your guitar or banjo or play it on your recorder. If you do not play an instrument, sing it! "Changing" is a good song, and it was meant for you.

The best thing about this song it that you can carry it with you in your head. It is portable. Take it to the park and teach it to your rock group or play it with friends at home. (The photographs on the opposite page give some idea of how much fun those activities might be.) Why not make your own variations on the music? And you can improvise on the lyrics, too, if you are a poet. Why not add some "changes" of your own? Think of all the things you know in the world that change—and sing about them.

The music world rocked with religion in 1972.

THE MUSIC SCENE

In years past, singing sensations, like Bob Dylan or the Beatles, appeared on the scene to shake up the world of popular music. In 1972, however, events—rather than new superstars, outrageous styles, or definite trends—held the spotlight. And some of the major events of the year even had a "left-over" quality to them.

Jesus Christ Superstar, which opened on the Broadway stage in October, 1971, played to packed houses throughout 1972. The musical extravaganza, which had started out as a widely acclaimed rock-opera recording, opened to mixed critical reviews and tremendous controversy. Pickets denounced the opera as sacrilegious, and the Reverend Malcolm Boyd disapproved of its "lack of soul." But *Variety* described it as "the biggest all-media parlay in show biz history." Young and old alike flocked to the theater box office.

Whether or not the success of *Superstar* stimulated or reflected the growth of the "Jesus People," or "Jesus Freaks," movement during 1972 was not known. But religion seemed to be the "in" thing with a large number of today's young people. The world of rock music echoed with religious or pseudo-religious overtones. Some of the more popular recordings were Lalo Schifrin's *Rock Requiem,* Decca's *Rock Mass for Love,* Galt MacDermot's *Divine Hair* (Mass in F), and Merle Haggard's country-oriented "The Land of Many Churches." A rock version of Handel's *Messiah* by David Axelrod drew considerable reaction from music critics. *The New York Times* denounced the work as a high point in "commercial cynicism, bad taste, musical ignorance, and all-round incompetence."

Leonard Bernstein's theatrical rock *Mass,* which opened at the John F. Kennedy Center in Washington, D.C., in 1971, went on the road in 1972. The flamboyant production of *Mass,* a mishmash of rock, jazz, and classicism, had a limited engagement in New York City at the Metropolitan Opera House. Regardless of how the public felt about the stage production (the show evoked much discussion), the record album of *Mass* appeared to be a popular item in record stores.

Stephen Schwartz's *Godspell,* a smash hit off-Broadway musical based on the Gospel according to Saint Matthew, also took to the road. The show attracted enthusiastic audiences wherever it played, winning praise as a "superior rock opera." The rave reviews carried *Godspell* to London, where it proved to be one of the hits of the theater season. In keeping with the theatrical success, the *Godspell* album triumphed as a hit among record buyers. Many songs were taken from the album and recorded as singles, but "Day by Day" seemed to cause the most excitement.

A YEAR OF EVENTS

In 1971 former Beatle George Harrison and sitarist Ravi Shankar organized a benefit concert to help the people of Bangladesh. The rock musical event, called Concert for Bangladesh, was held at Madison Square Garden in New York City. With the donated talents of such superstars as Bob Dylan, Ringo Starr, Leon Russell, Eric Clapton, and Billy Preston, the concert was one of the most successful benefits ever produced. A three-disc album of the event became a giant best seller, and a film of the entire concert was released in 1972. Harrison reported that between the concert itself, the record album, and the film, an estimated $25,000,000 was raised for the people of Bangladesh.

The closings of San Francisco's famous rock palace, the Fillmore auditorium, and its New York branch, Fillmore East, brought about the end of an era. But this sad event in the world of popular music did not go unnoticed. *Fillmore: The Last Days,* a three-disc album, and *Fillmore,* a film, presented the music of such major groups as the Grateful Dead, Quicksilver Messenger Service, Hot Tuna, and Santana.

One of the major musical happenings of 1972 took place in Hollywood, California. The motion-picture industry voted an Academy Award for Best Song of the Year to Isaac Hayes for his "Theme from Shaft." It was the first time in the history of the Academy of Motion Picture Arts and Sciences that an Oscar for Best Song had been given to a black composer.

Isaac Hayes accepts Oscar from actor Joel Grey.

Carly Simon won the 1972 Grammy Award for Best New Artist of the Year.

ON TOUR

The Rolling Stones, the sole remaining superstar group of the 1960's, made a tremendously successful American tour in 1972. The group rolled through 31 cities, finishing with sold-out performances at Madison Square Garden. The Stones' tour coincided with the release of their newest album, *Exile on Main Street.*

With feverish anticipation the rock world awaited the American debut of the new British sensation T. Rex. The quartet, under the guidance of its lead singer, Marc Bolan, had made a series of hits in England, and its appearances throughout Europe had been hysterically received. Many rock enthusiasts thought that T. Rex, and particularly Marc Bolan, would set the rock music scene ablaze. But despite the group's hit albums *Electric Warrior* and *The Slider,* Marc Bolan failed to establish himself as a competitor to charismatic Mick Jagger or Rod Stewart.

Neil Diamond was acclaimed as one of the music industry's reigning superstars.

SONGWRITER–PERFORMERS

In 1972, writer-performers rather than interpreter-performers caught the public's eye—and ear. Neil Diamond, fast becoming one of the recording industry's top-selling male singers, played a highly successful engagement at Hollywood's Greek Theatre. Because of the concert's excellent notices, Diamond took his show to New York in October for a limited Broadway run. His album *Moods,* for which he wrote all the songs, made the best-seller charts. "Song Sung Blue," also written and recorded by Diamond, was one of the year's top singles.

Paul Simon (without Art Garfunkel) came up with a hit single in 1972. His "Mother and Child Reunion," while not as appealing as his earlier "Bridge over Troubled Water," made the best-seller charts. Simon's first solo album, simply titled *Paul Simon,* was well received by the record-buying public. One of the year's major albums was *Simon and Gar-*

funkel's Greatest Hits, an anthology of the former duo's top-selling songs.

After two so-so albums of his own songs, Harry Nilsson came up with a Gold Record album, *Nilsson Schmilsson.*

Randy Newman, another composer-singer, has been hailed as possessing the "most original comic vision." His new album, *Sail Away,* was one of the most favorably reviewed albums of the year. But despite the critical acclaim accorded Newman, the sales of his recordings were a disappointment.

Other songwriters who became noted recording artists during 1972 include: Tom Rush ("Merrimack Country"); Bill Withers ("Ain't No Sunshine," "Grandma's Hands," and "Lean on Me"); Ray Davies, leader-songwriter of the Kinks ("Muswell Hillbillies"); and John Prine, a Kris Kristofferson discovery, hailed by many in the music world as the most important new country- and folk-oriented artist of the year.

In 1972, folk singer Joan Baez came more into her own as a singer-composer. Having made numerous albums of songs written by other composers, she wrote and recorded the album *Come from the Shadows.* The song "To Bobby," included in the album, was an appeal to folk/rock hero Bob Dylan to assume once again the role of social-protest leader—a position he had given up and left unfilled.

Liza Minnelli in a scene from the film *Cabaret.*

Superstar Carole King continued to make news in 1972. Her award-winning album *Tapestry* is on its way to becoming the largest-selling LP in the history of the recording industry. In the United States alone, over 5,500,000 copies of the album have been sold.

NEW VOICES

The year's most dazzling leap to stardom was made by actress-singer Liza Minnelli. Her performance in the film version of the Broadway musical *Cabaret* won widespread critical

Roberta Flack thrilled audiences with her distinctive sound and style.

Elvis Presley, the king of rock 'n' roll, made his New York debut with sold-out concerts at Madison Square Garden in June, 1972.

acclaim. The original sound track of the film became one of the runaway best-selling albums of the year. Other artists making news in 1972 included: Roberta Flack with her hit single "The First Time Ever I Saw Your Face" and the album *First Take,* Al Green with his single "Let's Stay Together," and Neil Young with his recording of "Heart of Gold" and the album *Harvest.*

Don McLean had a major hit single during the year. In his "American Pie," McLean sings about the uneasiness and lack of direction of young people today.

The newest singing sensation to hit the music scene is Gilbert O'Sullivan, an Irish former postal clerk. His record "Alone Again (Naturally)" climbed to the top of the charts shortly after its release in the United States. Success appears to be an absolute certainty for O'Sullivan. The young singer is being guided by Gordon Mills, the same man who launched Tom Jones and Engelbert Humperdinck on their way to fame and fortune.

▸ ESTABLISHED CHART–MAKERS

The Carpenters continued to dominate the popular-music scene during 1972. Their two hit singles, "Goodbye Love" and "Hurting Each Other," were included in the album *A Song for You.* Other groups making the charts were Chicago; Sly and the Family Stone; Santana; Led Zeppelin; Grand Funk Railroad; and Three Dog Night. Elton John, with his album *Honky Château,* and John Lennon, with *Imagine,* caused a great deal of excitement in music circles.

Donny Osmond of the Osmond Brothers, Michael Jackson of the Jackson Five, and David Cassidy of TV's "The Partridge Family" all developed a loyal following among the pre-teen and early teen-age set. They all had hit records, and their personal-appearance tours drew large audiences.

▸ MUSICAL NOSTALGIA

A bygone era went on the road in 1972. The Rock 'n' Roll Revival of the 1950's, a traveling show sponsored by Richard Nader and other producers, rolled across the country. The highly successful tour brought renewed fame, standing ovations, and new fans for such musical pioneers as B. B. King, Bo Diddley, Chuck Berry, the Drifters, the Coasters, Bill Haley, and Chubby Checker. These were the musical giants of the 1950's and the 1960's.

The Revival's continuing popularity helped to emphasize that rock music was still in a state of change. No new style had taken hold. The year ended much as it began—with music fans still waiting for someone to come along and start an exciting new trend in the world of popular music.

ARNOLD SHAW
Author, *The Rock Revolution*

1972 AT A GLANCE

JANUARY

On January 5, President Richard M. Nixon approved the building of a space shuttle, a re-usable manned space vehicle. It will be able to blast off like a rocket, circle in earth orbit like a spacecraft, and land like an airplane. The space shuttle will serve as a ferry between the earth and orbiting space stations, and will carry out various space missions in earth orbit. Plans call for the shuttle to be in operation by 1978.

At a joint swearing-in ceremony, on January 7, Lewis F. Powell, Jr., and William H. Rehnquist became associate justices of the Supreme Court. The occasion marked the first time since 1911 that two justices had taken the oath of office at the same time.

What the projected manned space shuttle will be used for.

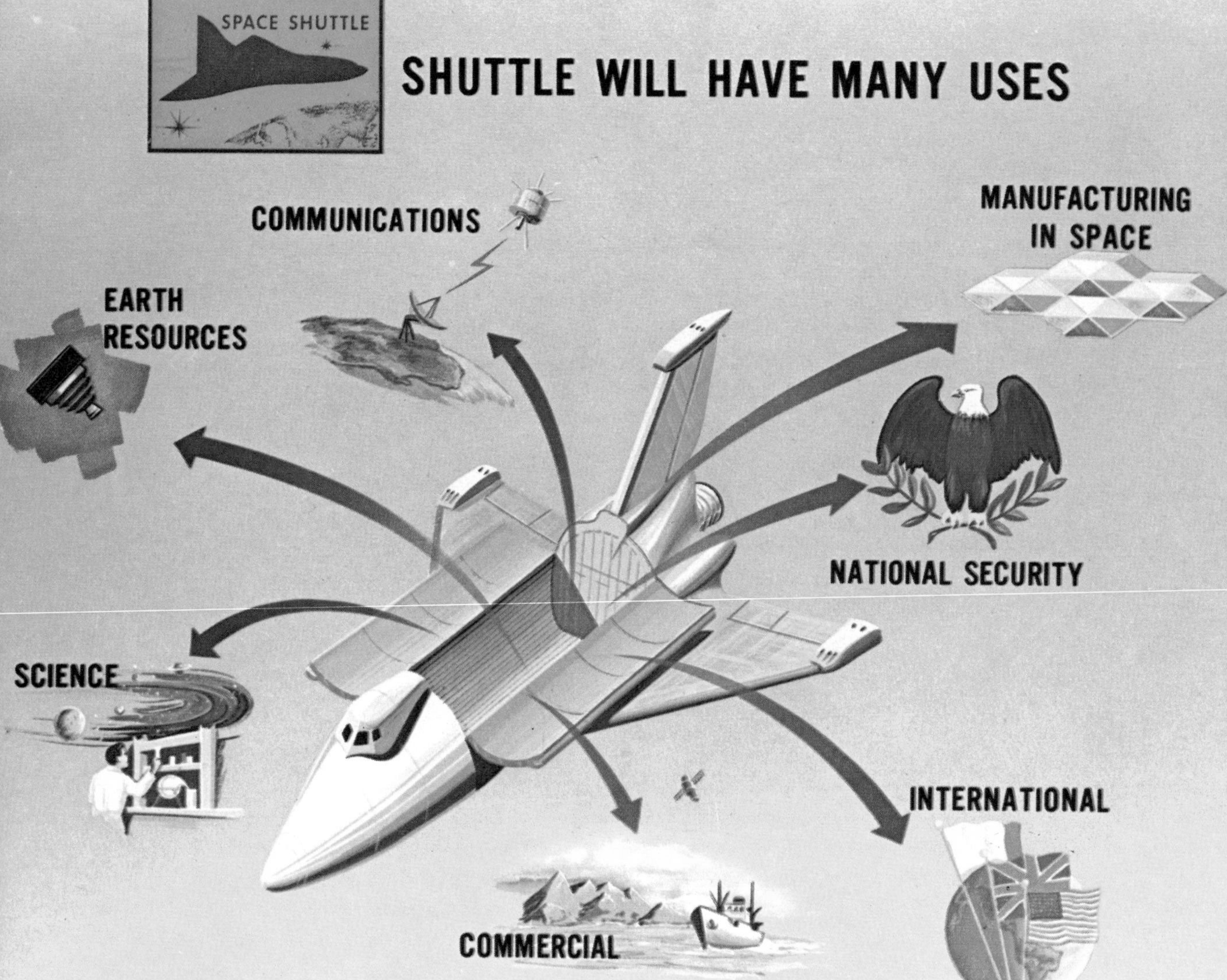

On January 7, Rome, Italy, ended a 9-day experiment in free transportation. The experiment was an effort to end the traffic chaos in the city's center caused by the large number of private cars jamming the narrow streets.

Mrs. Richard Nixon, representing the United States, ended an 8-day tour of West Africa on January 9. She visited Ghana and the Ivory Coast, and attended the inauguration of William Tolbert as president of Liberia, an African nation that had been settled, in part, by freed American slaves.

Sheik Mujibur Rahman returned to Bangladesh (formerly East Pakistan) on January 10. Sheik Mujibur, the leader of Bangladesh from the time it became a new nation, had been imprisoned in West Pakistan since March, 1971.

On January 15 a lovely princess was proclaimed Queen Margrethe II, the first reigning queen of modern Denmark. (An earlier Margrethe had ruled Denmark from 1387 to 1412.)

On January 22, ten Western European nations met in Brussels and signed the Treaty of Accession; the purpose of the treaty was to create an enlarged European Economic Community (Common Market). The treaty will have to be ratified by the four new member-nations—Britain, Denmark, Norway, and Ireland—before is can officially go into effect.

A Japanese World War II soldier was found in the jungles of the Pacific island of Guam on January 24. He had been reported dead on September 4, 1944, after the Americans had invaded the island. Not wanting to surrender, he had gone into hiding for 28 years.

Maurice H. Stans resigned as United States secretary of commerce on January 27. Peter G. Peterson, White House assistant for international economic affairs, was nominated to succeed him.

Upon learning that Britain, Australia, and New Zealand were going to recognize Bangladesh, Pakistan withdrew from the Commonwealth of Nations on January 30.

In Londonderry, Northern Ireland, 13 persons were killed by British troops during a civil rights demonstration on January 30. (The day has become known as "Bloody Sunday.")

The world's fourth largest suspension bridge will soon cross the Bosporus and link the continents of Europe and Asia. The cables of this bridge were hoisted in Istanbul, Turkey, in January.

FEBRUARY

A crowd of about 25,000 people burned the British Embassy in Dublin, Ireland, on February 2. The burning was a protest against the killing of 13 people by British troops in Londonderry, Northern Ireland, on "Bloody Sunday."

In an effort to control plane hijackings, a rule was put into effect on February 6 requiring the screening of passengers on all scheduled U.S. flights. The rule was issued on an emergency basis by the head of the Federal Aviation Administration.

Sir Keith J. Holyoake resigned as prime minister of New Zealand on February 7. He had held the post 11 years. A caucus of the National Party elected Deputy Prime Minister John R. Marshall to succeed Holyoake as prime minister.

Skaters Dianne Holum and Anne Henning, Olympic gold medal winners.

Mariner 9, in orbit around Mars, took photographs of the planet and sent them back to earth. The photographs, received early in February, reveal that there is a huge volcano on Mars, larger than any on earth. The volcano is named Nix Olympica, which is the Latin for "Olympic Snow." It covers an area 300 miles in diameter, and its opening is 40 miles wide.

The 11th Winter Olympic Games were held in Sapporo, Japan, from February 3 to February 13. More than 1,300 athletes from 35 nations took part. Dianne Holum and Anne Henning, two young U.S. skaters from the same hometown—Northbrook, Illinois—went home with four Olympic medals between them. There were three other Northbrook skaters on the Olympic team, as well. The whole town, which now calls itself the "Speed Skating Capital of the World," was out to welcome them home.

Scientists of the U.S. Navy have been experimenting with a novel approach to the problem of oil spills at sea: the use of bacteria to consume the oil. The Navy research became known in mid-February. Scientists have identified over 60 species of bacteria that devour oil. As the bacteria eat the oil the number of bacteria increase. In this process the oil is broken down into other compounds that are less harmful to marine life. So far, it would seem that the bacteria are more effective against marine diesel oil and less effective against crude oil.

A step toward keeping the Atlantic free of poisonous wastes was taken on February 15, when 12 European nations signed an agreement that their ships and planes would not dump mercury or cadmium into the northeast Atlantic. They also agreed not to dump, without special permits, such harmful wastes as lead and tar.

U.S. Attorney General John N. Mitchell resigned his post on February 15 in order to head the re-election campaign of President Richard M. Nixon. Deputy Attorney General Richard G. Kleindienst was appointed Mitchell's successor.

On February 17 the British House of Commons voted (309 votes to 301) to approve legislation that would allow the United Kingdom to enter the European Economic Community.

President and Mrs. Richard M. Nixon and a party of U.S. officials arrived in Peking on February 21 for talks with the Chinese leaders, Chairman Mao Tse-tung and Premier Chou En-lai. The President's historic visit included a trip to the Great Wall of China and the Ming Tombs in the north. The presidential party returned to the United States on February 28.

MARCH

Pioneer 10 began the longest journey of the Space Age on March 2. The unmanned spacecraft's journey to the planet Jupiter—620,000,000 miles from Earth—will take about 21 months. In late 1973, when Pioneer is closest to the planet, the first closeup photographs of Jupiter will be taken. Eventually, Pioneer will leave our solar system and journey endlessly through space.

Prime Minister Indira Gandhi of India campaigns for re-election.

State elections in India, held from March 5 to March 12, gave a great victory to the New Congress Party of Mrs. Indira Gandhi, India's Prime Minister. The New Congress Party already controlled India's central government. Mrs. Gandhi has been India's prime minister since January, 1966. At the time of the elections her personal popularity and political power were judged to be at an all-time high.

On March 11 the people of the vast Australian trust territory of Papua and New Guinea finished voting for a new legislature. The newly elected legislature will eventually be responsible for deciding when the territory will become an independent nation.

On March 26, Britain and its former colony of Malta signed a 7-year agreement permitting Britain to retain its military bases on the Mediterranean island. The agreement, which ended many months of debate, will permit British troops and their families—most of whom had been evacuated from Malta during the treaty negotiations—to return.

On March 29, for the first time in 6 years, West Berliners were permitted to travel beyond the Berlin Wall to pay Easter holiday visits to friends and relatives in East Berlin. For the 8-day holiday period, East German officials permitted West Berliners to visit not only East Berlin but, for the first time in 20 years, the East German countryside as well. Many Germans expressed the hope that this move marked the beginning of an era of easier relations between the two Germanys.

The British Government suspended home rule in Northern Ireland on March 30. Direct rule from London was imposed. British Prime Minister Edward Heath appointed William Whitelaw secretary of state for Northern Ireland. In this capacity, Whitelaw would hold both legislative and executive powers in the embattled northern counties. Prime Minister Heath said that this radical move was a necessary step in efforts to bring an end to violence between Roman Catholic and Protestant factions.

The Arctic Ice Dynamics Joint Expedition, a scientific team with the mission of exploring the world beneath the drifting ice of the Arctic, began a 2-month survey in March. Frogmen in newly developed "dry suits" (designed to protect them from extreme cold) form part of the team. Working from a base on an ice floe near the North Pole, scientists hope to learn more about the pressure and movement of ice so that safer routes for shipping can be charted through the region. After April, the spring thaw prevents aircraft used in transportation and supply from landing.

APRIL

On April 10, in ceremonies held in Washington, London, and Moscow, more than 70 nations signed a convention prohibiting the stockpiling and development of biological weapons of warfare. The nations also agreed to destroy their stockpiles of such weapons within 9 months or to divert them to peaceful purposes. The agreement also binds the signers to work toward a similar ban on chemical weapons. The hope was expressed that this covenant would be the first step in a genuine attempt to halt the arms race. Of the nuclear powers, the United States, Britain, and the Soviet Union signed the covenant. France and China did not.

John W. Young, commander of the Apollo 16 lunar-landing mission, hops from the moon's surface as he salutes the American flag.

On April 15, President Nixon and Prime Minister Pierre Elliott Trudeau of Canada signed a joint agreement to clean up the waters of the Great Lakes. The pact, known as the Great Lakes Water Quality Agreement, will unite the efforts and resources of the two countries to reverse the process of pollution that has seriously fouled these waters. Much study has gone into the pact. It offers a hope of future clean water to the millions of Canadians and Americans living on the shores of the five lakes.

The two giant pandas, Ling-Ling and Hsing-Hsing, presented to the people of the United States by the People's Republic of China settled into their new lair in the National Zoo in Washington, D.C. On April 20, they received their first visitors at the air-conditioned glass-walled quarters.

On April 22, John Fairfax, 33 and Sylvia Cook, 31, arrived at Hayman Island, Australia, after having rowed across the Pacific from San Francisco. Provisions for the voyage (which took almost a year) consisted of dried foods, 80 gallons of fresh water, and an evaporator for distilling seawater.

On April 27 three jubilant astronauts, Captain John W. Young of the U.S. Navy, Lieutenant Commander Thomas K. Mattingly of the Navy, and Lieutenant Colonel Charles M. Duke, Jr., of the Air Force, returned to earth from their 11-day trip to the moon. Astronauts Young and Duke had spent a record 71 hours on the moon. This included over 20 hours outside their lunar module, walking, working, and driving an electric car. Astronaut Mattingly spent the time in orbit, taking photographs to be used in mapping the lunar surface, and making various scientific observations. The astronauts brought back 214 pounds of lunar material, including the first rock samples from lunar mountains.

In April the Republic of Sierra Leone reported the finding of the world's third largest diamond, which has been named "Star of Sierra Leone." The two larger diamonds, both found in South Africa, were the Excelsior, discovered in 1893, and the Cullinan, discovered in 1905. The Cullinan weighed 3,106 carats, and the Excelsior, 995.2 carats. Both the Cullinan and the Excelsior were cut into smaller gems. The Star of Sierra Leone, 969.8 carats, and valued at about $11,700,000, will be kept intact.

In April, the new Asian nation of Bangladesh announced a plan to preserve wildlife within its territory. The population of one of its most spectacular species, the Bengal tiger, has shrunk to about 100. This figure was arrived at by various signs, including the "pugmarks," or footprints, of the tigers.

MAY

On May 8, President Richard Nixon announced that he had ordered the mining of all North Vietnamese ports. He also warned that measures would be taken to stop the flow of war matériel by rail to North Vietnam. All such acts of force would end as soon as North Vietnam agreed to return the U.S. prisoners of war and to accept an internationally supervised cease-fire.

Michelangelo's masterpiece the *Pietà* after it was damaged by a man wielding a hammer. The statue has since been fully repaired.

At a ceremony in Tokyo on May 15, the United States returned control of Okinawa and other islands of the Ryukyus to Japan. Okinawa had been captured by American forces in 1945, after one of the fiercest battles of World War II.

Governor George C. Wallace of Alabama was shot and wounded on May 15 while he was campaigning for the presidential nomination in a shopping center in Laurel, Maryland. Emergency surgery was performed, but it was feared that his legs would be paralyzed by a bullet that could not be removed. Arthur Herman Bremer, aged 21, was arrested and charged with the shooting.

John B. Connally, Jr., resigned as secretary of the treasury on May 16. George P. Shultz, director of the Office of Management and Budget, was nominated to succeed Connally.

One of the world's greatest sculptures, the *Pietà* by Michelangelo, was damaged when a 33-year-old man attacked it with a hammer on May 21. The marble statue, which shows the Madonna with the dead body of Christ in her arms, stood over an altar in St. Peter's Basilica in Rome. The left arm of the Virgin was shattered, and her face was chipped.

On May 22, the island nation of Ceylon broke its ties with the British crown and proclaimed itself the Republic of Sri Lanka. "Sri Lanka," meaning "great and beautiful island," is the ancient name for Ceylon.

President Richard Nixon spent the week of May 22–29 in the Soviet Union, conferring with Soviet leaders. The historic summit talks ended with a joint declaration of peace that promised a new era in Soviet-American relations.

Armed with automatic rifles and hand grenades, three Japanese gunmen attacked a crowd of about 300 people at Lydda Airport in Israel on May 30. Twenty-five persons were killed and 72 wounded. One of the gunmen was killed; one committed suicide; and the third was captured. The Popular Front for the Liberation of Palestine, an extremist Arab guerrilla organization, announced that it had been responsible for the attack.

Dawn Ann Kurth, an 11-year-old Florida schoolgirl, studied television commercials as part of a school project. On May 31, Dawn testified at a U.S. Senate committee hearing that she had found that commercials aimed at children were often dangerous and deceptive. She also thought that by the time children reach age 10 or 11, they no longer believe the commercials.

JUNE

Delegates from 112 nations met in Stockholm, Sweden, June 5–16, for the United Nations–sponsored World Conference on the Human Environment. In a series of meetings, the delegates studied ways of protecting the environment and conserving natural resources. Three recommendations designed to reduce pollution, and a proposed global air monitoring system, were endorsed.

Pottstown, Pennsylvania, was hard hit by Hurricane Agnes.

On June 13, for the first time since the Middle East cease-fire went into effect in August, 1970, Israeli and Egyptian planes engaged in an air battle. The clash took place over international waters about 25 miles north of the Sinai Peninsula.

Five men were arrested for breaking into the headquarters of the Democratic National Committee in Washington on June 17. They were said to have had in their possession complicated eavesdropping and photographic equipment. The incident became known as the "Watergate Caper" and figured prominently in the national presidential election campaign.

On June 23, President Richard Nixon declared five states eligible for federal help as a result of the destruction caused by Hurricane Agnes. In what was termed the worst flooding in United States history, floodwaters devastated large areas of Florida, New York, Pennsylvania, Maryland, and Virginia. Pennsylvania was the hardest hit, with the governor's mansion in Harrisburg standing in 8 feet of water, and the Susquehanna River surging over 38-foot-high dikes in Wilkes-Barre.

On June 25, France resumed atmospheric testing of nuclear weapons in the South Pacific, over the Mururoa Atoll. The tests were strongly condemned by several nations. (France and China are the only nuclear powers that did not sign the 1963 Nuclear Test-Ban Treaty, and the two nations continue atmospheric testing of such weapons.)

Ending a 5-month political crisis, Giulio Andreotti, leader of a three-party coalition, was sworn in as the new premier of Italy on June 26. The event marked the 34th time since 1943 that Italy had had a new government.

The transfer from Vietnam of more than 2,000 pilots and 150 planes to bases in Thailand was completed on June 26. The United States command in Saigon announced that the pilots and planes from the Danang air base had increased the number of American forces in Thailand to close to 50,000.

On June 29 the United States Supreme Court rendered a historic decision. In a 5 to 4 vote, the Court ruled that the death penalty as ordinarily enforced by the states was a violation of the Eighth Amendment prohibiting cruel and unusual punishment.

In June, archeologists excavating in Denmark claimed that new finds proved that hunters and fishermen had lived in southern Denmark as long as 60,000 to 100,000 years ago.

JULY

India's Prime Minister Indira Gandhi and Pakistan's President Zulfikar Ali Bhutto signed an agreement on July 3 after a series of talks in Simla, India. The talks were the first held by the two nations since the Indian-Pakistani War of December 1971. Among the terms of the agreement was a provision that the two nations would not use force to settle differences. There was also a provision for the withdrawal of troops from the nations' common borders.

North and South Korea revealed on July 4 that they had held a series of secret talks in Pyongyang and Seoul. The two sides agreed on three principles of unification, including an agreement to use peaceful means rather than force. A South-North coordinating committee was set up and a telephone linking the offices of the leaders of North and South Korea was installed immediately.

On July 5, President Georges Pompidou of France accepted the resignation of Premier Jacques Chaban-Delmas and named Pierre Messmer premier. Messmer is a follower of the policies of the late General Charles de Gaulle.

Left: The 1972 solar eclipse, as seen over northern Canada. Right: Two young girls view the eclipse the correct way—through exposed film.

Japan elected a new premier on July 5. He is Kakuei Tanaka, formerly minister of international trade and industry. Tanaka succeeded Eisaku Sato, who had announced his retirement in an emotional speech on June 17. Sato had suffered a blow to his prestige when U.S. President Richard M. Nixon had announced, without consulting Japan beforehand, that he would visit China in February.

President Richard M. Nixon announced on July 8 that the United States has agreed to sell $750,000,000 of wheat, corn, and other grains to the Soviet Union over a period of 3 years. The agreement for the sale of the grain was an outcome of the President's trip to the Soviet Union in May.

Residents of North America witnessed a rare event on July 10—a solar eclipse. The moon passed between the sun and the earth, totally blocking out the sun near the Arctic Circle for 2 minutes 36 seconds. In other places, the sun was only partly hidden. If you missed the eclipse, there will be another on August 21, 2017.

The Democrats nominated Senator George S. McGovern of South Dakota as their candidate for president. He was chosen on the first ballot, July 13, at the party convention in Miami Beach, Florida. Senator Thomas F. Eagleton of Missouri received the vice-presidential nomination.

U.S. and Soviet space officials meeting at the Manned Spacecraft Center in Houston, Texas, announced on July 17 the details of a joint U.S.–Soviet spaceflight slated for July, 1975. An Apollo spacecraft carrying 3 American astronauts is to dock with a Soyuz carrying 2 Russians. The astronauts are to exchange visits and to carry out various scientific experiments. The first international manned spaceflight had been agreed upon when President Richard M. Nixon visited the U.S.S.R. in May.

Egypt's President Anwar el-Sadat announced on July 18 that he had ordered Soviet "military advisers and experts" to leave Egypt immediately. The order was said to affect about 5,000 people.

A 1,965-pound unmanned satellite, the Earth Resources Technology Satellite, or ERTS, was launched on July 23. Its cameras have been taking pictures that should give scientists information about crops, forests, glaciers, and water pollution.

On July 31, Senator Thomas F. Eagleton withdrew as the vice-presidential candidate of the Democratic Party. Eagleton had disclosed on July 25 that he had been hospitalized 3 times for "nervous exhaustion and fatigue" and had had psychiatric treatment.

AUGUST

President Anwar el-Sadat of Egypt and Col. Muammar al-Qaddafi of Libya agreed on August 2 that their nations would work toward becoming one political unit by September 1, 1973.

On August 4 a Maryland court convicted Arthur H. Bremer of shooting Governor George C. Wallace of Alabama on May 15.

The lighting of the Olympic flame marked the start of the Summer Games.

R. Sargent Shriver was selected on August 8 to run as the vice-presidential candidate on the Democratic ticket after Senator Thomas F. Eagleton of Missouri had withdrawn as a candidate.

The 3rd Battalion of the 21st Infantry, the last American ground combat unit in Vietnam, was de-activated on August 11. Most of the battalion's 1,043 men were to be sent home within a few days, leaving in Vietnam only those members of the unit with job specialties still needed there, and those who had served less than 6 months in Vietnam.

King Hassan II of Morocco survived an attempt on his life on August 16. The King was flying back to Rabat, his capital, from Paris in a Boeing 727 after a trip to Spain and France. Moroccan Air Force jets sent to accompany the King's plane began firing on it as it flew over Moroccan soil, but they did not harm Hassan. On August 17, Defense Minister Mohammed Oufkir, accused of having planned the attack, committed suicide.

A 4-week strike of British dock workers that had forced the government to declare a state of emergency ended on August 21.

On August 22 the Republican Party, meeting in Miami Beach, Florida, again named Richard M. Nixon as its candidate for president and Spiro T. Agnew as its candidate for vice-president.

In August a balloon filled with hot air carried two men up, up, and across the Alps from Zermatt, Switzerland, to Biella, Italy. The 3-hour trip was the first successful crossing of the Monte Rosa chain by hot-air balloon. Scotsman Donald Cameron and his American co-pilot, Mark Yarry, flew their 120-foot-high balloon over Monte Rosa's 15,000-foot peak.

On August 25, China cast its first veto in the Security Council since its admission to the United Nations in October, 1971. China used its veto to bar Bangladesh from membership in the United Nations. The United States and the Soviet Union voted in favor of membership for Bangladesh.

Ceremonies were held on August 26 in Olympic Stadium, Munich, Germany, formally opening the 20th Summer Olympic Games. More than 8,500 athletes from 121 nations were there to compete. Earlier, black athletes from a number of African nations had threatened not to participate in the games if Rhodesia competed. The black athletes opposed the racial policies of Rhodesia. The International Olympic Committee met and voted Rhodesia out of the games on August 22.

SEPTEMBER

Beginning in early September, and continuing throughout the month, a stream of Asians, expelled from Uganda, arrived in Britain. In August, President Idi Amin of Uganda had announced that all Asians with British passports would have to leave the country within 3 months. His decision affected about 55,000 people, many of them owners of businesses.

Asians in Uganda crowd the office of the British High Commission in Kampala, seeking permits to enter Britain.

On September 1, Bobby Fischer became the world's chess champion. He is the first American ever to hold the title and the first non-Russian titleholder in 25 years. Fischer's opponent was Boris Spassky of the U.S.S.R., world champion for 3 years. The final score of the match, held in Reykjavik, Iceland, was 12½ to 8½.

A rare event, the birth of a gorilla in captivity, occurred in New York's Central Park Zoo on September 3. Lulu, the mother, a 7-year-old, 145-pound gorilla, announced the birth by grabbing her keeper's arm and holding up her 5-pound baby. The father is Kongo, also 7. The baby was named Patty Cake. (She was called Sunny Jim until her doctors found out she was a girl.)

Violence and death marred the Olympic Games in Munich, Germany, on September 5, when Arab guerrillas, demanding the release of 200 Arab prisoners in Israel, killed 2 Israeli team members and took 9 hostage. Later a gun battle left the 9 hostages, 5 Arabs, and a West German policeman dead. A memorial service for the 11 Israelis was held the next day in Olympic Stadium, and the Games were suspended for 24 hours.

Whales have been trained to go down to depths of 1,500 feet or more in the ocean and retrieve objects, such as torpedoes, the U.S. Navy announced on September 5. The whales had been trained in Project Deep Ops, begun in 1969 and carried out in Hawaii.

The heaviest air attacks since the 1967 Arab-Israeli War took place on September 8 when Israeli planes struck 10 Arab guerrilla bases and naval installations in Syria and Lebanon. The attacks followed the killing of the 11 Israelis in Munich on September 5.

On September 23, President Ferdinand E. Marcos of the Philippines declared a state of martial law; he imposed a curfew, put government controls on newspapers and radio stations, and banned the carrying of guns by civilians. Marcos said he took the emergency action because the country was in peril of "violent overthrow." There had been an attempt on the life of the Defense Secretary, and several bombing incidents in Manila.

In a 2-day national referendum September 24 and 25, Norwegians voted against their country's entry into the European Economic Community (Common Market).

Premier Chou En-lai of China and Premier Kakuei Tanaka of Japan signed a joint statement in Peking on September 29, officially ending the state of war that had existed between China and Japan, and establishing diplomatic relations.

OCTOBER

Visitors have come from all over the world to see Rome's most famous landmark, the Colosseum. However, during 1972 the ancient, 150-foot-high structure was crumbling badly, and huge chunks of stone crashed to the ground. In early October, it was announced that the Colosseum had been partially closed, and a network of scaffolding was placed around it.

Scaffolding protects passersby from Rome's crumbling Colosseum.

In a national referendum on October 3, the people of Denmark overwhelmingly voted to join the European Economic Community (Common Market). Following the referendum, Premier Jens Otto Krag, a strong supporter of membership, retired. He was succeeded by Anker Jorgensen.

United States bombing of North Vietnam above the 20th parallel was halted on October 23. Three days later, Dr. Henry Kissinger announced that a draft cease-fire agreement was being worked out and "peace is at hand."

On October 27, President Richard Nixon announced that 300,000 tons of corn, worth $18,000,000, had been sold to the People's Republic of China. This was the second U.S. sale of grain to China.

Ending several years of border clashes, the Asian nations of Yemen and Southern Yemen agreed, on October 28, to become united into one nation.

National elections were held in Canada on October 30. In a startling upset, the Liberal Party of Prime Minister Pierre Elliott Trudeau lost its parliamentary majority.

THE 1972 NOBEL PRIZES

The Nobel Prize in Chemistry was shared by three American scientists: Christian Boehmer Anfinsen, a biochemist at the National Institutes of Health; and Stanford Moore and William H. Stein, both professors at Rockefeller University.

The Prize in Physics was also shared by three Americans: John Bardeen, a professor at the University of Illinois; Leon N. Cooper, a professor at Brown University; and John Robert Schrieffer, a professor at the University of Pennsylvania.

The Literature Prize went to the West German novelist, short-story writer, and playwright Heinrich Böll.

An American, Gerald M. Edelman, a biologist at Rockefeller University, and a Briton, Rodney R. Porter, a biochemistry professor at Oxford University, shared the Prize in Physiology or Medicine.

The Nobel Memorial Prize for Economics was shared by an American, Kenneth J. Arrow, a professor at Harvard University, and a Briton, John R. Hicks, a retired Oxford professor.

There was no Nobel Peace Prize awarded.

NOVEMBER

President Richard M. Nixon and Vice-President Spiro T. Agnew were re-elected on November 7 in a landslide victory over the Democratic slate of Senator George S. McGovern and R. Sargent Shriver. The Republican team carried 49 states with a total of 521 electoral votes. The Democratic ticket carried only the state of Massachusetts and the District of Columbia, for a total of 17 electoral votes. It was the first presidential election in which 18–20-year-olds could vote.

A skull assembled from fragmented ancient bones may be a clue in dating the evolution of man's ancestors. The finding of the bones was announced on November 9. The hundreds of fragments were discovered embedded in solidified volcanic ash near Lake Rudolf in East Africa. The age of volcanic debris can be tested in various ways. Scientists can say with assurance that the material in which these bones were found was deposited more than 2,500,000 years ago. The assembled skull has many resemblances to that of modern man. According to Richard Leakey, a leader of the expedition that made the find, the skull may be proof that man's immediate ancestry is 1,000,000 years older than had been widely believed.

In federal elections held November 19, West Germans gave a vote of confidence to Chancellor Willy Brandt and his coalition government of Social Democrats and Free Democrats. (Brandt has been chancellor since October, 1969.) With more than 91 percent of the electorate having voted, the vote was seen as a clear mandate to Brandt to continue his policy of normalizing relations with East Germany and the other Communist nations of Europe.

In an upset, the Labor Party swept into office in New Zealand's general election on November 25. Norman E. Kirk was to head the new government, succeeding Prime Minister John Marshall.

After selecting and piecing together about 1,500 photographs, the United States Geological Survey drew a detailed map of the planet Mars. A reproduction of the map was released late in November. The selection had been made from some 7,000 photographs transmitted to earth by Mariner 9, in orbit around Mars since 1971. Until the early Mariner flights (Mariner 4 in 1965; Mariners 6 and 7 in 1969), the only knowledge we had had of Mars was gained by telescopic scanning. Since Mars is about 35,000,000 miles away from earth, even the most powerful telescopes did not reveal a clear view of that planet's topography. The early Mariners flew past the planet, photographing only a small portion of the Martian surface. Mariner 9 provided photographs of the entire surface of the planet. The position or angle of each photograph could be figured out from the tracking data of Mariner 9. With the aid of modern computers, it was possible to fit the photographs together, like pieces of a mosaic, to reveal a detailed composite.

In late November, President Richard Nixon began reshuffling his Cabinet for his second term of office. Elliot L. Richardson, secretary of health, education, and welfare, was nominated secretary of defense, to succeed Melvin R. Laird. Caspar W. Weinberger, head of the Office of Budget and Management, was nominated to succeed Mr. Richardson as secretary of health, education, and welfare. Peter J. Brennan, president of the Building and Construction Trades Council in New York, was nominated secretary of labor, to succeed James D. Hodgson.

PRESIDENT RICHARD M. NIXON'S PROCLAMATION OF THANKSGIVING DAY NOVEMBER 23, 1972

When the first settlers gathered to offer their thanks to the God who had protected them on the edge of a wilderness, they established anew on American shores a thanksgiving tradition as old as Western man himself.

From Moses at the Red Sea to Jesus preparing to feed the multitudes, the Scriptures summon us to words and deeds of gratitude, even before divine blessings are fully perceived. From Washington kneeling at Valley Forge to the prayer of an astronaut circling the moon, our own history repeats that summons and proves its practicality.

Today, in an age of too much fashionable despair, the world more than ever needs to hear America's perennial harvest message: "Take heart, give thanks. To see clearly about us is to rejoice; and to rejoice is to worship the Father; and to worship Him is to receive more blessings still."

At this Thanksgiving time our country can look back with special gratitude across the events of a year which has brought more progress toward lasting peace than any other year for a generation past; and we can look forward with trust in Divine Providence toward the opportunities which peace will bring.

Truly our cup runs over with the bounty of God—our lives, our liberties, and our loved ones; our worldly goods and our spiritual heritage; the beauty of our land, the breadth of our horizons, and the promise of peace that crowns it all. For all of this, let us now humbly give thanks.

DECEMBER

In national elections held in Australia on December 2, the Labor Party ousted the conservative coalition government of William McMahon, prime minister since March, 1971. The victory brought the Labor Party to power for the first time in 23 years. Gough Whitlam, parliamentary leader of the Labor Party, was sworn in as prime minister three days later.

Apollo 17 was the first manned space mission to be launched at night.

In early December, President Richard Nixon concluded the changes in his second-term Cabinet by announcing three new nominations: James T. Lynn to succeed George Romney as secretary of housing and urban development; Frederick B. Dent to succeed Peter G. Peterson as secretary of commerce; and Claude S. Brinegar to succeed John A. Volpe as secretary of transportation. John A. Scali, a former journalist, was nominated to succeed George Bush as United States representative to the United Nations.

On December 8, Time Inc. announced that *Life* magazine, published since 1936, would cease publication.

Apollo 17, the last planned lunar mission, blasted off toward the moon in the early morning hours of December 7. Aboard the spacecraft were Captain Eugene A. Cernan, Dr. Harrison H. Schmitt, and Commander Ronald E. Evans. During their 3-day stay on the lunar surface, Cernan and Schmitt carried out scientific experiments, and gathered 250 pounds of rocks and soil, perhaps finding both the oldest and youngest lunar samples. Orange lunar soil, suggesting possible volcanic activity, was an unexpected discovery. The astronauts unveiled a plaque to peace and dedicated a huge rock on the moon to the youth of the world. On December 19, Apollo 17 returned safely to earth, "the last, longest, and most successful of 7 manned lunar landing missions."

On December 13 the secret talks on a Vietnam cease-fire, which were being held by U.S. and North Vietnamese officials, were broken off. President Nixon ordered a full-scale resumption of the bombing of North Vietnam above the 20th parallel and of the mining of its harbors. The raids, which ended on December 31, were described as the heaviest and most devastating of the war.

East and West Germany signed a treaty on basic relations on December 21, formally ending more than two decades of mutual enmity.

Thousands of people were killed and most of Managua, the capital of Nicaragua, was destroyed when an earthquake hit the Central American country on December 23.

On December 26, Harry S. Truman, 33rd president of the United States, died at the age of 88.

On December 27, Lester Pearson, former prime minister of Canada and Nobel Peace Prize winner, died at the age of 75.

Roberto Clemente, Pittsburgh Pirates star outfielder, died on December 31 in the crash of a plane carrying aid to Nicaragua.

INTERNATIONAL STATISTICAL SUPPLEMENT (as of December 31, 1972)

NATIONS OF THE WORLD

NATION	CAPITAL	AREA (in sq. mi.)	POPULATION	GOVERNMENT
Afghanistan	Kabul	250,000	17,480,000	Mohammad Zahir Shah—king Abdul Zahir—prime minister
Albania	Tirana	11,100	2,226,000	Enver Hoxha—communist party secretary Mehmet Shehu—premier
Algeria	Algiers	919,593	14,769,000	Houari Boumedienne—president
Argentina	Buenos Aires	1,072,158	23,552,000	Alejandro Agustín Lanusse—president
Australia	Canberra	2,967,909	12,728,000	Gough Whitlam—prime minister
Austria	Vienna	32,374	7,456,000	Bruno Kreisky—chancellor Franz Jonas—president
Bahrain	Manama	231	220,000	Isa bin Sulman al-Khalifa—head of government
Bangladesh	Dacca	55,126	75,000,000	Abu Sayeed Choudhury—president Mujibur Rahman—prime minister
Barbados	Bridgetown	166	239,000	Errol W. Barrow—prime minister
Belgium	Brussels	11,781	9,726,000	Baudouin I—king Gaston Eyskens—premier
Bhutan	Thimphu	18,000	854,000	Jigme Singye Wangchuk—king
Bolivia	La Paz	424,163	5,063,000	Hugo Banzer Suárez—president
Botswana	Gaborone	231,804	668,000	Sir Seretse Khama—president
Brazil	Brasília	3,286,478	95,408,000	Emílio Garrastazú Médici—president
Bulgaria	Sofia	42,823	8,540,000	Todor Zhivkov—communist party secretary Stanko Todorov—premier
Burma	Rangoon	261,789	27,584,000	Ne Win—prime minister
Burundi	Usumbura	10,747	3,615,000	Michel Micombero—president Albin Nyamoya—premier
Cambodia (Khmer Republic)	Pnompenh	69,898	6,701,000	Lon Nol—president Hang Thun Hak—premier
Cameroon	Yaoundé	183,569	5,836,000	Ahmadou Ahidjo—president
Canada	Ottawa	3,851,809	21,786,000	Pierre Elliott Trudeau—prime minister
Central African Republic	Bangui	240,535	1,637,000	Jean Bedel Bokassa—president
Ceylon (Sri Lanka)	Colombo	25,332	12,669,000	William Gopallawa—president Sirimavo Bandaranaike—premier
Chad	Fort-Lamy	495,754	3,800,000	François Tombalbaye—president

NATION	CAPITAL	AREA (in sq. mi.)	POPULATION	GOVERNMENT
Chile	Santiago	292,259	8,992,000	Salvador Allende Gossens—president
China (Communist)	Peking	3,691,512	787,176,000	Mao Tse-tung—chairman Chou En-lai—premier
China (Nationalist)	Taipei	13,885	14,300,000	Chiang Kai-shek—president Chiang Ching-kuo—premier
Colombia	Bogotá	439,736	21,772,000	Misael Pastrana Borrero—president
Congo	Brazzaville	132,047	958,000	Marien Ngouabi—president
Costa Rica	San José	19,575	1,786,000	José Figueres Ferrer—president
Cuba	Havana	44,218	8,657,000	Fidel Castro—premier Osvaldo Dorticós Torrado—president
Cyprus	Nicosia	3,572	639,000	Archbishop Makarios III—president
Czechoslovakia	Prague	49,370	14,500,000	Gustáv Husák—communist party secretary Ludvík Svoboda—president Lubomír Štrougal—premier
Dahomey	Porto-Novo	43,483	2,760,000	Mathieu Kerekou—president
Denmark	Copenhagen	16,629	4,966,000	Margrethe II—queen Anker Jorgensen—premier
Dominican Republic	Santo Domingo	18,816	4,188,000	Joaquín Balaguer—president
Ecuador	Quito	109,483	6,297,000	Guillermo Rodríguez Lara—president
Egypt	Cairo	386,660	34,130,000	Anwar el-Sadat—president Aziz Sidky—premier
El Salvador	San Salvador	8,260	3,534,000	Arturo Armando Molina—president
Equatorial Guinea	Santa Isabel	10,830	289,000	Francisco Macías Nguema—president
Ethiopia	Addis Ababa	471,777	25,248,000	Haile Selassie I—emperor
Fiji	Suva	7,055	531,000	Ratu Kamisese Mara—prime minister
Finland	Helsinki	130,120	4,684,000	Urho K. Kekkonen—president Kalevi Sorsa—premier
France	Paris	211,207	51,260,000	Georges Pompidou—president Pierre Messmer—premier
Gabon	Libreville	103,346	500,000	Albert B. Bongo—president
Gambia	Bathurst	4,361	375,000	Sir Dauda K. Jawara—president
Germany (East)	East Berlin	41,610	15,954,000	Erich Honecker—communist party secretary Willi Stoph—premier
Germany (West)	Bonn	95,743	59,175,000	Willy Brandt—chancellor Gustav Heinemann—president
Ghana	Accra	92,099	8,858,000	Ignatius K. Acheampong—head of government
Greece	Athens	50,944	8,957,000	George Papadopoulos—premier Constantine II—king (in exile)

NATION	CAPITAL	AREA (in sq. mi.)	POPULATION	GOVERNMENT
Guatemala	Guatemala City	42,042	5,348,000	Carlos Arana Osorio—president
Guinea	Conakry	94,926	4,010,000	Sékou Touré—president Lansana Beavogui—premier
Guyana	Georgetown	83,000	736,000	Forbes Burnham—prime minister Arthur Chung—president
Haiti	Port-au-Prince	10,714	4,969,000	Jean-Claude Duvalier—president
Honduras	Tegucigalpa	43,277	2,582,000	Oswaldo López Arellano—president
Hungary	Budapest	35,919	10,364,000	János Kádár—communist party secretary Jenö Fock—premier
Iceland	Reykjavik	39,768	214,000	Kristján Eldjárn—president Ólafur Jóhannesson—prime minister
India	New Delhi	1,261,813	550,374,000	Indira Gandhi—prime minister V. V. Giri—president
Indonesia	Jakarta	575,894	124,894,000	Suharto—president
Iran	Tehran	636,294	29,783,000	Mohammad Reza Pahlavi—shah Amir Abbas Hoveida—premier
Iraq	Baghdad	167,925	9,750,000	Ahmad Hassan al-Bakr—president
Ireland	Dublin	27,136	2,971,000	Éamon de Valéra—president John M. Lynch—prime minister
Israel	Jerusalem	7,992	3,013,000	Golda Meir—prime minister Zalman Shazar—president
Italy	Rome	116,303	54,078,000	Giovanni Leone—president Giulio Andreotti—premier
Ivory Coast	Abidjan	124,503	4,420,000	Félix Houphouët-Boigny—president
Jamaica	Kingston	4,232	1,897,000	Michael N. Manley—prime minister
Japan	Tokyo	143,659	104,661,000	Hirohito—emperor Kakuei Tanaka—prime minister
Jordan	Amman	37,738	2,383,000	Hussein I—king Ahmad al-Lawzi—premier
Kenya	Nairobi	224,959	11,694,000	Jomo Kenyatta—president
Korea (North)	Pyongyang	46,540	14,281,000	Kim Il Sung—premier
Korea (South)	Seoul	38,922	31,917,000	Chung Hee Park—president Kim Jong Pil—premier
Kuwait	Kuwait	6,178	831,000	Sabah al-Salim al-Sabah—head of state Jabir al-Ahmad al-Jabir—prime minister
Laos	Vientiane	91,429	3,033,000	Savang Vatthana—king Souvanna Phouma—premier
Lebanon	Beirut	4,015	2,873,000	Suleiman Franjieh—president Saeb Salam—premier

NATION	CAPITAL	AREA (in sq. mi.)	POPULATION	GOVERNMENT
Lesotho	Maseru	11,720	935,000	Moshoeshoe II—king Leabua Jonathan—prime minister
Liberia	Monrovia	43,000	1,571,000	William R. Tolbert—president
Libya	Tripoli	679,360	2,010,000	Muammar al-Qaddafi—president Abdul Salam Jallud—premier
Liechtenstein	Vaduz	61	21,000	Francis Joseph II—prince
Luxembourg	Luxembourg	999	341,000	Jean—grand duke Pierre Werner—premier
Malagasy Republic	Tananarive	226,657	6,750,000	Gabriel Ramanantsoa—head of government
Malawi	Zomba	45,747	4,549,000	Hastings K. Banda—president
Malaysia	Kuala Lumpur	128,430	12,324,000	Abdul Halim Muazzam—paramount ruler Tun Abdul Razak—prime minister
Maldives	Male	115	110,000	Ibrahim Nasir—president
Mali	Bamako	478,765	5,143,000	Moussa Traoré—president
Malta	Valletta	122	325,000	Dom Mintoff—prime minister
Mauritania	Nouakchott	397,954	1,200,000	Moktar O. Daddah—president
Mauritius	Port Louis	720	836,000	Sir Seewoosagur Ramgoolam—prime minister
Mexico	Mexico City	761,602	50,830,000	Luis Echeverría Álvarez—president
Monaco	Monaco	0.4	24,000	Rainier III—prince
Mongolia	Ulan Bator	604,248	1,283,000	Yumzhagiyn Tsedenbal—communist party secretary
Morocco	Rabat	172,997	15,234,000	Hassan II—king Ahmed Osman—premier
Nauru		8	7,000	Hammer DeRoburt—president
Nepal	Katmandu	54,362	11,290,000	Birendra Bir Bikram Shah Deva—king Kirti Nidhi Bista—prime minister
Netherlands	Amsterdam	15,770	13,194,000	Juliana—queen Barend W. Biesheuvel—premier
New Zealand	Wellington	103,736	2,853,000	Norman Eric Kirk—prime minister
Nicaragua	Managua	50,193	1,912,000	headed by a triumvirate
Niger	Niamey	489,190	4,126,000	Hamani Diori—president
Nigeria	Lagos	356,668	56,510,000	Yakubu Gowon—head of government
Norway	Oslo	125,181	3,905,000	Olav V—king Lars Korvald—prime minister
Oman	Muscat	82,030	678,000	Qabus ibn Said—sultan
Pakistan	Islamabad	310,403	55,000,000	Zulfikar Ali Bhutto—president

NATION	CAPITAL	AREA (in sq. mi.)	POPULATION	GOVERNMENT
Panama	Panama City	29,205	1,478,000	Omar Torrijos Herrera—head of government
Paraguay	Asunción	157,047	2,386,000	Alfredo Stroessner—president
Peru	Lima	496,223	14,015,000	Juan Velasco Alvarado—president
Philippines	Quezon City	115,830	37,959,000	Ferdinand E. Marcos—president
Poland	Warsaw	120,724	32,749,000	Edward Gierek—communist party secretary Piotr Jaroszewicz—premier
Portugal	Lisbon	35,553	8,668,000	Marcello Caetano—premier Americo Thomaz—president
Qatar	Doha	8,500	81,000	Khalifa bin Hamad al-Thani—head of government
Rhodesia	Salisbury	150,333	5,500,000	Ian D. Smith—prime minister Clifford Dupont—president
Rumania	Bucharest	91,699	20,470,000	Nicolae Ceaușescu—communist party secretary Ion Gheorghe Maurer—premier
Rwanda	Kigali	10,169	3,827,000	Grégoire Kayibanda—president
Saudi Arabia	Riyadh	829,997	7,965,000	Faisal ibn Abdul Aziz—king
Senegal	Dakar	75,750	4,022,000	Léopold Senghor—president Abdou Diouf—prime minister
Sierra Leone	Freetown	27,699	2,600,000	Siaka P. Stevens—president Sorie I. Koroma—prime minister
Singapore	Singapore	224	2,110,000	Lee Kuan Yew—prime minister Benjamin H. Sheares—president
Somalia	Mogadishu	246,200	2,864,000	Mohammad Siad Barre—head of government
South Africa	Pretoria Cape Town	471,444	22,092,000	Balthazar J. Vorster—prime minister J. J. Fouché—president
Spain	Madrid	194,884	34,134,000	Francisco Franco—head of government
Sudan	Khartoum	967,497	16,087,000	Gaafar al-Nimeiry—president
Swaziland	Mbabane	6,704	421,000	Sobhuza II—king Makhosini Dlamini—prime minister
Sweden	Stockholm	173,649	8,105,000	Gustaf VI Adolf—king Olof Palme—prime minister
Switzerland	Bern	15,941	6,311,000	Roger Bonvin—president
Syria	Damascus	71,498	6,451,000	Hafez al-Assad—president Abdel al-Rahman Khalafawi—premier
Tanzania	Dar es Salaam	364,898	13,634,000	Julius K. Nyerere—president
Thailand	Bangkok	198,456	35,335,000	Bhumibol Adulyadej—king Thanom Kittikachorn—president

NATION	CAPITAL	AREA (in sq. mi.)	POPULATION	GOVERNMENT
Togo	Lomé	21,622	2,022,000	Étienne Eyadema—president
Tonga	Nuku'alofa	270	90,000	Taufa'ahau Tupou IV—king Prince Tu'ipelehake—prime minister
Trinidad & Tobago	Port of Spain	1,980	1,030,000	Eric Williams—prime minister
Tunisia	Tunis	63,378	5,137,000	Habib Bourguiba—president Hedi Nouira—prime minister
Turkey	Ankara	301,381	36,162,000	Cevdet Sunay—president Ferit Melen—premier
Uganda	Kampala	91,134	10,127,000	Idi Amin—president
U.S.S.R.	Moscow	8,649,512	245,066,000	Leonid I. Brezhnev—communist party secretary Aleksei N. Kosygin—premier Nikolai V. Podgorny—president of presidium
United Arab Emirates	Abu Dhabi	32,278	197,000	Zayd ben Sultan—president
United Kingdom	London	94,216	55,566,000	Elizabeth II—queen Edward Heath—prime minister
United States	Washington, D.C.	3,615,123	207,006,000	Richard M. Nixon—president Spiro T. Agnew—vice-president
Upper Volta	Ouagadougou	105,869	5,491,000	Sangoulé Lamizana—president Gérard Kango Ouedraogo—prime minister
Uruguay	Montevideo	68,536	2,921,000	Juan M. Bordaberry—president
Venezuela	Caracas	352,143	10,399,000	Rafael Caldera—president
Vietnam (North)	Hanoi	61,294	21,595,000	Le Duan—communist party secretary Ton Duc Thang—president Pham Van Dong—premier
Vietnam (South)	Saigon	67,108	18,332,000	Nguyen Van Thieu—president Tran Van Huong—vice-president Tran Thien Khiem—premier
Western Samoa	Apia	1,097	143,000	Malietoa Tanumafili II—head of state Tupua Tamasese Lealofi IV—prime minister
Yemen (Aden)	Medina al-Shaab	112,000	1,475,000	Salem Ali Rubaya—head of state Ali Masir Mohammad—prime minister
Yemen (Sana)	Sana	75,290	5,900,000	Abdul Rahman al-Iryani—head of state Abdullah al-Hagri—premier
Yugoslavia	Belgrade	98,766	20,550,000	Josip Broz Tito—president Dzemal Bijedić—premier
Zaïre	Kinshasa	905,565	22,477,000	Mobutu Sese Seko—president
Zambia	Lusaka	290,585	4,275,000	Kenneth D. Kaunda—president

DICTIONARY INDEX

A

Aquafarm. A place where fish and sea animals used as food are raised commercially. In particular, a building or group of structures located beside the ocean and equipped with scientific devices that make possible the growing of marine life under conditions free of disease and other harmful effects of water pollution. The term "aquafarm" means literally "water farm." Aquafarms are among the most modern developments in the hatching and cultivation of marine life.

B

Bait-and-switch. In advertising, the practice of offering certain products or services at bargain rates and then seeking to force a customer to take a more expensive item. The bargain rate is the bait to attract a buyer. The switch is the attempt to make him buy or contract for something much less reasonable. Merchants who employ such practices are sometimes charged with breaking the laws protecting customers. The federal government, for example, has successfully taken legal action against retail sellers of meat products who used such tactics. In 1972 the City of New York sued a large dance studio that advertised a short program of lessons at a small fee and then led students to switch to much more expensive instruction against their wishes.

Boilerplate. A model, or replica, of a spacecraft, whose weight is greater than that of the actual spacecraft used in flight.

Bottom out. In finance, to reach a low point in price or value and to level off at that point. This verb phrase is used to describe the decline of securities. When stocks or bonds, for example, have bottomed out, their prices, which have dropped steadily, cease to fall. Usually at that point a rise in price or value can be expected. During the drop, the supply of the item in question has been greater than the demand for it. When the item has bottomed out, the demand can be expected to increase. If it does, the demand will soon exceed the supply, causing the price or value to rise.

C

Chicano. An American of Mexican ancestry; a Mexican-American; especially such a person whose parents or one of whose parents was born in Mexico.

Counter culture. A culture or way of life that differs sharply from that of the majority of citizens in a given society. The term has been applied, in the United States particularly, to the way of life adopted by some members of the present generation of youth. Such a culture is always marked by goals or values that are strongly opposed to traditional values (those favored by earlier generations and handed down as models of conduct). Counter cultures therefore break with the conventions accepted by the majority and represent a form of revolt, though not necessarily one marked by violence. The counter culture of youth emphasizes personal freedom and the right of self-expression. This freedom takes the form of dress and hairstyle that differ from those of the majority. It is expressed in the right to behave largely as one chooses—to "do one's own thing"—in education, employment, and family life, so long as it does not interfere with the rights of others. It finds expression also in such things as drugs, rock music, and underground newspapers, books, films, and various kinds of theatrical productions.

Cyclamate. In chemistry, a salt of an organic acid whose formula is written $C_6H_{11}NHSO_3H$. Such a sodium or calcium salt is used as an artificial sweetner for foods and beverages. When the word "cyclamate" is used now, it usually means a sweetener of this kind.

D

E

Environmentalist. A person who is active or very interested in the study of human environment. Such a person seeks to improve the quality of people's lives by improving the physical quality of their surroundings. He is concerned especially about the condition of the earth as it affects all of us. He is therefore interested in purifying the air we breathe, in cleaning the rivers, streams, and oceans that supply water for drinking and bathing, and in protecting the land from the effects of droughts, floods, and littering. He is an active fighter against everything that pollutes the earth and its vital, life-supporting atmosphere.

F

Feedback. In technology, the return of part of the "output" of a system or process to the "input." Through this return, the input is controlled or corrected. More recently, as an informal term, "feedback" has come to mean information about the result of an action that is usable as a guide for further action. For example, if a storekeeper decides to discontinue giving trading stamps to his customers, his knowledge of the way the customers react is feedback. The public response in turn controls his action. If the response is favorable—that is, if there is no marked decline in sales—the storekeeper will probably do away with stamps permanently. If the response is not favorable, he will probably return to the policy of giving stamps to his customers with the goods he sells to them.

G

Green belt. A strip of land surrounding a city or town and containing public parks, farmland, or other areas covered with greenery. Usually such a belt is set aside by law. Commercial businesses and traffic are either forbidden within it or regulated strictly. A green belt is

H

I

J

L

M

Ms. Increasingly the most acceptable title for married and unmarried women in the women's rights movement in the United States. The acceptance of "Ms." (pronounced "miz") is based on the belief that calling women "Mrs." or "Miss," thus labeling them as married or unmarried, is in itself discriminatory, since all adult males are called by a single title, "Mr." (mister). Historically, in the English language, all women were once called by a single title, "mistress."

N

O

P

Playscape. An outdoor area designed for recreation. It is constructed so as to harmonize with such natural surroundings as trees, shrubbery, streams, or beaches. Special care is taken not to change or destroy the surroundings or to mar them with litter.

Position paper. A statement or report by a government official or by a candidate in a political campaign that sets forth in detail his position on a given issue or problem. A candidate's position paper on taxes or busing, for example, would describe the course of action he recommends on those matters. The phrase has also been applied to reports or statements prepared by persons in business, industry, or any number of other fields.

Pulsar. Any one of a number of heavenly objects in the Milky Way that give off radio pulsations, or electromagnetic waves. The radio energy is sent forth at high intensity during short, regular periods of time.

R

S

Skylab. The first U.S. space station, designed and built to travel in orbit around the earth. It is a form of manned orbital laboratory. The major part is a 100-ton workshop, remodeled from the third stage of a Saturn 5 rocket and launched from the earth with no astronauts aboard. The interior of the workshop contains both scientific laboratories and living quarters for the crew. The crew is carried to the workshop in a separate Apollo spacecraft, powered by a Saturn 1-B rocket and launched after the workshop is put in orbit satisfactorily. The Apollo craft, with the crew of three men, is designed to join the workshop by docking with it in outer space. When this is accomplished, the Apollo and the workshop travel thereafter as one craft for a period of 28 days or longer. The purpose of such a space-station flight is to test man's ability to live for long periods in the weightlessness of outer space and to permit the crew to carry out scientific experiments. The experiments deal with astronomy in outer space, including a study of the sun, and with observations of the earth. These include studies of the earth's geological formations, of its atmosphere and weather, and of problems relating to the pollution of the earth's natural resources.

Soft landing. A landing by a spacecraft on a body in outer space, such as the moon, in which the craft and its contents are unharmed. The landing is usually accomplished at a slow speed. A craft making a soft landing may carry human beings (astronauts) or scientific equipment or both. Usually the term has been applied to craft carrying only scientific equipment, which sends signals or pictures to earth.

T

Thermal pollution. Pollution of streams, rivers, or other natural bodies of water caused by the emptying of very hot liquid waste into them. The heated waste material (from a factory, for example) can harm the animal and plant life of the body of water into which it flows.

Z

ILLUSTRATION CREDITS

The following list credits, by page, the sources of illustrations used in THE NEW BOOK OF KNOWLEDGE ANNUAL. Credits are listed illustration by illustration—left to right, top to bottom. Wherever appropriate, the name of the photographer or artist has been listed with the source, the two being separated by a dash. When two or more illustrations appear on one page, their credits are separated by semicolons.

Cover photo: Gerry Cranham—Rapho Guillumette
10 UPI
12 John Dominis—*Life* magazine, © 1972 Time Inc.
13 UPI; Wide World
15 UPI
16 Smithsonian Institution
17 Smithsonian Institution; Beverly Rongren—San Francisco Zoo
19 UPI
22 New York Public Library Picture Collection
24 *The New York Times*
25 Brian Brake—Rapho Guillumette
26 Hugh M. Moss Ltd.
28 UPI
29 Wally McNamee—Newsweek, © 1972
31 UPI
32 Novosti Press Agency
33 L. Zhdanov; V. Nikulin
35 A. Makarova—APE; V. Shustov
36 Novosti Press Agency
37 Novosti Press Agency; UPI
38 New York Public Library Picture Collection
39 New York Public Library Picture Collection
40 New York Public Library Picture Collection
41 New York Public Library Picture Collection
44 Paolo Koch—Rapho Guillumette
44–45 Tass from Sovfoto
45 Tass from Sovfoto
46 Richard Alcorn
47 Richard Alcorn
48 UPI
49 Wide World
50 UPI
51 UPI
52 UPI
53 UPI
54 UPI
55 C. J. Zumwalt—Pictorial Parade
56 Mimi Forsythe—Monkmeyer
57 Mimi Forsythe—Monkmeyer
58 Russell Reif—Pictorial Parade; UPI
59 Mimi Forsythe—Monkmeyer
61 Jason Laure; George Buctel; Bernard Pierre Wolf—Alpha
62 Shostal; Jason Laure; Jason Laure
64–65 Jeff Meyer—Rapho Guillumette
66 Ron Church—Rapho Guillumette
68 Ron Church—Rapho Guillumette
69 U.S. Naval Photographic Center
70 General Electric Company
71 General Electric Company
72 Ron Church—Rapho Guillumette
73 General Electric Company
74 Copyright © 1968, by D. C. Heath & Co. Reprinted by permission of the publishers.
75 Copyright © 1968, by D. C. Heath & Co. Reprinted by permission of the publishers.
76 Lydia Murphy Savage
77 Stuart Struever—Foundation for Illinois Archeology
78 Lee Balterman; Stuart Struever—Foundation for Illinois Archeology
79 Lee Balterman
80 UPI
81 Wide World
82 Nikos Kontos
84 NASA
85 NASA
86 NASA
87 NASA
88 Boy Scouts of America
89 Environmental Protection Agency
90 Phyllis Marcuccio—National Science Teachers Association
92 Becket Academy Staff
93 *Look* magazine
94 Future Farmers of America
96 John Launois—Black Star Photos
97 John Nance—Panamin, Magnum
98 John Nance—Panamin, Magnum
99 John Launois—Black Star Photos
100 John Nance—Panamin, Magnum
101 John Launois—Black Star Photos
103 Miller Pope
105 Miller Pope
106 Miller Pope
107 Miller Pope
108–109 Courtesy of New York Zoological Society
110 UPI; Courtesy of Paramount Television
111 UPI; UPI; Carl T. Gossett—*The New York Times*
112 Walter Chandoha
113 Walter Chandoha
114 Walter Chandoha
115 Walter Chandoha
116 Walter Chandoha
117 Walter Chandoha
119 Alexandre Georges—Courtesy of the New York Zoological Society
120 Courtesy of the New York Zoological Society
121 Charles Shapp
122 Courtesy of the New York Zoological Society
123 Courtesy of the New York Zoological Society
124 Charles Shapp; Courtesy of the New York Zoological Society
125 Courtesy of the New York Zoological Society
126 Courtesy of the New York Zoological Society
127 Courtesy of the New York Zoological Society
128 Reprinted by permission of Farrar, Straus and Giroux, Inc., from *Dominic* by William Steig, © 1972 by William Steig
129 Reprinted by permission of Farrar, Straus and Giroux, Inc., from *Dominic* by William Steig, © 1972 by William Steig
130 Reprinted by permission of Farrar, Straus and Giroux, Inc., from *Dominic* by William Steig, © 1972 by William Steig
131 Reprinted by permission of Farrar, Straus and Giroux, Inc., from *Dominic* by William Steig, © 1972 by William Steig
132–133 The Netherlands Information Service
134 Tom Kaib—*The Plain Dealer Sunday Magazine*
135 Donna Dennis
136 Tom Kaib—*The Plain Dealer Sunday Magazine*
137 South Street Seaport Museum
138 Tom Kaib—*The Plain Dealer Sunday Magazine;* William E. Sauro—*The New York Times*
139 Tom Kaib—*The Plain Dealer Sunday Magazine*
140 South Street Seaport Museum
141 South Street Seaport Museum
142 Donna Dennis
143 Donna Dennis; Charles Shapp
144 Geoffrey Gove
145 Geoffrey Gove
146 Geoffrey Gove
147 Geoffrey Gove
148 Lent by the Millicent A. Rogers Memorial Museum, Inc., Taos, New Mexico, to the exhibition "The Navajo Blanket" organized by the Los Angeles County Museum of Art; Lent by Anthony Berlant to the exhibition "The Navajo Blanket" organized by the Los Angeles County Museum of Art; Lent by William H. Claflin, Boston, to the exhibition "The Navajo Blanket" organized by the Los Angeles County Museum of Art
149 Lent by Anthony Berlant to the exhibition "The Navajo Blanket" organized by the Los Angeles County Museum of Art
150 Private Collection
151 Denver Art Museum
152 American Museum of Natural History
153 American Museum of Natural History
155 Denver Art Museum
156 Museum of the American Indian
157 Museum of the American Indian; Museum of the American Indian; Museum of the American Indian; American Museum of Natural History
158 American Museum of Natural History
159 American Museum of Natural History
160 Denver Art Museum
161 Denver Art Museum
162 Reprinted by permission of Julian Messner, Inc., from *The Story of Corn* by Peter R. Limburg, illustrated by Paul Frame
164 Reprinted by permission of Julian Messner, Inc., from *The Story of Corn* by Peter R. Limburg, illustrated by Paul Frame
166 B.O.A.C.
167 B.O.A.C.; British Tourist Authority
168 British Tourist Authority
169 British Tourist Authority
170 British Tourist Authority
171 Henry I. Kurtz
172 Netherlands National Tourist Office
173 Netherlands National Tourist Office
175 Netherlands National Tourist Office
176–177 Courtesy of The Macmillan Company
179 Lawrence Frank—Rapho Guillumette